Who Dares Sells

Who Dares Sells

Patrick Ellis

Thorsons
An Imprint of HarperCollins*Publishers*

Thorsons
An Imprint of HarperCollins*Publishers*
77–85 Fulham Palace Road,
Hammersmith, London W6 8JB

Published by Who Dares Sells Publications 1991
This revised edition published by Thorsons 1992
1   3   5   7   9   10   8   6   4   2

*Every reasonable attempt has been made to ensure a
high degree of accuracy throughout the book. The
author regrets neither he nor the publishers can be
held responsible for any unforseen errors.*

A catalogue record for this book
is available from the British Library

ISBN 1 7225 2718 7

Typeset by Harper Phototypesetters Limited,
Northampton, England
Printed in Great Britain by
HarperCollinsManufacturing Glasgow

This book is dedicated with ever loving affection to my children, Richard and Rowena – two born sales heroes; my mother Marjorie; my wife Norma; Jeffrey, Phillip, Claudia, Theo, and a family friend, John T-B.

Contents

Preface

The reason for this book is clear as daylight: to provide a book that will make any reader a fortress of a salesperson when communicating with others.

WHO DARES SELLS not only examines in detail the science and art of selling, and the psychology of the human mind, but also looks at the philosophy of living. With a strong moral and ethical framework, WHO DARES SELLS combines powerful selling ammunition with a sense of fair play and a concern for the well-being of others and of the environment. You don't have to be unscrupulous to win sales, but you do need to know the tricks of the trade. In WHO DARES SELLS, everybody can be a winner.

WHO DARES SELLS is *the* book on how to win the sales battle, and how to win the battle of life. There has never been and there never will be another WHO DARES SELLS. Read it, live it, and you can be a winner too.

Acknowledgements

No man is an island. Without the courtesy and cooperation of so many individuals and organizations, I would never have been able to produce this book even with the strongest will and self-motivation in the world. Some of these people who assisted me were experts with a capital E and others were supporters with a capital S. At times some of them were difficult with a capital D and on other occasions they were simply great with a capital G. But the truth is they were all friends to me with a capital F. I love them, warts and all, and although they have at times had to put up with some of my more outlandish methods I hope they will bask in the reflected glory this book will produce.

I am extremely thankful and deeply indebted to every one of these individuals and the respective organizations for the kindness and assistance given to me during the compilation of the manuscript: N.M.T. Ellis, J.M. Thalben-Ball, Cliff Port, Ram Chandel, Nick Swindley and Staff, Tony Buzan, Tony Nevard, David Gaster, Theo Gimbel, Gordon Wainwright, Renna Nezos, Gavin Deans, Dr Susanne Bano, Dr Barry Cripps, David Leigh-Howarth, Alec Bater, Daire O'Gallagher and many, many others. I wish to thank Allan Pease for permission to reproduce material in Chapter 7 from his book *Body Language* (Sheldon Press, 1981).

I wish to convey my thanks to the following organizations for their kind assistance given in compiling Chapter 16.

The Religious and Moral Education Press and Sarah Thorley.
Franklin Watts Publishers.
The London Liberal Synagogue and Rabbi Hillel Avidan.
The Board of Deputies of British Jews.
The London Mosque and Mr A.L. Khan.
The Vishwa Hindu Mandir, Southall.
The London Buddhist Vihara.
Thomas International Management System (Europe) Ltd.

Introduction

Everybody, everywhere, everyday is selling or buying products, services or ideas. Individuals, groups, companies and governments partake in this fundamental and most important function that can offer achievement, power, fame, fortune and success to those who excel in it. Non-achievement, powerlessness, mediocrity, poverty, despair and despondency lie at the other extreme for those who fail at it because selling and buying are the two vital arms in the "people business". And it can either be a very simple or a very complicated process.

The infant crying for its mother's attention is selling. A school child trying to avoid being reprimanded by the teacher for not doing his homework is selling. A candidate for employment or a job promotion is selling. A boy wooing a girl or a girl wooing a boy is selling. A politician canvassing for votes in a constituency or a government offering its policy to the country is selling. A musical entertainer or an orchestra is selling. The pastor in the pulpit is selling. A lawyer in a courtroom arguing a case is selling. The patient in a doctor's surgery complaining about aches and pains is selling. A high-powered team attempting to negotiate a major contract for plant, machinery or aircraft is selling. And so the list goes on. The end result will either be that the sender's (seller's) message is received and acted upon by the receiver (buyer) or it will fall on deaf ears, depending on how effectively the message is sent through the spoken word, written word or through non-verbal means. The result is Success or Failure, Win or Lose.

Whatever your background and from whichever country you originate, WHO DARES SELLS will show you step by step how to maximise your chances of success and minimise your chances of failure when selling or buying anything. Every thought-provoking section provides new pieces of the jigsaw puzzle. The complete book, packed with humour, inspiration and motivation, gives you a clear, honest picture on how to win with others.

Of the many books written on the subject of selling WHO DARES SELLS dares to go further, beyond the place where others have stopped, incorporating some of the latest techniques from all over the world. Even seasoned old hands at selling and buying will find some very useful information.

WHO DARES SELLS will show your mind and mouth how to behave in any selling situation, anywhere in the world, using the "twist drill" approach: you apply the correct sales pressure with the appropriate drill bits (the selling skills) to enable you to bore through even the toughest of woods (difficult buyers). First you start to learn gradually under guidance and assistance, as if you were in the shallow end of a swimming pool. As your knowledge, skill, confidence and experience grow the book acts as a lifebuoy, enabling you to go deeper and deeper until you are at the deepest end and can hold your own. However, it is always at hand to provide vital support when required.

As a veteran salesman I have put an ocean of knowledge into a teacup, using unambiguous language to provide you with the unadulterated facts of professional selling in an enlightened and (I hope) entertaining way.

In WHO DARES SELLS I redefine what used to be called Salesmanship as **Salespersonability**, or in other words: **a skilled battle fought by the SELLER to influence a BUYER's mind to win sales of products, services or ideas through Persuasion, Motivation, Manipulation or Negotiation by evaluating the buyer's spoken word, written word and non-verbal signals to**

produce a desired result which may be of greater or lesser benefit to Buyer or Seller or of equal benefit to both.

WHO DARES SELLS is about creative dynamic selling – the psychology of sales success. It is the most powerful tool you can use to achieve measurable results. Years of painstaking research, academic and practical experience have been used to compile this book and it will undoubtedly be invaluable to anyone who conscientiously applies the lessons within. Whether you earn your living by selling or buying, managing or directing others, whether you are in a decision making capacity, or in a professional occupation, WHO DARES SELLS will be an indispensible reference book. When you have all the knowledge WHO DARES SELLS has to offer firmly locked into your system, you can coast through life as if you were on the crest of a wave.

I would like to justify the above statements. I do not mean to be unkind when I say there are a vast number of books by many well-meaning authors on the subject of professional selling which contain some excellent ideas peppered with a vast amount of rubbish. The reason for this is that these are experienced, theoretical and armchair salespeople who have gleaned their knowledge from other books and sources without having applied it in the field.

Now of course there are masterpieces, but they are few and far between. What this book gives you is practical advice.

It leads you to the truth on whichever rung of the success ladder you are. It shows you how to triumph and remain successful in the exciting and lucrative business of professional selling. It reveals the unadulterated facts, scientific know-how and artistic skills against a background of theoretical considerations and tried and tested practical experience. This book contains the latest expertise from the developed West, where salespeople are highly trained, and the instinctive and intuitive skills of the East where selling is often part of survival.

The choice is yours. Study, enjoy and implement the information given in this book to your advantage, or disregard it to your disadvantage. I have spent many hours studying books, tapes, videos, training courses and seminars and observing other high flyers in action in a relentless search for the best output from the world's experts. I have personally tested everything you are going to encounter in this book. From the knowledge I have gained and applied to live selling situations all over the world, I have produced phenomenal results. You are therefore going to derive the benefit of my enormous experience.

I am going to give you an arsenal of techniques, some of which have been created by myself; others which have the backing of other sales, marketing and management experts. No person can live in a fool's paradise and call themselves the best, because there will always be someone who is better, but without doubt there are a selected few who are infinitely better than most in a specific field and it is those supreme individuals one has to emulate in pursuit of excellence. You cannot afford to be complacent, there will always be someone waiting to usurp your position. Consider the record breaking mile run by Roger Bannister on 6 May 1954 in Oxford. It has been broken many times since then.

The only way to improve is by acquiring the knowledge and the skills of those who are better than you, together with wide exposure, keen observation and rigorous practical application.

If you are not yet convinced, my advice is think once, think twice, and think again – you must never judge a book by its cover! Humble yourself, become a lifelong student of selling, and the sky is truly the limit. Knowledge and skill taught by experts coupled with experience is better than knowledge and skill gained the slow and painful way because it gets you to your destination more quickly. WHO DARES SELLS will be your companion and friend all the way to becoming a top flight sales professional.

Professional selling is like war, played out on the business battle field. A soldier fights with live bullets; your weapons are words. But unlike the amateur who uses the shot gun method, spraying an area with bullets and hoping one will meet its target, the professional salesperson, like a trained marksman, shoots with precision and accuracy – reaching the target every single time. The days of the canned sales pitch are over. What is needed today are structured presentations or demonstrations with logical and emotional appeal designed to satisfy the needs of buyers for specific benefits, supplemented with razor sharp objection handling techniques, slick negotiating and closing techniques, to persuade, motivate or manipulate buyers into making decisions of mutual benefit.

Today's buyer is sophisticated and cautious, with a mass of counter measures and avoidance strategies to ward off unprofessional, amateur, would-be salespeople. The sales battle needs to be fought word-for-word, bullet-for-bullet. Success on today's business battlefield is survival of the fittest, and the only insurance policy is total professionalism. If you want to win, WHO DARES SELLS will give you this professionalism – a small premium to pay for huge benefits.

In my research for this book I have sought assistance from experts in the various fields of psychology, graphology, colour science, neuro-linguistic-programming, religious education and science, as well as a few hand-picked masters of selling and management.

We all know someone who is a 'Jack of all trades but master of none', but I can claim to be a Jack of all trades and master of one – SELLING! and, through selling – BUYING! Consequently, my big thanks go out to the hundreds upon hundreds of buyers all around the world – the Good, the Bad and the Ugly. More often than not I have won, and sometimes I have lost, but these people have taught me more about selling than any academic textbook or classroom training could ever do.

WHO DARES SELLS is an unrivalled combination of expert knowledge and practical experience, the essence of several lifetimes of selling from the four corners of the world. Read it, apply it, and I assure you will be a winner.

I am offering a prize to anyone who can present to me in writing a better system of personal success. If you have the courage of your convictions, put your chest forward and hold your chin up high and prove your knowledge to me is based on the "real world" and not a "make believe" one I would welcome it wholeheartedly. If that is the case, I will declare you the champion of champions and you will have in me a faithful disciple for the rest of my life – I look forward to hearing from you.

I wish you luck and may your successes go from strength to strength.

Patrick Ellis

THE MAN WHO DARES
The man who decides what he wants to achieve
and works till his dreams come true
The man who will alter his course when he must
and bravely begin something new
The man who is determined to make his world better
who is willing to learn and lead
The man who keeps trying and doing his best
is the man who knows how to succeed
WHO DARES SELLS!

CHAPTER 1

You were born to be a winner, but face the facts of life first!

Whoever you are, wherever you may be, whatever your circumstances, take time to consider that your life is a process from womb to tomb. How you live and make use of that precious gift of life once you reach the age of reason is what determines success or failure.

Success covers many facets of life; not just financial success alone. The person who views success purely in terms of monetary success and power at all costs – important as those factors may be – is ultimately going to be a failure, as you will discover in the following chapters. Success is the difference between power – in all its forms – and wisdom.

If an animal is brought up from birth in an exclusively human environment instead of being nurtured in the wild by its natural parents it makes good progress and acquires many skills, but is bounded by definite limitations.

However, human babies that have been snatched by wild animals such as wolves or gazelles and reared in the wild – feral children – were able to make relatively good progress in learning speech, and reasoning creativity when discovered and brought back into civilisation.

There are well documented true-life cases of Kamala and

Amala, the wolf children of Midnapore, Ramu the wolf boy of Lucknow, and the Gazelle boy of Egypt, and many other stories.

It is reported that the wolf children Kamala and Amala were snatched by a she-wolf and taken into the wilds where she nursed the children with her cubs on her milk and fed them with raw meat. The children, when discovered many years later, barked like wolves, ran on four feet, chased a prey (a chicken), were covered in hair, had long fingernails and in every way behaved like animals. But, because they were human and in spite of their terrible disadvantages and deprivation, they were able to adjust to civilisation.

Whatever our circumstances we can better them because we are mentally superior to animals and are uniquely human. It is therefore the paramount duty of all parents to give their children the best mental and physical nourishment to equip them for life and, if they cannot for whatever reason provide this, to seek life-enhancing assistance from elsewhere.

When my first child, Richard, was born in 1979, my wife used to buy a maternal magazine called "Mother and Baby". In it I came across an excellent poem about the impact of adult behaviour on children:

If a child lives with criticism, he learns to condemn.
If a child lives with hostility, he learns to fight.
If a child lives with ridicule, he learns to be shy.
If a child lives with shame, he learns to feel guilty.
If a child lives with tolerance, he learns to be patient.
If a child lives with encouragement, he learns confidence.
If a child lives with praise, he learns to appreciate.
If a child lives with fairness, he learns justice.
If a child lives with security, he learns to have faith.
If a child lives with approval, he learns to like himself.
If a child lives with acceptance and friendship, he learns to
find love in the world.

The inner child syndrome is deeply rooted in every adult, and in every one of the adults you see today is an overgrown baby still in nappies!

Now that you have made your entry on to this planet, assuming

WHAT IS LIFE?

you have had the minimum requisites in life and have reached a level of understanding necessary for comprehending this book, may I ask you whether you have planned to get what is best for yourself on your journey through life?

Are you ready for your exit which can happen at any time?

It is never too late to get into gear and GO FOR IT.

Act now, because it is only a matter of time before you make your exit. Life is a battle, and so too is selling. While you are battling you will either get rapped on the knuckles for being bad or get pudding for being good. One of the ironies of life is that many people end up being kicked in the shins for being good and receiving the gold medal for being bad. But what really counts is not the battling (which is what I call the action part) but whether you WON or LOST.

Many people aimlessly float through life accomplishing nothing. Just before they pass on, they curse and say, 'Life's a bitch', and they turn around and die. It will not be the same for you when you have read, understood and applied the contents of these pages, from cover to cover. WHO DARES SELLS will help you achieve your dreams, goals and ambitions – *and* win the ultimate battle of life.

I wish you the best of good luck for your journey through life. May you arrive at your destination with a smile upon your face, through the power of WHO DARES SELLS.

THE FACTS OF LIFE

Who are you?

Whether you are brown, yellow, black or white, originating from Asia, Africa, Europe, Australia or America, a tinker, tailor, soldier, sailor, richman, poorman, beggarman, salesperson, policeman, thief, academic, skilled person, genius or plain good-for-nothing – you name it . . . I have a little secret to tell you, "CONGRATULATIONS MY FELLOW BROTHERS AND SISTERS, AS HOMO SAPIENS, YOU ARE, BECAUSE YOU HAVE BEEN CREATED UNIQUE, SIMPLY INCREDIBLE!"

Homo sapiens is derived from Latin: Homo meaning Man, and

Sapiens meaning Wise – Possessing Intelligence. It means Man is differentiated from other members of the animal kingdom, particularly those of his own order and family, namely monkeys and great apes, by his distinct ability to reason.

Nobody else on this planet has your unique physical and mental characteristics such as your personality, handwriting, intellect, scientific and artistic talents, build, postures and gestures. You may be described as highly polished, eloquent, well educated, brilliant, debonair, suave, or, an outright rough and tough, stupid, uneducated, filthy, evil, lazy, uncouth scoundrel. Whatever expression is used to describe you, fear not! Because we are all part of the human race variation exists, and you may find the worst in the best of us and the best in the worst of us. To put it another way *all that glisters is not gold*, and *to every cloud there is a silver lining*! Between these two extremes you will find people I refer to as the genuine gems of life blessed with a lot of goodness in them, but remember:

- There are none so blind as those who do not wish to see.
- Two men looked through prison bars, one saw mud and the other saw stars.
- Confucius said, 'Everything has its beauty but not everyone sees it'.

What I am specifically talking about is your attitude.

The process of creation is a miracle. From all the millions of healthy sperms that swam up the fallopian tubes, one and one only was responsible for you being born. Now, isn't that simply fantastic?

Not even the most sophisticated computer ever made can match the creative potential of the human mind. Computers are very quick at mathematical calculations and step-by-step logical processing, but this is infinitesimal when compared with the ability of the human brain. The main difference between the brain and the computer is that the brain works not only in a linear fashion, but also does parallel processing, integrates and synthesises information and abstracts generalities.

There are computers that have been developed that can recognize a simple object such as a cup from a collection of around ten or so other objects. That takes several minutes, while the human brain can recognise a face in less than a second. Furthermore, computers cannot recognise every object, only certain types. Even if the advanced technology today could develop a transistorised computer capable of doing all the human brain can do, then such a system would weigh more than ten tons, and would hardly fit into the massive Carnegie Hall in America. Did you know that the whole of the world's telephone system is equivalent to only 1 gram of your brain, roughly the size of a pea. Furthermore, reseach has shown that we are still today only using less than one tenth of a percent of our brain.

Another most outstanding feature of the excellence of the human brain can be seen in the functioning and developing of the human baby. Far from being a little helpless and incapable mass of mind and body, it is the most extraordinary learning, remembering and intellectually advanced being. Even in its early stages it surpasses the performance of the most sophisticated computer. Most babies learn to talk by the age of two or even earlier, something which is taken for granted by us all, but if the process is examined carefully it is extremely complex indeed.

Here is an example to prove the point. Try listening to someone speaking in a different language: if you have no knowledge of the language and the subject matter being discussed what happens when you try to make sense of it? You will come up against a mind bender, but every baby has overcome this – learning to speak properly by sorting out what makes sense and what does not. When someone starts saying things in a musical voice like – 'what a sweet little darling baby you are' – isn't it a wonder how he or she makes sense of it? The baby's ability to understand its mother's or father's loving words involves nature's inherent blessing to the child: the ability to understand rhythm, mathematics, music, physics, linguistics, spatial relationship, memory, integration, creativity, logical reasoning and thinking, or in other words, left and right brain interaction from the cradle. This is something that will be covered in greater detail further on.

Anyone who doubts his or her own abilities must be reassured by now by understanding that they too learned to read and write, that the human brain is capable of infinitely more complex tasks, and the only thing we have to do is increase our level of aspiration and remove the blinkers which are preventing us from exploiting our minds and creative potential to the fullest.

Body and mind are inseparable – what affects the body affects the mind, and vice versa. So, it is important to keep both in tip-top condition. Pay sensible attention to exercise, diet, rest, relaxation and recreation and always maintain a positive, cheerful and happy outlook whatever your circumstances.

I know of an old man who was still working at the ripe old age of 85 and was physically fit, active and very healthy. He had been married three times, had fifteen children and God only knows how many grandchildren and great-grandchildren. He lived life to the fullest and had a 30-year-old girlfriend. I asked him what his secret for successful living was. Here was his reply:

'I HAVE *SUMMER* IN MY HEART'
(for this happy, youthful outlook on life)
'I HAVE *AUTUMN* IN MY CHEEKS'
(for the wrinkles on his face)
'I HAVE *WINTER* IN MY HAIR'
(for the white hairs and loss of hair on his head)
and 'I HAVE *SPRING* IN MY BOTTOM'
(now we all know what that means!)

Where are you heading?

If you do not know where you are going, any bus will take you.

Take the example of a commercial airplane pilot who wants to take an aircraft from one airport to another.

Before he takes off a flight plan will be required, which means that the pilot will have to:

1. know the distance.
2. know the payload, i.e. the passenger and/or cargo weight, and the corresponding fuel requirements.
3. assess weather conditions at departure and arrival airports and at diversion airports, if necessary.
4. allow for contingency measures, such as diversion alternatives.
5. have maps for departure, en route and arrival.

6. be a manager of his crew, ambassador for his country, have a wide range of knowledge of his aircraft, airport and operating procedures.
7. at all times be prepared to expect the unforeseen and be able to cope efficiently and accurately with any problems that could occur, for which the training is precisely tailored.
8. make instantaneous decisions: see, think and act in all eventualities while occupied in flying.
9. psychologically accept mundane, routine flying duties and be fully prepared to cope with the occasional emergency that may arise.

Similarly, if you want to reach a destination in life you have to know where you are going, you have to know how to get there, you have to be prepared to pay the price, and you have to accept and be ready for all eventualities. This means you have to set yourself goals, become goal-orientated and a goal achiever. Otherwise you will drift through life like a ship with no rudder. We will discuss Time Management and Goal Setting in later chapters.

What have you been in the past? What are you now? What do you want to achieve in the future?

There is only one person who can honestly answer these questions – yourself. Whatever you have been in the past must be used to your advantage and this can only be done by making an honest appraisal of yourself.

The hardest thing to do is to put yourself under the microscope and examine yourself in minute detail, but it has to be done in order to identify your strengths and weaknesses. The objective must be to improve and capitalize on your strengths and conquer your weaknesses.

Whatever you have been in the past can have only two influences on the present: either positive (strengths and

INTERNATIONAL LIFE EXPECTANCY FIGURES

LIFE EXPECTANCY FROM BIRTH

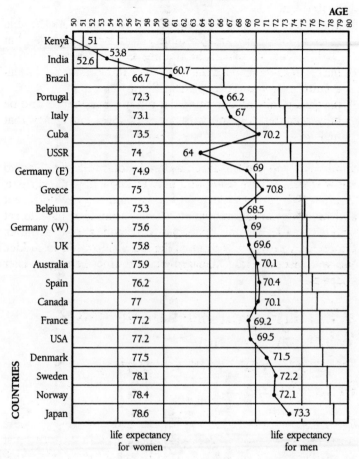

life expectancy
for women

life expectancy
for men

By kind permission of Thames & Hudson.

This graph shows average life expectancy for men and women from different parts of the world. We all have a limited amount of time available to achieve whatever we want in life. So it is up to us to utilise every hour productively to fulfil our hopes and dreams and achieve our ambition and goals.

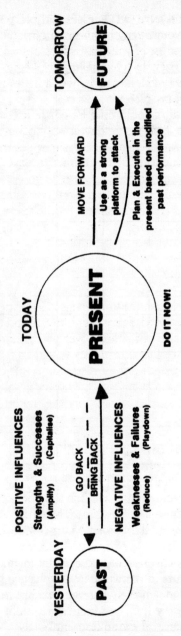

SUCCESS MODEL

YESTERDAY **TODAY** **TOMORROW**

PAST **PRESENT** **FUTURE**

POSITIVE INFLUENCES
Strengths & Successes
(Amplify) (Capitalise)

GO BACK
BRING BACK

NEGATIVE INFLUENCES
Weaknesses & Failures
(Reduce) (Playdown)

DO IT NOW!

MOVE FORWARD

Use as a strong
platform to attack

Plan & Execute in the
present based on modified
past performance

N.B. TODAY IS TOMORROW'S YESTERDAY

successes) or negative (weaknesses and failures). Now what you do is amplify your Strengths and reduce your Weaknesses. You also make the most of your past successes and play down your past failures. Then by channelling it all into the present you attack the future fearlessly to achieve a better tomorrow. See the Success Model on p.28.

Remember, you should only be concerned about the present and the future. Take it one day at a time, learn from your past mistakes, unfortunate experiences, successes and failures. Empty all the good you can derive from the past into the present, ignoring any undesirable factors that you cannot change and with a reinforced platform in the present, attack the future with the utmost zeal and enthusiasm. People fear the future because they lack three important things — knowledge, understanding and control of their own emotions.

There are a few practical things that can help anyone overcome fear of the future.

1. As long as you have knowledge and understanding of the present you can visualize the future. If you are prepared and able to exercize self control over your emotions, you will be able to face the future fearlessly – and even attack it with vim and vigour. Continuously setting and achieving goals is the answer. Invest in *knowledge*, the powerful self-defence weapon you can use against fear. Empty the money in your purse to feed your mind with knowledge in the present and your mind will reward you handsomely in the future. Trust your subconscious computer-like mind to find you solutions.
2. Live your best today and take one day at a time. Love life and respect all other forms of life: the good, the bad and the ugly. Life is a precious gift. We can't all be kings, and queens, Picassos, Chopins or Einsteins. The world would be a strange place if we were all the same. Nature has designed life in such a way, quite outside our control, so that there is a pecking order, and inequalities *do* exist. What may be to one person a piece of cake is a nightmare to another. Or, as the saying goes one man's meat is another man's poison.

Here are some real examples:

- A policeman who was a winner of a medal for bravery in disarming an armed robber on the ground was mortally afraid of heights because he suffered from vertigo.
- A soldier who was decorated for gallantry in active service in the front line in the Second World War was so afraid of his petite wife that he would tremble if she raised her voice even slightly in anger.

The cardinal rule to be aware of is that whatever good or bad circumstances we are in at present we can always improve our situation when we know how to tackle it. Life is ever changing. Just observe the clouds above you: blue skies one moment; dark clouds the next. Whatever has happened in the past has no bearing in the future provided we seek to remedy any errors in the present and segregate what cannot be changed from our master plan or blue-print for success, which we are formulating today to launch into the future. The only permanent thing in life is death and that is not my specialist subject. I am not a prophet of doom or gloom. Sure, we all have problems, small, medium or large, but what really matters is how we react to them and how we solve them.

I love life, and I would like you to love and enjoy your life too, because that is what life is meant to be, solving problems and making the most of each day. Give reasonable care and attention to your daily problems, work hard and play hard!

I have written a song, which you may have heard – an inspiring, powerful song which summarizes this book and the secret of selling in less than four and a half minutes:

WHO DARES SELLS
(Lyrics)

CHORUS
Who Dares Sells, Who Dares Sells, Let's really learn how to sell,
Who Dares Sells, Who Dares Sells, We can learn how to sell,
We'll practice and observe the secrets of a Super salesman.

Verse 1
The right mental attitude, is the first thing you require,
A will to win must also be desired,
Sharpen your mind and act like a professional.

Chorus (repeat)
Verse 2
When you start to win, more and more success flows in,
You'll find your way of life and future start improving,
Inspire yourself and have the fighting spirit.

Chorus (repeat)
Verse 3
Battle on and on, even when all hope is gone,
Changing your ways to handle all your problems,
By helping others gain, the salesman moves along.

Verse 4
Watch for reaction and respond with affection,
Doing what you should with a lot of dedication,
So clinch that deal and leave without hesitation.

Chorus (repeat)

Here's a secret. When you are in search of authoritative knowledge on any subject, something that should be an obligation you owe to yourself as a mature person, under no circumstances should you simply accept advice from anyone, however close that person is to you, even when it is given with the best of intentions. Of course, always pay the courtesy of listening to everyone, but terminate politely, in the shortest possible time and as tactfully as you can, if you suspect the advice is incorrect. When your thinking is sharp (something which can be developed), you will instinctively get a gut feeling if your adviser is full of balloney!

You will also be amazed if you remove your blinkers what fantastic ideas you can glean on how to work around corners and get to the heart of the matter from ordinary experienced people in life.

If you have to make a choice between the experience and intelligence of two advisers to solve a problem for you, then I would say experience is better than intelligence any day. However, an adviser who has experience and intelligence combined together is the last word! Obviously, if a problem is of a complicated nature, then take it to an expert and be prepared to pay for the advice. A really good expert does not come cheap, but it could be a tremendous help and saving to you in the long run. To be sure that you are on the right track with the advice given to you ask at least three knowledgeable people for their opinion. If all three confirm the same opinion, you are OK. If two say it is not OK and one says it is OK, on the balance of probabilities get a fourth opinion to be on the safe side. If all three say it is not OK – it is a no go. If two say it is OK and one says it is not OK you will have to decide yourself whether two are right and one is wrong depending on how you value the advice. But get a fourth opinion in any event.

Whatever happens your decision to proceed must only be made after carefully evaluating the advice given based on facts rather than emotional reasons. You may upset some people in doing so, but may save yourself some headaches and heartaches. Look after yourself – you are the most important person that exists on this planet. This is your world. You've got to know where you are going and how to get there in the shortest possible time. But remember – the most important by-product of success while you are climbing or when you have made it to the top of the ladder, is your ability to help others come up. You can only do that from a position of strength – not weakness. Those who do that are the truly good people of this world.

When do you want to arrive at your destination? When should you make the move?

Make your decisions now, and make your plans now. Those who fail do so not because they plan to fail, but rather because they fail to plan. Figure out every detail in your mind's eye: what you want to happen.

- how are you going to achieve it (be realistic)
- what is required
- how long it will take
- what it will cost
- any problems you can forsee
- how you intend to solve them
- what contingency measures you will have on standby.

Write down your total plans on paper. It is absolutely necessary to do so as you will learn in later chapters. On reaching each intermediate stage of your plan, cross it out as you achieve your objective.

Prior to embarking on your plan, get the advice and feedback from others who have already taken the plunge, for the best way to learn and do things is with OPM:

Other People's Mastery
Other People's Mistakes
Other People's Money
Other People's Materials
Other People's Methods

This is the only way you can get going if you don't have the know-how or the money of your own to get started. But whatever happens, you must take a calculated risk, get started, and you will learn as you go along. Don't jump in at the deep end. Start at the shallow end, learn how to float and swim and then go deeper. If your confidence level is high and you feel you know better than others, do plunge into deeper water straight away. At this point one of three things will happen:

1. You will sink if you cannot float or swim.
2. You might float if you don't know how to swim, because Archimedes' Principle states that when a body is wholly or partially immersed in a fluid it experiences an upthrust equal to the weight of the fluid displaced. You can use this principle to survive if you can keep your cool.
3. You will swim and make headway in any direction you want, to accomplish what you desire.

If (1) happens, you should have adequate contingency safeguards to bail you out. If you have no contingency safeguards you are a fool.

If (2) happens, you will soon be able to learn how to swim, as you will be able to keep your head above water. There is a saying in selling: *If a piece of decaying wood can float, so can a lousy business person.*

If (3) happens, you will be in a prime position desired by a great many people. You will be able to write your own pay cheques and depending on how good you are, you could be eating cream buns every day. You could also consider yourself very lucky to be in this position without any preparation.

Don't procrastinate – do it now. Start the ball rolling and you can cross your bridges when you come to them.

Combine positive expectations with a state of readiness to face the unexpected. Do not be afraid of making mistakes. If you do not make mistakes, how can you learn?

This is the challenge and the fun of being enterprising. This is the spirit of all optimistic and progressive people. Gloomy, pessimistic and negative thinking will get you nowhere.

Your undying will to win will supersede any adverse influences, provided you religiously follow the rules and methodology offered in this book. If you don't understand the rules, don't participate in the game, for you will make an ass of yourself and head straight for trouble.

Why change?

Simply because by doing so you can avoid headaches, heartaches, pitfalls, roadblocks, prevent drawbacks and get to your destination quickly and safely. Your destination or objective must be firmly fixed in your mind's eye, but your *modus operandi* must be subject to alteration as and when required.

Let's look at driving a car from point A to Point B. To get motion you have to change gears, accelerating or decelerating according to the terrain and road condition. Even motor cars with cruise control for the highway cannot have constant speed for long because road conditions vary from place to place all the time – uphill, downhill, overtaking vehicles, traffic lights, pedestrian crossings, railway intersections, floods and other hazards.

Likewise in selling, people are different – no two sales are alike. So use different strokes for different folks.

People buy the same products, services or ideas for different reasons. You have got to change your strategy, techniques and tactics constantly to enable you to communicate at different levels and styles, but your prime concern must be to make the sale. Only a prize idiot keeps to an unchanging course of action and ends up in disaster.

I have seen and read of numerous accidents and tragedies that have occurred because people by virtue of their rigid thought processes could not respond and react to danger signals. People have literally driven into brick walls with their eyes wide open. This argument can be extended into other areas such as chronic alcoholism, compulsive gambling, excessive smoking, overeating, drug abuse, high risk sexual exploits and so on. Too much of anything is good for nothing. Change now, and change for the better.

Likewise in selling, countless sales have been lost by salespeople saying and doing the wrong thing with their eyes wide open. Their total inflexibility and inability to respond to the buyer's strategy and counter measures means that these salespeople are walking and talking disasters who need to get their heads examined. Get on the right track and on to the gravy trail! This book will show you how. Even though you may think you are on the right road, don't insist on your right of way. For even though you may be one hundred per cent correct on an issue, you cannot go around telling people you are right and they are wrong – you just won't get anywhere with this approach. You need the WHO DARES SELLS selling approach.

Change is desirable because change attracts attention. All humans who have their thinking faculties in order are competing for attention from others. They do it with cars, clothes, homes, cosmetics, gestures, postures, facial expressions and in many other ways. Infants are born in total dependence and crave for their mothers' love and attention for their survival. This is why they cry when in pain or are hungry. So the surest way to get people thinking and reacting towards you is by doing things which cause a change in your attitude, clothes, personal grooming, sales talk, possessions, gestures, postures and facial expressions. The list can be very large indeed depending on what you want to achieve.

Change is also a natural process in life. We are constantly changing as we grow older, and during these phases we undergo mental, physical and spiritual change. The human animal, which is built for achievement, needs to change in order to survive.

Change breaks monotony and adds colour to our lives. Change banishes the boring and mundane. The old saying *variety is the spice of life* is absolutely true.

Finally, civilization and progress are dependent on change. When we are contemplating change or undergoing change, review the objective – the change must be for the better – don't jump from the frying pan into the fire!

> As you move on through life fighting, let it be your goal
> To keep your eye upon the goal posts – don't move them
> And kick the ball skilfully into the net!

How to get there – and how soon!

I have no apology to make when I say that whether you are born privileged or deprived, you have to fight for your survival. As in the law of the jungle it is simply a case of survival of the fittest.

In the wild, conditions are harsh and nature curbs the population explosion by eliminating the weak, the sick and the old. Have you seen those wild life films where predators like lions, tigers and cheetahs hunt the samba, gazelle and wildebeest? The big wild cats have to fight for their prey – their food – by precision, planning and executing the chase, and in response, the ultra-sensitive prey are equipped to detect even the slightest variation in sight, sound and smell to set them fleeing from danger. Both predator and prey are fighting for survival. When cornered in a life-threatening situation, even a little rat will thrash out with the utmost ferocity.

Let us make no bones about it – the human animal behaves in just the same way and can be just as ruthless depending on the environment and the situation. However, what distinguishes us from animals is that we have a conscience, and can exercise control, reason, creative thinking together with the ability to turn adversity into profitability and prosperity. And given that human life is a miraculous and precious gift we have to act responsibly, respect it, give it dignity, irrespective of what it looks like, feels like, smells like or sounds like. The strong have to protect the sick, the weak and the innocent who need the protection, support and guidance from those who are stronger in order to create a just and fair world. This does not mean you have to walk through life with a halo around your head. Indeed, sometimes you will have to kick like a mule, bite like a crocodile, charge like a rhinoceros as well as being gentle as a lamb when putting your point across. But what must stand out in all your actions are your good, sincere intentions, caring motives and concern for other people. It is the callous disregard for another's well being that must be fiercely resisted.

> *Might is not right, but Right is might!*
> *We all have to eat and live.*

Attack to appease, not to destroy is the vital skill you have to acquire in life to succeed. Delivering blows with controlled force means that you have to be in control of yourself. To rush around haphazardly in pursuit of your objectives, knocking everything down in your path and leaving a trail of destruction like a hurricane is something any idiot can do, but to be able to get to your destination, leaving everything intact, requires considerable skill and know-how. It has got to be learnt and requires an effort.

When I say you have to fight to get up and stay up, this is what I mean:

1. You have to fight to maintain good physical and mental health.
2. You have to fight to get a good education, food, clothing, shelter and recreation.
3. You have to fight to maintain superiority and keep ahead of the competitors and those who are trying to undermine your well-being.
4. You have to fight and be prepared to protect yourself and your loved ones against physical and mental attacks when required,

which could happen at any time in any place without notice.
5. You have to fight all negative influences that will deter you from reaching your goals and achieving your ambitions.
6. You have to fight to overcome the roadblocks and setbacks that you will encounter in life.
7. You have to fight to be financially solvent.

For some fortunate people the fight can be easier, but for others it is a hard struggle. That's tough luck, but you do have an opportunity in life to succeed and you have to grasp the opportunity with a come-hell-or-highwater attitude – Just Go For It! Some of the factors that stand in your way may be self-imposed (the enemy within) whilst others come from outside.

Contrary to popular belief, you don't have to be born with a silver spoon in your mouth to become rich, famous, powerful and successful. How many rags-to-riches stories have you come across? Abraham Lincoln, former President of the USA was a shoe shine boy!

In fact, when you come up the hard way, the stronger, more experienced and less vulnerable you become. The sooner you accept that life is not a bed of roses and is a fight all the way from the cradle to the grave the better. Just as in the jungle, the faster you can prepare for the unexpected the better you can survive the traumas and hardships in life.

Some people end up battered, bruised and bewildered from the fight. Others come home, shrug it off and lick their wounds, refusing to let it worry them at all. Others behave as live cowards, running away from problems and achieving very little, while some through their unselfish, daredevil and adventurous spirits meet problems head on and pay a heavy price, ending up as dead heroes. Yet another breed is those I call born survivors who will wheel and deal, twist and turn, duck and dive, and propel themselves against insurmountable obstacles and somehow keep rolling.

Whichever cap suits you, wear it! Whichever beat of drum you march to, then do so; as long as there is a bona fide reason for your actions. Everyone, whichever route they choose and whatever end result they produce, will have supporters, objectors and sympathizers. There are no rights and wrongs, but what will stand out in the final analysis is your motive. Think about that carefully. All is not necessarily fair in love and war. Strengthen yourself mentally and physically and do anything and everything that is necessary to protect yourself, your loved ones, and your property. For good to survive, evil must not be allowed to thrive.

One of the greatest leaders of all time was Sir Winston Churchill, who during the Second World War, when his country was threatened by the German Army, told the British people, 'We *shall not flag or fail. We shall fight in France. We shall fight on the seas and oceans. We shall fight with growing confidence and growing strength in the air. We shall defend our island, whatever the cost may be. We shall fight on the beaches. We shall fight on the landing grounds. We shall fight in the fields and in the streets. We shall fight in the hills. We shall never surrender.'*

In life we do not have bags of time available to get what we want and to achieve what we desire. Some people use the '*slowly, slowly catchee monkey*' principle, others use the hare and tortoise approach, while another group works the fast way: see, think, act and achieve. The important thing to realize is that we are in a race against time, and if you slow down others will overtake you to win the trophy. Slow, deliberate, cautious, methodical and conclusive is not necessarily better than fast, accurate, powerful and precise. By all means plan, but then act.

It is often perceived by many that being fast causes error. People who get into the fast lane without preparation, training and experience will hurtle headlong into oblivion.

Some projects, by virtue of their complexity, do take longer than others, but an unpardonable offence is the colossal wastage of precious time that a vast number of people practise as a way of life and which can be prevented.

Time waits for no man!

And never forget that time is a great teacher and healer, but she finally kills all her pupils!

To get to your destination as soon as possible, avoid traffic jams, avoid roadblocks, get as much information as you can on the project prior to embarkation, use the side roads and back streets, and above all be prepared to alter course at the earliest opportunity when you see a warning or hazard ahead. I have often seen people in head-to-tail traffic jams, highly stressed, wasting precious time and money, burning fuel with their engines running and possibly missing an important appointment as a consequence, when all they had to do was make a small detour to get to their destination with the minimum of fuss and bother, and arrive smiling and in the right frame of mind to do business rather than exhausted and anxious.

To whom should you look for guidance, reassurance and support? Who should you blame when things go wrong?

On your journey to success you will and must expect disappointments and obstacles. The process is very much like learning to drive a car. While learning you encounter difficulties which you overcome, and even though you may know how to drive, accidents may and do happen. Nothing is perfect.

When you first learn to drive a car, in order to learn the correct procedures you receive instruction from a competent instructor who will do the following:

1. provide instruction in a car that has dual control.
2. point out the various controls and gauges in the car and tell you what they are and what they do, explain how to start the car, how to drive observing the highway code, paying due care and attention to road signs, traffic signals, parking and, above all, how to manoeuvre while observing the safety of other motorists, pedestrians and yourself.
3. ensure that you carry 'L' plates to indicate to other drivers you are a learner.

Now, even though you may be fully familiar with the controls, it does not mean you can drive the car competently in densely populated areas and on the high roads and motorways. That skill will come gradually, and before you can relinquish your provisional driving licence and throw away your 'L' plates you will have to pass a test to demonstrate your competence to an examiner before a Full Driving Licence is given to you.

The whole thing has been a learning process: the person who was originally responsible for your success was the instructor and you were the one who made the effort.

There are many professional advisers who are competent to give advice. Always seek guidance from experts, and make it a rule of thumb that you deal only with qualified people. Always express your problem as you see it and ask them for their opinion and how they would recommend you solve it. The answers they give must not be taken in blind faith, but rather you must insist they explain in simple terminology if they talk in professional jargon – their job is to convince you that they are the right people to handle your problem. If you do not understand what they say, ask what they mean. If they are not prepared to give you this service, then obviously they do not deserve your business. When you are the buyer the onus is on them to sell to you. Be business-like and honest in your approach and very often they will either submit to your request and give you want you are looking for or they will tell you to find another adviser. This is better for both parties.

Under no circumstances should you take professional advice from unqualified people, however close or friendly they are to you. This is business not friendship. There are many people who like to give the impression that they are the masters on the subject you are seeking advice on, but the information they give you can get you into a lot of hot water. Remember, you are the one who is buying – you do things to please yourself first. It is your problem, your well-being and your money. You are entitled to the service you are paying to get. Go about it politely, but in a professional manner.

If your problem is recurrent, ongoing or getting more difficult day by day, go for reassurance to your expert. Bother him, that is what he is being paid for, make it his headache. Get a second opinion if you are not satisfied or still worried, but change only when you have been convinced that there is no light at the end of the tunnel and no solution in sight and you feel you have been wronged. Take it up with higher authorities or controlling bodies responsible for professional conduct and sue, if necessary, for damages.

Never make a decision based on emotional reasons, but rather by:

- the content (the logic behind the sweet talk)
- the motive (the intention)
- what is done (the actions).

Many professional advisers can be blunt, to the point, and might not be liked very much for their manner. Beware of forming erroneous opinions! And bear in mind, when professionals have a problem they take it to another expert. What happens when the psychiatrist goes bananas? He is taken to another psychiatrist for treatment.

Now, the people you do turn to for support are family and friends. What they can give you is a buffer to handle all the knocks, a shoulder to cry on or an outlet for your feelings. If you are a salesperson who lacks the support of your partner, either change your job or change your partner's thinking.

This will be one of the primary indicators of your ability to pursue a sales career and all the ups and downs which go with it. It would be a formidable task and it is only the psychologically super-tough and non-caring individual who can go ahead regardless of emotional support, and I suspect such a person could not make it to the top.

If we focus on the medical profession, here is the way they operate. Doctors are trained to diagnose illness, but it is the nursing profession that offers the care. This is why doctors are usually hurried in surgeries. They want to collate all the facts on their patients and make a diagnosis. Do not misunderstand their role when they act hurried. Have faith and patience. Take your time, be patient when you are buying, but when you are selling you move fast. In this instance the seller is the professional adviser – he controls the time you spend in consultation with him, but you control his livelihood.

If things go wrong who is to blame? The answer is nobody else but yourself. *Caveat Emptor* means buyer beware! The ultimate responsibility for fouling up lies on your shoulders. If you are selling and a sale is lost, the harsh truth is that responsibility for losing that sale lies in the hand of the salesperson. This topic will be covered later in the book. Never blame others, start by looking for the solution in yourself. When things go wrong, as they sometimes do, even with the most precision-built machines and the finest of human beings, even the best of trained experts can and do fail. Look at what happened to the Titanic and the American Space Shuttle Columbia which exploded in mid-air.

What is crucial is the ability to put the whole incident aside, treat it as a temporary setback, learn from your mistakes and bounce back into business.

IF

IF you can keep your head when all about you
Are losing theirs and blaming it on you;
IF you can trust yourself when all men doubt you,
But make allowance for their doubting too;
IF you can wait and not be tired by waiting,
Or being lied about, don't deal in lies,
Or being hated don't give way to hating,
And yet don't look too good, nor talk too wise:

IF you can dream and not make dreams your master;
IF you can think and not make thoughts your aim;
IF you can meet with Triumph and Disaster
And treat those two impostors just the same;
IF you can bear to hear the truth you've spoken
Twisted by knaves to make a trap for fools,
Or watch the things you gave your life to, broken,
And stoop and build 'em up with worn out tools:

IF you can make one heap of all your winnings
And risk it on one turn of pitch and toss,
And lose, and start again at your beginnings
And never breathe a word about your loss;
IF you can force your heart and nerve and sinew
To serve your turn long after they are gone,
And so hold on when there is nothing in you
Except the Will which says to them: "Hold On!"

IF you can talk with crowds and keep your virtue,
Or walk with Kings nor lose the common touch,
IF neither foes nor loving friends can hurt you,
IF all men count with you, but none too much;
IF you can fill the unforgiving minute
With sixty seconds' worth of distance run,
Yours is the Earth and everything that's in it,
And, which is more, you'll be a Man, my son.

Rudyard Kipling (1865–1936)

Footnote -

 IF you can follow all the above advice readily, I predict you will be a successful salesperson.

CHAPTER 2

Creative dynamic selling

WHO DARES SELLS is about Creative Dynamic Selling, the most powerful psychological techniques you can use to achieve measurable results in the selling, buying and self improvement business.

What is Power?

Positive Thinking is Power
Happiness is Power
Personality is Power
Activity is Power
Skill Is Power
Knowledge is Power
Belief is Power
Confidence is Power
Enthusiasm is Power
Dependability is Power
Courage is Power
Forgiveness is Power
Punctuality is Power

Money is Power
Health and Fitness are Power
Quality is Power
Kindness is Power
Courtesy is Power
Creativity is Power
Position is Power
Honesty and Sincerity are Power
Integrity is Power
Intelligence is Power
Memory is Power
Discipline is Power

Love and Understanding are Power

Simplicity is Power

Persistence is Power

Awareness is Power

But the person who possesses the ability to **sell** and **buy** products, services or ideas **knowledgeably**, **skilfully** and **profitably** by evaluating people **scientifically** to create wealth or achieve tangible results by persuading, motivating, manipulating or negotiating for **mutual benefit** holds **ultimate power**.

CREATIVE DYNAMIC SELLING (C.D.S.)

Creative means using your mind in an imaginative way, or using your powerful computer-like subconscious mind to win in all kinds of sales situations.

Dynamic means being forceful, active, energetic, conveying a sense of power and transmitting energy. Nothing happens in business until the sales force makes it happen!

Selling means the ability to persuade, motivate, manipulate or negotiate with a buyer or buyers to invest in products, services or ideas for mutual benefit. A result of mutual benefit to both buyer and seller must be the objective.

Therefore, **Creative Dynamic Selling** means using your mind in an imaginative way to be mentally and verbally forceful, active, energetic and creative, radiating a sense of power and transmitting energy to persuade, motivate, manipulate or negotiate with a buyer to invest in products, services or ideas for mutual benefit. The whole thing can be summed up as the science and art of **winning** in business and life.

Creative Dynamic Selling starts with a tough 'I will not fail to make this sale' attitude, also known as a Positive Mental Attitude (PMA). It requires the salesperson to see a sales situation, think about the pros and cons and act rapidly to solve it in the most effective and professional manner. In doing so, the salesperson has to consider the buyer's welfare as the most important aspect of the sale, because it is the buyer who helps the salesperson and his company stay in business.

The professional salesperson helps buyers make decisions they are fearful or reluctant to make. A strong sale can only ensue when buyers place their total dependency on the salesperson to solve their specific problem and this the salesperson can only do by winning the buyer over psychologically and ethically.

To facilitate this, the salesperson will have to have the nose of a bloodhound to be able to sniff whether a need exists for the product, service or idea or whether it can be created. When the need has been identified and confirmed by both buyer and seller, the salesperson will then proceed to show the buyer how the product, service or idea will satisfy the need and be of benefit. The salesperson will have a thinking process and a talking manner to get the buyer to say **Yes** to the offer made rather than **No** or **Maybe**. In other words this means getting the buyer to accept the proposal rather than objecting or being indifferent to it.

You will learn specific techniques to handle various situations as they crop up because the raising of objections and the handling of those objections is the normal process in which decisions to buy are made. And these decisions may be favourable or unfavourable to you depending on how clever you are in dealing with the situation. The techniques you will apply will be dependent of course on each particular buyer and their motives.

The salesperson will have to judge the buyer's personality, study the moves made and adapt to changing situations. No two sales are alike and the process of making the sale can vary from day to day depending on the mood and the emotions of the buyer. The salesperson must have the skin of a rhinoceros to be able to withstand verbal laceration, unpleasant insinuations and unsavoury remarks that occasionally come from some buyers.

The salesperson will be courteous, polite and civil to the buyer at all times up to the point at which the buyer tries to take kindness for weakness (some do). At this point the salesperson will fight on a tit-for-tat basis to demonstrate to the buyer who is who. If you show the buyer a reflection of his or her behaviour in your behaviour (also known as the mirror effect) he or she will tone down.

After regaining the status quo, make sure you let the buyer feel he has come out on top, even though it may be the other way around. Imagine the buyer as the master and the salesperson the dog. If you let the buyer take control, you could end like a dog on a lead, being told to sit and smacked on the paw if you do not get your act together. This is an extreme situation, but it does happen from time to time – be warned, be prepared, be a likeable, faithful and affectionate dog, but not an underdog!

I have cited extreme examples in this book for good reasons. If you work on the understanding that you are ready, equipped and trained to tackle the most difficult situation, then the less difficult will be a piece of cake!

In 1976 I went to Canada to the Montreal Olympic Games. I also had the opportunity of visiting the world's tallest (at that time) free-standing-structure, the CN Tower in Toronto, built in 1975. The tower is 1815 ft tall, weighs 130,000 tons (which approximates to 23,214 large elephants) and you can see up to 74.5 miles when you get to the top – a phenomenal engineering feat and an example of outstanding human courage to build. It dwarfs its other famous counterparts, the Eiffel Tower in Paris (1052 feet) and the Empire State Building in New York (1250 feet). To maintain stability of the CN Tower, engineers were confronted with working out how to withstand the turbulent, treacherous winds that exert a twisting, destabilizing effect. The most fascinating outcome was this. The engineers studied the effects of winds of 130 mph that were statistically likely to hit the tower once in a thousand years. Although 114 mph winds were the highest recorded that century, CN Tower Limited built it to withstand a wind of 260 mph – doubling the safety margin. Which just goes to show that you can never be over-prepared.

WHO DARES SELLS will overprepare you for all your sales battles. For just as an iceberg floats one-ninth of its mass above the surface of the water and eight-ninths below, in reality you may only use one-ninth of the information contained within its pages. However, should you require it, you have another eight-ninths in reserve to fall back on.

The buyer either needs – or can be skilfully made to need – your product, service or idea as much as you need the buyer's business. Clearly it is advantageous to accomplish the sale on favourable grounds and on friendly terms. However, if strained feelings do exist, you can still proceed with the sale to the buyer's satisfaction. This is the hallmark of true professionalism – the show must go on, whatever the prevailing conditions. Deal with unpleasant buyers with courtesy and politeness, ignore negative emotions and give them the respect fellow human beings deserve. Quite apart from anything else, this will leave the door open for your repeat call. And remember: a wounded buyer can be a dangerous animal. Aimless retaliation can harm you more than a lost sale, and is the last thing a professional salesperson would attempt. Never create an opening that might cause trouble for yourself. Do not leave yourself exposed and always act with a high degree of skill.

> *Never trouble trouble, till trouble troubles you*
> *For if you trouble trouble, you will double up in two.*

What you should aim for is to get the buyer thinking favourably about you, without perhaps knowing why they are doing so. I have often heard people say to me, 'Your product is the most expensive, but you are the only salesman I have sat down with and discussed my problem, and although many have tried and failed you are the one who has managed to sell me the whole lot, when I only wanted the one item!' Beware, however, the buyer who sweet-talks you, but never gives you the order.

If you cannot close the sale on the first interview due to 'Circumstances beyond your control' it might mean that you do not close the sale this time. Nevertheless, try to leave the buyer with a good impression about you. 'There is something special about that salesperson, some magic I can't quite put my finger on. I cannot use that product right now, but I must have it. I must have it when I am ready to buy.' If you can conquer the buyer's mind the sale will inevitably follow.

Psychological Pressure

Enthusiasm and Motivation are like the two pedals of a bicycle.
Logic and Emotion are the Wheels.
Adaptability is the Gears.
Empathy the Brakes.

On the road to success in sales you have to apply what I call Cycle Logical Pressure on yourself and the buyer to overcome inertia and get momentum going. Once you do this you adapt by changing to situations using different strokes for different folks and empathising with the buyer. When you have whipped up a tremendous amount of motivation and enthusiasm and have fully charged yourself up like a human dynamo and have transferred your feelings on to the buyer with a sales talk that has the right amount of logic and emotional appeal, then you will see the buyer's mood swinging from negative to positive.

I have often made buyers go from a totally negative mood to a crazy buying spree where I have literally had to stop the buyer from ordering more than I had expected them to do. Now isn't that amazing? On the rare occasions where you find an apathetic buyer, you will be advised to give a heavy dose of enthusiasm and motivation with regular intermittent doses of empathy and logic to enable you to fan even the smallest flicker of interest or a ripple of indifference into a mighty flame of desire to help you make that sale.

The following limerick illustrates my point amusingly:

> *An ambitious Salesman from California*
> *Wanted desperately to become a millionaire*
> *His glib talk was a farce*
> *The sales did not last*
> *And the cowboy wound up in prison a failure!*

And the **moral?** Never assume buyers are dumb just because you dazzle them with brilliance and baffle them with bull. Buyers are people and people are buyers. Some of them may give you the impression they are naive, but they will pull the rug you are standing on from under your feet without you even knowing it. Then there are others who will make mince meat out of you in a flash if you try to be too smart with them, while others, if they think they have been conned will crucify you without any remorse.

Think before you play dirty and act too slick with others. Be warned and be cautious in this respect for your own good and for the good of others. Abraham Lincoln said, 'you can fool some of the people all of the time and all of the people some of the time, but you cannot fool all of the people all the time'.

Attack is the best form of Defence

Attack! Attack the problems of life. Attack your work with the utmost zeal and enthusiasm. Attack your negative attitude. Winners attack, they don't run away. Attack must be a way of life. Attack is a way of replacing complacency with positive action. It is a state of readiness to demolish obstacles with aggression, but the aggression must be controlled and channelled in the right direction. The medicine used must cure and not kill. You must be ruthless in business, but it must be based on fair play. Do unto others as you would they should do unto you.

Sometimes in selling you will encounter unjustified aggression on your product, service, ideas, yourself or your company by a dominating buyer who has cultivated a style that has paid off well with other salespeople. Such a buyer can be devastating if you do not know how to handle their tactics. They will intimidate openly or use subtle innuendos and discourtesy to show their opposition to you. For this type of buyer you will have to adopt a strong defence line to be able to handle the onslaught. You can use two different strategies:

1. **The Karate Approach.** If some one attacks you, go straight for the vulnerable parts of the body (offensive self defence) with kicks, blocks, punches and chops.

2. **The Aikido Approach.** What you do here is deflect his attack, disarming him by using his force against him. Tell him 'look chum, calm down, I am not here to make war with you but I'd like to discuss a matter that will be of great benefit to you.'

I always prefer the latter kind of approach. Even the most difficult of buyers will respond by at least giving you a brief hearing, which should be sufficient to pave the way for a subsequent meeting or communication to discuss the matter further. As long as you can impress on the buyers, without reacting to whatever they say or whichever manner they come over, that they are the ones who are going to benefit from the offer, you have created an opening for further discussion. Many a time such a buyer has said something like, 'what a cheek you have. Come and see me again or write to me'.

Tender Loving Care

This comes after the sale has been won, but until then you have to be prepared to use every tactic, every manoeuvre to persuade, motivate, manipulate or negotiate with the buyer to get that sale. Don't kid yourself or the buyer who will soon know what you are after and will stop you if she does not want you selling her. But take notice of this: if your tactics are sound, even though the buyer may know full well what you are up to they cannot stop and will not stop you, as long as they can see they are going to benefit from the outcome. Only an outright weakling or a dumbo of a buyer will say **Yes** when they mean **No**, and if you sell to this type of buyer without qualifying, crosschecking and getting feedback that the buyer's needs will be satisfied by your product, service or idea, that it meets all the requirements and the buyer is pleased with the decision made then the **real dumbo** for making such a sale is yourself, for you risk the buyer subsequently stalling, or cancelling the contract. A good, strong sale should never fall out of bed!

You must do everything within your reasonable capability to make the sale for if you do not, somebody else will, and why should it be so? Your buyer's wellbeing, your company's and your survival are the foremost considerations. All's fair in love,

war and selling, so as long as the buyer has the Money, Authority and Need for your product, service or idea, then kick the competition out by selling the advantages of your proposal while not denigrating the competition.

The buyer in most instances will respond to the positive, vibrant, articulate salesperson and, for the relatively few who do not warm up to your approach you will quickly get body language signals to indicate to you that you should change your *modus operandi*, which any professional salesperson will quickly do to suit the buyer's personality. You should go to the sales interview to speak courteously, supremely confident and happy. If and when the circumstances become very tough you quickly discard your straw hat, put on your soldier's helmet, get ready for a battle of wits and fight all the way to the finish – and fight to win the sale!

When you enter the sales arena with a Positive Mental Attitude you will soon get them dancing to your sweet music of penetrating sales talk, just like the Pied Piper of Hamlin who made all the rats dance to his seductive flute music until they all ended in the river. But never forget that in the selling business it is the buyer who pays the piper and will therefore name the tune!

Tender Loving Care means the salesperson looks after the buyer like a good mother looks after her baby, caring for it, nursing it, standing by it through thick and thin, for better or for worse. In other words, a longstanding, committed relationship which may mean sacrificing your time and making an effort to give your buyer your best. This may include going out of your way on occasion to be of assistance on non-business matters.

No doubt, if your product, service or idea has major competitive disadvantages it will have to be modified in order for you to stay in business and you will have to resell to your buyer the new features and corresponding benefits in order to keep the wolves (competitors) at bay. However, having initially 'got in', it is an easier task for you to convince the buyer of the suitability of your product with its improvements rather than for your competitor. You will find that if you adopt this strategy you need not fear the competition; they will never be able to get in –

or at the very least they will have to put on a superlative show to oust you. Let me show you why in the following example.

I have a client who has a very prosperous business selling consumer repeatables. This client usually commissions me to develop a Christmas promotion to boost sales during the festive season every year, in my capacity as sales, marketing and management consultant to all kinds of businesses, handling their advertising, marketing, image building and professional sales training requirements. The package I had undertaken to provide my client for this particular Christmas was advertising leaflets, a particular high street promotion using people wearing a sweatshirt with the company logo and a brief sales message, plus with a door-to-door distribution in the client's catchment area. A printer had approached my client having heard that he, historically, during the Christmas period did publicity, something which, incidentally, I had pioneered. He was eager to grab my client and to entice him offered to do the entire deal for thirty percent less. I gathered my client was going to make a decision in favour of this cheaper deal. No sooner had I heard about this than I immediately made an appointment with my client and went to see him to re-educate him, even though I had been doing good business with him for many years and had a good working relationship with him. I told him he was dealing with the Rolls Royce of sales promoters, that I had invested in a lot of knowledge, acquired enormous skill and a vast amount of experience, and that what I was offering him was a very personalised service against which I assured him the printer could not compete. I convinced him that a Rolls Royce only runs on 4 Star petrol and not on 2 Star. He owned a Rolls Royce himself, and saving money was important to him, but was not on its own the deciding factor. The outcome was that my client gave me the go ahead at my price. Can you see why? The reason was he trusted me, respected my work and to him the devil he knew was better than the devil he didn't, the new person with whom he had no previous dealings. This is one of numerous instances where this same tactic has helped me keep hold of my clients in the face of competition.

The buyer must be made aware that everything in life has a

price attached to it, and when you and your product, service or idea is worth it then they must be prepared to pay.

Here is the famous sales story of a young man who set his sights on a key role in a movie, having gone to stage school in the USA, and having dedicated himself to practising and rehearsing constantly with a view to get the leading part in the film. After going for many auditions he failed to get the break which he desperately wanted. He became so depressed he was on the threshold of committing suicide. Fortunately, a close friend called on him and he confided his predicament. Let's call this desperate individual Mr Miserable.

Mr Miserable's friend, on hearing his buddy's plight, told him not to do anything foolish to himself and suggested he contact another person – a powerful figure with a great deal of influence in the right places. Let's refer to him as Mr Fixit. An appointment was made for Mr Miserable to meet the influential Mr Fixit in his office. They met and exchanged courtesies, and Mr Fixit asked the troubled Mr Miserable what his problem was. He related the story of how he had spent all his life's earnings training hard with a view to reaching stardom as the leading man in the movie. Now that things had not worked out for him as planned, it was pointless carrying on, and he simply wanted to end it all. Mr Fixit listened patiently and in a reassuring tone of voice told him to relax and that he would do all he could do to help him out. He paused for a moment, picked up the phone, dialled a number and had a half-hour conversation with the person at the other end to no avail. Mr Miserable watched all the action subdued and motionless. Mr Fixit picked up the phone and dialled his second number, and on this occasion the call lasted for twenty minutes. Again the answer was no. On the third attempt to yet another contact the call lasted only ten minutes. This time there was success. Mr Fixit then turned to Mr Miserable and said, 'I have good news for you, you are in.' He immediately reached to his drawer for his invoice pad. Mr Miserable was overjoyed and profusely thanked Mr Fixit until he saw that the invoice was for $25,000. When Mr Miserable saw the figure he almost collapsed with shock, and in a bewildered voice told Mr Fixit, 'I am ever so pleased with what you have done for me, Sir, but all you did was make three telephone calls lasting an hour in total, and you are charging me $25,000 for it!' To which Mr Fixit promptly replied, 'It is not the three telephone calls I made on your behalf that I am charging you for, my friend, but for my twenty-five years of experience as an entrepreneur which enabled me to give you what you so desperately wanted.'

This is how the buyer must see you – a Master. When you can truly say your product is excellent or you are a master of your particular speciality go out and tell the world. Soon people will come chasing after you, for there are many who will be prepared to pay a high price for something good, especially if they have been using something inferior. If a buyer uses a particular brand and repeatedly buys that brand, when she switches to an upgraded version or downgraded version of that brand, all she is doing is exercising a *change of heart*. The professional salesperson who can influence her to invest in a brand that is totally different from what she is used to, is the champion. That salesperson has made the buyer *change her mind*.

Selling fridges to the Eskimos, sand to the Arabs and cars to the Japanese can be done when you decide to programme your powerful subconscious mind that you are going to tackle the impossible and win. But the way you speak to your sub-conscious mind is to talk to it positively and in the present. As it works like a computer it will then instantly set about finding you a solution to your problem. This solution will come to you as an answer, a directive or an inspirational message. Remember always to programme your subconscious mind in positive terms and in the present. For example, if sales are bad, you are heavily in debt, and you are having problems at home, say to yourself *My situation, as bad as it may be, has been caused either by my own negligence or by factors outside my control.* This is not the end of the world but a small setback, and when I have solved it, it is going to pave the way for bigger and better things for me soon. Compare this with *This is it. I am finished. I do not have a hope in hell and I will never make it any better.* Use the Positive and Present, not the Negative and Future method of programming. Try this system and watch the magic in your subconscious mind working to your advantage. Whatever you tell your mind will happen, will happen. So remember IBM's slogan GIGO, which means if you put Garbage In you get Garbage Out.

Reverting back to my client in Consumer Repeatables, our relationship is close, but sometimes bumpy as most normal relationships are. However, from time to time when required I help out in numerous little ways and act like a family friend. I have created my own security and business stability by doing the little things that go a long way. As a result I sleep well at night and do not fear the competition. This is what I mean by Tender Loving Care. This client who is a tough businessman has contested other sales organisations and sought legal redress when they have failed to deliver what they promised.

It is better to have a relationship that starts up badly and ends up well, than one that starts off well and ends up badly. If you are an outright devious or pathological liar, and cannot be honest to your buyer irrespective of what the outcome is going to be, the sale and future sales are doomed from the start. The occasional white lie to keep things ticking over may be necessary and it happens all the time. I do not believe there is such a thing as *one hundred percent* honest business person. Play the game the way it has to be played like a professional and you will often come out the winner. Your task is to do business, not to discover liars. To err is human: to forgive is divine.

Throughout this book I am going to give you controversial ways of dealing with various sales situations, some of which you may accept and some of which you may be reluctant to use. If you are the timid type of salesperson you will be afraid to venture, and therefore you may fail to achieve; but if you are the brave, leader type then you will have to have a bash at it. The only way you will know is to suck it and see for yourself. Is it sweet like honey, sharp like lemon or bitter like ale?

My conclusions on this topic are, *Fight the great fight with a prospect with all your might until victory is achieved. If you don't understand the rules, don't play the game, and always treat your customers like gold dust, because they are the ones that feed you.*

DON'T YOU QUIT

When things go wrong, as they sometimes will,
When the road you're trudging seems all uphill
When the funds are low and the debts are high,
And you want to smile, but you have to sigh,
When care is pressing you down a bit,
Rest, if you must – but don't you quit.

Life is queer with its twists and turns,
As everyone of us sometimes learns,
And many a failure turns about
When he might have won had he stuck it out;
Don't give up, though the pace seems slow
You might succeed with another blow.

Often the goal is nearer than
It seems to a faint and faltering man,
Often the struggler has given up
When he might have captured the victor's cup.
And he learned too late, when the
night slipped down,
How close he was to the golden crown.

Success is failure turned inside out
The silver tint of the clouds of doubt
And you never can tell how close you are,
It may be near when it seems afar;
So stick to the fight when you're hardest hit,
It's when things seem worst that you mustn't quit.

Anon

Sales Humour

It has become a sort of religion with me that whenever I talk
to anyone outside my family and small circle of close friends,
I always now, by virtue of my conditioning, look for an
opportunity to SELL and BUY. This has forced me to become

versatile. I am Jew to the Jew, Arab to the Arab, Asian to the Asian, European to the European, Yank to the Yank, African to the African. Prior to meeting with any national, I would learn as much as possible about their food, clothing, religion, customs and mannerisms. My observations from experience are so finely tuned that I can literally pinpoint what part of the world a person comes from no sooner than I hear the accent and see their facial features. I open out with a greeting that they identify with and immediately copy their ways of communication to build up a subconscious rapport during the initial part of the meeting. Subsequently I revert back to being myself after I have built up the confidence level. Even though my knowledge of foreign languages is near zero, as a general rule, I deliberately speak in basic English if their knowledge of English is not very good, with a lot of hand, head, body and foot movements to simulate the prospect's own kind of people behaviour so he can identify with it. This kind of behaviour on my part invites me into his brotherhood as one of his own and prevents him treating me as an outsider. This is how you can break down the psychological barriers before starting work on making the sale.

I would start off with an opening greeting like this:

Buon giorno	–	To an Italian
Coma esta	–	To a Portuguese
Bonjour	–	To a French person
Hi	–	To an American
Zdrazdvite	–	To a Russian
Hello	–	To an English person
Zdravo	–	To a Yugoslav
Sawadee	–	To a Thai
Salam ale Kum	–	To an Arab

This is a tremendous ice breaker and from there on it is a matter of living on your wits. Using this approach I have sold to many different nationalities. If on the rare occasion I say Bonjour to a Spaniard and he says No, I say Espanol?, they will soon confirm as to whether I was right which allows me to move straight into a broken English sales talk if their command of the language is poor.

Some years ago I was doing freelance work selling newspaper advertising space. I had sold a quarter page advert to a restaurant. The deal was signed on a Friday with the restaurant owner who wanted the same advert which appeared in a competitive newspaper to appear in my company's newspaper. He said he would bring a copy of the newspaper on the following Monday evening by 6.00 pm, to enable us to lift the artwork and reproduce it in the advert. I arrived at the appointed time, only to discover he had forgotten to bring the newspaper. Copy deadline for my newspaper was Tuesday by noon. To add fuel to the fire, the restaurant was full, the owner was short of staff and was running around like a cat on a hot tin roof busily serving his customers and paying little attention to me. My situation was also unenviable as I had to get the copy – he knew it and I knew it. I plucked up courage and decided to follow him until he gave me a decision. He had just picked up some dishes from the table onto a tray which he was holding in one hand and was literally running into the kitchen. I gave chase, and when he saw me coming he hesitated, and in the process the tray struck the edge of the door and down came the hot curry like molten lava on his clean white jacket. He was furious and turned around and told me in no uncertain terms where to go. I stood my ground and said, 'You rascal! You have the audacity to book space in the front page, and as a result somebody else had to forfeit this opportunity. You have let me down while I bent over backwards to get you the best deal. Now it's up to you to give me the copy or pay for the blank space on which we will print only the name of your restaurant.' He got the point, told me to sit down, gave me a fantastic courtesy dinner plus cash on top of the deal, and signed for a new advert to be created and designed through me for the newspaper, which I got done post haste through an external design studio. We both ended up being very pleased.

In my early days in selling, I worked as a sales representative for a very big international company which specialised in manufacturing and selling business equipment. My previous experience in selling was limited even though I had plenty of academic experience and a vast knowledge of people and places having spent a period of time in the Merchant Navy. My company was eager to pull the business from another large company and all previous sales efforts by other representatives had blown out. I took on the task and quickly realised that the departmental head of this particular company had a close affiliation to our competitors. He had been using their equipment on a lease basis for seven years and had therefore built up loyalty to their products and sales representatives. I was fully aware that my competitor's equipment had disadvantages as well as advantages, unknown to the departmental head who was away on holiday I managed to arrange a demonstration with the section head and his three assistants who were going to use the equipment. I told them that as far as the boss was concerned, he really did not care about their wellbeing because it was they who were going to do all the mundane work, but by golly if the workload was not completed on time, every time, they could be in for a rollocking and, what's more, it could possibly mean the boot! I noticed the expression on their faces! I then went on to demonstrate all the features of our machine by talking only in terms of benefits that would save them time and effort and contribute to efficiency of the department, and boy, did I make that demonstration like a West End theatrical show! The audience was enthralled. I let each of them try their hand at operation – they just loved it! I left the system on trial under no obligation because during that time a big workload came in and our machine just handled it with ease.

I had won, and having made the initial break, went on to motivating the staff, with whom I had a good rapport, to get more ancillary product sales. My relationship with the departmental head was formal and business-like – but I came home to a hero's welcome at my office, which really meant something to me.

I left the machine for three days, checking daily that things were running smoothly. I soon realized the staff had fallen in love with my system. One afternoon about the time that the workload usually started to build up, I purposely went and removed the system, much to their dismay. I then told them that since they needed the superior benefits of my machine, they should all make a concerted effort and make representations to the departmental head when he returned. I made a lunch appointment with the section leader and gave him a treat that made him think about me long after I had left. I also told him

I would be writing a report, together with a quotation, for the departmental head advising him what had transpired and giving him my observations and recommendations, saying that the section staff would back up what I had recommended. I had laid the foundations for ousting the competitor's machine. The lease on the competitor's machine was up in the December, in approximately one year's time. Every month I would regularly call the departmental head asking how things were going. Sometimes he would show his annoyance at my persistence, but that did not worry me – I wanted the sale and his staff wanted the equipment. Finally in mid-December I received a Christmas card at the office with an order tucked inside it for the purchase of the system, which gave me a fat commission cheque. The card read: *Mr Ellis, here is that bloody order you have been chasing for so long – now that you've got it, I do not want to see you for another year. Have a good Christmas.*

Customers make pay days possible!

Who is a Customer?
- A Customer is the most important person whether he comes in person, writes to us or telephones.
- A Customer is not dependent on us, we depend upon him for our living.
- A Customer is not an interruption to our work, he is the purpose of it. He is doing us a favour by giving us the opportunity to serve him.
- A Customer is not someone with whom to argue or match our wits. No one has ever won an argument with a customer.
- A Customer is a person who comes to us because he needs certain goods. It is our job to provide them in a way profitable to him and to ourselves.
- A Customer is not a cold statistic, he is a flesh-and-blood human being with emotions and prejudices like our own.
- A Customer is the most important person in this firm, for without him there would be no business!

Mahatma Gandhi

IT'S ALL IN YOUR ATTITUDE

You Are What You Think

If you think you are beaten, you are.
If you think you dare not, you don't.
If you like to win, but you think you can't,
It is almost certain you won't.

If you think you'll lose, you're lost,
For out of the world we find,
Success begins with a fellow's will
It's all in the state of mind.

If you think you are outclassed, you are,
You've got to think high to rise,
You've got to be sure of yourself before
You can ever win a prize.

Life's battles don't always go
To the stronger or faster man,
But sooner or later the man who wins
Is the man WHO THINKS HE CAN!

Anon

As long as the trunk is firm, worry not over the branches swaying to the wind.

A Chinese Proverb

If you mean to profit, learn to please!

Charles Churchill

There are no hard times for good ideas! The customer is always right!

H. Gordon Selfridge

What you do not use yourself, do not give to others – for example . . . advice!

Sri Chinmoy

CHAPTER 3

Creative mechanical buying and selling

We are all fruit and nut cases to a greater or lesser extent, therefore selling and buying can be reduced to a creative mechanical process.

The best way I can explain this phenomenon is to look at a chestnut which I always think looks like the human brain. It's got a hard skin like the skull and a white kernel patterned like the two hemispheres of the brain. Now to enjoy the delicious chestnut, you have to give it a roasting. Once you peel the layer of the skin off, you can place the succulent chestnut in your mouth, chew slowly and enjoy its superb taste. The degree of

Chestnut before roasting

Chestnut after roasting

roasting will be dependent on how tough the skin is.

Similarly, when communicating in Selling or Buying you have to penetrate the other person's own unique outer, put-on psychological barrier and capture their inner mind to get to the real person within. Only then can you enjoy and relish the relationship. The more you know and understand about the person, the more predictable will be the results. And if you can predict the outcome with reasonable accuracy based on experience and the input to your senses from the feedback given by the other person, then you can manipulate that person. You can drive them bananas or make them nuts over you to achieve precisely what you want. This happens all the time to everyone, often without one being aware of it.

Because someone reacts differently, do not automatically assume that person is a fruit and nut case. You may not have any experience of dealing with such people; you may not understand how they think. So no matter how awkward or strange they may appear to you, do not assume that they have the brains of a rocking horse, as in reality they may be millions of miles ahead of you in their thinking and capabilities. And even if your initial reactions are right, you must always try to treat people with love and respect, and only react against them as a last and final resort, and that again only to show your disapproval for their behaviour, and not because you despise them as people.

By not harbouring bad feelings against other humans your tough selling job will be made so much easier. This is not an easy thing to do but can be learnt. If you adopt this philosophy towards life you cannot fail anywhere in the world.

Most of us have used or heard the expression *I couldn't penetrate his thick skull*. This is because the communicator has not understood what makes the receiver think and act favourably to the message and when some unusual feedback was produced, is lost on unfamiliar ground.

The next section will give you an insight on how to deal with this situation.

THE GOLDEN RULE TO PERSUADING, MOTIVATING AND MANIPULATING OTHERS FOR MUTUAL BENEFIT:

"Every closed door has a key that will unlock it, and he who holds the right key to the other person's heart can open the door to enter."

Having all the attributes and qualifications to satisfy a specific requirement does not give you an automatic right of entry to a place you eagerly desire or richly deserve in life. This is why some victims of injustice who may otherwise be the nicest people on the face of the earth sometimes resort to violence, and barbarism to correct the injustice. They get convinced that the door is shut for good when one key did not open it. If they had looked for another key they would not have had to blast the lock. The key to success is to persevere and be flexible in the face of adversity. And if you can't do that you are inviting and encouraging failure.

This is why you see some people less qualified than you in better positions. These are the successful people who have been able to worm their way to the top despite all obstacles. This is why you see some sons and daughters of the rich and famous who had every opportunity but sadly end up as junkies and drop-outs, and sometimes even end their lives tragically. Here are the failures. This is why you see some brilliant well-educated people end up on the scrap heap. I once heard of a genius who was just such a wizard, but could not find himself a job, and eventually lived his life on the dole. Here is a failure. These are the people who do not believe it is possible to change. It is, as I will demonstrate, easy to win in life when you know how and that's the beauty of it.

Learn to fight, because from birth to death life is one continuous struggle for survival.

I cried when I had no shoes until I met a man with no feet. Remember there is always someone who is many times worse off than you. Toughen up your mental strength and reflexes to respond like a hot knife cutting through butter. Accept the truth of life: it is not a bed of roses and is loaded with all kinds of anxieties, misfortunes, drawbacks and disadvantages. Ruthlessly fight all negative thoughts and influences which stand in the way of you conquering those things that cause unhappiness. Always look forward and never look back. Depressive states are a result of looking back with regret at your past. Anxiety states are a result of looking fearfully at the future. Draw a happy medium between the past and the future and live for the present, live for today. Fight every battle second by second, minute by minute, hour by hour and day by day and you will automatically win the war of life. Never shut yourself out from others, because no man is an island.

Search for the right key to open the door of any person from whatever walk of life they come, and they will have some good to offer you. Never pass judgment on any person, however disturbing or threatening their behaviour, conduct or way of life, for in doing so, you will alienate, isolate and compartmentalise another human being. All problems start from this point, and you will find you have made a rod for your own back. Look for ways to get on with others however difficult they may be. Do not try to prove people evil, bad or wicked. Ignore that and only search for the good. Use the power of good to win over evil. Good will, can and must triumph over evil.

Persuade, Motivate, Manipulate and Negotiate – do all you can to win, for you can when you are psychologically prepared. I promise you every lock has a key, but you must find it and try it – there is no easy way in. If someone makes a mistake, and you make another which you think will produce a favourable result, then it is your foolishness when it does not. Your task must be to emerge the winner. That is what this book is all about.

If, for example, you are in a life-threatening situation confronted by an armed fugitive, don't try to fight physically while you are unarmed even if you are stronger. This can only be a win-lose situation. Use psychological pressure instead to outwit even the worst of scoundrels. In this way you will both win. Only bring your opponent to the floor with the most devastating rugby tackle when everything reasonable, decent and good has been tried and failed.

If you can adopt this method of dealing with even the worst of humanity they will somehow act honourably towards you. I know because I have tried both ways and I can tell you honestly the latter is much better. If someone wants to match a sword with a sword let them do so, they will go about it the hard way. I am offering you the easier and better way. Keep cool.

If you can defeat your opponent psychologically there is no better medicine. I will always raise my hat to such a person. For organisations that are geared to matching force with force as long as their motive is good we must give them our wholehearted support. When the Fire Brigade is called in to put a fire out, they will automatically break down doors and windows to save lives first and property later. The job of repairing the place is left to others to do.

For heaven's sake, keep smiling!

Out of the gloom a voice said unto me
"Smile and be happy, things could be worse!"
So I smiled and was happy and indeed,
Things did get better!

All sellers please take note of the importance
of smiling in selling!

A SMILE

A smile costs nothing, but gives you much.
It enriches those who receive,
without making poorer those who give.
It takes but a moment, but the memory of it lasts forever.
None is so rich or mighty that he can get along without it,
and none is so poor but that he can be made rich by it.
A smile creates happiness in the home,
fosters good will in business
and is the countersign of friendship.
It brings rest to the weary,
cheer to the discouraged,
sunshine to the sad
and is nature's best antidote for trouble.
Yet, it cannot be bought, begged, borrowed or stolen,
for it is something of No Value until it is Given Away.
Some people are too tired to give you a smile.
give them one of yours, as none needs a smile so much
as he who has no more to give!

Anon

- Smile – and give your face a holiday!
- Smile – unless you are in the business of carrying coffins.
- Smile – and the whole world smiles with you, cry and you cry alone.
- On the telephone, always DIAL-A-SMILE!
- A smiling jackdaw is better than a laughing jackass.
- An insincere smile is more readily welcomed than a sincere grouse, but still better give a sincere smile, it will last for a long time.

- The face is the mirror of your heart and a smile is the reflection of a happy soul.
- Smile once in the morning and get going with it.
- Smile at a stranger without saying a greeting and you could make him nervous.
- Laugh every day and keep ulcers away.

He who laughs, lasts!

CUTE REPLIES WORK WONDERS IN SALES

If your reflexes are ultra sharp and you can come back like a boomerang on to the buyer twisting her negative statements to something that would be to her advantage and to yours too, then you can win her heart. Children are particularly good at this because it comes out naturally and unexpectedly.

I will never forget the clever reply my little six year old daughter gave me. When she refused her lunch I asked her to think about the starving millions who had nothing to eat. My daughter's instantaneous reply to this was, 'why don't you give my food to them then?'

As a sales promoter, I often get random business from retailers in high streets using below and above the line advertising. On one occasion, I had two similar retail businesses who wished to publicise Easter bargains in the same area and about the same time. One of these businesses was all in favour and made his decision to do the campaign immediately whilst the other was dilly dallying. Neither of the two knew I was handling the other's publicity. My intentions were to do my best for both.

I signed the deal with the business who was all set to go ahead – call them Client A – and started work on the project. To the client who was procrastinating – Client B – I said, 'soon there will be activity in the area and if you do not make up your minds and do something shortly, a competitor could be launching a campaign and would have the edge. You will be like Nero playing the fiddle while Rome burned,' at which Client B made an instantaneous decision to have the campaign done at double the cost of Client A immediately. My loyalties were to both business owners as I liked them both and they in turn liked me too. But my prime loyalty as a businessman was to cash. As I am self employed, I rise every morning unemployed, and hungry for business. I believe money doesn't just talk, it swears, and I know because I have been through some hard times myself.

Client B's campaign started off well with smart leaflet distributors wearing customised sweatshirts handing out leaflets on the high street. The next week, Client A also had a similar style campaign. Being the campaign organiser, things went dreadfully wrong for me when I received a telephone call from Client B saying his competitor had distributors handing out promotional material on his doorstep and having spoken to the field supervisor was advised that the promoter of this event was myself. He was so angry he could have chopped my head off! I had to explain that I had given the field supervisor's promotion agency clear cut instructions about how and where to distribute and it was obviously not properly conveyed to the team and this was the cause of the problem. Through the grapevine, Client A got to know I had promoted Client B the previous week and that made him upset too because he claimed it affected his sales as they did not do as well as expected. I was able to persuade both clients that, like a doctor, I was treating two patients to the best of my ability and in an ethical manner. As my father used to say, if you drink a glass of milk under a palmyrah tree, some people will say you are drinking toddy, a white intoxicating liquor produced from this tree which resembles milk. This time a cute reply helped me in an awkward situation. There are numerous instances where it can work wonders to help you to make sales, keep customers and bail you out from unforeseen trouble when used spontaneously and intelligently.

In another case I was handling the training and promotion of a high-tech retail outlet. I had just finished a professional sales training course for the directors and staff and had embarked on an advertising campaign. The Managing Director was keen for new instantaneous leads (most of his current business was primarily servicing and selling to existing clients) to put his training into practice. However, he did not wish to increase the advertising to the level I had recommended. He had full faith in my abilities, but due to his budget limitations he no longer wanted to speculate further. I was face to face with him in his office and asked him, 'Why is it that you see a cornflakes advertisement appearing on television time after time, day after day? It is like using a nail and a hammer – you hit the nail on the head and it goes into the wood thus far, then you hit it again and it goes in further and you hit it again to go in even further. In other words it reinforces the message. All you have done is a limited amount of advertising, which has produced some results. I am no miracle worker, but for advertising to work it must be seen often and depends on dropping the right thing, in the right place, at the right time, to the right people and at the right price. Your products are speciality products which are bought infrequently. One campaign is not enough; you have to do it again and again for it to work – people need to be reminded about your company and its standing in the market place or else they will make the purchase when the need arises from your competitors. You know we have spent a long time creating your advertising. Nobody can criticize its content or visual impact. I have done everything to help you succeed, you know that. I am now, have always been and will always be backing you to the best of my ability and now you are backing out! Now it's up to you to make your mind up.' I just stood still, silent and looked at him straight in the eyes. He promptly gave me a re-order and went even further in ordering promotional gifts to give away as handouts. Cute replies work wonders when you know what, when, how and whom to use it on for mutual benefit.

Dare to use them in *your* sales efforts to see what magic results they can produce for you. Get cracking and good luck!

A Word of Caution

When driving a car the Rules of the Road say that while overtaking another vehicle or changing directions to the right or left, the sequence to follow is:

Mirror – Signal – Manoeuvre

In Selling the Rule is:

Put Brain in Gear before you put Mouth in Action

Fish 'n' Chips

There is a close parallel between selling and fishing. To catch fish (make sales) you put your chips down (pit your expertise against the elements) and when you succeed (make money), then you can eat (have a better standard of living). A professional fisherman who lives by catching fish treats the sport as a business. Fish have to be caught and sold to provide an income. He must be both a dreamer and a realist, living in a world of his own but with a goal to achieve everyday. He cannot afford to make mistakes, for although the prize for success is glorious, the penalties for failure are severe. The professional fisherman cannot expect to treat his job lightly, for if he does it will affect his livelihood. He dreams of nothing but the ripples of the water, the battle with his catch, the sound of the spinning reel and the ultimate victory of man over fish (his quarry). The same is true in hunting and other blood sports. Whilst I do not advocate or contribute to blood sports in any way, I cannot but acknowledge the fact that there is an element of supreme skill present in all such sports. The salesperson who closes a complicated sale demonstrates a comparable degree of skill and expertise.

The professional fisherman needs to know and do much before he can take a prized catch. For instance, he must know how to handle his tackle, his rod, reel and line and he must know how to present the bait (food on the hook) or lure (an artificial device that attracts fish by guile). He has got to know how to set the hook, play the fish and finally land it.

If you want to become an expert angler, then you have to learn the skills from the professionals, reading books and watching others, and you have to be diligent and persevere. There is a favourite expression used in sales training, *Give a man a fish and you feed him for a day; teach a man to fish and you feed him for a lifetime.*

Knowledge, skill and experience are the raw materials of the success trade. Acquire them for heaven's sake by hook or by crook if you want to achieve your goals. A fish will not come out of its natural habitat easily. It will fight for its life and will use a lot of tricks to break free. Once hooked, it will surge, jump, rush and try to free its mouth from the lure, and the fisherman will have to play it by keeping the line taut and releasing the pressure as appropriate until the fish is worn out and can be hauled in. The same is true in selling. The salesperson will play the buyer like a cat and mouse game. I do not care what type of sales animal you are, just as I do not care whether the cat is black or white as long as it catches mice! The salesperson will guide the buyer to make a favourable decision that the salesperson wishes the buyer to take. The salesperson would do this by

- talking (asking questions)
- listening (to feedback given by the buyer)
- replying (giving pertinent information back)
- handling objections (overcoming sales resistance)
- closing (getting commitment to buy from the buyer).

> *Mighty whales, the big fish of the oceans,*
> *are easily harpooned when they are spouting.*

The more information the buyer gives when talking, the easier it is for the salesperson to do the closing. For a professional fisherman to be successful, he will have to go about his business in an organised manner. The following information makes a comparison between selling and fishing and is not intended to be a treatise on fishing. Hence the professional fisherman will:

1. Have an objective
   - stream fish (trout, salmon, grayling)
   - big game deep sea fish (marlin, swordfish, tuna).
2. Have a method
   - a natural bait like worms, crayfish or insects are attached to the hook which will lie beneath the water surface until the fish bites.
   - trolling – here the hook with a bait or artificial lure is drawn through the water in a boat which can be sea, river or lake.
   - casting – a rod is used with a live bait or artificial lure in fresh water or salt water to catch fish.
3. Be well prepared
   - he will have a positive attitude towards making the catch

and he will be self motivated to achieve his goal. He will also study such things as weather conditions and read fishing magazines and journals to improve his knowledge.

4. Have the right equipment
   - he will have a selection of lures just like a golfer who has an assortment of clubs for different putts, but restricts the use to two or three primarily. Fishing rods are available as extra light, light, medium and heavy. He will also use the right bait to attract the fish he is trying to catch. He might use a live bait such as a mayfly. Alternatively, he might use a dry fly which floats above the surface of the water and imitates insects while a wet fly is designed to move below the surface.

5. Have the right knowledge
   - if he wishes to catch trout, he will either have to use a live bait or mayfly or use an artificial lure that imitates the action of the mayfly. If he lacks knowledge of the trout's feeding habits, how to cast the line and which other fish are likely to be attracted to the bait, even the best of equipment will not help him. When in search of game fish, the object is to imitate the action of a small fish being chased by a larger pursuer so that the game fish makes a grab for the bait. When catching bass the bait should lie at the bottom. A surface lure is used to catch pike, and a shallow running lure to catch fish in shallow waters, while salmon are usually caught using a prawn bait.

6. Go to the right places
   - He will go to the waters where the particular type of fish are found. Salmon are found in abundance in Scotland, Ireland and certain select areas of the British Isles. Trout, bream and carp in the River Thames. Trout in particular can be found in large quantities in Normandy, while Florida is famous for big game deep sea fishing.

7. Be there at the right time
   - During the day or night, dusk, dawn, spring, summer, autumn or winter. Fish bite better at certain times of the day and year, just as it is easier to sell ice cream in summer than in winter.

The above shows you clearly the analogy between selling and fishing. To be successful in both requires a planned system of action and a lot of expertise. Just as a beginner can become an expert angler by applying himself, learning the skills and having the correct attitude of mind, so an amateur can grow into a top flight salesperson. You first start as a small fish in a small pond, then as you grow further you become a big fish in a small pond, finally becoming a big fish that swims in the mighty ocean.

THE FUNNEL TECHNIQUE

In selling what you have to do is to keep driving your buyer systematically, skilfully and scientifically into an imaginary funnel, gradually converging the buyer's escape options. All you have to do is to put a bucket at the other end and the buyer jumps right in, giving you the decision to go ahead.

This technique must not be interpreted as being negative or unethical. It is very much like trying to get a hen to lay an egg. What you do is you catch it and put it in a straw basket, cover it with a lid and it will lay an egg for you because you have induced it to do so by creating the right environment and conditions.

The reason I say you have to *drive* the buyer (the driving force being provided by the seller) is because conscious, unconscious and subconscious factors which come out as logical and/or

emotional words and non-verbal communication reflecting her likes, dislikes, fears, predjucices and perceptions could restrict the buyer from making a favourable decision. She may like to make a favourable decision, but cannot without assistance for reasons she may or may not be aware of. Your job is to find out what these reasons are, and overcome them. This reluctance on the part of the buyer to move further into the funnel once you start the sales process means that you have to either persuade, motivate, manipulate or negotiate, depending on the type of buyer, of your good intentions by helping her to make the decision, convincing them it will improve their wellbeing, success and wealth. This is the seller's job and an obligation the seller owes to the buyer.

The following example shows how the Funnel Technique can be applied.

A patient comes to you, a dentist, for a routine dental check up. You look at her teeth, take an X-ray and then tell her she has a tooth which is rather badly decayed and needs filling. Your patient then replies, 'come on, are you kidding? I've had it like that for many years, I feel no pain, and I do not think I need a filling'.

You reply, 'From my professional view point, I recommend you do have it filled now because a little bit of drilling and a little bit of filling can save you a painful extraction later!' You as the dentist are the seller and the patient is the buyer. You are the master of your profession, not the patient, and she depends on your expertise to sort her problem out, if she has got one. If the patient responds by refusing to have it done, either through fear, outright ignorance or concern about personal appearance, the good professional dentist who knows his business inside out must know how to persuade, motivate, manipulate or negotiate with this patient to prevent further damage. Indeed, not to do so would be tantamount to professional negligence. Even though the patient (the buyer) has the final say, the professional adviser (the seller) must, in the interest of the patient, sell that individual the recommended advice and encourage her to make a decision to use the product, service or idea. Never treat a difficult customer with indifference.

The buyer may find hundreds of reasons not to go ahead, but

the seller need find only one good reason that the buyer sees as being beneficial to him, and home in on it till a favourable decision is made. Only if the buyer gives an outright 'no', and the seller has gone as far as possible must the selling stop.

Cowboys, Crooks and Confidence Tricksters

The recipe for lasting success is provided by basic ingredients: good motives. People will judge you not by what you have got, but rather by how you got it; not by what you say but how you said it; not by what your family connections are but rather by who you are. Each person is responsible for himself. Whatever the human mind desires and believes it can achieve, by fair means or foul – but what will stand out in the final analysis is your motives.

Robin Hood stole from the rich to give to the poor. His acts are judged by some to be noble while others would say he was wrong.

A friend of mine recently visited Australia and had a strange encounter while over there. She went to a department store to buy some items of clothing. After browsing through various selections, she was approached by an elderly woman who said in a tearful voice, 'Excuse me dear, you look so much like my daughter, your sweet face resembles hers in every way, but the saddest thing for me is that she does not contact me anymore. I am so very miserable – I miss her so much.' She pulled out a handkerchief and looked as if she was about to sob her heart out. Turning to my friend, she said, 'May I ask you a request? When I leave will you just wave your hand to me and say, "Cheerio Mummy"? It would make me very happy.' My friend was glad to agree. As the old lady made her way to the exit my friend waved and shouted, 'Cheerio Mummy!' and walked towards the cashier to pay for her goods. The cashier totalled up her bill and said, '$60 please, plus $40 for your mum – a total of $100 please.'

'I beg your pardon, she is not my mother, I just met her for the first time' said my puzzled friend.

'Come on madam, who are you trying to kid? I heard you call and wave to that lady saying "Cheerio Mummy",' the cashier angrily retorted.

In the end my friend had to pay the bill to save face.

Unfortunately, unscrupulous people abound. Some people are prepared to risk everything and take a chance, but woe be unto the ones that are pursued relentlessly by the authorities, finally found out and have to pay dearly for their folly. Is it worth it?

On one of my trips to Sri Lanka, I stopped at a wayside cafe to have a cool drink. There was another man seated on the opposite side of the table. He was poor with an emaciated appearance, but the thing that really stuck out was the fearful look on his face. He looked really terrified. He kept staring at me, so I summoned the waiter to ask him why this man was looking so hard at me. Apparently this man had walked into the restaurant about a half an hour before I arrived, ordered some food and drink through terrible hunger, had eaten his meal but did not have money to pay for it. He was fearful of what the management might do to him. My heart just melted when I heard this. I walked up to this man and told him I would pay the bill, and gave him a few rupees as a gift. The man was overjoyed. He thanked me repeatedly, and with tears in his eyes literally worshipped me for saving him from his predicament. This was a genuine case that deserved sympathy but some ruthless business owner may have hung this man as a wolf when he was only a lamb.

In business we have to be tough but ethical, flexible and adaptable. You cannot sell to an unscrupulous person by playing it according to the rule book. I do not care what anybody says, as a professional salesperson, you must be able to run with the hare and hunt with the hounds. This is why you hear the armed forces talk of 'covert operations', and sometimes you hear of police mingling with criminals. But even when you have to act the thief to catch a thief, it does not mean we have to change our legal, moral and ethical values.

If you are born a leopard, you can never be a cat. If your upbringing has been respectable, you will certainly carry those hallmarks and they will not change. You may use all the tactics, wear a different cloak and use a different dagger to achieve your objectives, but when the task is accomplished, you revert back to your true self. I say this from first hand experience, having sold to the good, the bad and the ugly all over the world. To be ethical means you fight the great fight, fight to win and win the fight, but when you see your opponent down on the canvas you do not beat the hell out of him. You fought fair. You won. You respect him and you don't blow your own trumpet. You simply treat it as part of your normal daily activities, just like the professional fisherman who catches fish, or like the lawyer who wins a case. It is your job and you move on to the next one. This is the way to think and act as a true professional.

If you claim to be a professional salesperson, then you must be legal, decent, honest and ethical. If you do not and merely masquerade as one, then all you will do is tarnish your image and bring the profession of selling into disrepute. Life assurance, double glazing, electronic showers and others have all taken their fair share of criticism in the buying public's backlash to unethical selling practices.

Only you will know whether you are engaging in nefarious selling practices, and don't expect to get away without getting caught. Consumer protection laws and buyer awareness mean that even the sharpest shooters cannot hope to be lucky all the time. As Abraham Lincoln said, 'You can fool some of the people all of the time, but you cannot fool all of the people all of the time.'

In Malaysia, the penalty for drug trafficking is death – the ultimate price. While drug trafficking may be a lucrative business for the trafficker, look at the heavy price the addict has to pay. Think of the poor souls who get hooked on it. Life is meant for living, loving and laughing; not dying in such a horrible manner. Financial success is every business person's right, of course it is, but we must seriously consider how we wish to attain our goals. Are the practices we are engaging in ethical or unethical? Live and let live, is a universal requirement, and we must only deal a crushing blow when our own lives are threatened, in defensive attack. We have to be fair to all our brothers and sisters of the universe irrespective of colour, creed or religion, because they are part of our extended selves. What lies beneath the outer skin of all races, whether caucasian, negroid, mongoloid or polynesian is red blood, and all our biological needs and reactions are the same.

Travelling to foreign lands and experiencing the beauty, culture, food, way of life and religion is part of the magic of living. Why destroy the planet and its life forms and cause untold pain and suffering? Power is the reason, and acquiring power is natural and good. But exercising destructive power is against life itself. To harness and use creative thinking and power to benefit others is the finest thing a human can give to all other living things. No one can change the world, but if each of us can seriously examine ourselves and try to make an effort to improve first ourselves and then make a useful contribution to others, then the world will be a better place.

There are hundreds of enjoyable and useful occupations that will benefit you and your fellow beings, rather than indulging in dangerous or high-risk activities that serve little or no useful purpose. The laws of nature remain a mystery and apply to one and all without fear or favour. You cannot violate her laws and not expect to pay the price, for in nature there are neither rewards nor punishments, just consequences. In the pursuit of power one can become insensitive to the other's feelings and wellbeing. Herein lies the danger – for the very thing that you possess can be your downfall, just like the spider that spins a web to catch flies and insects and eventually gets entangled in its own web and perishes.

And while we are on the subject of catching flies, a teaspoon of honey is better than a barrel of vinegar. This means that in selling it is much better to use a little kindness, a professional and friendly approach rather than resorting to a mountain of dirty tricks. The truly professional salesperson should know when and how to respond and what to use in any selling situation.

No opportunity is lost; the other fellow takes it.

Anon

A wise man hears one word and understands two.

Yiddish Proverb

Adversity reveals genius, prosperity conceals it.

Anon

WINNERS AND LOSERS

A Winner makes mistakes and admits 'I was wrong.'
A Loser says, 'It wasn't my fault.'
A Winner credits his good luck for winning, though it wasn't luck.
A Loser blames his bad luck for losing, but it wasn't luck.
A Winner works harder than a loser and has more time for leisure.
A Loser is always busy – too busy staying a failure.
A Winner goes through a problem; a Loser goes round it.
A Winner shows he's sorry by making up for it.
A Loser says he's sorry but he does it again next time.

What are you? – A winner or a loser?

The Professional Salesperson's Credo

- I believe that I am the greatest salesperson that exists in this town, city and country. My belief is based on my total dedication to the profession of selling and on hard-earned knowledge, skills and experience, not on an illusion or false premise.
- I will not fail in my duty to put the buyer first and foremost as the most important person in any transaction and will use all my expertise to help the buyer solve problems or situations, so that the buyer will ultimately profit from the business deal. Consequently, my company and I will also benefit.
- I will be ethical and always perform my tasks to the highest professional standards and operate to a just and fair code of business conduct.
- I will live in the hard, down-to-earth world of reality rather than the pie-in-the-sky world of make believe. I will not shirk work but I will have my share of rest, relaxation and enjoyment.

- I will be kind, sincere and sensitive to the thoughts and feelings of others and I will not fail to be persistent, to use tact, to persuade and motivate others to buy me as a person and my products, services or ideas.
- I will be a tough and resilient negotiator, manipulative if necessary and will develop a keen sense of observation and practice the vital skills of listening and interpreting body language signals.
- I will constantly improve on my selling skills and be fully prepared to meet and deal with any eventuality during the sales interview.
- I will plan and execute my work with military precision.
- I will set realistic short, medium and long term goals and work religiously and diligently to achieve them.
- I will not be jealous, envious or vindictive towards my fellow brothers and sisters, and I will use the enormous creative power of my mind to harness my full potential to fight all the way to the winning post.
- I will eliminate all the negative emotions and influences that surround me and replace and enrich my mind with all that is positive and good. In doing so, I declare myself a winner in the business of selling and in the game of life.

Negative and Positive People

Negative People:
- are miserable
- worry
- have no goals
- make no plans
- fear failure
- see false ceilings
- see problems
- blame others for failure
- cheat themselves
- tear down others' goals

Positive People:
- are enthusiastic
- smile
- have goals written down
- have plans
- are self-confident
- expand their minds
- see opportunities
- analyse themselves
- have self-knowledge
- inspire others

CHAPTER 4

When you pay peanuts you get monkeys!

I was once dealing with a financial adviser regarding investing in US property in America. He was a close friend of a friend of mine who said he would be very reasonable when it came to charging me. In fact it was at my insistence that he agreed to be very modest in his charges. I put it like this to him: 'As you are a very close friend of my friend, I hope you will not hit me with the sledge hammer, but just give me a gentle tap with your mallet!' He then proceeded to advise me strongly against investing in the US property market. Having studied that market carefully and having clients already investing over there, he believed there was insufficient growth. This really disappointed me because I liked the American lifestyle and I was hell-bent on investing in a retirement home over there. I suspected that the adviser was giving me incorrect advice, because if I put my money in the UK market and did the transaction through him he would get commission. I questioned him further and asked him whether he was hitting me back with the same weapon I was using on him. 'Are you giving me monkey advice because I am paying peanuts?'

The financial adviser found great amusement in this cheeky question (I was fully ready to defuse the situation should he have reacted adversely) and went into hysterical fits of uncontrollable laughter – I had caught him out. Five minutes later out came the real truth with facts and figures. Only moments earlier he had been trying to do the salesman on the salesman. I hit his 'panic button' and he had to come out with the truth or lose face. Having got all the facts, I then went on to invest in the USA. He offered not to charge me for his monkey talk, so I entertained him to a good business lunch; but that was all.

I strongly believe in this philosophy. If you are good, then you can and must get paid what you are worth; you cannot buy a Rolls Royce at Ford Escort prices. If you are good, then you can and must blow your own trumpet and demand your just dues. Muhammad Ali did it. He certainly beat his own drum and the world loved it. The US marines have a saying *when you are good, it's hard to be humble.*

I know of a door-to-door distribution company that advertised its services by starting off saying, 'We are the most expensive door-to-door distributors in Greater London. We are also the best door-to-door distributors in Greater London.' These are powerful words that build confidence.

You must use similar techniques when you are good and prospective buyers must be educated to pay you for your expertise, products, services or ideas, when it is worth it. I sell my expertise sometimes double or treble the price of my competitors and I have lost very few clients over the years.

There is an old Indian saying: *When you buy an expensive product, you may cry only once, but if you buy a cheap product you may cry often.*

If the buyer's needs are fully met and satisfied, they will be happy and pay you on time, every time, unless of course they are crooks, in which case you must play them at their own game, and play to win.

WINNING TIPS

The more you learn
The more you will know
The more you know and understand
The more you will use
The more you try and the more you use
The more you will sell.

Who Dares Sells!

Don't be led on a wild goose chase

Cut your losses. It is said you must not go wildly chasing a man or a woman blindly, because like buses, there is always one following. Unrequited love, like unreciprocated buyer behaviour is a futile and worthless effort, particularly when your offer is strong and superior and the buyer is weak and pig-headed.

A very close friend of mine fell head over heels in love with a young woman, even though she did not have the slightest inclination towards him. She emigrated and fell in love with a young man whom she married three years later. But, from the time of her departure until the day she married, this lovesick man used to send her two to three love letters every day plus the occasional gift, although she had requested him from the start not to. He did not receive a single reply. It cost him dearly – money, time and mental health. They say love is blind, but what sort of stupidity is this?

Just the same thing can happen in selling. What you have to do is concentrate on good, qualified prospects and look after them like gold dust. Eliminate the time wasters politely, firmly and quickly. Use the Pareto Principle: *20% of your buyers will give you 80% of your business, so spend 80% of your time with 20% of your buyers.*

If you aim to be professional then do not waste time with prospective buyers that have not got the Money, the Authority or the Need.

Very often in business you find the egotistic buyer who likes to give the impression that he or she is the decision maker when they are simply the influencer in the decision-making process. These people are very important in enabling the final decision to be made and can either make or break the sale, but you must not let them take control in any event.

When the influencers are procrastinating or dragging their feet, maybe because they are fearful of giving the wrong advice to their superiors, fearful of being reprimanded, and subconsciously fearful of losing their jobs, then your strategy is to manipulate the influencers to act to safeguard themselves, to look better in the eyes of their superiors and benefit the organization for which they work. In this way you build up goodwill and get results.

As an expert in your field, you do not want to waste time unnecessarily wooing people who cannot say Yes or who are impeding a final outcome that will be profitable to both buyer and seller. Your time is far too precious and valuable to be larking about – unless they are paying you for your time.

I see a business relationship like a marriage partnership. If one partner is not getting their share of satisfaction (benefits), then he or she may seek it elsewhere. Remember you are in business to keep your company and yourself in business by helping others to benefit. The prospective buyers have to appreciate this fact, or you may have to educate them to see you in this light. You are not in the charity business and if that's what they are looking for, tell them to find a turkey from some other benevolent organization that would be prepared to sit and talk with them for free. Subtly let them know you are a high flyer and that your normal playing ground is where eagles fly. If you have done a good selling job they will want to come fly with you and reward you handsomely for your expertise.

For buyers who move slowly, I sometimes spin a yarn like this, 'It may be desirable for us to get this matter processed as soon as possible, for you to enjoy all those benefits I told you about, to avoid suffering a financial loss, and to prevent those disadvantages. I am here at your service to enable you to do just that, even though I have prearranged appointments to see at least five other buyers to-day to complete some transactions to help me pay my bills. As you may know, I am self employed, which therefore means I get up every morning unemployed, and that's real tough for me as I do have liabilities – a wife, two small children, three dogs, five cats and a pet python to feed,' which gets the message across in a friendly way.

I conduct business in the way that benefits both my buyer and myself most. I sell them first class know-how, products or services at competitive prices. I make sure I always get paid in one way or another. I get fantastic discounts for my personal use on the products or services I promote on behalf of my clients, plus other perks like being invited to private functions, weddings and parties. My relationship is so strong and healthy with my buyers that I never fear the competition. Indeed, I have a motto I work to and keep to myself which is: *when I eventually get in, the competition gets out and stays out by courtesy of the buyer.*

I do not use dynamite to bring down the brick wall but pull out one brick at a time till I have the whole wall demolished. This way neither the buyer nor the competition fully realise I have got in and have consolidated myself. I never try to put on airs and graces and speak frankly, honestly and sincerely, calling a spade a spade. At times you may have to rub their noses into it to make them see sense, but surprisingly they usually respect my candid talk and respond, because the truth is what really matters. I know because some buyers have told me so.

The reason why many a salesperson fails to capture a buyer's mind and heart and make the sale is that they come across to the buyer as being 'cosmetic' – they try to give the impression that they are the 'cream' when in reality they are perceived by the buyer as a 'clot'.

One buyer, the managing director of a large company, told me openly, 'I see many salespeople from many top companies, but nobody has even dared to speak to me like this. I'd like to kill you – I really do not know why I am giving you the business. But you are different, and I like you.' He is now a good friend. In other words, I carve out the destination I want to reach with the buyer, I then put on a skilful demonstration or presentation and I scientifically and artistically either persuade, motivate, manipulate or negotiate with them so that they do not know what really hits them; they are sold – hook, line and sinker. They cannot take me on a wild goose chase even if they wanted to. Why not do the same? They will either love you or leave you!

A USEFUL SELLING POINT

Buyers love sellers who talk a lot about benefits and justify the cost or price.

Fit for Selling?

To climb the success ladder and stay there, you are well advised to pay sensible attention to physical fitness, and apportion at least a few minutes a day to regular exercise, just as you are devoting precious time to learning the psychological techniques and verbal skills for success in selling. You need not go overboard to become a fitness fanatic but rather spend some time each day by engaging in any one of the popular physical activities listed below. Eliminate or reduce smoking, keep drinking to a minimum and watch your weight. Rest and relaxation are also very important.

If you have any serious medical condition or disability, always consult your doctor first and take professional advice from a trained instructor before you start any rigorous physical activity. Keep a check on your stress levels, and keep them under control. The following check list is provided for your information.

What level of stress are you under?
(All questions relate to the last year of your life, except where specified.)

	Points
● Has your life partner died in the past three years?	20
● Have you divorced or become separated in the past three years?	15
● Has a close relative died in the past three years?	13
● Have you been in hospital because of injury or illness?	11
● Have you moved house?	11
● Have you got back together with your partner after a separation?	10
● Have you discovered that you are soon to become a parent?	9

Points

- Has there been a major change either for better or worse in the close health of a close member of your family?   9
- Have you retired or been made redundant?   9
- Is trouble with your partner causing tension within the family?   8
- Are you experiencing any sexual difficulties or any dissatisfaction with your sex life?   8
- Has your family acquired a new member either by birth or through a new relationship?   8
- Has a close friend died?   8
- Have you become financially much better off or much worse off?   8
- Have you changed your job?   8
- Have any of your children left home, started or finished school or become unemployed?   6
- Is trouble with your partner's family causing you tension?   6
- Do you frequently suffer from premenstrual tension?   6
- Is there anyone at home or at work whom you strongly dislike?   6
- Have you had meteoric success, such as a rapid promotion at work?   6
- Have you experienced jet lag at least twice?   6
- Has there been an upheaval such as moving house or some building work taking place (but not including a change in the family relationships)?   5
- Have you had problems at work that may put your job at risk?   5
- Have you taken on a large mortgage or other debt?   3
- Have you had a minor brush with the law?   2

This is how you rate: Under 30 low, Over 60 higher than normal.

Height		Men	Women
4'11"	(150cm)	7st 2lbs (100lbs)	6st 6lbs (90lbs)
5'0"	(152cm)	7st 7lbs (105lbs)	6st 11lbs (95lbs)
5'1"	(155cm)	7st 12lbs (110lbs)	7st 2lbs (100lbs)
5'2"	(157cm)	8st 3lbs (115lbs)	7st 7lbs (105lbs)
5'3"	(160cm)	8st 8lbs (120lbs)	7st 12lbs (110lbs)
5'4"	(163cm)	8st 13lbs (125lbs)	8st 3lbs (115lbs)
5'5"	(165cm)	9st 4lbs (130lbs)	8st 8lbs (120lbs)
5'6"	(168cm)	9st 9lbs (135lbs)	8st 13lbs (125lbs)
5'7"	(170cm)	10st 00lbs (140lbs)	9st 4lbs (130lbs)
5'8"	(173cm)	10st 5lbs (145lbs)	9st 9lbs (135lbs)
5'9"	(175cm)	10st 10lbs (150lbs)	10st 00lbs (140lbs)
5'10"	(178cm)	11st 1lb (155lbs)	10st 5lbs (145lbs)
5'11"	(180cm)	11st 6lbs (160lbs)	10st 10lbs (150lbs)
6'0"	(183cm)	11st 11lbs (165lbs)	11st 1lb (155lbs)
6'1"	(185cm)	12st 2lbs (170lbs)	11st 6lbs (160lbs)
6'2"	(188cm)	12st 7lbs (175lbs)	11st 11lbs (165lbs)
6'3"	(191cm)	12st 12lbs (180lbs)	
6'4"	(193cm)	13st 3lbs (185lbs)	
6'5"	(196cm)	13st 8lbs (190lbs)	
6'6"	(198cm)	13st 13lbs (195lbs)	

Check Your Ideal Weight
(Height is measured barefoot and Weight is measured without clothes on.)

Get Some Exercise
The following activities are graded from 1–3 according to the degree of suppleness, strength and stamina each gives. Choose an activity which appeals to you and get started as soon as you can.

Once you embark on a programme of physical exercise and the right diet you should experience weight reduction, increased physical fitness and stress reduction, something that can also be reduced by proper diaphragmatic breathing and meditation. No longer will you need to complain and say, 'Poor me, I am overweight and unfit, everything I eat turns to fat,' but rather you can get into shape by balancing your calorie intake with your energy output. Now you are well on your way to being a winner through and through!

Physical Activity	−	Suppleness	+	Strength	+	Stamina	−	Total Points
Swimming	−	3	+	3	+	3	−	9
Disco Dance	−	2	+	3	+	3	−	8
Keep Fit	−	2	+	2	+	3	−	7
Squash	−	3	+	2	+	2	−	7
Cycling	−	1	+	2	+	3	−	6
Running	−	1	+	2	+	3	−	6
Football	−	2	+	2	+	2	−	6
Housework	−	2	+	2	+	2	−	6
Judo/Karate	−	2	+	2	+	2	−	6
Badminton/Tennis	−	2	+	2	+	2	−	6
Climbing Stairs	−	1	+	2	+	2	−	5
Walking Briskly	−	1	+	1	+	1	−	3

The Sales Competition

Casanova and Don Juan were two top flight, dedicated sales professionals. Both were extremely hardworking, competitive and close buddies working for the same company. One day Casanova challenged Don Juan that he could outshine him in spheres outside selling, namely womanising, at which both were also very good. The challenge was eagerly accepted by Don Juan and the rules of the competition drawn up. They were both to go to a forthcoming event, sit at the same table, and for every amorous liaison each arranged he would tap the other's foot. The winner would be the one with the most taps after half an hour.

On the day of the event, both arrived smartly dressed, took their positions at a centrally located table, and there entered into the hall many beautiful women. The competition was going ahead at full speed for 28 minutes on an even footing, tap for tap, indicating both had been successful with the same lady. Suddenly Don Juan's wife and daughter arrived at the function. Don Juan made one tap, and Casanova followed with two taps.

The Profession Called Selling

Let it be spelt out loud and clear, professional selling may appear to be easy but it certainly is not. It is not an occupation which will make you rich quickly, become an overnight success and achieve fantastic results by a stroke of luck. It takes years and years of dedicated hard work, practice and learning in the classroom and through experience to become a top pro. A great many enterprising people get into selling thinking they can amass a quick fortune. Very few do; most don't. Those who make it cannot be classed as being lucky. There is no such word in professional selling. Luck happens if you nominate a number on a roulette table and the ball falls in the slot you chose. It is your good fortune you won and it was success thanks to chance. But on the other hand you can do certain things in a systematic and scientific way to achieve predictable results which is not luck but skill. You *can* create your own success.

Certain non-salespeople view the professional salesperson's job with envy. They believe it is:
- Easy (you only need the gift of the gab)
- Glamorous (fancy cars, wining and dining, the finest hotels)
- Lucrative (you can earn big ticket money and live in luxury like lords).

This is absolutely true for top-flight sales professionals, just as in all other professions. But for the vast majority of mediocre salespeople, this is not true. For people who think selling is easy, the only way you will know is to try it out. You could be in for a rude awakening.

Your first hurdle will be to pass the interview and convince your employer, who could be a sales manager, sales director or a panel that you are the one for the job in preference to the other applicants. You may be subjected to a psychology screening process known as psychometric analysis which will scientifically tell your employer about your suitability. You would be required to provide references and be expected to have the right qualifications for the post. Having got the job, you will have to undergo training to learn about the company, the products, selling skills, and the competition. When you are out in the field you have to produce results, because if you don't, you will discover that no company can afford to carry passengers.

In selling, what you have to realize is that you are literally self-employed, even though you may be on the company's payroll. Unless you produce results, your company doesn't earn and you don't eat. Your belief and your activity, knowledge and skill are what determines your success.

Psychometric Testing

Psychometric tests consist of Human Job Analysis, and Personality Profile Analysis. The following questions and answers will, I hope, deal with most of the questions you might have about this important method of selecting candidates for jobs. I am grateful to Thomas International Management Systems for their help in compiling this information and providing sample questionnaires.

- **What exactly are Human Job Analysis and Personality Profile Analysis?**
  The Human Job Analysis (HJA) is a structured questionnaire for use by anyone in industry and commerce who is involved in job assessment or role specification. Its twenty-four questions concern themselves with the human requirements of the job role, rather than skills or qualifications, and thus it is applicable across the board to all functions be they shop floor, administrative-, sales-, marketing- or management-orientated. On completion, the instrument provides a benchmark to measure and assess information gleaned from the interview and the Personal Profile Analysis (PPA).

  The PPA again is a structured questionnaire which is applicable to the individual rather than the job. It is completed by a candidate applying for a particular position. It measures the same criteria as the HJA, but in a different way, allowing the results of both instruments to be compared for compatibility or deviation. It allows the information gleaned from the HJA to be measured in an objective way.

  The information gathered from the two instruments not only provides a compatibility comparison, but also brings to the surface any anomalies and suggests a line of questions to be asked at the interview which may not normally be accessed by normal interview procedures.

● **How is the HJA used?**

The line manager or supervisor rates the role to be filled according to a Likert Type Scale (a rating system) on the HJA. From this data a visual profile of the job is drawn up. This process takes about 15 minutes.

● **How is the PPA used in Sales selection?**

The Personal Profile Analysis is applied to the candidate and a comparison is made between the resulting Personal Profile Analysis and the Job profile. The Personal Profile Analysis is easy to apply and takes approximately 7 minutes to complete and a further 10 minutes to score and read, providing a wealth of information for the interviewer in no more than 17 to 20 minutes.

● **Who can use it?**

Anyone who has been trained in the use of the system. Users do not need to be psychologists, but training is necessary for competent use of the system. Alternatively, the system can be applied and the results telephoned or forwarded direct to a team of trained analysts at hand who either provide spontaneous verbal feedback, or a written report.

● **Is the PPA reliable?**

The PPA when applied at intervals of no less than three months will reliably measure individuals and reveal similar or dissimilar characteristics (if they have cropped up) in the interim period. The questionnaire is said to be reliable if it is consistent over a period of time.

● **Are the PPA and HJA systems valid?**

The in-built validity of the PPA is high. In an experiment analysing data from 500 subjects, looking at the validity of the PPA with two other well known instruments, all the instruments were saying similar things about the same people. The predictable validity of the system is also very high (around 87%) when it is matched with the HJA.

- ## What are the other uses of the PPA/HJA system?
  Its other uses are in career guidance, management development, compatibility, identification of training needs, and in examining managerial, administrative and sales efficiency, performance and potential. It can identify stress, frustration and lack of goals or direction within the working environment.

- ## Can it be used for counselling?
  The PPA/HJA system is a work-based instrument and as such is an excellent tool to use in the Job and Career Counselling field. It should not however be used for counselling abnormal behaviour or any other form of clinical counselling.

- ## How should these instruments be used in industry and commerce?
  The PPA/HJA system should be used alongside a standard interview procedure. In this way it will provide a means of enhancing the objectivity and reducing the subjectivity of standard interview techniques. It should never be used in isolation and must be seen for what it is – an efficient, cost effective and practical managerial aid for the improvement of any form of work interview be it for selection, redeployment, training and development or counselling. It cannot and should not be used to remove or reduce managerial responsibility but to aid the manager in his or her decision making.

> *'To achieve successful results in selling,*
> *Think carefully before you act,*
> *Act fast after you have thought!'*

Human Job Analysis

This Analysis Matches the Person with The Position

NAME

POSITION *SALES EXECUTIVE - FIELD*

EVALUATED BY *Edward*

DATE *Nov 88*

I RATE EACH QUESTION THINKING OF THE JOB BEING PERFORMED MOST SUCCESSFULLY. PLACE A DOT IN APPROPRIATE BOX, VERY LOW, LOW, SIGNIFICANT, HIGH OR VERY HIGH, BASED ON THE RELATIVE IMPORTANCE OF THE JOB.

	VERY LOW	LOW	SIGNIFICANT	HIGH	VERY HIGH
1. Must concentrate on detailed work easily			●		
2. Must make unpopular decisions in carrying out job			●		
3. Must have persistence to plug steadily at routine work		●			
4. Must have ability to organise various types of people				●	
5. Must be diplomatic and cooperative				●	
6. Must be able to act without a precedent					●
7. Must have ingenuity to create new ideas				●	
8. Must have the ability to deal with strangers					●
9. Must be steady in following an established work pattern	●				
10. Must work directly under supervision	●				
11. Must have poise and mastery of language in expression				●	
12. Must be able to follow a system to perfection		●			
13. Must be able to help others solve human problems			●		
14. Must be able to stay at one work station or area	●				
15. Must develop rhythm and coordination in repetitive work	●				
16. Must be able to handle interruptions and changes					●
17. Must be able to exercise caution in calculating risks		●			
18. Must have ability to motivate others				●	
19. Must have the ability to overcome objections					●
20. Must have vision to plan ahead on a large scale				●	
21. Must have skill to persuade others to his/her point of view					●
22. Must exercise caution in making policy commitments			●		
23. Must have patience to follow detailed instructions	●				
24. Must be satisfied to stay at this job level		●			

II Ignore dots in centre column. Count 2 points for very high, 1 point for high.

(a) Count the number of points in purple squares ☐ 8

(b) Count the number of points in red squares ☐ 7

(c) Count the number of points in black squares ☐ 0

(d) Count the number of points in green squares ☐ 1

III Ignore dots in centre column. Count 2 points for very low, 1 point for low.

(e) Count the number of points in purple squares ☐ 0

(f) Count the number of points in red squares ☐ 0

(g) Count the number of points in black squares ☐ 10

(h) Count the number of points in green squares ☐ 4

THOMAS INTERNATIONAL
MANAGEMENT SYSTEMS (EUROPE) LTD

Hams House,
17 West Street,
Marlow,
Bucks SL7 2LS,
England.
Tel: (06284) 75366

Your **Human Job Analysis**	**From P.P.A.** **How Others See You**	**From P.P.A.** **How You See Yourself**
D I S C	**D I S C**	**D I S C**

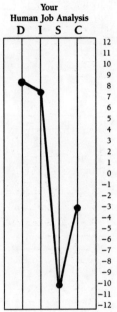

Human Job Analysis graph scale:
12, 11, 10, 9, 8, 7, 6, 5, 4, 3, 2, 1, 0, −1, −2, −3, −4, −5, −6, −7, −8, −9, −10, −11, −12

From P.P.A. How Others See You

```
D      I      S      C
2 0    1 7    1 9    1 5
1 6    1 0    1 2    9
1 5    9      1 1    8
1 4    8      1 0
1 2                  7
1 0    7      9      6
9             8
8      6      7      5
       5      6
7             5
6      4      5      4
5             4 3    3
4      3
3      2      2
2             1      1
       1      0
1
0             0
```

From P.P.A. How You See Yourself

```
D      I      S      C
2 0    1 7    1 9    1 5
1 6    9      1 1    7
1 5    8      1 0    6
1 4    7      9      5
1 3    6      8      4
1 2    5      7      3
1 0    4      6      2
9      3      5      1
8      2      4      0
7      1      3     −1
5      0      2     −2
3     −1      1
1     −2      0     −1
0     −3     −1     −2
−2    −4     −2     −3
−3    −5     −3     −4
−4           −4     −5
−6           −5     −6
−7    −6     −6     −7
−9    −7     −7     −8 −1 9
−1 0  −8     −9 −1 0
−1 1         −1 0   −1 1
−1 3   −9 −1 0  −1 1
−1 4  −1 0  −1 2 −1 2
−2 1  −1 9 −1 9 −1 6
```

IV D Subtract (e) from (a)   **8**
    I Subtract (f) from (b)   **7**
    S Subtract (g) from (c)   **−10**
    C Subtract (h) from (d)   **−3**

V Graph D I S C on the above Human Job Analysis graph.

VI Match the person with the position by completing either **VII** or **VIII**

present employees

VII Transfer numbers from P.P.A. Graph I (How Others See You) to the above. Determine if graph is similar to Human Job Analysis. If it is different from this, person needs to have job clarified or defined.

job selection only

VIII Transfer numbers from P.P.A. Graph III (How You See Yourself) to the above. Determine if graph is similar to Human Job Analysis. If it is different decide if difference is acceptable.

The Personal Profile Analysis

DIRECTIONS: Each of the following boxes contains four descriptive words. Examine the words in the first box and give your first spontaneous reaction. Place an M in the box to the right of the word if that is what you are most. Place an L in the box to the right of the word if that is what you are least. For every four words you should have one M and one L. The individual in the example to the right perceives of himself as most original and least gentle of the four descriptive words. **Use ball point pen or pencil. Please press hard.**

REMEMBER:

1. The analysis is not a test. There are no 'right' or 'wrong' answers.

2. The profile must be completed in isolation and without interruption.

3. Be certain you complete the Personal Profile thinking of yourself in your current job; if you are not working, then think of yourself in your last job. If you have not worked, then think of yourself at home

---

PLEASE PRINT

FORENAMES _PAULINE_   SURNAME _?_   DATE _16 JAN 89_

POSITION APPLIED FOR _SALES EXECUTIVE_

PRESENT/LAST POSITION HELD _SALES EXECUTIVE_

ADDRESS _19   ALFRETON_

EXAMPLE

gentle	L	persuasive		humble		original	M

gentle		persuasive	M	humble	L	original	
attractive		God-fearing	L	stubborn	M	sweet	
easily led	L	bold	M	loyal		charming	
open-minded	M	obliging	L	will power		cheerful	
jovial		precise	M	courageous	L	even-tempered	
competitive	M	considerate		happy		harmonious	L
fussy		obedient	L	unconquerable	M	playful	
brave		inspiring	M	submissive		timid	L

Trait		Trait		Trait		Trait	
sociable	M	patient		self-reliant		soft-spoken	L
adventurous	M	receptive		cordial	L	moderate	
talkative		controlled	L	conventional		decisive	M
polished	L	daring	M	diplomatic		satisfied	
aggressive	M	life of the party	L	soft touch		fearful	
cautious	L	determined		convincing	M	good-natured	
willing		eager	L	agreeable	M	high spirited	
confident	M	sympathetic	L	tolerant		assertive	
well disciplined		generous	L	animated		persistent	M
admirable		kind		resigned	L	force of character	M
respectful	L	pioneering	M	optimistic		accommodating	
argumentative	L	adaptable		nonchalant		light-hearted	M
trusting		contented	L	positive	M	peaceful	
good mixer		cultured	M	vigorous	L	lenient	
companionable		accurate	M	outspoken		restrained	L
restless	M	neighbourly		popular		devout	L

MEETS HJA
REQUIREMENT IN FULL
X.R. PERSONNEL DEPT.

THOMAS INTERNATIONAL
MANAGEMENT SYSTEMS (EUROPE) LTD.

Hams House,
17 West Street,
Marlow,
Bucks SL7 2LS,
England
Tel: (06284) 75366

1972 Thomas Management Systems Inc.

Revised 1981 Thomas International Management
Systems (Europe) Ltd.

Instructions for Developing the Profile

1   Count the number of M's in the completely enclosed purple boxes M and the number of M's in the boxes with the top purple line M̄. Add them together and place the total number in the purple square of the tally box under the I column.

2   Count the number of L's in the completely enclosed purple boxes L and the number of L's in the boxes with the bottom purple line L̲. Add them together and place the total number in the purple square of the tally box under the II column.

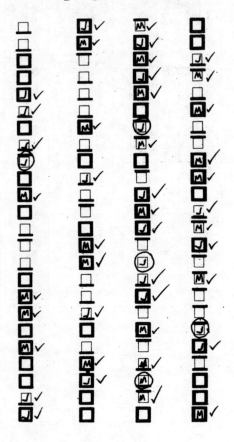

TALLY BOX

23 I	20 II	III
13	2	+ 11
6	3	+ 3
0	7	- 7
4	8	- 4

3 If the number in the purple I column is greater than the number in the purple II column, subtract and designate this as a plus number in the tally box under the purple III column. If the number in the purple I column is less than the purple II column, subtract and designate this as a minus number in the tally box under the purple III column. Example of this procedure: The total number in Column 1 is 8, the total number in column II is 4. The result to be placed in column III is +5. It would look like this:

I	II	III
8	3	+5

4 Continue by counting the number of M's and L's in each of the remaining colours (boxes red, black, green). Follow the identical procedure as you did in Steps 1, 2 and 3 with the purple boxes. Upon completion you should have filled in the tally box on page two.

5 Transfer the numbers to tally box overleaf.

	I	II	III
D	13	2	+11
i	6	3	+3
S	0	7	-7
C	4	8	-4

COMMENTS

SUGGESTED STRENGTHS

DIRECT APPROACH
GOOD CLOSER
GOOD OPENER
PLENTY OF WORK ENERGY
PLENTY OF PACE
INDEPENDENT but will COMPLY
IN LONG RUN
POINTS TO REVIEW AT INTERVIEW

GETS VERY Stubborn UNDER
PRESSURE (check @ INTERVIEW)
Small STRESS SHOWING, QUESTION
@ INTERVIEW
WHY "C" FACTOR ABOVE LINE
ON GRAPH 1 @ @ INT.
PRESS ON ADMIN LIKELY
TO bE POOR.
Will NEED TO bE CHALLENGED
NEEDS STRONG but DEMOCRATIC
MANAGER

6 Plot and graph the numbers from
   the tally box in Step 5 to the bar
   graphs I, II and III below. Each
   graph has lines of D.i.S.C.

7 Determine what characteristic is
   the highest above the centre line
   and what characteristic is the
   lowest. Enter in the box at the base
   of the graph.

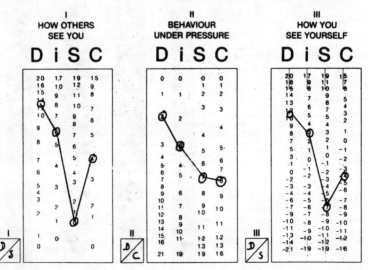

THOMAS INTERNATIONAL
Management Systems (Europe) Ltd.

Harris House,
17 West Street,
Marlow, Bucks.,
SL7 2LS, England
Tel: (06284) 75366
Fax: (06285) 24226

=========== "Bringing People and Ideas Together" ===========

<u>PRIVATE & CONFIDENTIAL</u>   9 March 1989

<u>PERSONAL PROFILE ANALYSIS</u>

Pauline P

D	13	2	11
I	6	3	3
S	0	7	-7
C	4	8	-4

File Ref.DI.17

<u>SELF IMAGE - GRAPH III</u>

This is an assertive person who can take a creative idea and make it serve a
practical purpose. She uses a direct method but still considers people
and can convince them through persuasiveness when necessary. Aggressive and
confident, this person is goal-minded and harnesses people to help obtain
goals. She generally plans well ahead and integrates activities to
assist in getting results. This versatile, eager self starter acts
positively in both the competitive and social environments. Ms P may
be impatient and irritable when things do not happen fast enough, but she
is an excellent director of people to achieve results. Ms P seeks
earned respect from associates, needs variety and change. She strives
for the independence of a wide scope operation and loves challenging
assignments that will offer the opportunity to move up the management
ladder. Ms P requires negotiated commitments on a man-to-man basis
and an opportunity to vent drive and freedom of expression.

<u>SELF MOTIVATION</u>

Ms P wants prestige, authority and position. She likes to run an
operation where tangible, measurable results can be shown and progress can
be demonstrated. Seeks earned respect from associates.

<u>JOB EMPHASIS</u>

<u>Managing work and people for a profit</u>
Ms P's job should ideally require tangible results to be obtained
through people. The individual should be under pressure to produce and
frequently be required to apply pressure to others. Planning, problem
solving and organising should be key responsibilities. Authority to make
decisions and the independence to act should be vested in this person, as
well as the need to delegate to others. The working environment should be
relatively unpredictable and should call for several projects to be kept
going concurrently. Although operating policies should exist this person
should frequently be able to act without a precedent.

<u>DESCRIBING WORDS</u>

Self starter, direct, decisive, demanding, self assured, confident,
friendly, verbal, active, mobile, alert, restless, firm, independent, strong
willed.

HOW OTHERS SEE YOU (MASK) - GRAPH I

Whilst the very low compliance factor in the self image suggests that this
person will be strong willed and independent, there are clear signs in the
work mask that she modifies her behaviour a little in the work
situation.

The indicators are that at work she may not be quite as strong willed and
independent as the self image suggests. This is not likely to have a major
effect on her basic characteristics.

BEHAVIOUR UNDER PRESSURE - GRAPH II

Whilst under normal circumstances all the indicators are that Ms P
can be stubborn, strong willed and opinionated, the suggestions are that
under pressure she may become even more so.

The likelihood therefore is that Ms P becomes defiant and immovable
in pressure situations.

GENERAL COMMENTS

There are some minor stresses or frustrations showing within this person's
profile.

Such stresses appear to be work related, but should not have a major effect
on job performance.

We do recommend that the situation be carefully monitored to ensure that
future major problems do not arise.

Ms P is motivated by a combination of power, prestige, popularity and
freedom. Additionally, a wide scope operation and direct answers are
important to her, as is public recognition to indicate her ability
and favourable working conditions.

Ideally she needs a boss who is committed to negotiating objectives and
timescales with her on a person to person basis, and then allowing
her the authority to act and the freedom and responsibility to go away
and get the job done.

HJA COMPARISON

In comparison with the HJA, Ms P appears to meet in full all the
requirements as described. Your HJA is calling for a person who is direct
in approach, forceful, demanding, people orientated, verbal in approach,
friendly, outgoing, quick in pace, active, alert and independent in
approach, yet will comply in the final issue. This does describe Ms P's
characteristics in full and we would suggest that the match between her and
the position is almost ideal. However, all our comments in the above
paragraphs should be taken into consideration before appointment.

Person meeting HJA

"To achieve successful results in selling, Think carefully before you act, Act fast after you have thought!"

Sales Management Techniques

Some tough-minded managers use fear tactics to motivate their salespeople. I've met and experienced a few. I knew one who used to summon all his slow or non-producing salespeople on a Monday morning to his office and say, 'I am firing you now, but I am giving you until Friday to get your job back, so get out there and do your best or you won't be working for us soon.' Others do the firing in a sweet way. A sales manager told me when I first started selling and was producing atrocious sales figures, that I was not cut out for selling and I should find another job: 'Patrick, it's been nice knowing you, and I wish you all the very best in your future occupation. Drop in and have a cup of tea with us when you are around next.' With these parting words which came as a devastating blow to me, he gave me my last wage packet. I left almost in tears and terribly ashamed of myself, vowing to fight back all the way to the top. During my early days as a novice, I have been kicked by both buyer and company bureaucrat because of my greenness and naivety. That was the price I had to pay for making it in the business of professional selling. When I hear unqualified comments from those who laugh and sneer and say selling is easy – I suggest they go and learn their ABC!

When I was at the receiving end in those dark days, I always thought to myself that the business of selling only attracted and employed people who were mercenary in their outlook and had no understanding of human sentiments. It seemed a very wrong practice. But now, several years later, older, greyer and more mature, I fully appreciate the difficulties one has to endure in the profession of selling and I am thankful for the lessons I learnt in those bad days for the plentiful good days I now enjoy. I also readily acknowledge the fact, having run my own business, that profit is not a bad word and is the motive of all business. For if you do not produce the goodies, out you go!

When you are young, you live to learn,
When you are old, you learn to live!

Say to yourself, *I am getting older and better day by day. My climb to the top is going to be slow and steady. I can't do business sitting on my ass – business means busy . . . ness, and nothing happens in business until a sale is made. Every day I will face my obstacles fearlessly and with relentless zeal and enthusiasm. I will invest my time to acquire the know-how to tackle my job, and I will always be responsive to the fact that when the going is easy, I may be going downhill. I will live and die by the concept of fair play, success and winning above all. I will shun the plague of procrastination from morn till night and I will pledge myself to hard work, rest and play for every single day of my existence, as I realize this is what makes a winner in the business of selling and the battle of life.*

The Process of Selling

The process of professional selling and winning a sale or sales is analagous to the following occupations and professions:

- It is like a soldier or a battalion of soldiers engaged in a battle with the common purpose of winning the war.
- It is like a fisherman or a group of fishermen participating in a fishing exercise to make a catch or haul a net.
- It is like a surgeon or a team of surgeons involved in an operation on a patient to save life or relieve suffering.
- It is like a matador tiring out a raging bull before he destroys it with his sword.
- It is like a driver of a car going from one point to another encountering hazards and unroadworthy conditions en route and steering clear to reach a desired destination.
- It is like a footballer running with the ball and overcoming opposition to score a goal.
- It is like a student preparing herself with intensive study to pass examinations.
- It is like the captain of a ship leaving his berth in the safety of a harbour and sailing into high seas to reach another port of call.
- It is like a politician making a prepared speech to put a point of view across to get the support of her electorate.

- It is like an actor reading his lines to maintain continuous audience attention and interest.
- It is like a boxer in a ring fighting a bout with an opponent to win the contest.

Each of the above analogies demonstrates different aspects of selling, and there is a common denominator to all the above: success or failure.

You will need knowledge and skill, plus dedicated hardwork in order to excel in each sphere of endeavour. At the end of the day you are not judged by whether you made a tremendous effort, but whether you won or lost. Also-rans and runners-up are a separate category that can be used to manipulate or support a cause depending on the objective and circumstances. The end justifies the means to achieve success only provided the means justifies the end. So don't use a sledge hammer to crack a nut, take unfair advantage or resort to foul methods in pursuit of profit.

If you are not prepared to pay the price for success and accept either the glory of success or the penalties for failure, having earned it the easy way you are well advised to reconsider the current line you are pursuing or how you acquired it. The ethical considerations are paramount to lasting success in all our endeavours. If you cannot stand the heat, do yourself a favour and get out of the kitchen!

Using Your Brain

On one of my regular visits to the USA I saw a notice displayed on the wall of a busy New York office which is very relevant to my favourite subject, Selling:

> *When God created us, He gave us two ends,*
> *One to sit on and one to think with.*
> *Success depends upon which end we use most,*
> *Heads we Win and Tails we Lose.*

Eminent psychologists tell us that Talented or Not Talented depends on how effectively we use the two sides of our brains.

If we are weak in the area of thinking creatively – which is paramount to success in selling in a highly competitive and astute buying market place, the good news is you *can* develop the quality of creativity by understanding the function of the human brain.

The two sides of our brains have different functions. The right side is the feeling side; the left the thinking side. Thus, with the right side of our brain we are sensitive to music, colour, pattern, rhythm, and use this side for creativity and imagination. We use the left for logical reasoning, language, numerical work, and analysis. Scientists tend to be left brain dominant, while artists and musicians appear to be right brain dominant. However, research has shown that when people are encouraged to develop a mental area that they thought was weak, all areas of mental performance improved dramatically. Some fascinating findings on Einstein reveal that he failed maths at school and engaged in other activities such as violin playing, sailing, art and imagination games. It was his imagination games that he credited for his more significant scientific insight. It is said he was day-dreaming on a summer's day when he imagined riding sunbeams to the far extremities of the universe, quite illogically, saw the universe was curved and realized that his previous logical training was incomplete. The numbers, formulas, equations and words with which he surrounded this new image are known as *the theory of relativity*, a good example of right and left brain synthesis.

Likewise, great artists were also discovered to be using both sides of their brains rather than using haphazard methods of daubing paint on a canvas. On examination of their diaries, notes like this were found: *Got up at 6 a.m., spent 17th day painting 6 of the latest series. Mixed 4 parts of orange with 2 parts of yellow to produce colour combination which was placed in upper left hand corner of canvas to act in visual opposition to spiral structure in lower left hand corner, producing desired balance in the eye of the perceiver.* One man that really stands out is Leonardo Da Vinci, who was arguably the most accomplished man in a range of different disciplines: Art, Sculpture, Physiology, General Science, Architecture, Mechanics, Anatomy, Physics and Invention. Rather than separating these different areas of his abilities, he combined them. His scientific note books are filled with three dimensional drawings and images, but most interesting were his paintings combining straight lines, angles, curves and numbers – a truly remarkable use of the right and left hemispheres of brain activity.

Since professional selling is the science and art of persuading, motivating, manipulating and negotiating with others to make decisions that will benefit themselves and the seller, learning to think creatively, using both sides of our brains and selling dynamically while applying the principles and techniques of Salespersonability will help you to achieve spectacular results. If you want to fly with eagles, then don't behave like a turkey!

Are you a professional salesperson or an order taker? The job of the professional salesperson starts when the customer says No. Your job is to convert a No to a Yes, because if all buyers

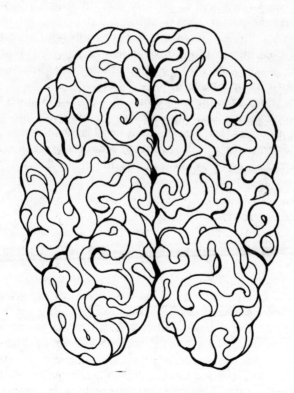

The two sides of the brain

said Yes from the outset there would be no need for salespeople. Nothing comes easily in life.

Creative   means using your mind

Dynamic   means being forceful

Selling   means exercising skill as both science and art to influence another person's thinking to produce a mutually beneficial result.

Most importantly of all, Creative Dynamic Selling requires a positive Mental Attitude.

When you see a glass half filled with liquid do you see it as half full, or half empty? To be successful in selling, you must accentuate the positive. See it as half full.

Always get into the habit of expressing things in a positive manner even though things may appear negative. If you break something, don't say, 'I'll never find another one,' Instead say, 'How can I fix or replace it.'

When you start expressing things in a positive manner you start programming your subconscious mind with the right thought processes. The subconscious mind is the most powerful computer on the face of the earth and produces positive results if programmed correctly. So it is very important that you feed

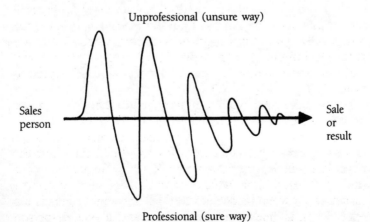

your powerful subconscious mind with positive thoughts and it will automatically provide you with the right way to solve various selling situations and problems.

Having the correct attitude plays a major part in winning at selling, but you also have to possess skill. The following illustration shows the unprofessional route to making a sale which is haphazard, while the professional route is direct. The professional salesperson understands the psychology of the sales process and is in control of the interview, whereas the unprofessional trusts to luck, hopes the buyer will buy, and is at the total mercy of the buyer.

PROFESSIONAL OR UNPROFESSIONAL?

The professional is able to get to the sale in the shortest possible time whereas the unprofessional often fails. On the rare occasion he scores a hit, he may have to pay a big price for it, having wasted a large amount of valuable time. The professional salesperson's sale is rock-solid, while the unprofessional's sale is very shaky and could collapse. Selling is not a game of luck but unquestionably a game of skill.

Luck has hardly a place in professional selling, but if you arm yourself with know-how, and are prepared to grasp the opportunity when it arises, or create opportunities for yourself then your skills will enable you to make your own luck. On the roulette table you trust to luck and your chances of winning are remote. In bullfighting, a game of skill, the matador trains to win and has to win, because if he does not win he will be gored to death.

The matador trains with a dummy bull in the form of a cart on two wheels with a straw table top which is pushed by an aide towards him to simulate the charging bull. Some sales experts compare the selling interview to a bull fight where the buyer (the bull) has the power to say Yes or No in his own office (the bull ring) and from which he can sling the salesperson (the matador) out when he decides he does not want to pursue the offer. He can intimidate openly or subtly, and all the salesperson has at her disposal is her training to fall back on to persuade, motivate, manipulate or negotiate with the buyer for a sale – just like the matador lures the bull to its doom.

From my own experience in selling, I fully agree with the concept that the selling interview is like a bullfight. The salesperson has to win and most professional buyers expect the salesperson to be trained. They will want to have a meaningful discussion and thrash out all the relevant pros and cons before they make the decision to purchase – which they will gladly make, or can be influenced to make, when they realize they are going to benefit from the transaction. *I use the bullfighting example to illustrate the point.*

Training makes the difference between success and failure. I am not suggesting that buyers should be provoked and demeaned in the way bulls are in some bullfights. The task of professional salespeople is clearly defined. They have chosen a career to make sales and earn money by helping buyers to benefit by making an investment in the proposal offered to satisfy their needs, so they have to be totally professional about their job.

So why does the salesperson have to battle for the sale? The answer is because anything we want in life we have to make an effort for – nature has made it that way. Even animals have to fight for their food. If products sold themselves, then you would not require salespeople. In the buyer/seller situation two or more different persons have to argue, discuss and weigh the advantages against the disadvantages of a proposal, and after evaluating those factors, the decision-maker will finally have to decide whether he should purchase or not, depending on how skilfully the sales demonstration or presentation is put across.

When there is a product demonstration or service presentation in which two or more people are exchanging views there will be a polarisation of negative and positive thoughts and words. The salesperson will have to take control, influence and convince buyers to make a commitment to purchase based on the positive factors (merits) and ignoring or playing down the negative aspects (demerits) of the offer.

The salesperson will have to overcome the buyer's own psychological barriers, which means the salesperson will have to battle against:

1. The buyer's beliefs, or what the buyer thinks is true about the proposal.
2. The buyer's emotions, or what the buyer feels is true about the proposal.
3. The buyer's actions, or what the buyer sees as true about the proposal and will finally act on.

When you can make headway on these three aspects, then you are well on your way to making a solid sale.

Buyers can, broadly speaking, also be classified into three groups: Realists, Cynics and Idealists. Each group has its own perceptions of what the world is and how they relate to it.

The Realist is a down-to-earth person who sees the positive and negative sides of an argument and can be influenced by straight talking, facts, persuasion and negotiation.

The Cynic believes that salespeople are crooks, a Doubting Thomas who has preconceived ideas and only sees the negative aspects. The Cynic can be handled by re-education and manipulation.

The Idealist is one who sees only the positive side in everything and therefore can easily be motivated into making favourable decisions.

In the process of battling for your order, you the salesperson will encounter three different responses from the buyer:

● Acceptance of the proposal (Yes)
● Objection to the proposal (No)
● Indifference to the proposal (Maybe)

Order takers only do the most uncomplicated of all tasks: take an order after the buyer has decided to purchase, in which case no real selling is involved. Professional salespeople have a thought process and a voice habit, and right from the word 'go' they are overcoming simple and complex sales resistances with ease and style, moving towards their goal of making the sale. When sales resistances come into play, part of the normal buying process, the professional relies heavily on the training and know-how to pull through to get the order. When you can embrace the idea that the product, service or idea is irrelevant as long as there is an existing need, or a need which you can create, and can then show the buyer that your product, service or idea will satisfy their dominant buying motives, then you must sell using this principle.

If you lack the personal qualities essential to build up a rapport with the buyer, but you nevertheless have the know-how, although you are going to find it harder to make the sale you could still win. If you are endowed with some of the traits of the successful salesperson, you will make it more effectively, more productively and much more quickly to the top. The underlying principle still remains the same: know-how is paramount to success! And if you have the personality without the know-how you may end up on the scrap heap unless some tactical adjustment is made. For example, Gerry Dorsey did not become a big hit until he changed his name to Engelbert Humperdinck, although his personality and singing style was the same.

To build up a reputation as a super salesperson takes a lot of effort, but unless you have that thing called know-how all your efforts will be in vain. Your progress must also be satisfying. When you finally make it to the top, then it is up to you to maintain your position, or you could come tumbling down. It is up to you to build your own success and sensibly maintain it. Life is a funny thing: people do not judge a surgeon by the number of successful operations performed, but let her fail one and it will soon be the talk of the town!

Sow a thought and you create an act, sow an act and you create a habit, sow a habit and you create an attitude!

PROFESSIONAL SALESPERSONABILITY AND COMMANDO SALESMANSHIP

The English Dictionary describes Professional Salesmanship as *Someone who engages in an activity to earn money by exhibiting skill in the selling of products or services.*

This in my opinion is an outdated definition for the professional salesperson of the 90's and beyond. 'Salesman' is a term of the past when selling was primarily a male occupation.

The suffix -*ship* denotes a brotherhood or a clan, as in friendship, comradeship, brinkmanship, statesmanship and kinship. Selling in the past was conducted without the highpowered selling skills, training and psychology of today and had to depend on guts and bravado to produce results. The job was very tough those days, and there were many hungry salesmen around who found consolation by supporting each other. The job today is still as difficult, but the salesperson has superior combat aids at his or her disposal. WHO DARES SELLS is one of them. Professional selling today is a distinct skill, or an **ability** – the salesperson thinks and acts on his or her feet to produce results using scientific know-how and artistic skills.

Professional Salespersonability is the activity of selling products, services or ideas of benefit to buyers, to earn an income by engaging in a skilled psychological and verbal battle to influence the buyer's mind to win sales through persuasion, motivation, manipulation and negotiation by evaluating the buyer's spoken word, written word and non-verbal signals.

Furthermore, a **commando salesperson** is a crack salesperson put into a new market for a limited period to intensify the selling effort of a new product or service, to provide a back up to the existing sales force or to spearhead a launch.

A commando has a profound understanding of the science and art of selling and can literally be put into any place, anywhere and can be depended upon to produce sales results. They are usually lone rangers, born survivors who will constantly adapt to meet new developments during the sales interview. They treat the sales process as if they were driving a car: changing gears, accelerating and decelerating according to the road conditions until they reach their destination. They live in the real world and have reached a high degree of professionalism through experience, training, analyzing their previous successes and failures and constantly striving to better themselves. They have all the qualities of a trained expert, oozing with confidence and personality. They can take the rough with the smooth and will never be deterred from reaching their objectives and goals. They fight battles and win sales. They do not win battles and lose sales. They respect the buyer and show courtesy, no matter how difficult or awkward the buyer may be. When dealing with the unscrupulous buyer, the commando salesperson uses an arsenal of tactics and techniques to defeat or outsell the opponent. They do not look for praise for their heroic efforts and sales results, but when the task is completed to both the buyer's and their company's own satisfaction, they accept the monetary remunerations and acknowledgements with gratitude and grace. And like some commando soldiers who perform many daring feats of human skill, disappear without mention. Their pride is in their achievements and is not derived from outside praise.

Set your sights and standards to reach the degree of excellence of the elite group of commando salespeople, and you will never fail in selling.

The 26 Qualities of the Professional Salesperson

1. Intelligence
2. Perception
3. Self-Motivation
4. Enthusiasm
5. Integrity
6. Discipline
7. Resilience
8. Appropriate Dress
9. Self-Criticism
10. Empathy & Love for Others
11. Ambition to Succeed
12. Punctuality
13. Ability to Listen
14. Persistence
15. Confidence
16. Courtesy
17. Belief in Product/Service/Company/Self
18. Knowledge (Of Product/Service, Company, People, Competition and Self)
19. Communication Skills
20. Diligence
21. Sincerity
22. Loyalty
23. Do-it-Now
24. Survivor
25. Cunning
26. Excellence in Persuasion, Motivation, Manipulation and Negotiation

IF NOBODY CARED

If nobody laughed and nobody sang
And nobody cared about anything
If nobody spoke a word of cheer
To help a long day through
If all the joy went to the great
And nothing remained for the small
Then surely the world would be upside down
And life hardly worthwhile at all

I AM I AND YOU ARE YOU

I do my thing and you do yours
I am not in this world to live up to your expectations
And you are not there to live up to mine

You are you and I am I
And if by chance we find ourselves amiable,
Amicable and beneficial to each other
That's great, it's beautiful

On the other hand, if we don't click and see eye to eye
That's understandable, so be it
For you are you and I am I
Let's agree to live and let live

Anon

CHAPTER 5

The four stages of a typical sales interview

The professional salesperson will use the Attention – Interest – Desire – Action formula.

Opening
1. Exchange of courtesies
2. Salesperson's opening remarks
3. Arouse interest
4. Develop interest

Stage 1
Capturing the Attention, awakening buyer Interest. Breaking through any pre-occupation. Creating or Satisfying the need.

Presentation
5. Commencement of selling proper
6. Demonstration/ presentation
   a. introduction of product, service or idea
   b. explanation of selling points

Stage 2
Stroking the emotions. Creating Desire.

c. operation of product
   by salesperson
d. operation of product
   by buyer
7. Discussion of price
8. Countering of objections

Closing	**Stage 3**
9 Commencement of close	Moving towards Action.
10. Persuasion and trial close	Getting the commitment
11. Decision making	
12. Order taken – purchase complete	

Departure	**Stage 4**
13. Completion of details	Sealing the sale so that it
14. Closing courtesies	stays closed. Leaving –
15. Departure	making sure everything is
	buttoned up.

If the above is the structure of a typical sales interview, then the following selling equation will tell you what you need to do to achieve your sales results, and it will also give you an insight into your performance and the reasons why you are failing if you are not reaching your pre-planned sales targets. Use it as a ready-reckoner.

The Selling Equation

$$\text{ACTIVITY} \times \text{SKILL} \times \text{KNOWLEDGE} = \text{RESULTS} = \text{£'s}$$

Let's say you want to achieve a sales result of £10,000 next week, and let's assume 100% of activity, 100% of skill and 100% of knowledge would produce this income.

100%		100%		100%			
Activity	×	**Skill**	×	**Knowledge**	= **Results**	=	£10,000
(i.e.		(i.e.		(i.e.			
Your work		How talented		Product,			
output)		you are in		Service,			
		dealing with		People,			
		different types		Company,			
		of buyers)		Competition			
				and Self)			

Now, mathematically speaking, the left hand side of the equation must equal the right hand side. To make this possible, what I have done is to give each component a rating to balance the equation.

100% of Activity = 50
100% of Skill = 20
Therefore, 100% of Knowledge = 10
i.e. $50 \times 50 \times 10$ = £10,000.

If, say the activity level drops to 50%
the skill level drops to   75%
the knowledge level drops to   50%
Then the following week's sales would be:
$25 \times 15 \times 5$ = £1,875.

What the selling equation tells you is that activity, skill and knowledge levels must always be at peak to produce top class sales figures, and if any one of these areas starts to drop it will affect the end result. So take note and use this equation which is suitable for any type of selling, whether telephone, retail or direct, to produce super sales results.

Why People Buy

People buy products, services or ideas because they will satisfy their needs. Buyers make purchasing decisions emotionally and justify them logically. Ask someone how many tons of concrete were used to build their house, and they would be clueless. But ask them what colour their house is, and the answer would come out easily.

A professional salesperson can either sell to a need, or create the need.

Products are tangible: items that can be seen, touched and operated by user, such as motor cars, videos, hi-fi's and business equipment.

Services are intangible: anything that is labour intensive and uses knowledge, and/or appliances and fuel, such as carpet cleaning, minicabbing, tailoring, hairdressing and car repairs.

Ideas are intangible and creative: a process by which academic knowledge and/or practical skill is passed from seller to buyer, such as in advertising, consulting and professional occupations, writing and teaching.

30 reasons why people buy (buying motives)

1. To satisfy the need to look and feel good, often to impress the opposite sex.
2. Because they see it advertised.
3. To keep up with the Joneses.
4. To be in vogue.
5. To show their love and affection for others.
6. As a gift.
7. From habit.
8. From a recommendation.
9. Satisfaction with past performance.
10. In order to sell on and make a profit.
11. To save time, money and effort.
12. Due to persuasion, motivation, manipulation and negotiation skills exercised by the salesperson.
13. To make a donation to charity.
14. For security and protection.
15. For comfort and convenience.
16. For prestige and style.
17. Because they are getting a bargain.
18. Due to the persistence of the salesperson.
19. To maintain competitive superiority.
20. To gain efficiency and increased value.

21. For better health, hygiene, cleanliness, happiness and enjoyment.
22. As a contingency measure.
23. To avoid pain, criticism or trouble.
24. To copy others.
25. To satisfy curiosity or appetite.
26. To be popular and gain praise.
27. To be individualistic.
28. To protect their reputation.
29. To make work easier.
30. As part of an expansion plan.

The 9 P's – The Hallmark of the Star Salesperson

Positive	Precise	Prepared
Persuasive	Polite	Punctual
Patient	Planning	Practical

The Different Types of Buyer

Buyers are people and people are buyers. The psychological make-up of a buyer can be very complex indeed. The professional salesperson must quickly size up what type of buyer he or she is confronting and read that person like a book in order to be able to formulate a sales strategy.

Consider the different epithets we give to different animals. I have always felt it is possible to see buyers in the same light: there are many different types with different characteristics. The following list demonstrates a few typical character traits:

The intelligent dolphin	The sleek panther
The gentle lamb	The stubborn mule
The brave lion	The praying mantis
The fierce bull	The courageous bear
The timid dormouse	The jumping frog
The cunning wolf	The unforgetting elephant

The vicious serpent

The strong ox

The clumsy whale

The lazy hippo

The stupid ass

The poisonous scorpion

The smelly skunk

The prolific rabbit

The slow tortoise

The slippery eel

The fast hare

The silly goat

The stinging bee

The ignorant pig

The wise owl

The faithful dog

The proud peacock

The graceful swan

The talkative parrot

The singing bird

The scared chicken

The wild boar

The galloping horse

The sly fox

The charging rhinoceros

The laughing jackass

The stupid sheep

The deadly shark

The camouflaging lizard

The wriggling worm

The gnawing rat

The regal eagle

The scavenging hyena

The peaceful dove

The busy beaver

The keen-eyed hawk

The hard-working ant

The elusive butterfly

The fighting cock

The performing sea lions

The pea-brained ostrich

The clever monkey

The playful kitten

The friendly cat

The cheeky mouse

The sensitive deer

If you were trying to capture each one of these animals you would need to tailor your approach accordingly. You would have to outfox the fox with a snare; wear grip-tight gloves to catch the slippery eel; shoot the lion with a tranquillizer dart, and throw a ball for the playful puppy to chase.

Similarly, in professional selling you need to adopt different methods of handling the sales interview depending on the buyer's make-up, in a cool, calm and collected fashion as you move towards your objective – which may be to get a sale or another positive result. It is up to the seller to adapt to the circumstances and control the interview and outcome – rather than the other way round.

Now let's look at some of the different types of buyer make up and how to deal with them in a bit more detail.

63 DIFFERENT TYPES OF BUYER

1. The Silent Buyer

This is the person who stays silent and apparently glum and who is probably more disturbing than any other to the new or inexperienced salesperson.

How to handle him/her:

- Do not get flurried or panic. Try to establish the cause. It may be due to the buyer's belief that silence is the best weapon against high-powered or persuasive salespeople.
- Break through the silence by using tact, asking questions and waiting for feedback. If you make a selling point, repeat it twice and get the prospect's opinion.
- Meet silence with silence, as a gap of half a minute can seem eternal and will very often force the prospect to say something.

2. The Phlegmatic or Imperturbable Buyer

These are the cool, calm and collected buyers. Adapt your sales talk accordingly. Continue with your demonstration or presentation until you are ready to close. If the buyer still makes no comment, try to provoke him or her with a remark such as, 'I take it you have agreed with what we've been discussing, so I am putting you down for 50 Kg of Product X and 30 Kg of Product Y.' You will soon find out what this buyer's views are.

3. The Talkative Buyer

Talkative buyers are not without value because by talking they reveal a lot about themselves. Whales are caught when they are spouting.

- Let them carry on, provided that what is said is relevant to the sale.
- They are almost certainly to be flattered by having a good listener, and may well sell your proposition to themselves sometimes better than you even would.
- Whenever they wander from the subject, bring them tactfully and firmly back to the point.
- Let them talk as long as their talking is helping you. When it isn't, stop them as soon as you can.

4. The Argumentative Buyer

This type requires extreme tact in handling. They thrive on arguments even when there is nothing to argue about. The cardinal rule to apply is: the customer is always right, even though they may be wrong. Your job is to sell, not to prove he or she is wrong because winning the argument and losing the sale is certainly not a professional salesperson's way of achieving results.

The argumentative buyer is a very troublesome type who will dispute every statement you make and question every opinion you put forward. They will test the thoroughness with which you have prepared your sales presentation. Whatever you do, don't get involved in an argument but make sure you have all your facts at your fingertips. Keep to definite statements and do not get heated. Exercise patience and restraint.

5. The Disbelieving Buyer

Closely related to the argumentative type, this type does not generally argue, but clearly implies or quite openly states their disbelief for the salesperson's statements. The only answer is to give them proof. If they still disbelieve, then it becomes an irrational thing and should be treated accordingly. You could defuse the situation with a joke: 'If you were in the middle of the Sahara desert dying with thirst and I offered you a glass of cool water, you would say I am giving you poison, wouldn't you?' Establish the reason for their disbelief, answer it convincingly and get back to proper selling. Disbelieving buyers need to be made to see the light. Don't let them bump along the bottom and give you a hard time. Draw them to the surface in any way you can and you can do a deal with them.

6. The Irrational Buyer

The irrational buyer is exasperating to deal with. It stems from either emotional insecurity or immaturity. The best way to tackle this type is to play ball with the buyer by talking in emotional language. When a rapport is created, use the built-in-error selling technique. Take a feature of your product or service, convert it into a benefit that you have determined is important to the buyer and say something like this, 'During the course of our conversation we discovered that this benefit is what is important to you, and that this is not what you are looking for, is that right?' By this method you can really make him see how silly he is.

7. The Indecisive Buyer

There are many buyers who fall into this category. They may ask you to show them everything and then stand back and be unable to make up their minds. The reason they cannot make up their minds is because they are uncertain of themselves and afraid of making mistakes, so it is up to you to inspire confidence and convince them that you are recommending the right purchase. The indecisive buyer can be erratic, reserved or timid. Indecision arises usually from one of two main causes: over-conscientious or unable to concentrate.

The way to handle this type of buyer is to:

- Let him see that nothing is being kept back. Explain everything very clearly and relate your explanation to his particular situation.
- You must be involved with the buyer's weighing up of the offer. Try to stop him going off at a tangent. Delay with this type of buyer is dangerous, go all out to get a decision on the spot. Use flattery, a well timed display of firmness, and special inducements to win this buyer over.

8. *The Ill-Mannered Buyer*

Rude buyers are a fact of life. It is hopeless to try and cure them, and the only thing to do is to bear it with a grin for as long as you can unless the rudeness either becomes personal or an open attempt at intimidation. Do not give in or retaliate but if the rudeness becomes unbearable try to withdraw from the interview with dignity. Much of the time rudeness on the part of the buyer is more apparent than is intended. A good tactic that I have used with enormous success is to tell the buyer: 'please don't insult me, I am ignorant.'

9. *The Guileful Buyer*

The buyer who flatters the seller but does not buy is the most difficult to type to deal with. They confess to being tremendously impressed and convinced by the demonstration or presentation and other proofs put forward. They agree that the product or service is extraordinarily good value for money but will not order. This type of buyer is very slippery. Your one course of action is to find the real reason for the person's obstinacy: does he simply not want it and is taking the line of least resistance, or can he not afford it but won't admit it?

10. *The Pompous Buyer*

The buyer that has an inflated idea of his or her own importance is quite an easy person to tackle as they are susceptible to flattery. But do practise a degree of subtlety in your flattery. Ask them for their advice and treat them as an authority whose opinion is respected.

11. *The Suspicious Buyer*

This type of buyer believes that all salespeople tell lies just to make sales. Even though they may feel that you are telling the truth, they will automatically adopt a defence mechanism against

what they secretly fear is unscrupulous selling practice. They may be nervous or afraid, because they are not as well informed about the product, service or idea, that the seller will take advantage. The thing to do is to stick rigidly to facts, supported by proof. Suspicious buyers are usually suspicious for a reason – perhaps due to a bad experience with unprofessional salespeople. Maintain eye contact, be open and aim to reassure that you are a genuine salesperson and that your intentions are honest and sincere.

12. *The Price Cutting Buyer*

Stand firm on price, justify the cost, and if you still cannot close switch from selling to negotiating. A good tactic I have used with this type is to say to the buyer, 'Dealing with you is more harmful to me than smoking a cigarette. It is said smoking can seriously damage your health, but doing business with you can seriously damage my wealth! The rock-bottom price you are offering me is way out of line, so I am going to recommend that you don't buy and let me say Goodbye.' Wait for the response before you react with a devastating close.

13. The Know-All Buyer

These buyers waste no time in letting the seller know that they know all about the seller's products, services or ideas and they may give the impression that they also know all the answers to life's problems. They may very well do. Close as soon as possible in the most knowledgeable way by securing their agreement that the product, service or idea will satisfy their needs or has competitive advantages. Whatever you do, don't pretend that you know all about the matter in question if you don't. Say something like 'You seem to know all about my product, and you certainly have made my job very easy. I'll put you down for (whatever it is), how's that?'

14. The Two Buyer Situation

When two people come to buy a product, service or idea, one is the decision maker, the other tags along as a friend or expert. The friend may prove to be a real nuisance and take delight in contradicting whatever the seller says. Sell to them both as one using the techniques of professional salespersonability, and when agreement has been reached on the benefits of your offer, ignore the **expert** and concentrate on the **decision maker**.

15. The Nervous Buyer

Undersell, rather than oversell. This type of buyer is frequently inexperienced and is scared of making a mistake. Offer him or her the opportunity to do business and make friends.

16. The Stupid Buyer

This is the type of buyer who, if you say $1+1=2$, will say $1+1=5$. Don't try to prove him wrong. Tell him you are impressed with his wisdom, that you really have learnt something from him, and as a token of gratitude you are going to give him a fantastic offer he cannot refuse. You then give him a discount or an incentive to buy, and close hard.

17. *The Miserable Buyer*

This type of buyer has nothing but gloom to talk about and can very well attempt to demotivate even the most positive of salespeople. It is best to tackle this type with humour. Tell them that investing in your product is a licence to print money, then close with 'Whose pen would you like to use to OK this contract for me, yours or mine?'

18. *The Confused Buyer*

Ask plenty of open-ended questions to try and find out what the confusion is all about. Once you've determined the cause you can use specific questions to establish the reason for the confusion. You will then be equipped to deal with the mental blocks and move forward to a close.

19. The Dominating Buyer

Dominating buyers try to get you to submit to their whims and fancies. What you have to do is to play the game the way that they want to play it, as if you were playing a game of tug-o'-war with a dog pulling a rubber ring from the other side, occasionally tugging back, jerking him hard for them to feel the pull from your side, until you wear him out. You will then be able gradually to bring the buyer around to your way of thinking.

20. The Intelligent Buyer

Use their intelligence to your advantage. Let them get into the driving seat and you sit on the passenger seat. Let them do the driving and find the direction, while you give the instructions for the ultimate destination.

21. The Friendly Buyer

Business first, friendship later. First close the deal, then be the best of friends afterwards.

22. The Naïve Buyer

Educate this buyer by giving him or her the benefits of your proposal, playing up the strengths, and ignoring or playing down the weaknesses if they are brought up by the buyer. When the buyer gives you back positive feedback implying that the offer is understood and liked then that is the time to persuade the buyer to make a favourable decision towards your proposal.

23. The Religious Buyer

This type of buyer tends to be humanitarian, and will be on your side even though he or she may not be fully convinced about your product or service. You can motivate this buyer by giving him or her the honest, sincere story of how the product or service will satisfy their needs and how they would benefit by investing in it. If you also tell them that you are not doing too well in your selling job, it could be in your favour. Your demonstration or presentation must be low key rather than overtly showy.

24. The Politically Conscious Buyer

This type of buyer will try to drag you into a heated political discussion which could well be your downfall if you get involved. What you have to tell the buyer is that you are a business-person, and that you will gladly discuss all aspects of the buyer's business, but you would rather leave the politics to the politicians.

25. The Educated Buyer

These buyers have a string of qualifications after their names. What you do is underplay your qualifications if you have any and emphasize the importance of theirs. You can say something like this: 'You have obviously spent a great deal of time educating yourself and amassed numerous letters after your name which I respect enormously. As for me, I have a PhD which means I Passed high-school with Difficulty. The only useful qualification that I have is a degree from the University of Finance and the letters that I have after my name are M.O.N.E.Y. Let me show you my expertise in that field, which is to show you how to make money, how to increase your sales and multiply your profits.'

26. The Sceptical Buyer

This type will always find some reason not to buy. Heavy motivation is required, and if he still does not dance to your sweet music make a suggestion like this, 'I have done everything within my power to convince you and we seem to have reached a dead end. What else have I got to do, apart from jumping off the Tower of London, to make you change your mind?' The onus is then on the buyer to tell you how he would want to proceed.

27. The Responsive Buyer

In this case the Golden Rule is: *don't waste time, get in, demonstrate/present, close, thank and get out!*

28. The Indifferent Buyer

As the seller, you will need to probe with various open-ended questions to try to establish why the buyer is indifferent. Once you discover the hidden objections you may deal with them using the objection-handling techniques I will provide further on. You can then isolate the objections and treat them as final objections as a prelude to closing.

29. The Buyer Who Objects to Your Offer

This is a buyer who flatly refuses an offer based on an important objection or a series of objections. Assuming the seller has built up a good rapport with the buyer and that she gives good reasons for not wanting your proposal, this is your chance to bring creative selling to the forefront, coupled with the philosophy that when the buyer says NO you can turn it around and keep ON (persistence).

For example, you are taking in a photocopier for demonstration at the buyer's request and in response to some information furnished in advance. She actually sees it being brought into her office for the first time by you and before you can even start the demonstration she comes out with an objection saying that the machine is too big.

Now the whole sale could be threatened from the start if you do not know how to handle this objection. Your challenge is to wriggle out of it by finding a suitable space for her to keep it in her office.

30. The Intimidating Buyer

Keep one step ahead of intimidating buyers so that they know who is in charge. In response to indimidating behaviour you can either:

- Ignore it totally.
- Use the mirror effect: reflect the buyer's behaviour back at him. If he shouts, you shout back; if he stares, you stare back. This will unnerve him.
- Do something contradictory. If the buyer tells you to sit in a particular place, you explain that there is too much light reflecting on your face in that position, or that your eyesight is not all that good, and that it is better for you to sit in the position that you have chosen.
- If the buyer says, 'Quick, I am giving you five minutes to tell me all about it,' you say, 'I will finish in four and a half minutes and if I stay any longer it will be because you asked me to, so let's get cracking right away.'
- If the buyer tells the seller to do something for her in order for her to do a certain thing, you can reply, 'If I do this, would you do that, that and that for me?' In other words you put pressure on her to give you more than you are prepared to give her because of her awkwardness. You come out with a better deal as a result.

If the buyer is intimidating you by being seated behind a large desk, perched at a higher level, looking and talking down to you, what it means, in effect, is that the large desk represents an extension of the buyer's body space. Do not sit directly opposite unless you have enormous amount of personal power to deal with this type of buyer. Create an opportunity for you to move around on to the side of the table the buyer is seated or, if the buyer is standing, stand up too. As a result the buyer will lose control and you can communicate as equals rather than accepting the position.

31. The Deceptive Buyer

Some buyers thrive on leading sellers up the garden path by being untruthful. The golden rule in selling is to believe the buyer, until he shows signs of deception. By playing along with him you will give him enough rope to hang himself. You must always play the good detective looking for clues, and when you can prove his deception has caused you trouble that is the time to hit back and hang him with the very rope you gave him. In other words wear the deception as long as it is helping you, when it is not, turn their deception on them so that they will pay for their gullibility.

32. The Angry Buyer

When a buyer is angry for any reason, keep quiet, incline your head to one side with a surprised look on your face, as if you do not understand the reason for the buyer's anger. Keep a safe distance and hear her out. Then try, 'I understand how you feel and I am sorry you feel this way for the reasons you have mentioned,' whether they are bona fide or not. This will take the sting out of the buyer's anger and after she unleashed her feelings on you – which as a professional you should be able to take on the chin – you can get to grips with the real cause of the anger and resolve it. Under no circumstances should you exchange cross words as nothing will be resolved if you do, and you will cause more trouble for yourself.

33. The Complaining Buyer

Complaining buyers are giving you the opportunity to keep their business provided you resolve their complaint satisfactorily.
The standard procedure for this is:

- Listen, observe and jot down what the buyer is complaining about.
- Show concern for the buyer's complaint.
- Do not admit liability automatically.
- Probe to find out the facts behind the complaint.
- Make an apology only if there is a bona fide reason to make the apology.
- Decide with the buyer what you are going to do to put the complaint right and how you are going to go about it.
- See it to its conclusion until the complaint has been resolved.

34. The Impulsive Buyer

Say little and let the product, service or idea sell itself, which it will usually do without much fuss and bother with this type of buyer. Try to go for the large order with a bigger sales value.

35. The Unforgiving Buyer

This type of buyer may have a personal dislike or vendetta against you or even a grudge against your company, which may be the result of some previous petty affair of no real significance. The buyer will consequently attempt to take revenge when the opportunity arises. He may well demand an apology from you, by saying you are wrong, even though you may not be, and could possibly cause a considerable amount of trouble for you if he choses to.

What you can do here is to apologise to the buyer and make an act of overwhelming generosity such as a free sample or gift, a lunch or dinner which will leave them puzzled and get you off the hook. When you have done that and paved the way to win their heart and business, move in like a hurricane.

36. The Professional Buyer

Do not even attempt to see and talk to this buyer without having planned your sales presentation, collated all the files about her and her company, and identified the range of problems and possible solutions well in advance of the sales interview. This buyer will have no hesitation in stopping you dead in your tracks if you do not have all the information. The professional buyer is an extremely time-conscious person and will require your proposal in writing to study the contract specifications in detail prior to giving her commitment to purchase. Be businesslike from start to finish, be well versed in your product, service or idea and any competitors' merits, downfalls or activity, if any. These buyers will test all your abilities to the limit but if your tactics, techniques and offer are strong, you are well on the way to getting their business.

37. The Unsuspecting Buyer

When you have successfully extracted an order from an unsuspecting buyer whom you have scientifically and skilfully won over, but who subsequently realises that he has made a decision to purchase something he is now uncertain about, and you get an indication that they want to change by the way they speak to you, you have to reassure the buyer that he has made a good decision and that he will be pleased with the benefits he will get. You should clear any residual objections if there are any, get agreement once again that they are satisfied with the purchase, wind up the conversation rapidly and get moving! Don't wait for idle chit-chat or you might end up talking yourself out of the sale which you have already completed. Don't risk it!

38. The Dreaming Buyer

The buyer who is dreaming of bettering herself and does nothing about it can have the reality of the situation pointed out by your saying something like: 'You are taking it easy and losing out while your competitors are rapidly moving ahead, look at them increasing their efficiency, productivity and profits by investing in this product, service or idea. How long do you want to go on like this, for now and forever?' This should spur them into positive action.

39. The Aggressive Buyer

These buyers are easy to deal with. They will openly tell you their likes and dislikes, giving you the opportunity to find an opening and sell to them. Do your selling job like a professional and the sale is yours for the asking.

40. The Moody Buyer

This buyer will swing from the normal to the ridiculous to the sublime. When they are crazy you have to be patient and handle them with the utmost care and firmness until they swing back to normality. If you don't keep your cool and if you lose your head, the sale is dead.

41. The Attacking Buyer

This buyer will attack you like a guard dog when you enter her premises on a cold-call without even knowing anything about you, your company, or your offer. How you can respond is with **fight**, **flight** or **submission**, depending on your personality. If you stand your ground and fight back (trying to sell) you will either be slung out or listened to when the buyer has mellowed.

In a flight situation, use the stun gun technique: quickly say 'Sir/Madam, I am leaving right now. Maybe I have called at an inappropriate time, but before I leave here is some free information for you to browse through (give them a brochure or leaflet) I will talk to you later, bye for now!' Take the name of the business when you are out of the premises, or get hold of a compliment slip or business card. Do not stay there when you are ordered to leave or you will be trespassing and they could call in the police to get you out or they could physically throw you out and you would not have a leg to stand on! Ring them back later.

If you choose submission you become an underdog with no control, and will most likely lose your self-esteem plus the sale. Don't forget that very often you may find an entirely different reaction the next time you call. Life is strange: one moment it is like the Battle of Britain and the next it is like a symphony orchestra.

42. The Timid Buyer

Don't frighten him. Talk to him gently and put your hand on his shoulder like a friend not a fiend, and build up their confidence. If you have given cause to trust you, your company, the product, service or idea he will make the decision in your favour when he is ready to buy.

43. The Competitive Equivalent Comparison Buyer

This buyer will ask many companies to present a product, service or idea and will never give a decision on the spot. As a professional salesperson you will ask the buyer as a matter of routine what other products, services or ideas they have seen in the market. You should also ask her if she plans to call in any more companies. If she says Yes, tell her that you can offer her the best deal going after she has seen the rest. This will oust the competition and you will be able to present and close the sale then or after the buyer has evaluated the competition. Once you have sown the seeds of doubt about the competition the buyer will be doubly impressed by the benefits of your product, service or idea from your presentation. When you achieve any one of these two objectives sell your product, service or idea like a true professional, get the order and get out!

44. The Sly Buyer

The sly buyer only wants to pick your brains – this you will soon gather. You must determine his objectives with careful questioning. You might get them to see eye to eye with you by saying something like this in a friendly tone of voice, 'Come on, let us be frank with each other. I do not know what your game is, but whatever it is I will play ball with you. As you well know even amongst hardened criminals there is a code of ethics, one crook does not try to "do" another crook. Please don't make it hard for me!' This approach, though controversial, will make the

sly come fly with you. That is what true selling is all about. I
know – I have done it.

45. The Evasive Buyer

For the buyer who is avoiding giving you a decision, remember
persistence pays. When you do make contact, make her feel bad
about her actions by telling her that you did not expect a person
of her calibre to waste *your* time as you are not in the business
of wasting *their* time and money uselessly. Rather you are
spending your time to help her make money and become
successful.

46. The Stubborn Buyer

You can make the stubborn buyer move by appealing to his need
or greed, and by coaxing him. Patience is a virtue when dealing
with this kind of buyer and persistence will produce the result
you want. This type of buyer will not budge or give in easily once
they dig their heels in, so use extreme tact and eventually you
will come out with flying colours.

47. The Cunning Buyer

These buyers will try to get the best deal they can get out of the
seller. In other words they will do a selling job on the
salesperson, and will want to get much more than the seller is
prepared to give them, such as extra ancillary equipment, extra
supplies, more frequent maintenance calls, more for their money
and so on. What you must do here is draw the bottom line to
show how far you are prepared to go, and stop any further
advances fast or you may end up a lean and hungry salesperson.
The cunning buyers can snatch your profits, just like a fox who
steals a farmer's chickens or like a thief that operates in daylight
(daylight robbery) unless proper care is taken to protect your
belongings.

48. The Negotiating Buyer

This buyer will not automatically pay you your asking price or accept your terms. She will look for the best possible terms for herself or her company. Unless you know the tactics and skills of negotiating you could fail miserably to achieve the best deal for yourself or your company and you could very likely blow yourself out of a deal.

49. The Slow Buyer

If you try to expedite a slow decision-making buyer you could lose out heavily, because these buyers are like grazing cows – they chew the cud before they swallow it. Likewise, these buyers like to chew things over and ponder their decisions, looking at all aspects of the transaction before they give their approval. They are usually thorough and accurate. You have to be the same in order to do good business with these buyers.

50. The Entertaining Buyer

Here is the buyer who says, 'Come on in, let's open a few cans of beer and leave the business for another day.' What you do is go for a quick close, catch them when they are in good spirits and say something like this, 'What a fantastic idea, let's hang the business and enjoy, because that is what life is all about, but before I do that let me just tell you that today just happens to be the closing day of this month's business for me and it also happens to be the last day that I can get you the best possible deal'. A little white lie in business is permissible but if you get caught a second white lie may be necessary – smile and tell them that the expiry date has been extended! 'So if you can please authorise this purchase for me, you won't be disappointed and I will be happy, and we can then go on to celebrate with a clear head.'

51. The Fast Buyer

This buyer will try to get the whole deal concluded soon (for their own benefit of course) but you could end up with terrible problems, awful comebacks or disadvantages if you have not got all the terms and conditions buttoned up. The buyer may be morally of good character and look great on the surface but legally he could tie you up in knots if you have not been careful. Know your subject inside out, and from every angle before you let the fast buyer pressurize you into finalizing the deal quickly.

52. The Busy Buyer

This buyer is usually working under a lot of pressure and will make a quick decision to go ahead if you can get to the point rapidly and accurately, but will usually say no if they smell something fishy. It all depends on how you present yourself, and on the nature of the proposal. I am very capable of securing decisions from busy buyers in my area of speciality even though they may not have had time to study everything in detail because they trust and respect me for my expertise. And respect is something that you earn.

53. The Hard-Working Buyer

These buyers will want to see you sweat for your order because they are firm believers in hard-work, being hard-workers themselves. Take your job seriously and show them your devotion and love for it and they will reward you. Do the opposite and they will soon get rid of you.

54. The Criticising Buyer

This buyer will openly tell you that you are useless if you, or your company, your products, services or ideas fall short of their expectations. You can learn a lot from this buyer and if you haven't got the right product, service or idea to offer them but something close to it, you may do what is called negative selling. Ask them how they would have gone about selling it if they were doing your job, and when they reveal their approach you humble yourself and apologise profusely for making such a diabolical mistake. They may give you the order out of sympathy, but at any rate they will have highlighted some shortcomings in your offer from which you can learn.

55. The Cheeky Buyer

This buyer will say a lot of things that affront you during the sales interview such as:

- Now that's correct!
- You really do not know what you are talking about, do you?
- Get your facts right before you waste my time!
- You are wrong!
- Where did you get the notion from?

The cheeky buyer is not being rude but challenging your authority all the time. The thing to do is to take no notice and carry on regardless until you get the order. A problem will arise if you get angry or lose your cool.

56. The Curious Buyer

This kind of buyer may only be wanting to satisfy his or her curiosity. If you are an inexperienced salesperson you may well go through a complete presentation with the curious buyer and having done so, you may very well end up having an educated buyer but no sale. The secret here is to make sure they have Authority and Need. In other words, confirm with the buyer that if you can show them that the product, service or idea will be of benefit to them, they will give you the order. If they will not agree, do not bother with the demonstration.

57. The Jealous Buyer

A prospective buyer who is jealous of his competitors is easy to convert into a customer. All you have to do is to explain all the great things the competition is doing and how it is going to affect them if they remain static and do not take any positive action to improve their circumstances by investing in the product, service or idea which you are offering. They will then see your product as to safeguarding their interests, and keeping up with the competition.

58. The Crooked Buyer

With experience you will soon know from the way the sales interview is going that the buyer's intentions are to play you out. What he really wants is to get the products or services without paying, which is the hardest blow the salesperson can get. The thing to do here is to stimulate the buyer to make the purchase by using every tactic of salespersonability, bring him or her to the point where they would pay you something up front to cover your costs if things go wrong later. It is better still to get full payment in advance. If you have got a deposit and you are having difficulty getting the balance it must be done very diplomatically if you want to continue to maintain a working relationship with the buyer, which can go sour and spoil future prospects if you use legal or other forms of pressure to get your money. I have sold to a few crooked buyers (also known as bad debts) that other companies and salespeople I knew did not dare touch, with a 95% success rate. I usually get the payment upfront by saying something like this: 'Listen, even the undertakers nowadays are selling plots of burial ground which you and I will need in the future, inflation-proof and at today's prices, but in order to avail yourself of that offer you have to make the purchase on their pay-now-and-die-later scheme. We also like to operate our business in that way. Would you like to pay for it in whole or give me at least 50% now?' I usually succeed.

59. The Noisy Buyer

This is the type of buyer who usually shouts – whether on the telephone, communicating with staff or during meetings with customers. This is a show of authority intended to scare others. What you must understand is that barking dogs seldom bite. Throw it a bone to keep it quiet and then muzzle it. In other words offer an incentive to buy such as a discount or an invitation to lunch that should keep the noisy buyer quiet and on your side.

60. The Lazy Buyer

Show lazy buyers how the product or service will make life easy for them and they will want it as soon as possible.

61. The Charitable Buyer

This buyer has a good heart and caring attitude. Play the role of a victim of tough circumstances and sympathy for you should help you get the order.

62. The Inexperienced Buyer

This is a buyer who may be new to the buying scene and is totally dependent on the seller to guide him or her to make the right decision. Use:

- Honesty
- Integrity
- Motivation
- Empathy
- Respect to help them buy your product.

And finally . . .

63. *The Perfect Buyer*

This buyer says immediately: 'Hello stranger, what have you got to offer me today?' You talk enthusiastically about your product, service or idea. The buyer says, 'That sounds wonderful, how much does it cost?' On hearing the price, the perfect buyer's response is: 'Tell you what, as I like you, your company, the product, service or idea so much and I haven't to date seen anything like it please do not bother to demonstrate or present it to me, I will have it right away. I will pay you ten per cent more than the asking price and throw in a weekend trip to Paris for you and your wife with free accommodation in a five star hotel for all your kind efforts. How's that? Here is my cheque now. Off you go – have a nice time and thanks for all your help!' . . .

Of course you know I am only joking – I have never met such an animal as a perfect buyer and cannot hope to, unless by some freak occurrence in a million years. This last buyer simply does not exist. Concentrate on learning how to tackle all the other buyers above and you will be the perfect salesperson.

HOW TO SELL YOURSELF

People buy people first. In low cost items purchased on a one off basis, the buyer can afford to make a purchase and sometimes does so even if the salesperson is lousy and when there is no ongoing relationship to be had. In big ticket sales, which can take anything from two months to five years or more to conclude, and which can run into five or six figures, the professionalism of the salesperson is paramount. The buyer or buyers will be very selective about the type of salesperson they are going to deal with.

A truly professional salesperson must be in control of the transaction, using logical and emotional appeal, offering competitive advantages over other products available in the marketplace to stimulate buying decisions, or else the sale may fall out of bed to the competition.

It can be assumed with a reasonable degree of certainty that no matter how good the product, service or idea and the reputation of the company, if the buyer takes a dislike to the salesperson the chances of making the sale will be played on very unfavourable ground. What you must do is to aim for the buyer to like and respect you, no matter what the buyer's make-up is.

Some sales experts suggest that the first thirty seconds in the interview are critical in the buyer's evaluation of the seller. I don't think so. What I am firmly convinced about is that if you have the skills of persuasion, motivation, manipulation and negotiation, then the seller is the one who controls the buyer, and could even fan a dying ember (an unlikely sale) into a mighty flame (a lucrative one). I know so – I have done it.

Here are some good guidelines on how to sell yourself:

- Bear in mind that the first 30 seconds could play a part in the outcome of the sale, but it is not the ultimate deciding factor. Being aware of it can only offer a positive influence and contribute to your state of preparedness and professionalism.
- Make sure you are appropriately dressed for the occasion.
- Your body language must convey your intentions to the buyer. You are primarily there to do business for mutual benefit.
- Be like a Karate expert – see, think and act by sizing up the buyer and his or her surroundings, and then decide what strategy and techniques you are going to use. Do find out also if your competition is wooing the business.
- Try and stop any distractions that may be interfering with the discussions, such as the TV, radio, cassette player, or other people.
- Use the AIDA formula (Attention Interest Desire Action) to break through the buyer's preoccupations.
- Use open-ended and specific questioning techniques to establish the need.
- Concentrate on taking the features of your product, service or idea and converting it into benefits. Applying the WIIFM, or What's In It For Me? formula from the buyer's point of view meaning, and showing how it will satisfy the buyer's needs. Get agreement as you go along.

- Listen carefully to every word the buyer utters to formulate a picture behind those words.
- Study and respond to all the non-verbal cues as recommended in chapters 7 and 8.
- Use all the selling skills that you will learn in this book to get the business and ask for the order at the appropriate time.
- Work towards the idea of getting the buyer to like you as a person and respect you as a knowledgeable business person.
- Always be in control of the conversation.
- When selling watch out for feedback in facial and body expressions as to how the buyer is responding to your sales patter.
- Try to figure out what personality the buyer has. If you get a glimpse of the buyer's signature or handwriting, chapter 12 on Graphology will be an additional string to your bow to help you sell better.
- Try to touch the buyer if possible whilst you are talking to him or her as a sign of friendliness – if you like people you might do this naturally. Research has shown that touching has a profound effect on most people, for it forms an emotional bond between buyer and seller. Make sure the timing and circumstances are right. This approach does not work with all buyers.
- Be natural, smile and shake hands on your first visit if you think the buyer will respond. Only arrogant buyers would not put a hand out in a friendly gesture.
- A little bit of showmanship will not hurt and goes hand in glove with salesmanship.
- Show interest in the buyer's business and well-being.
- Remember: a cardinal rule of selling is, it is not what you say in selling that matters, but it is the way that you say it.

Reading Your Prospective Buyer

Prospective buyers will give you various signs. Your success as a salesperson will be greatly enhanced if you read these signs effectively, by observing their

- appearance
- facial expressions
- gestures
- mannerisms
- speech

These will all combine to convey their

- beliefs (what they think is true about your proposition)
- emotions (what they feel is true about your proposition)
- actions (what they see as true about your proposition and what they will finally do)

Make the reading of these indicators your constant study, and you will start to perfect your abilities to persuade, motivate, manipulate and negotiate your way to success. You will find they fall into three distinct categories, in what I call the three sides principle (see below). Learn to visualize each prospective buyer and his or her characteristics from this list.

The Three Sides Principle

A	B	C
Unhappy	Contented	Happy
Objection	Indifference	Acceptance
Infant	Child	Adult
No	Maybe	Yes
Pacifist	Moderate	Activist
Frowning	Straight-faced	Smiling
Stupid	Fairly intelligent	Very intelligent
Vague	Clear	Precise
Sickly	Healthy	Radiant
Uninteresting	Interesting	Captivating
Hostile	Businesslike	Friendly
Uneducated	Educated	Intellectual
Unscrupulous	Fair	Scrupulous
Left wing	Moderate	Right wing
Silent	Reserved	Talkative
Backward thinking	Static thinking	Forward thinking
Depressed	Cheerful	Ecstatic

A	B	C
Silent	Quiet	Noisy
Lean	Medium built	Fat
Amateur	Semi-professional	Professional
Rude	Accommodating	Polite
Untrustworthy	Opportunistic	Trustworthy
Unreliable	Irregular	Reliable
Shy	Confident	Over-confident
Dull	Plain	Sparkling
Humble	Modest	Pompous
Past	Present	Future
Negative	Neutral	Positive
Unpredictable	Stable	Predictable
Barbaric	Civilised	Cultured
Irrational	Emotionally stable	Rational
Disapproving	Accepting	Supporting
Erratic	Stable	Orderly
Timid	Calm	Aggressive
Lazy	Active	Energetic
Moody	Good-tempered	Vivacious
Uninterested	Unenthusiastic	Enthusiastic
Non-competitive	Semi-competitive	Competitive
Illogical	Partly logical	Logical
Mad	Strange	Sane
Hysterical	Emotional	Phlegmatic
Over-anxious	Anxious	Relaxed
Miserly	Generous	Extravagant
Unskilled	Semi-skilled	Skilled
Lies	White lies	Truth
Evil	Bad	Good
Weak	Resourceful	Strong
Poorly dressed	Presentable	Immaculate
Quiet	Forthcoming	Pushy
Serious	Businesslike	Playful
Sloppy	Smart	Elegant
Non-negotiating	Open to negotiation	Negotiating
Disagreeable	Non-committal	Agreeable
Sleeping	Seated	Standing
Dreaming	Attentive	Concentrating

A	B	C
Unfriendly	Distant	Friendly
Trusting	Shrewd	Sly
Indecisive	Evaluating	Decisive
Loser	Runner up	Winner
Attacking	Defending	Welcoming
Inattentive	Attentive	Listening
Tired	Rested	Active
Late	Time-conscious	Punctual
Pessimistic	Realistic	Optimistic
Impatient	Restless	Patient
Afraid	Cautious	Brave
Indisciplined	Fairly disciplined	Disciplined
Atheistic	Agnostic	Theistic
Poor	Comfortable	Rich
Uneducated	Proficient	Well educated
Powerless	Weak	Powerful
Non-technical	Semi-technical	Technical
Skiver	Plodder	Hardworker
Non-commitment	Excuses	Commitment
Cold	Warm	Hot
Backwards	Stationary	Forwards
Resting	Standing	Walking
Can't afford	Just about afford	Can afford
No authority	Some authority	Has authority
Careless	Careful	Meticulous
Shocked	Startled	Unperturbed
Weak willed	Pliable	Strong willed
Alcoholic	Moderate drinker	Teetotaller
Smoker	Occasional smoker	Non-smoker
Gambler	Spasmodic gambler	Non-gambler
Lethargic	Takes exercise	Exercise fanatic
Loner	Fairly good mixer	Gregarious
Dirty	Clean	Spotless
Non-risk taker	Chancer	Big risk taker
Delay in paying	Staggered payments	Prompt payments
Worker	Supervisor	Manager
Employee	Manager	Managing Director
Argumentative	Accommodating	Agreeable

A	B	C
Unconcerned	Concerned	Over concerned
Hate	Love-hate	Love
Unfit	Fit	Peak fitness

I'm sure you will be able to add to this list. All buyers, and all people, are made up of characteristics from each column, and the challenge for top salespeople is to learn how to deal with every type of person. If you can duck and dive, wheel and deal, twist and turn, run with the hare and hunt with the hound, kick like a mule and dance like a peacock, bite like a crocodile and be as gentle as a lamb . . . you will be able to number yourself amongst the top salespeople of the world. This ability to change like a chameleon and adapt to each new situation must always be framed within a civilized code of conduct, legal and morally acceptable. Learn to duck and dive, but not away from the law.

This is what makes the selling profession so demanding – requiring as it does people with strong personal qualities – and so envied and respected, offering high earnings for the top achievers. There is no doubt about it: selling is hard work – mentally, emotionally and physically!

Sales Talk

> *'O Lord, please help me to keep*
> *my big mouth shut until I*
> *know what I am talking about!'*
> *(The Moral: Think Before You Speak)*

As a salesperson you probably try to convey a certain impression to the buyer through the way you act: happy-go-lucky, easy-going, serious, tough, jolly, aggressive . . . while in reality you may be quite the reverse. You can fool your buyer quite well through outward appearances, as looks and behaviour can be deceptive. No buyer can make an accurate judgement of you, your company or your product without some kind of oral communication, no matter how much extra influential material is available to convey a message. That is why there will always be the need for sales people to act as assistant decision makers to buyers in the evaluating of products, services or ideas and to offer them guidance in the decision making process.

Thus, even if you lack a good appearance or personality, or if you even have a poor quality product, service or idea to offer, but have the power to convince others with your sales talk, you cannot fail to win. Smart dress and good behaviour are not the be-all and end-all of selling, as they are sometimes made out to be. It is an advantage but not a disadvantage. I know because I have tried and tested both – in fact I would say that businesslike dress in preference to casual wear can be a major disadvantage in some instances and I am of the opinion that some people who pay great importance to dress have little of value to offer in other areas. Consider the politicians, your workmates, doctors, solicitors, and managers to whom you either pay attention or ignore. Was it done on dress and behaviour alone? Obviously not. How did they occupy a place in our minds and in our hearts? Whichever way you look at it the influencing was done through the spoken word. You may be a brilliant person but if you cannot communicate your knowledge or ideas with an objective, you will be a misfit – a square peg in a round hole. Do not be a lighthouse in a bog – brilliant but useless!

Then again, if you are talking rubbish, remember it is better to be silent and be thought a fool than to speak and remove all doubt! If you have the chance to say something productive and you say nothing, then silence is the virtue of fools. But if you are in a closing situation, silence is golden.

Today the astute buyer is all too aware of mind games sales people play. What is required is sales talk with an objective, structured with logical and emotional appeal. Your job as a professional salesperson is to persuade with sales talk, to motivate with sales talk, to manipulate with sales talk, to negotiate with sales talk. The great Muhammed Ali clearly showed the world his greatness through the spoken word, his punching fists and dancing feet.

Wherever you are in the world an articulate person can achieve unimaginable results. And it is possible to learn how to become articulate and fluent, provided you take the time and trouble to acquire the knowledge and skills. When selling, the professional salesperson uses word bullets every time he or she says something, until the target is hit and the sale is made. Analysis of the following diverse examples of sales talk and communication shows that all roads lead to the same destination – a sale or desired positive outcome.

A Medicine Man's Bazaar Presentation

'Now, may I have your attention please, ladies and gentlemen? I have good news for you. Whenever you are troubled with anything such as a pain, or ache, or ailment like a headache, a cold, flu, loss of appetite, bad breath, rheumatism, premature greying, or when you hear the agonizing cry of your neighbour's young son or daughter complaining of stomach ache, all you have to do is open up this little medicine bottle, put a few drops into a glass of water and give it to the poor child and hey presto, the discomfort's vanished, the pain is gone and the kid is cured! Now if there is anyone interested in making a purchase at five Rupees per bottle, then they should come forward immediately because in a few minutes I will be closing my medicine box and will not open it, even for one thousand Rupees.'

The result is that the medicine man grabs the audience's attention and creates tremendous interest and desire so quickly and skilfully that some gullible peasant buyers (not even really knowing what is in the miniature bottles) cling to his sales talk like ants attracted to a lump of sugar, and volume sales are made instantly.

The Case of Stolen Perfumes!

I was spell-bound once at a Sunday market in London, by the rhetoric, wit and charm of a young Jewish salesman who appeared from nowhere with a case of what he called stolen perfume. It may have been a gimmick of his but by golly he did pull a crowd and motivated them to purchase. From what I can recollect from his sales talk this is what he said, with a bottle of the perfume in his hand. He was nothing if not dynamite.

'Ladies and Gentlemen, you are not buying cold tea, lemonade or diet cola. This one is called SECRETS, and it retails at £30 a bottle. Forget paying anything like it. I'll give this one away No Charge, F.R.E.E., FREE! Now watch what I do; on top of the

SECRETS I'll go a stage further and give you this bottle of SEDUCTION complete with spray and atomizer; it costs £40 a bottle.

'Ladies and Gentlemen, they are advertised on television seven nights a week. It is advertised on Crimewatch. We don't call it Crimewatch, we call it free advertising. Now, there is £70 worth of stolen perfume in the box, no charge and I don't stop there, I go a stage further and as I go a stage further it is like sex, the further I go the better it jolly well gets.

'Now you see that bottle over there? It is called TANTALIZER, and it was never meant to be sold in the gutter. It was meant to be sold by the PRESTIGIOUS COMPANY. There is only one problem, at the PRESTIGIOUS COMPANY, they call you madam, they call you sir, they show you the PRESTIGIOUS COMPANY colour magazine and charge you £60 for a bottle of TANTALIZER. I think it is a bloody outrage. I am no liar, I went to the PRESTIGIOUS COMPANY yesterday.

'Last but by no means least I am going to make you pay for the cream of the cream, the icing on the cake – the ROYAL perfume priced at £100 a bottle. It does not come from the Tower of London. It comes from the world of beauty. Work it out for yourself with me. Work it out with the PRESTIGIOUS COMPANY. £30 for the SECRETS plus £40 for the SEDUCTION equals £70 plus another £60 for the TANTALIZER equals £130 plus another £100 for the ROYAL perfume equals £230 worth of stolen perfume.

'Late last night when Prince Charles was busy getting hold of Lady Diana, I was busy getting hold of this stolen perfume. Now think about it – £230 worth of stolen perfume is yours for the asking in this box containing four of the finest range, for my price, the fair price [and here he hit the box with his hand] of only £23. I don't sell any empty boxes. If you want an empty box go see an undertaker.

'Ladies and Gentlemen, for just £23 you can take home with you £230 worth of stolen perfume in this box containing four of the finest range; SECRETS, SEDUCTION, TANTALIZER and the ROYAL perfume. Now if you want one off me, all I say is do it quickly and sharply. Get your money ready. I am not supposed to be here. I am a bit nervous. If the boys in blue come around, me and my little business we run like Sebastian Coe down the road the other way.'

You can bet your bottom dollar it was the quickest sale of the century I have ever seen.

The African Witch Doctor

'Friends, I am Chief Goat-Head, your great witch doctor, astrologer, herbalist, spiritualist, magician, healer and occultist, here with you today. Thank you for coming and a very warm welcome to you. I would like to ask you a quick question if I may. What do you want out of life? Do you want success in friendship, romance, marriage, sex or education? Do you desperately need freedom from enemies and unhappiness? Do you want an assurance against disloyalty or unfaithfulness? That is no problem. All you have to do is buy my magic rings or talismen that are graded according to price and benefits.

'Here they are, the magic rings for a happy future and success. You can have a grade 1 happiness ring for $25, or the superior quality grade 2 one for $35. Alternatively, you can have the happiness and success ring grade 3 for $75 or the better quality happiness and success ring grade 4 for $100. I also have this magic talisman that will bring you luck for $50, and the mysterious talisman for love and good luck which you can have for $75. If you want to become successful in business why not try my magic talisman for business priced at $100, and if you are dreaming of becoming rich then this magic talisman for riches at $150 is a must. If enjoying sex is of concern to you why not wear this magic talisman for love and faithfulness for a once only payment of $200 – your partner will love you so much and be faithful to you and will never go out with anybody else, so that every time you make love you will enjoy it so much and will be so tired that you will have to keep a glass of water by your bedside to revive you!

'Please hand me your money now – remember the more you pay the better you get. If you are not satisfied with the goods your money will be refunded in full – and that is guaranteed!'

These three examples are amusing and a little outrageous; I am not suggesting that you follow them to the letter, but take note of the spirit – notice how they capture attention, create interest, desire and action in double-quick time. You will probably not be operating in a street market, but rather in the sophisticated business environment of business and commerce. There are many different ways of selling and communicating a message, and if it can produce a positive result for you, then don't hesitate to use it. The following method is widely used in the Western world.

Steps the Professional Salesperson Would Take to Make the Sale

Suspects	Cold calls people who may be considered as potential buyers (a suspect).
Prospects	Arranges an appointment with the suspect to demonstrate or present the product, service or idea. The suspect becomes a prospect when the seller creates the opportunity to sell by identifying a need or creating a need with the suspect.
Qualification	Determines whether the prospect has the Money, Authority, Need and also if the competition is vying for the business.
Demonstration or Presentation	Takes the features of the product, service or idea and converts them into benefits, and shows the prospect (buyer) how the benefits will satisfy their needs. Please note you *demonstrate a product* and you *present a service or idea.*
Objections	The buyer will want to clarify doubts, fears and relevant queries he or she may have on the offer, which the salesperson will have to answer, overcome and provide reassurance for the buyer, in order to pave the way for closing.
Closing	The seller gets commitment from the buyer to proceed with the offer. The salesperson will have to ask for the order or guide the buyer to make the buying decision in a skilful manner. After closing, there is an opportunity to get referrals.

Steps the Professional Buyer Would Take to Make the Sale

The professional buyer will weigh up many factors before a decision to purchase is made. This would cover factors such as

- Price
- Cost
- Delivery
- Quality
- Value
- Functionability
- After-sales service
- Warranty/guarantee
- Billing and invoicing system
- Competitive advantages/disadvantages
- Persuasion exercised by the salesperson and degree of professionalism
- Discounts
- Availability
- Brand name

SUCCESS

Success is speaking words of praise,
In cheering other people's ways,
In doing just the best you can,
With every task and every plan,
It's silence when your speech would hurt,
Politeness when your neighbour's is curt,
It's deafness when the scandal flows,
And sympathy with other's woes,
It's loyalty when duty calls,
It's courage when disaster falls,
It's patience when the hours are long,
And perseverance all along.

Anon

FURTHER STYLES OF SELLING

Here are some samples of sales messages found in pubs in Ireland that are often packed with customers. One landlord told me these motivational messages help cheer up the drinkers and keep them in good spirits, and provide him with good sales.

When we drink, we get drunk
When we get drunk, we go to sleep
When we go to sleep, we commit no sin
When we commit no sin, we go to heaven
So let's all get drunk and go to heaven!

*

Prevent hangovers, stay drunk!

*

Everyone entering this place makes us happy
Some when they arrive and some when they leave!

*

Our bank manager assures us that
He will not be selling beer or spirits
We have agreed not to
Cash cheques or operate a loan department!

*

I would like to help you out, which way did you come in!?

*

Credit will only be given to
Persons over 85 years of age
Accompanied by both grandparents!

*

In God we trust
But all others pay cash!

*

You are cordially invited to
Drown all your sorrows in booze!

In selling, what breeds success is that it is not what you say to get your point across that really matters, but rather it is how you say it that counts. Furthermore, it is not the size of the company that you represent that matters but how effective you are as a salesperson.

I would like to finish off this chapter with a sales interview that was so funny and doomed from the start that it ended up in disaster for both my buyer and me.

I was urgently requested to visit a company that traded in used cars and was doing very badly. The owner had heard about my expertise as a sales promoter and called me in to discuss what I could do for him to boost his sales. When I called on him he looked very depressed sitting behind his desk. I said, 'Hello, I am Patrick Ellis, and as you have already told me a part of your story over the phone, let us get down to business right away. How many cars do you sell in a week?'

He grunted and said 'Huh, it should be more like in how many weeks do I sell a car?'

I replied, 'That must be pretty bad for you, but don't worry, I'll get your sales going for you with a good advertising campaign.'

'That's good,' he said, 'and what do you think will be the *outcome*?'

I said, wondering whether he had any money to pay me with, 'That will of course be dependent on your *income!*'

He said, 'FORGET IT!' and that was the end of that encounter and the end of this chapter.

CHAPTER 6

Time management and goal setting

Time – The Irreplaceable Resource
Goals – Success means achieving them

The watch of life is wound just once,
And no one can predict when the hands will stop.
To become successful takes longer
Than it takes to be a failure.
Time waits for no man so hurry now,
For there is limited time to achieve our goals.
Plan your time, respect time, be on time,
Ration time and eliminate the time wasters.
And don't rush around madly,
Trying to accomplish the impossible.
Or you could end up on troubled waters,
And even dead on time.
So watch your life and do watch out.

Patrick Ellis

When selling the key word to think about is 'Watch'

Words (watch your words)
Actions (watch your actions)
Thoughts (watch your thoughts)
Character (watch your character)
Heart (watch your heart)

I do not believe anybody can teach you how to manage your time except yourself, even though there are many interesting books written on the subject offering elaborate theories and time organising systems. Theoretically one can plan one's time to the last second of the day, but as a matter of practicality the human animal being logical and emotional, but more emotional than logical, will always for a multitude of reasons end up deviating from the plan of which it was the architect. Those reasons are often unforeseen and usually outside the person's control. However there are useful guidelines which we can learn and use to control our time and achieve our goals quicker. Time is nature's free gift to everyone on this planet and given to all of us in exactly the same number of units. These are:

60 seconds = 1 minute
60 minutes = 1 hour
24 hours = 1 day
7 days = 1 week
52 weeks = 1 year
12 months = 1 year
365 days = 1 year
366 days = 1 leap year

And we've all heard of the nursery rhyme:

30 days hath September
April, June and November
All the rest have 31
Except February alone
That has 28 days clear
And 29 in each leap year

What I want to emphasize here is the units of time we have available to us. How we utilise this precious gift will determine whether we are successful or not, and I am not just referring to financial success alone but to all aspects of success.

The average person can expect to live as long as possible in their country of origin and/or domicile as shown in the life expectancy table at the beginning of this book. These figures of course would vary significantly depending on nutrition, stress, exercise, physical and mental health and the availability of good medical care.

However what we can take from the longevity statisticians, efficiency and time management experts, is a basis to plan our time and lives so that we may control it in such a way as to be able to achieve our goals, dreams and ambitions in the most productive way possible. Put another way, it is managing ourselves and controlling our destiny, just like harnessing the flow of water through a tap: you can either let it drip slowly to fill a number of containers or fill them faster by opening the tap fully – it is all a matter of time before you achieve your objective.

Goals and Objectives

By the age of forty, most people should have achieved eighty percent of their goals. It is up to you whether you want to burn the candle at both ends to achieve your objectives sooner rather than later, but be warned this will involve stress and its side effects. On the other hand, if you withdraw from imposing challenges on yourself you could end up dissatisfied, miserable and depressed at the age of forty, when others are making headway in life. I can relate the lack of self-esteem, chronic alcoholism, drug-taking and negative thinking in adult life to poor time management and objective-setting skills early in life. Failure to set goals leads inevitably to failure, while success comes by taking control of your life. Having the fighting spirit will help you become a winner.

Forty is by no means the end of the road, and at any age you can decide to get your skates on and start afresh. But if you are set in your ways you will find it difficult initially to get going.

It's not that you can't teach an old dog new tricks, but that it becomes slightly harder to teach an old dog new tricks!

The later on in life you set your goals, the faster you have to work to achieve them because the watch of life is ticking away, and every second it ticks by we are getting closer to the date of departure from this world. We have only a limited amount of time to make it, the Bible says, no one hath control over the day of death. So whatever you may be thinking of doing, do it now, don't procrastinate.

Goals can be divided into

Short-term (nought to five years)

Medium-term (five to ten years)

Long-term (ten to twenty years plus).

The important thing about setting goals is to have them written down on paper and to make them realistic. By all means dream about your goals but they must be attainable. Let your imagination run riot for a while and it will certainly help to formulate a fantastic idea which you can make your goal. The logical side of your mind will find constructive ways to attain it.

Visualize Your Goals

Vividly imagine in your mind the luxury holiday home you wish to own, or that world record you wish to break, or the world cruise you wish to go on, or the Rolls Royce you will be owning and driving one day, and put these and other dreams you may have onto paper as your short, medium or long term goals so that they may become a reality. Once you firmly commit yourself to a particular goal and feed that thought in a positive manner into your subconscious mind, which acts like a computer, it will automatically set about the task of helping you achieve it in the most effective manner.

For those who have given up the race, this book is here to give you encouragement to reverse your negative thinking. If, in spite of all the guidance you are receiving now, your negative thoughts still dominate your thinking and your life and you still say things like, 'but ah, I left it too late', 'I am too old now, I can never make it,' or 'it will all be the same in a few years time', my honest advice is stop reading this book and continue on your downtrodden track, you poor thing! Failure owes you a big handshake and will welcome you with open arms. Good luck to you for having made your choice. Only you will enjoy all the rewards for that decision which is an anti-phase to successful living. Alternatively you may need to seek help from a therapist or counsellor if you want to get back onto the springboard of life.

This book has been written for those positive thinkers who want to take the long, hard, sure road to success as opposed to the 'get rich quick' route advocated by some books. There are only a few people who have become overnight successes, and then such success is only cosmetic if you haven't worked for it. If success comes easily, it can go easily. You need the foundation, life experience and level headed thinking to handle it. For the vast majority of people life is an ongoing battle and the experience you gain along the way is irreplaceable. Now, if you can add know-how to that experience of yours from others who have taken the plunge, then you are going to be all the wiser and better off in life.

It is true that we will all end up in the same destination some time in the future – dust to dust, ashes to ashes – but while the negative thinkers are going on the painful road of doom and gloom, the positive thinkers will be fighting all the way on the exciting route to success, winning and losing and enjoying themselves every second, every minute, every hour, every day to the fullest. As humans we are built for achievement, and if we can only embrace the idea and cultivate the fighting spirit life can truly be fantastic. Putting control into your life is a must for every person.

'It is far better to dare mighty things, to win glorious triumphs, even though checkered by failure, than to rank with those poor spirits who neither enjoy much nor suffer much, because they live in the grey twilight that knows not victory nor defeat'

Theodore Roosevelt

Another good system in planning your time is to plan for the year and then convert the yearly plan into a monthly plan and then to a weekly and daily plan, and then work one day at a time to achieve your goals. Achieving your short term goals will

The Things I Must Do Today DAY
DATE / /

Item No.	Description	Urgent	Completed (Tick)
1			
2			
3			
4			
5			
6			
7			
8			
9			
10			

Item No.	Description	Urgent	Completed
		(Tick)	
11			
12			
13			
14			
15			
16			
17			
18			
19			
20			

be the realization of your five one-year goals. As you keep achieving all the component parts, stage by stage, which you have written down on paper in your master plan that go to make up your short term goals, you must cross them off the list as you move forward, reviewing your actions at regular intervals, then doing a progress report on yourself and taking corrective action if necessary, but sticking to your course in spite of all obstacles. Repeat the procedure for your medium term and long-term goals. It is as easy as that.

When working on a day-to-day basis write down the six most important things you have to do the following day. Review it before you go to sleep and your subconscious mind will work on a problem-solving procedure for you to operate on the following day that will provide the best solutions for your requirements. Start with the priorities first and only after you have achieved your objective on your priority must you move on to the less important ones, to prevent mental chaos, fatigue and failure.

Remember, every minor goal you achieve contributes to your overall success and helps you to achieve your main goal to which you have committed yourself. You may have heard of the saying, 'little drops of water, little grains of sand, make the mighty ocean and the pleasant land.' Achieving success through achieving goals is just like that!

A sample list of THE THINGS I MUST DO TODAY is provided here to help you with your goal achievement.

Tips to Manage the Time of Your Life

- Do one thing at a time and do it well.
- Learn to say politely, 'sorry, you are disturbing me', or 'I am already engaged', when someone encroaches unduly on your time or tries to unload a problem on you that really belongs to them.
- Learn to delegate.
- Don't go on wild goose chases.
- Plan your following day's work the night before.
- I have a business colleague who has a tough philosophy: any

prospective buyer is only worth two phone calls and one visit after which if they do not respond they can go take a dive. Try it if you like it.

- Don't waste too much time on the telephone on idle chatter.
- There is a time and a place for everything in life. Don't watch TV for too long when other important things have to be dealt with.
- Time is money. Use it wisely, and if you manage your time well you will make a profit.
- If there is a short cut, take it.
- Don't procrastinate. Cultivate the habit of doing it now.
- You will have all the time in the world to do nothing when you are dead. So do something useful when you are living on borrowed time.
- Positive thinking can save you time and make you money.
- Take one day at a time.
- Make the best use of your time, work while-u-work, play while-u-play!
- In between calls don't waste your time idling, do something productive instead.
- Avoid time wasters like traffic jams, queues, airline, train and bus delays when possible, by keeping your eyes and ears open through TV, radio, press or a phone call. To be forewarned is to be forearmed.
- Speed-reading and developing a super memory can save you bags of time.
- Allocate your time to business, but spend time with family and friends.
- Use driving time productively by listening to educational, motivational and inspirational (self-improvement) audio cassettes.
- Finally, there is a time for you to disappear – called sleep – and a time to reappear – called waking up. Please don't fail to do that or you will end up dead on time!

'*All the world's a stage,*
And all the men and women merely players;
They have their exits and their entrances,
And one man in his time plays many parts,
His acts being seven ages. At first, the infant,
Mewling and puking in the nurse's arms.
Then, the whining school-boy, with his satchel
And shining morning face, creeping like snail
Unwillingly to school. And then the lover,
Sighing like furnace, with a woeful ballad
Made to his mistress's eyebrow. Then a soldier,
Full of strange oaths, and bearded like the pard,
Jealous in honour, sudden and quick in quarrel,
Seeking the bubble reputation
Even in the cannon's mouth. And then, the justice,
In fair round belly with good capon lin'd,
With eyes severe and beard of formal cut,
Full of wise saws and modern instances;
And so he plays his part. The Sixth age shifts into the lean and
slipper'd pantaloon,
With spectacles on nose, and pouch on side,
His youthful hose well sav'd, a world too wide
For his shrunk shank, and his big manly voice,
Turning again toward childish treble, pipes
And whistles in his sound. Last scene of all,
That ends this strange eventful history,
Is second childishness, and mere oblivion,
Sans teeth, sans eyes, sans taste, sans everything.'

Shakespeare *As You Like It*

And that is what life's all about, as it was then, is now, and will be in the future. Even with the most sophisticated scientific advances, we are all born to die, and when your Creator calls you, whoever you are, you go! As Tennyson said about the Light Brigade, 'Theirs not to reason why, Theirs but to do and die.'

So make the best of every day, plan your time, plan your life, and aim for success.

ADVANCE WARNING TO ALL SALESPEOPLE!

Beware the mentally sick salesperson's blues, fear, negative thinking and failure syndrome. Very contagious to order-takers, the new and inexperienced and especially the unsuccessful members of a sales team.

Symptoms: The victim continually complains by blaming lack of success on bad sales management, poor territory, a useless firm, bad luck, inferior products, services or ideas, bad weather and non-purchasing buyers.

The patient has a blank expression, tends to roam around the office aimlessly and hide in pubs. At most times he or she is deaf to the sales manager, successful sales people and well-meaning colleagues.

They criticise the winners and become artistic liars, even to their nearest and dearest. They display little or no motivation to meet buyers and to do the selling job. They have no clearly defined goals and are ineffective time managers. They frequently refer to sales manuals but that's about as far as they go. They hang around in golf courses, cinemas, restaurants, clubs and betting shops, spending someone else's money, and are often in debt. They sit longer than usual in front of the TV and make discreet phone calls to colleagues to compare performances and obtain the latest gossip from the office.

Quarantine: This is a very infectious disease, immediate isolation is necessary.

Treatment: Rigorous mental hygiene to include attitude correction by switching to positive thinking, belief in oneself, self-motivation, and a big injection of enthusiasm. Physical exercise to be had by making sales calls. Sales training to be given to improve the affected selling skills and knowledge areas. The victim must face up to his or her fears and do what s/he fears most in order to build up confidence. If a bout of psychosomatic illness such as a panic attack occurs the best drug to take is to face the facts fairly and squarely with a calm assuredness, and using the following autosuggestion mental and physical action. 'I can, I will, I must win in this matter' and substitute fear with positive, mental and physical action. If that does not work see a medical practitioner who may refer the patient to a psychiatrist (a head-shrinker).

Prognosis: The patient will usually show improvement under this management scheme. Sacking is not recommended unless condition is severe. If termination of employment is caused by the salesperson's massive self-inflicted attitude injury, then make sure s/he gets a grand send-off with a bouquet of flowers (a wreath) to mourn the death of yet another salesperson with a brief message: *With our deepest sympathies to the greatest sales disaster our company has known in recent times, may you RIP – 'Repent In Private and not Return If Possible'. Bad news but Good luck and all the very best in your future working life. THE MANAGEMENT!*

Convalescence: During convalescence the recovering salesperson must be segregated from the losers and made to move only with the winners to prevent a relapse.

Permanent cure: Is possible with an initial vaccination of self-motivation and sales training and then with booster doses of ongoing training coupled with occasional jabs of recognition. When the salesperson reaches peak sales performance give him/her a congratulatory testimonial of achievement, a certificate of selling fitness such as YOU ARE NUMBER 1. Success will then automatically breed success.

THE PSYCHOLOGY OF THE SALE

Demonstration, Presentation and Ideas Selling Techniques

As I mentioned earlier you demonstrate a product, you present a service, and you use creative techniques to sell ideas. In fact you must use creative techniques to sell products and services as well to become a champion salesperson because they all originate from ideas. Products are described as tangibles. Services and ideas are described as intangibles.

Products are **Tang-ibles** that can be   Jet planes, Ships, Capital equipment, Power tools, Motor cars, Business touched and operated by hand equipment, Fork lift trucks, Microwave ovens, Electronic showers, Computers, Video recorders, TVs, Hi-Fis, Double Glazing etc.

Services are **Intangibles** that require a combination of both factual know-how and Practical skills. It involves mental and physical work but is usually more physical work than mental. There tends to be more public contact with services. Car repairs, Laundry and dry cleaning, Shoe repairing, Tailoring, Undertaking, Carpentry, Building work, Carpet cleaning, Gardening, Teaching, Consulting, Driving School, Chemist, Clergy, Pest control, Theatrical and Showbusiness work, Musician, Surgeon, Police, Fire and Ambulance work, Receptionist, Nursing, Photography & developing, Restaurant business, Estate agency, Selling, Hair dressing, Travel agency, Physician, Politician, Plumber, Painting and decorating, Jeweller, Watch repairing, Electrician, Child minding, Videographing etc.

Ideas are **Intangibles** that are more scholarly, academic, artistic, abstract and creative by nature, and which require greater mental prowess, factual knowhow and more practical skill but less public contact Administrators, Analysts, Planners, Copywriters, Journalists, Teaching, Management and Training, Marketing, Consulting, Fiction and Non-fiction writing, Research and development, Artists, Composers, Pilots, Painters, Sculptors, Designers, Creative thinkers, Computer programmers, Public Accounting, Medical, Legal, Engineering and allied professions etc.

In order to sell to or from each of these three categories, first look at the FEATURES of the sellers' offer:

● What is it? Shape, form, chemical composition, physical characteristics, speed, distance, time, length, width, height, texture, expertise and so on.

● What is its purpose? Its Function and objective
  and convert them into BENEFITS.

What will the product, service or idea features do for the buyer?
 How will those features satisfy a buyer's needs (needs that
either pre-exist or which can be created)? Remember you cannot
take a horse to water and make it drink, but if you make it thirsty
and then offer it water, it will drink.
 When selling against a competitor, use the FAB approach –
Feature, Advantage, Benefit – which means how do the features
of your product, service or idea compare with the competition.
Its advantages and the corresponding benefit to the buyer.
 When a seller can understand and embrace the concept that
buyers are only interested in how they are going to benefit when
they make an investment in a product, service or idea and are
not interested in features, then the seller can structure the whole
sales demonstration or presentation to sell the offer in terms of
benefits so that it will draw the buyer to the sales talk like a moth
to a flame and naturally produce a sale.
 The only people who are really interested in the features of
a product or service are those involved in manufacturing or
creating it. For example, in the case of a motor car, the design
and production engineers would be interested in the **features**
(such as sensitive and sharp braking). In terms of buyer benefits,
this translates to smoothness and safety. Similarly, a benefit of
car repairs is trouble-free motoring and peace of mind.
 Earlier you read about **why people buy** and the **different types
of buyer**, which means you should now find it very easy either
to identify a need or create a need to enable you to make the sale.
There are however other interim steps which you will have to
observe and take before you get to closing. The sequence of the
sales interview, which is given at this stage only to provide you
with an overall view is as follows. A detailed explanation on each
topic covering the steps of the sale will follow on in later chapters.
 You identify a need or create a need by **Probing**, which is the
technique of asking questions in the form of **Open-Ended
Questions** (to get feedback) and **Specific Questions** (popularly
known as closed-ended questions to get the buyer to say yes or
no). When the buyer responds to your questions s/he will reveal

certain needs. Listen intently to what the buyer says. There are two ways of listening: **Active Listening** and **Passive Listening**. At this stage you will be able to pinpoint the type of buyer you are dealing with and know how you should tackle him or her. Some sales experts say that 80 percent of the talking should be done by the buyer and 20 percent by the salesperson. I have to disagree with this, and I suggest the ratio should be as follows:

Sequence	Salesperson (Talking)	Buyer (Talking)
Opening (Buyer is least interested)	80%	20%
Body (Buyer is more interested)	60%	40%
Close (Buyer now wants it)	30%	70%
Departure (Salesperson says least and gets out soon with the order)	20%	80%

In professional selling the salesperson has to talk to overcome a multitude of sales obstacles initially. If you do not talk and sit like a dumb clot in front of the buyer how can you control the sales interview? Once the sales resistance is overcome and control of the interview has been gained, then the seller starts to scale down the sales talk proportionately. You have to build a rapport, penetrate smokescreens, inform and educate the buyer and also either **persuade, motivate, manipulate** or **negotiate** with him/her depending on what type of buyer you are dealing with. In Order taking the buyer does the talking and the seller does the closing.

Ron Holland in his book *Talk and Grow Rich* says, 'no matter how brilliant an idea, product or service is the one way to sell it is with the spoken word'.

If the thing being sold is of a protracted or complicated nature and cannot be closed on the second visit then, on the third or subsequent visit the salesperson must do approximately 40 percent of the talking and the buyer should do approximately 60 percent till the final closure is accomplished.

In a live selling situation, unless the seller is skilful enough to know how to handle the buyer's personality, and properly interpret and respond to the verbal and non-verbal responses given – even though the seller's presentation may be excellent – it would still have a detrimental effect on the seller. So, before the seller reaches the point of saying little and executing the maximum pressure of silence, s/he would also have to watch out for non-verbal cues in conjunction with the verbal response and react accordingly until given a favourable decision.

Let us move on further into the sales interview itself. By now you should have a good idea of the type of buyer to whom you are about to demonstrate your product, present your service or sell your idea. It is at this point that **salespersonability** and **showmanship** go hand-in-hand. You really have to give your best at this stage. The curtain has gone up and the show has begun. You must deliver your demonstration or presentation by playing the sweetest music for the buyer's ears, just like a snake charmer tantalizes the snake with his flute. Every move the snake charmer makes up and down and from side to side with the flute the snake, usually a cobra, dances in strict obeyance.

You must also strongly appeal to the buyer's other five senses apart from hearing. These are sight, smell, touch, taste and intuition. When you have succeeded in exerting the magnetic pull on the buyer to make a decision then the buyer is likely to raise **objections** which are not put offs or excuses, as unprofessionals might think, but rather they are a request for more information or a clarification of a selling point. If correctly understood and answered by the seller, this should aid the buyer to make a positive decision in the seller's favour. Objections are a favourable sign that the buyer is interested in one way or another, for without objections it is highly unlikely that you would make a sale.

Once objections are handled properly you then have paved the way for closing. The best way to deal with objections is to kill them before they come up – in other words pre-empting the objection, bringing it up and dealing with it before the buyer does. The salesperson must study the buyer's non-verbal communication throughout the sales interview to gauge the buyer's response behaviour and change accordingly to suit the situation at hand.

The sole objective of the seller must be to build up desire for the product, service or idea.

When the buyer gives you a buying signal such as 'when can I have it?' you then close by saying 'how quickly do you want it?' If the buyer wants your product, service or idea but doesn't want to pay your price because s/he can get it cheaper elsewhere then you switch from selling to negotiating, which is another skill in its own right.

I have to stress this point very clearly; right throughout the sales interview the salesperson must be in control and more often than not be in command and red-hot in evaluating and responding to what the buyer is saying and doing. Salespeople should have their selling skills sharpened to razor-sharpness to capture the minds and hearts of the buyer and to enable them to come home with the trophies, it is just like the spider that weaves its web and catches the fly. It may sound hard, but that is the reality of the selling business. You either make the sale or you don't, you either win or you lose, and there is no place for runners up.

Resolutions For Any-time, Especially During Selling Time

Speak to people, there is nothing as nice
As a cheerful word of greeting.
Smile at people, it takes 72 muscles to frown
But only 14 to smile.
Call people by name, the sweetest music to anyone's ear
Is the sound of his own name.
Be friendly and helpful. If you want a friend,
Then you must be one.
Be cordial. Speak and act as if
Anything you do is a genuine pleasure.
Be interested in people, you can like everybody if you try.
Be generous with praise, but always cautious with criticism.

Be considerate of the feelings of others, it will be appreciated.
Be thoughtful of the opinion of others, you are not always right.
Be alert to give service. What counts most in life,
Is what we do for others.
Courtesy is the least expensive but the most valuable
Commodity we have, try it.

Anon

These words of wisdom have an equally important message to offer to anyone seeking the status of the professional and it has been introduced here specifically for that purpose. When you can incorporate both of the following selling skills **Probing** and **Listening** – into your selling style *and* adopt a philosophical approach, it is only then that you become a real master in selling and in life.

PROBING

I am going to let you into the most important and often used success producing secret – one which all professional salespeople rely heavily on to make sales. It is so important, not only if you want to make a success in selling but also for anything and everything in life. I strongly recommend that you commit it to memory, living and breathing it for the rest of your life. These are the six most commonly used words in everyday questions:

What, Why, When, How, Where, Who

It is as simple as that. But as to how many of us do make it part and parcel of our daily arsenal for solving life's dilemmas, tribulations and daily problems, that's another question. Rudyard Kipling wrote:

> *I keep six honest serving-men,*
> *They taught me all I knew and*
> *their names are What and Why and When,*
> *How and Where and Who*

In fact, the whole sales process is based on a questioning and answering sequence. There are many fancy titles and methods given by different authors and sales trainers to the different types of questioning techniques all revolving around the six honest serving-men which look impressive and sound good in theory, but in the real world it is impractical material to use and in some instances downright useless. I can say so because I have been through the sausage machine trying out much of the stuff I acquired from various books and training courses, much to my bitter regret in certain cases. That is why I have been rather critical about some of those sources at the beginning. While I must admit that I did learn a little from those sources (where there is muck there is brass), it did me more harm than good in the long run, thinking I was being led by the masters of selling only to discover they were the servants. This book, you would have gathered by now, is different because it comes from the real and not from the make-believe world of selling. I was no longer going to be made a fool by these self-appointed maestros, the overnight successes, and how I learnt to sell was from the buyers, playing with live bullets, in the thick of full-blooded selling doing what came naturally (both the conventional and unconventional), and it was there that I really found out what worked and what did not.

We know that Logic makes people think and Emotion makes them act. What you are doing by asking the right questions is getting your buyer to respond and reply in a predetermined and expected manner and then screen and scrutinize the answers to see whether the buyer is responding logically and/or emotionally. Based on the answers given you use the techniques of professional selling to **persuade, motivate, manipulate** or **negotiate** with them.

While the principles remain the same for selling tangibles and intangibles, the techniques and tactics to be used can vary for different types of buyers. It is those salespeople who are well trained and go about their business professionally, and have a profound understanding of the psychology of selling that are the ones who will *sell* and *sail* through troubled waters.

A defending attorney in a court of law would interrogate both plaintiff and defendant to uncover information. Once s/he obtains the information s/he would use it to achieve the objective which is to prove in court

- the defendant was innocent and/or the plaintiff was guilty
- the defendant was not guilty and has been wrongly accused
- the defendant was guilty but there were mitigating circumstances to reduce the sentence.

How the attorney would go about this job would be dependent on which side s/he is representing (defendant or plaintiff) and what s/he is trying to accomplish (the objective).

The principles of selling (the code by which we operate) to the seller are similar to the legal framework within which the attorney works. How we juggle the system to suit the circumstances to our advantage is up to us and our individual abilities. If you are good at it, you can expect to win and if you aren't, you can expect to lose. This means your success will be dependent on how good or bad you are at applying the tactics and techniques of selling to make sales or achieve desired results.

Open-Ended Questions
Must be designed around the six honest serving men, for example:

- What is it that is causing you concern?
- Why do you think it has been like this for so long?
- When are you going to have the funds available for this project?
- How do you feel about it?
- Where do we go from here?
- Who will be using this system and what sort of experience does that person have?

Specific Questions (closed-ended)
Are designed to get a **Yes** or **No** response. I call them control questions, for example: 'Seeing that lack of sales turnover is what is causing you concern, if I can solve that problem for you and

if the price for my proposal is right, you would be prepared to go ahead wouldn't you?'

Remember when using your control questions you must phrase them in such a way as to get more 'yes's' than 'no's'. The more 'yes's' you get the closer you are to getting a favourable decision, and the more 'no's' you get the further you are from making the sale. Successful selling is much like building a brick wall: you lay the foundation and keep piling layer upon layer of bricks until you finish the job.

This is all you will need to know on probing to enable you to extract information and control the sales interview – pulling the buyer towards you and then pushing him or her towards making a decision to benefit themselves and yourself. Having given you some information on probing, the most powerful medicine for better selling and successful living, what follows is complementary to it, which is the vital skill of listening.

Listening

Many people confuse listening with hearing. Let me make that point clear. You hear with your ears but you listen with your mind. Most people in selling have heard the well known expression:

When God created us he gave us two ears and one mouth so that our ears may work twice as hard as our mouth.

> *It is the province of knowledge to speak,*
> *But it is the privilege of wisdom to listen.*

Oliver Wendell Holmes

Listening, being a mental activity, is paramount to successful selling. It is only by careful listening that the salesperson can accurately pinpoint the buyer's needs and skilfully offer solutions.

If your sales talk is strong, clear, well presented and delivered fearlessly buyers will fall for your magnetic pull, but in order to make sure that the medicine you have to offer is the right stuff for the problem at hand, you have first to get the diagnosis correct, which you can only do by proper listening.

Your job is to ask question upon question upon question, not in a Gestapo-style fashion but in a friendly and professional manner, and then you listen and listen and listen mentally to analyse every word the buyer says, the way in which they say it, and above all to capture the 'picture' behind the words, before you get into the full swing of the demonstration or presentation.

Only the unprofessional shoots straight into a 'verbal diarrhoea' type of delivery without collating the facts. It is like using the machine gun technique – spraying the area with a hail of bullets hoping one will strike the chosen target. That is not professional selling, that is stupidity at its best.

The professional salesperson uses the rifle technique first identifying the target, then waits and watches, and when the time is right carefully takes aim and wallop, scores a direct hit.

There are two types of listening:

- **Active Listening**
  Is where you remain silent, involved in full concentration on what the buyer is telling you, particularly after you have asked him or her an open-ended question to get an idea of the buyer's views, opinions, feelings, and logical and emotional expressions, so that you can formulate the total picture behind the words.
- **Passive Listening**
  Is where you are partly concentrating on what the buyer is saying and partly thinking and formulating sales strategies, tactics and techniques, working out which is the best way to approach the problem or situation. In passive listening, you will be thinking, talking and listening to feedback at the same time, as if with a *third ear* in your mind.

In selling and in all other aspects of communication, if your listening skills are ultra sharp you can rest assured you will evaluate the problem or situation correctly and you should, as an expert, be able to offer the right remedies to the buyer. This, anyway, is your job as a professional salesperson. If buyers could and wanted to solve their problem on their own without outside help, they would! They need your assistance and therefore they will be only too grateful for good solutions to their problems and reward you proportionately. By employing the skill of listening in all your sales interviews and in all areas of verbal communication you can expect to witness the rising tide of sales success.

MURPHY'S LAW

Anything that can go wrong, will go wrong.
Anything good in life is either illegal, immoral or fattening.
The light at the end of a tunnel is the headlamp of an oncoming train.
Celibacy is never inherited.
Never sleep with anyone crazier than yourself.
Beauty is only skin-deep, ugliness goes to the bone.
Never play leapfrog with a unicorn.
If everything seems to be going well, you haven't got a clue what the hell is going on.
Never argue with a fool, people might know the difference.
A short cut is the longest distance between two points.
Friends come and go but enemies accumulate.
Everyone has a scheme for getting rich that will not work.
Murphy's Golden Rule: Whoever has the gold, makes the rules.
The race does not always go to the swift, nor does the battle go to the strong, but that is the way to bet.
Anything that you try to fix will take longer and cost more than you thought.
In order to get a loan you must first prove you do not need it.
The repair man would often say, 'I have never seen a model quite like yours before.'
No matter how long or hard you shop for an item, after you've bought it, you will find it on sale somewhere else cheaper.
The chance of a piece of bread falling with the buttered side down is directly proportional to the cost of the carpet.

MURPHY WAS AN OPTIMIST

Negotiating Tactics

*Negotiate without fear
never fear to negotiate
Tactics are the key to survival*

I live by selling, bargaining and negotiating. I love it, it is my life-blood and livelihood. I will negotiate in a Chinese takeaway or even the biggest of department stores in the country. I would negotiate on anything from a tiny pin to purchasing a house or motor car. It is has become part and parcel of my attitude to life and has bought me some excellent advantages.

I once had a car that required certain repairs to be carried out in order to pass its MOT (Ministry Of Transport) test for roadworthiness. A car repair firm known to me was chosen so that I could negotiate a deal. I had previously done some successful advertising for this firm.

The firm wanted me to carry out more advertising for them, and quoted a higher cost for the repairs than their competitors. They wanted me to help them promote their advertising, and they wanted my car repair business. I wanted their business, and the repairs to my car and the MOT certificate. I got them to lower the price of the MOT repairs to less than their competitors' price, while I agreed to charge the same as I had before, but for less much work on my part! I got a better deal for myself than they would have liked me to have. I do this all the time. Most people when they are negotiating only hear each other's noise. All they do is break the sound barrier. They are like oil and water; they do not mix. They should really be trying to break the thought barrier and price barrier. I believe I am the world champion at this! My alias is Mr Discount – I have a reputation to live up to. One very successful tactic of mine is to say 'I like you, but I do not like your price!' This breaks the thought, price and sound barriers. People think in words, when you have the words you move their thinking and then you have them!

The difference between selling and negotiating is that in selling the salesperson needs to build up desire in the buyer from what may start off as a *tiny flicker* of interest, and the salesperson has to fan it into a *mighty flame* of desire. If we take the AIDA formula shown previously as Attention, Interest, Desire, Action and carefully look at the stages involved, then what we are doing at the attention stage is starting off by grabbing the buyer's full attention from any other preoccupations he/she may be having. We then develop the buyer's *interest* by appealing to the buyer's *logical side.*

Where many salespeople fail is in building up the interest by appealing to the buyer's logical side and assuming that because the buyer is interested s/he will buy. This is not the case. What you have to do is switch from creating interest to creating *desire.* Desire is *emotional* and it is only when the buyer is emotionally involved with the product, service or idea that you will be able to get to the Action stage. You cannot force people to buy, but if you whet their appetite and act as a human dynamo, charging them up all the time with your power, wherever they try to hide in their mind or whatever unfair idiosyncratic game they try to play, you will be able to root it out and crack it. This is the real selling game that the true professionals play.

Now let's assume that the buyer in front of you has fallen head over heels for the product, the service or the idea you are offering and wants it, but is not prepared to pay your price. What do you do now? Stuck? Don't panic – it is negotiating time! Let us look at an example. Suppose your product is being offered at £1,800 and the buyer wants to pay £1,500 for it. To try and push for £1,800 would be foolish. In the first instance, it may reveal a weakness in your selling effort because had you done a good selling job you should be able to get the full asking price of £1,800. If that is not the case, and you are up against a tough cookie of a buyer who refuses to budge, here is an appropriate negotiating strategy:

Seller: So what you are prepared to pay is £1,500, is that right?
Buyer: Yes.
Seller: And what I am asking for is £1,800. Now Mr/Mrs Buyer, I can understand your point of view. If I was in your position I too would be looking for my pound of flesh if I could get it. Incidentally, in this instance the difference between what I am asking and you are willing to pay happens to be my livelihood. Obviously you, as a fellow human being who also has to work and earn a living like myself, would not want me to go broke

(just as I would not wish it on you) would you? So what we are talking about here is a £300 difference. Suppose you meet me half way I would like to work out a nice little deal with you.

Or you could crack a little joke: 'You know, even in the criminal world as in the forces of law and order there is always a sense of fraternity. They always try to help one another – they are all as it were birds of the same feather that flock together. To see what I can do to help you, I am going to take a coin out of my purse and I am going to toss it so that both of us will have an equal chance. Now you may call heads or tails. If you win I will meet you half way and let you have the product £150 cheaper than I originally wanted. If however I win then you pay me the full asking price of £1,800. OK!'

And you immediately get out your coin and toss. I have found many buyers will agree to gamble, and either way you make the sale and come out the winner (very often I have got my full asking price by winning the toss).

For those who dig their heels in and will not budge you can play it like this:

● Take the £300 and cost justify it.
● Use the if/then strategy, in which you are prepared to bargain for a mutually acceptable figure so that both the buyer and you can benefit from the deal:

Seller: What you are looking for is the best price, isn't that right?
Buyer: Yes.
Seller: And am I correct when I say you are in business to make a profit?
Buyer: Of course.
Seller: Likewise you would also agree that my company and I are in business to make a profit, isn't that so?
Buyer: I guess so.
Seller: Now what you are asking is that I should give you some of my profit so that you can end up better off than me, which I don't object to you trying to get, because if I was in your position I too would have looked for the best deal going. But what I am saying to you is, take my product (service or idea) by all means but let me share my profit with you where you can have some

of it and I can also have some. Now isn't that fair?

Here are the golden words to use now.

IF you can meet me at some reasonable point, at say £1,725, THEN we can shake hands. Now would you like to settle at £1,800 or £1,725?

Should the buyer still refuse to take it at £1,725 you can then say, 'If that's the way you feel about my product (service or idea), then don't have it,' (knowing very well they do want it but what they are really trying it do is knock you down on price). Wait for the reply. S/he may accept your price or make you an offer.

This offer may be above or below the minimum profit point you have fixed. If it is above, you gain. If it is below, you then tell the buyer what your minimum profit point is in this manner. 'That's my final figure, take it or leave it.'

This is the final pressure point you can use and if the buyer has let you carry on that long it is more likely that the deal would have been concluded favourably.

In negotiating what you have to do is destabilize the buyer's thinking from a '**No**, I won't budge' attitude, to a '**Maybe** I will listen to this salesperson because s/he is offering me a sensible and convincing argument and it is likely that I am being too rigid in my demands for the best deal for myself.' When you can shift the buyer's thinking into a more flexible and favourable ground then you can use the following approach to move his or her attitude under your command so that the buyer will eventually say **Yes**.

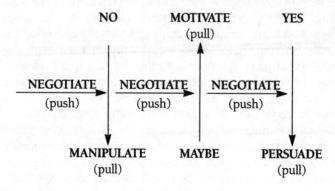

The NO-MAYBE-YES model

1. When the buyer says **No**, the seller uses the pulling power of **manipulation** to move the buyer from **No** to **Maybe** by using the pushing power of negotiation. The skill of **Manipulation** can be described as the methods by which the seller gets the buyer to invest in a product, service or idea, which the buyer was initially totally opposed to, by clever and cunning manoeuvring of the buyer's mind for the benefit of both parties.
2. When the buyer says **Maybe** the seller uses the pulling power of **motivation** to move the buyer from **Maybe** to **Yes** using the pushing power of negotiation.
3. When the buyer says **Yes** the seller uses the pulling power of **persuasion** to close the sale, and the pushing power of **negotiation** (if required at this stage) to seal the sale so that it stays closed.

Example

My prospective client happened to be a specialist eating house/ leisure establishment. The key person who was negotiating with me on behalf of this prospective client was the General Manager, a very intelligent, upright, eloquent, and pompous person. There were others involved in the decision-making process too, namely the Catering Manager and the Master Chef.

My first interview was for one hour with the Catering Manager, a well qualified, well travelled and pleasant person. I went over with him in detail what their current level of turnover was, staffing levels, previous advertising campaigns and their outcome, what investment the company had made to refurbish and modernize the place to an exceptionally high standard, and what problems they were encountering. I discovered they were having problems in pulling customers. I then told him what I could do to help them multiply their sales and increase their profits in terms of professional sales training, advertising, marketing and image building, tailor-made to suit their corporate culture. He was impressed and arranged a subsequent meeting with the General Manager and his Master Chef.

The meeting was held in the board room. It took one and a half hours with the General Manager chairing, or totally dominating the meeting with side support from the Catering

Manager and Master Chef. They were impeccably dressed in suits and ties and, being a lovely summer's day I strolled in in comfortable casual wear.

Contrary to what most sales trainers teach I do not believe it is always necessary to wear business dress. As a result I stand out, and I never fear to display the courage of my convictions and uphold my views no matter what others may think. My hidden power lies not in the way I dress (sometimes I dress to kill but my preference is to be relaxed in dress and to be mentally lethal) but rather in my ability to know what is in the buyer's mind, how s/he is reacting to me, and how I should deal with the situation to make the sale. If you work for a company that insists that you conform to a dress code, so be it, you have to obey. I did too when I was an employee. This is one of the reasons I quit, because I believe in freedom, to deal with people the way I want, to say what I want and to whom I want, and to be held personally responsible for my thoughts, words and deeds. I wanted to develop at my own speed, I wanted to earn what I wanted, to start work when I wanted and have holidays for as long as I liked and when it suited me. I wanted to dress the way it pleased me and above all not to let others control my life and destiny.

Coming back to my negotiating story, I sensed that the company was not pleased with the previous publicity done by another advertising agency. After having spent vast sums of money they were anxious about their low sales turnover. I reassured them that I could rectify the situation if they took my recommendations. There was a lot of hard talking done, followed by a smooth sales presentation which left them in no doubt that I was the one to do the job, although there were four other companies competing.

The General Manager then requested that I send my proposal in writing showing what problem areas I saw and how I intended to sort them out. I made it a point to talk to many members of staff to get a more detailed picture. I told the General Manager that the proposals would be on his table by a specific date. When I returned I then set about compiling the proposal which entailed giving a detailed outline of how I was going to promote the business. I had to contact graphic designers, photographers, printers, door-to-door distribution companies, direct mail list suppliers, balloon companies, and so on. This took me a further three hours. The actual drafting and typing of the letter and compiling the advertising leaflet took four and half hours. A total of ten hours.

I then included the following final paragraph into the detailed proposal and had it hand delivered to the General Manager. It read, *A fixed consultation fee of £1,500 + VAT is required to cover briefs, compilation of quotations, visits, etc, in addition to all the above itemized costs for all background work done to date, and to be provided on this project in the future, should you proceed with this package. However should you decide not to go ahead, a consultation fee of £350 is requested for all work done so far, as I have already devoted ten hours to this project. This, however, can be overlooked if you decide to proceed.* I worded the letter like this because I had a strong feeling that I would get the deal, but in reality I had to fight tooth and nail, and negotiate to get in – there was strong competition who were trying hard to get the business.

Here was the outcome. I rang the General Manager three days after the letter was delivered. He had scrutinized its contents carefully and in principle liked what he saw even though he thought the overall cost for promoting their business, which came to £20,000, was too much for them. He did not object to paying the £1,500 had they gone ahead (because they were contemplating selling the business at that time and to promote was the alternative had they decided to keep it) but he took much offence at the fact that I wanted to charge them £350 if they did not go ahead. He had not decided at that stage to give me the business because he wanted to compare my proposal with the others received. This is how I handled it and negotiated a satisfactory outcome for myself. One of the primary reasons he objected in principle to giving me the £350 was because I had approached them and not the other way around. Secondly, his company policy was not to pay any organization quoting to try and get business, for if every company charged for that service it would mean a loss to his organization.

I told him I was glad that he brought this matter to my attention but that I was confused as to why he reacted like this. On the question of me contacting them at a trade fair, it was my usual practice and it was nothing new to my way of doing business. I had already a three hundred and fifty strong self-generated user-base, many of whom were approached in a similar manner and, like an octopus, I was always wanting to spread my tentacles further, looking for non-user and competitive-user business (which he was) for my consultancy work. He agreed that it was a good thing.

I told him that the very fact that his company was participating in the trade fair showed that they were doing the same as I was – trying to get new business or hopefully some repeat business.

I also told him that I was going to have a super advertising leaflet printed for him and distributed by high street promotion girls to passers by and that they would be trying to create business for his company just as I was as a salesman doing for mine.

I also explained that I had already spent ten hours on his company's project first to diagnose the problem and then offer a solution. I told him that time is money, and that I had set aside all other important tasks that would have provided me with lucrative earnings in order to deal with his matter exclusively rather than delegating it to someone else. I also told him he was paying for my knowledge, skill and experience for without it I could not solve his problems, and for me to acquire that know-how my time and a small fortune had to be invested on intensive training and exhaustive learning. I told him that his whole campaign was going to be launched under my personal supervision. And I mentioned to him in passing that to see a medical consultant for a quick check up just to be reassured that you are OK would cost you around £60 for a twenty minute consultation – something presumably he would have paid without hesitation.

Similarly, it was an unwritten business code that he should expect a specialist in another field to charge him for their expertise.

The general manager agreed that it was not my expertise which was in question, but he was still not in favour of paying me if they did not proceed.

I then suggested to him that he would not open his front doors to the public to come in to wine and dine gratis just to taste his food and drink to tell him it's good or bad. I then rammed it home loud and clear that I was a professional and professionals did charge money and that it was only amateurs that did not. He was literally in the palm of my hand. I then went on to close the deal by saying that he had all the information necessary for him to come to a decision and that if he gave me the firing orders then I would execute his campaign with military precision and look after his promotion like a good mother looks after her baby, that I wanted to see his business succeed, for his success was mine, and I knew that if it worked he would come back to me for more and more.

I then said to him, 'Do you want me to handle your whole campaign and put your business on the road to profitability, or would you rather pay me the £350 for all the grafting that I have done to date? Naturally, if you take the package I can overlook the £350.'

The end result was that he decided to take my proposal after the next board meeting in which they were going to decide the fate of the company, whether to sell or keep the business. I won my point through **persuasion, motivation, manipulation** and **negotiation**.

When you are negotiating you must also use tactics to pre-empt the buyer's response to your sales talk and be ready to adapt at a moment's notice to meet that response. Both you and the buyer must benefit from the transaction, because negotiation is not a one-sided thing and those who are skilful at it can make the pointer lean more heavily to their side.

By tactics I mean something like this. Kemal Ataturk, the Turkish army officer who became his country's first president from 1923 to 1938, decided to abolish the customs of the Ottoman Empire and wanted to make Turkey more attuned to western ways. One of the customs prevalent at the time was that Turkish women wore a veil, called a purdah, to cover their faces to seclude them from the sight of men. Ataturk then passed a decree saying that the only women who were allowed to wear veils in Turkey were prostitutes, so the practice soon stopped.

My little son Richard has already got into the habit of using tactics and negotiating by listening to me. Children always try to be one step ahead of you.

While I was busy writing this book he came up to me and

asked me for a few blank sheets of paper as he was going to write a book of his own called **The Winner**. I just picked him up, gave a him a cuddle, and here is one of his tactics he pulled on me.

He said, 'Daddy, I bet you I can make you say the word "black"!'

'I bet you can't,' I replied.

'I bet £100 I can get you to say the word "black",' he said. 'Try it.'

'What are the colours of the Union Jack?'

'Blue, red and white,' I answered.

'Told you Dad I could get you to say the word "blue"!'

'No, you said "black" to me son.'

'Thanks, Dad, you just said it.'

I was astonished. If he at his young age of six could use tactics and win why can't and why shouldn't you?

AN INTRODUCTION TO HUMAN PSYCHOLOGY, THE HUMAN AURA AND BODY LANGUAGE

There is a vast amount of knowledge available today in the field of behavioural psychology and body language to help sales people understand buyers and people better and therefore make their task easier.

This section is not intended to be a source of detailed information on these topics but seeks to give you an overall view on what is necessary, relevant and useful, ignoring the trivia, to help you understand others and achieve your objectives. I strongly recommend that you visit a good bookshop or library to read further material to enhance your knowledge.

It must be said that you need not be an expert on these subjects to be able to sell and be a mediocre salesperson. But if you have in-depth knowledge in these areas you can without question become a super salesperson, a battleship of a seller that is ready to meet with any type of buyer, take the rough with the smooth and give back tit for tat, butter for fat, if they hurt your dog, you hurt their cat! You will also be able to have stronger customer relationships, earn better money, keep the competitors at bay, prevent cancellations and reach your objectives quicker. However, to become good at these topics you may have to devote a great deal of your lifetime to learn to be an expert at it. And even if one were to become an expert, it does not automatically follow that you will be very successful in selling unless you also know how to **persuade, motivate, manipulate** and **negotiate**.

Body language is practised by everyone either by conscious, unconscious or subconscious direction to varying degrees of effectiveness. Over the thousands of years many of the basic gestures, postures and positions have hardly changed, but may have become a little more refined with modern civilization.

The signals used to communicate non-verbally, generally speaking are pretty much the same, in principle, all over the world. For most types of meetings involving two or more people, the gestures, postures, positions and reactions from the six senses vary here and there, from country to country depending on the culture, customs, religion and habits.

Those who can understand the everyday psychology of people and are skilful in reading their body language signals, and can also control and use their own body language will profit the most in selling. Those who lack this vital skill of interpreting and reacting to the buyer's body language may be doing it naturally and producing reasonably good results without any conscious effort and formal training, but for any degree of success learning and practice are vital.

For those who want to score direct hits in selling and want to greatly improve their sales performance and figures, the more you know about your own body language, and that of others, the greater will be your sales effectiveness – that's business!

To enable you to become more successful and competent in understanding yourself and others here are some facts and figures on body language.

Researchers have discovered that a message, when communicated, is part verbal, part vocal and part non-verbal. Experts differ as to the relative percentages of each, but they are unanimous that non-verbal means, or body language, convey over fifty per cent of the message. This means that you must pay more attention to body language than what is actually being said.

The verbal message is formulated by the conscious mind, and can be distorted; the non-verbal messages come from the subconscious mind and hold the true meanings.

The Human Mind

The **Conscious Mind** is where our thinking and daily decision-making is done, based on reason, judgment, and an instinct for survival. The conscious mind works in the present.

The **Unconscious Mind** rules our actions and reactions, which are emotional and based on childhood experiences. Our unconscious minds are responsible for producing the Good, the Bad, the Mad and the Sad people of this world. The unconscious mind works in the past.

The Subconscious Mind is the human bio-computer and the most powerful of all the minds. It operates subliminally, outside conscious control and works by programming and imagination – negative thoughts produce negative results, and positive thoughts generate positive results. The subconscious mind can be looked upon as a person's conscience that always wants to speak the truth and is always accurate in its outcome. Its function is to search and provide creative ideas to enrich our lives and provide solutions to our problems. The subconscious mind works for our *future wellbeing* if it is programmed with *positive thoughts* and for our *future destruction* if it is programmed with *negative thoughts*.

In terms of buying decisions, twenty per cent will be conscious and eighty per cent subconscious or unconscious. People make decisions to purchase based on emotional criteria, then they justify their decisions logically.

Let us assume a seller is presenting a new chocolate bar to a retailer. One mode will dominate their reaction. These are very brief description of possible conversations, but watch how the seller tailors the response accordingly.

1. Visual Mode
Buyer: It looks good; I like the design.
Seller: You said it! Our creative designers have put a lot of

thought and effort into making the wrapper look very attractive. How many shall I put you down for?

2. Auditory Mode

Buyer: It sounds good and melts easily when you bite into it, rather than being crunchy. It is better than some of the cheaper brands that cause a mini explosion in your mouth!

Seller: I couldn't agree with you more; in a noisy world everything must be made as quiet as possible – we have done it here using a special soft confectionery base that is so smooth you can hardly believe you are chewing it. When would you want this product to start making money for you?

3. Kinesthetic Mode

Buyer: I like the way this chocolate bar feels; the shape is great. I would like to see it displayed on my counter.

Seller: It is very popular with many of my customers, and we have a special counterpack for display purposes. Shall I put you down for six dozen, or more?

4. Olfactory Mode

Buyer: What a wonderful chocolate aroma – it smells delicious!

Seller: Yes, many years of research went into formulating the secret recipe that is responsible for the special aroma. And as you have shown you have a good nose for chocolate, I imagine you also have a keen nose for profit. When would you like your first delivery?

5. Taste Mode

Buyer: Mmm . . . It's mouthwatering.

Seller: Yes, I agree it tastes wonderful, and market research has shown that your customers will also agree with you. When would you like to start selling it to them?

6. Intuitive Mode

Buyer: I've got a strong feeling this will sell.

Seller: Our extensive media campaign will ensure that it will, and you'll need a large quantity to meet the demand. Would you like your first delivery of, say, ten gross this week or next?

There are six ways in which people process information through the six senses. These are:

1. The **visual** (sight).
2. The **auditory** (sound).
3. The **kinesthetic** (touch).
4. The **nasal/olfactory** (smell).
5. The **taste bud** response (taste).
6. The **intuitive** response (intuition).

The response from the receiver (the buyer or seller) to the message from the sender (the buyer or seller) will be dependant on which may they process information.

During a sales interview a buyer could move through all of the six modes above but the decision to purchase will be based on one dominant mode. What the salesperson must do after identifying each mode is to adjust the sales talk to suit the processing mode and then follow up by getting commitment (closing).

The Human Aura

Every human being from birth until death is said to have an invisible personal zone that surrounds the body called an **aura**.

The human aura, an electro-magnetic life force emanating from the body, is known to be both ethereal and luminous. It is thought that the brain controls the aura which it is said can be seen by the naked eye in laboratory conditions as a fragmented dust cloud swirling around the body using a process known as **Kirlian photography**, which was discovered by a Russian husband-and-wife team of scientific researchers named Semyon and Valentina Kirlian in 1939. It was developed further and in 1960 it was given official recognition by the Soviet government. Today its main purpose is to diagnose a person's physical, mental, emotional and spiritual states by studying the patterns produced on photoghraphic paper and changes in the auric colour.

Auric colour	Emotion or meaning
Bright red	Anger, force
Light red	Passion, sensuality
Brown	Greediness, miserliness
Rose	Affection
Yellow	Intellectuality, creativity
Purple	Spirituality
Blue	Religiousness
Green	Deceit, jealousy
Dark green	Sympathy
Dark aura	Approaching death
No aura	Death

The aura may be responsible for our interaction with others. For example we have heard the expression, 'She has magnetic attraction' or 'I just don't feel comfortable with that guy' or 'He turns me off' may very likely be due to the following reason.

If we look at the laws of physics we can relate them to the human situation and postulate a theory from which we can discover a remarkable similarity between these two different worlds. The **first law** of magnetism states that **like poles repel and opposite poles attract**, which means that if you put two bar magnets (one of which is freely suspended) close to each other, if there are two similar poles, i.e. North and North, the magnets will **repel** each other. If there are two dissimilar poles, i.e. North and South, **attraction** will take place (see diagram).

Another possibility is that since the aura is electro-magnetic, a field exists around the body. If we take this rule from physics

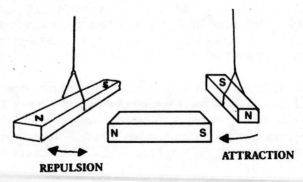

REPULSION   **ATTRACTION**

and apply it to two bodies that are in close proximity to each other, the two fields will cause forces which in turn will produce a motion towards attraction or repulsion depending on whether the people concerned are unlike poles (dissimilar) or like poles (similar). If two people have similar characteristics the tendency is for them to move apart and seek dissimilar ones, thus verifying the first law of magnetism in the human parallel. This theory fits in with all kinds of people with opposite or similar physical and mental attributes. The contributing factor that makes people want to get closer or move away from one another may be the force of attraction or repulsion caused by the human aura.

Another factor that reinforces this argument is that the further

The invisible air space that surrounds every living thing is the HUMAN AURA, an electro-magnetic life force emanated by the body which is both ethereal and luminous.

Intimate Zone	15 to 45cm	Only lovers,
	6 to 18 ins	close friends
		and family
		allowed to
		enter
Social Zone	46cm to 1.2m	Distance we
	1½ft to 4ft	maintain on
		social
		occasions
Business Zone	1.2m to 3.6m	Where
		business
	4ft to 12ft	is usually
		conducted
Public Address Zone	3.6m and more	Where a
	12ft and more	speaker
		communicates
		with an
		audience

apart two bodies are from one another, the less they feel threatened or ill-at-ease. The reason for this may be that the effect of the magnetic field directed from one person to another is much weaker and neutralized with distance. The aura can be strengthened or weakened by mind control, which would be how a smaller person can psyche themselves up and cause a strong aura to be generated to produce a stronger field around the body with a stronger force, and thereby weaken the field of the bigger person by intimidating or sweeping him off his feet subliminally, and cause the bigger opponent to surrender (attraction).

I would like to close this section by relating an incident that happened to me which involved interpretng body language signals and saved the day for me.

One of my job descriptions as a sales consultant is to provide small, medium and large businesses of various descriptions advertising advice and a media buying service. Apart from selling the concept of advertising on various media to my clients, I also write copy and scripts for them and when necessary I also provide the 'voice over' part, for which I bill them accordingly. My contact at a particular media company was the Managing Director who was very capable and intelligent, but a ruthless and unpredictable task master who would try to take your arm and leg if he could get away with it.

My client, a small business owner, wanted to keep his costs down and deal with the media company himself. I told him what to do and how to do it. So in my absence he went to the media, made a booking for the space and made the advertisement, telling the Managing Director of the company that it was I who had recommended his company to him.

The following day I visited the Managing Director to agree my commission. He tried to fob me off, saying he had done all the work and would not give me anything for it.

'You must be kidding', I replied. He then said all he was prepared to give me was a token amount for a lunch. I told him to get lost; either he had to give me my 10% commission as agreed or he would not get any more business from me and I would see him in court. I also told him that I was the front-line man that had created the sale for him in the first instance and

if that was the way in which he was going to reward my efforts
it did not speak very highly of himself or his organization. I told
him it was I who had directed the businessman to his company
telling him the benefits of advertising in their publications in
preference to others, and I had told him precisely what to put
in the advert. At this point the Managing Director went
temporarily crazy, banging his hands with palms facing
downwards onto the table (aggression), shutting his eyes (not
wanting to see my point) and raising his voice (intimidating).

Instinctively, I too raised my voice, banged the desk hard and
used my hypnotic eyes with a penetrating gaze that would have
sent a dagger through him.

I then said calmly, 'You can't be like Hitler, making

unreasonable decisions and expecting me to sit back and take it lightly after I did my best to get you business. What do you take me for, some kind of turkey? Come off it, two can play at that game; for every Hitler there is a Churchill!'

This threw him completely off balance – he mellowed and smiled and offered to give me my 10 percent commission immediately. I left on friendly terms, having shown him clearly that I had benefitted his media as much as it had benefitted me.

Had I not understood this man's non-verbal communication I would have left his office minus everything. But, by keeping cool and scientifically evaluating and responding to my opposite number I scored a decisive win by getting paid and retaining the goodwill.

The harp is a beautiful but difficult instrument to play, and the only way you can produce sweet music on it is by *pulling strings*. Similarly, in the tough selling business if you want to succeed and get the best out of the buyer then you will also have to *pull strings* – just like a puppeteer does to a puppet. Occasionally, while remaining in control, you will have to *change tactics* and play the role of the puppet and *let the buyer pull the strings*.

In the next chapter you will learn how to respond to different types of body language.

CHAPTER 7

How to respond to non-verbal communication (body language)

This chapter reveals some fascinating facts and figures about body language. It covers the most common gestures, postures and positions you can expect to encounter in your day-to-day experiences out of a staggering one million non-verbal cues researched by behavioural scientists since Charles Darwin produced his work on the expression of emotions in man and animals in 1872.

We have all seen the inborn gestures children use when lying, or being lied to, or when reprimanded, or when they want to prevent any unpleasant message from entering their mind. They act it out by playing . . .

SPEAK NO EVIL – they cover their mouth with their hands
HEAR NO EVIL – they shut their ears with their hands
SEE NO EVIL – they close their eyes with their hands.

These gestures become cleverly masked or disguised in adult life, but they can still be seen in hand-to-face body language signals – primarily when lying or deceit is involved, but also when there is doubt, uncertainty or exaggeration by the sender or receiver. As a generality it is worth noting that, the more educated a person is, the fewer gestures they will use to express themselves.

One of the special benefits of body language when communicating is that the sender can read any negative response signals and take corrective action before they are verbalized – it is difficult to change a verbal negative (No) to a positive (Yes).

A golden rule in body language is never to enter a person's territory unless permission has been granted for you to do so, either verbally or non-verbally. If, for example, your buyer has chosen to sit behind a square table for a discussion, you can assume the interview to be formal. If it is a round table you can assume the interview to be informal, and if it is conducted at a rectangular table, it is authoritative. The reason for this is that the table acts as a shield to the body, which in primitive times was open to attack from wild animals and invaders if not protected. Clothes, cars and houses also serve this function.

We will now look at various gestures, postures, positions and signals a buyer could give to a seller and their interpretation. The following list is based on the book *Body Language* by Allan Pease (published by Sheldon Press). What I have done is to recommend ways for the seller to deal with that non-verbal communication based on research, and my knowledge, skills and experience. It covers how the seller should respond to that non-verbal communication and the likely reaction/outcome the seller could expect from the buyer in that situation.

It must be very clearly stressed that casually looking at a buyer in a live selling situation and trying to interpret their non-verbal communication will never make you a wizard at reading what others are thinking. You have got to spend a great deal of time studying people and referring back to this chapter and the next. With practice coupled with patience you will get a true picture of what they are actually saying with their bodies to help you communicate better for mutual benefit. Moreover, a gesture must not be interpreted in isolation. It must be evaluated in terms of a cluster (a group of gestures), just as, if you want to find the meaning of something, you look at the structure of the sentence, not just the individual words.

Sender's (buyer's) posture, position or signal (non-verbal communication)	Receiver's (seller's) interpretation of that non-verbal communication & meaning	How seller should respond to that non-verbal communication	The likely reaction/outcome seller could expect from buyer
Smile	Happy or false expression	Always smile back	A positive reaction
Frown	Anger, doubt or disbelief	Toss the head to the side and frown back	A verbal response
Baring teeth	Attacking	Stay at a safe distance and try to reason with open palms, and look puzzled	De-escalation of hostility
Open palms	Honesty	Ask for commitment	You should get what you asked for
Pointing finger	Attacking or intimidating	Either meet a sword with a sword until dominance is achieved or side-step the issue by moving out of the way of the pointed gesture and playing a game of Russian roulette that leaves the buyer baffled and guessing	Cessation of aggression to pave the way for a less heated discussion
Shoulder shrug	Lack of comprehension	Educate the buyer with audio-visual aids to suit their level of comprehension	A favourable response
Making a ring with thumb and forefinger	Everything's OK	Do the same	The wind is blowing in your favour

Sender's (buyer's) posture, position or signal (non-verbal communication)	Receiver's (seller's) interpretation of that non-verbal communication & meaning	How seller should respond to that non-verbal communication	The likely reaction/outcome seller could expect from buyer
The tight grip handshake	Acting the tough guy	Either squeeze hand and push forward to show you are equally tough or pretend buyer has broken your hand	Either of these actions will help you take control of the situation
Thumbs up	No worries	Do the same	Buyer is in favour of your offer
'V' sign with first and second fingers, thumb and other fingers folded over palm and facing outwards	Victory	Make a clapping gesture with your hands to acknowledge the buyer's victory. The buyer makes this sign because they feel they have won with you. Smile and ask for the order	A pat on the buyer's back will put money in your pocket
'V' sign with first and second fingers, thumb and other fingers folded over palm and facing inwards	Up yours!	Ignore the insult and keep on selling, but if it happens again confront the buyer and bluntly ask why they are doing it	More often you will find that such behaviour does not have any deep-rooted and sinister motives but is intended to 'wind up' the seller
Open palms and shrugging shoulders	Honesty but there is doubt	Good sign. Use open palms to communicate. Provide facts to clear doubt and ask for the commitment	You will know where you stand with this buyer, whether it is positive or negative

Sender's (buyer's) posture, position or signal (non-verbal communication)	Receiver's (seller's) interpretation of that non-verbal communication & meaning	How seller should respond to that non-verbal communication	The likely reaction/outcome seller could expect from buyer
Limp handshake	Milk sop	It is due to insecurity or a weak personality. Play a submissive role and use open palms to communicate	Buyer won't feel threatened and may very well react favourably
Hand over the mouth	Lying – the subconscious mind is instructing the body to cover up the lie	Smile and make a joke of the issue	Buyer will feel at ease but confused at your reaction and will fall with ease into your trap
Eye rub	Buyer is either lying or thinks he or she is being lied to. It is also used when the sender does not want to see unpleasant things	Force the issue by proceeding with the demonstration or presentation	There are none so blind as those who do not wish to see. By pursuing this course of action you will hopefully force the buyer to see the truth
Neck scratch	Uncertainty	Reassure the with a pat on the back	This will give the buyer confidence and pave the way for a positive outcome
Collar pull	The buyer possibly feels ill-at-ease for telling a lie and therefore responds by tugging at the collar	Smile and carry on regardless till you make the buyer change from negative to positive	When you can do this the sale is yours
Fingers in mouth and palms under chin	An anxious buyer who needs to be reassured	Smile, look the buyer straight in the eyes and use confidence-building sales talk	This should build up confidence in the buyer who will begin to put faith in you

Sender's (buyer's) posture, position or signal (non-verbal communication)	Receiver's (seller's) interpretation of that non-verbal communication & meaning	How seller should respond to that non-verbal communication	The likely reaction/outcome seller could expect from buyer
Palms placed flat under the chin and the fingers spread open over the cheek	Bored	Remain silent and serious until the buyer expresses feelings. Then deal with those sentiments	By playing the waiting game till the buyer talks, you can determine what objections there are and deal with them
Thumb supporting chin; first finger pointing vertically upwards with other fingers partly folded in front of chin	Negative evaluation	This necessitates more enthusiasm and explanation. Use an aggressive approach, even to the point of ridiculing the buyer's negativism	This approach will put pressure on the buyer to alter their negative thinking
Chin stroking	Buyer is trying to make a decision. Silence is golden here	Ask for a commitment and remain silent	If you have done a good presentation and have either created a need or are selling to an existing need, then the sale is yours
Puts pipe, fingers or spectacles into mouth in a closing situation	Buyer is stalling to make a decision	Say little, or stay silent	Buyer should respond by stating objections or may even take a decision to go ahead
Thumb supporting chin with first finger folded under lips	Buyer has evaluated the message negatively and is not interested	Some unexpressed feelings are of concern to the buyer. Try to squeeze them out tactfully and then offer reassurance	Buyer will be impressed with your empathy and will be swayed to look at the proposition in a more positive way

Sender's (buyer's) posture, position or signal (non-verbal communication)	Receiver's (seller's) interpretation of that non-verbal communication & meaning	How seller should respond to that non-verbal communication	The likely reaction/outcome seller could expect from buyer
Rubbing the back of the neck	A negative sign. Buyer is either lying or frustrated.	Be very guarded about what is said and how it is said. The objective must be to get the buyer to trust you even though they may be distorted thinkers themselves	If trust is established, anything is possible
Rubbing forehead	Positive sign signifying openness	Use it to produce positive results	A positive result could be expected
Hitting forehead	Forgetfulness	Seller should try to jog the buyer's memory	It will help towards producing positive results
Hitting back of neck	Displeasure	Keep a safe distance and try to argue your case. Do everything to justify your point, even to the extent of shouting back or showing the buyer that they are crazy because of their pig-headedness and failure to listen to your valid arguments and to take advantage of your genuine offer. Be prepared to make a quick exit if the situation deteriorates but keep the pressure on for as long as you can	What you are waiting for is an opening to get the hook in; if and when you do so, tug hard

Sender's (buyer's) posture, position or signal (non-verbal communication)	Receiver's (seller's) interpretation of that non-verbal communication & meaning	How seller should respond to that non-verbal communication	The likely reaction/outcome seller could expect from buyer
Rubbing hands	Enthusiasm and excitement	Close quickly	Ask and you should receive
Clenched fist	Frustration	Relax buyer with humour and emotionally soothing words	You can then get down to business – like selling
Steepled fingers	Authoritative, superior, know-it-all	Praise, flatter and get this buyer off guard before the real selling starts	Get agreement by letting this buyer lead, but you must ask the right questions
Folded arms	Defensive gesture	Tread cautiously. Do not attempt to push the buyer at this stage. Seek to persuade the buyer and wait till the arms are unfolded before proper selling or the countdown to closing starts	When the buyer is in a non-defensive state then the deal can be closed, whereas in the defensive state any attempt to sell or close will be futile
Looking away	Lack of interest	Make a rude remark	It will make them want to take notice
Both hands behind back with one palm gripping the other forearm	Extreme frustration	Sympathise with the buyer	You will gain a place in the buyer's heart and also the sale
Both hands in front pockets and thumbs sticking out	Dominance	Dominance must be tackled by destabilizing the buyer by tactfully showing that you are in command though you let them feel that they are calling the shots	When equal positions of negotiating power are maintained then selling can start in earnest and the sale be concluded

Sender's (buyer's) posture, position or signal (non-verbal communication)	Receiver's (seller's) interpretation of that non-verbal communication & meaning	How seller should respond to that non-verbal communication	The likely reaction/outcome seller could expect from buyer
One or both hands gripping sleeve with thumbs sticking out	Submissive	Direct the buyer honestly to the benefits of the purchase without without leading them astray	This buyer will respect the seller who leads them to make a good purchase
Smiling cynically, with fingers closed and thumbs pointing upwards and backwards and displaying a forwards and backwards movement	Ridiculing	Confuse the buyer with intermittent bouts of seriousness and laughter to show that you are not affected	When the buyer realises that you are not going to be affected then move in hard
Arms folded with fingers tucked in between inner biceps and ribs and thumbs sticking out and pointing upwards	Negative	Negativism is a state of mind that can only be counteracted with bags of enthusiasm and motivation	Once the buyer has been pulled out from this frame of mind, sell like an ace
Hand over mouth with thumb pressed against cheek	Lying or being lied to	Give the impression that you are enjoying the lies. Play the buyer at their game until they have been won over	If the buyer feels that you are swallowing their lie pills, then you are on the buyer's side and can aim to get what you want
Nose rubbing	Lying or being lied to	A similar reaction to the previous example is recommended	A similar outcome to that in the previous example

Sender's (buyer's) posture, position or signal (non-verbal communication)	Receiver's (seller's) interpretation of that non-verbal communication & meaning	How seller should respond to that non-verbal communication	The likely reaction/outcome seller could expect from buyer
Left arm folded over right arm, or vice versa, with one hand tucked between the biceps and rib cage	Defensive	Defensive buyers have an underlying reason for their defensiveness. Reassure the buyer and exercise persuasion	The door opens and the way is paved for better business
Left arm over right arm, or vice versa, with fists clenched in between inner biceps and rib cage and pointing downwards	Hostility	Two approaches are recommended here: either (i) meet hostility with full hostility, but only if you are confident you can handle the aggression or (ii) meet the aggression with confusion tactics, in order to take control of the situation	As long as control is achieved and maintained, then selling to this buyer is possible. Failure means that you had better pack your bags and go
Left hand folded over the right hand, or vice versa, with palms gripping biceps	Receiver is saying 'I will not budge from my decision'	Ask probing, then closing questions and remain silent	This buyer can be pushed to make a decision only by the pressure of silence and non-verbal techniques, e.g. the use of the eyes in prolonged episodes of staring

Sender's (buyer's) posture, position or signal (non-verbal communication)	Receiver's (seller's) interpretation of that non-verbal communication & meaning	How seller should respond to that non-verbal communication	The likely reaction/outcome seller could expect from buyer
One arm folded and hand holding the elbow of the other arm which is hanging straight down	Defensive	Defensive buyers usually dread something bad happening to them if they commit themselves. This can be easily handled when it is known why it happens	Selling is a human occupation. All humans have weaknesses, some more than others, and this must be borne in mind when selling
Crossed legs	Could mean either relaxed or defensive	If relaxed, smile and ask for commitment. If buyer is not relaxed then seek to relax them before proper selling starts. The buyer will reveal that they are relaxed when they unfold their legs	It is only when the buyer is relaxed that proper selling and closing can be done. If it is done without the buyer being relaxed, then a cancellation is likely to follow
One leg folded and crossed over other knee and reading a book or document	Evaluating	When a buyer is evaluating, the biggest drawback is to interrupt. Feed the buyer with facts and intermittent doses of closing and silence till agreement to purchase has been reached	Wait patiently till a positive result is obtained

Sender's (buyer's) posture, position or signal (non-verbal communication)	Receiver's (seller's) interpretation of that non-verbal communication & meaning	How seller should respond to that non-verbal communication	The likely reaction/outcome seller could expect from buyer
One leg folded and crossed over other knee and and both hands gripping shin	Scorning, disregarding, will not yield	Any buyer that wilfully displays unfriendly behaviour can be and must be tackled by non-friendly methods till they resort to more acceptable behaviour	This is the acid which differentiates the men from the boys. Good luck - 'Who Dares Sells'
Standing, leaning against wall or support with hands folded against chest and legs crossed over	Defensive	Try to establish if the reaction is caused by a personal interaction or is due to the buyer's general disposition to all salespeople and the outside world. Reassure the buyer	Seek to eliminate fear and you conquer defensiveness
Ankles crossed one over the other	Tense, nervous and withholding information or facts	Probe, praise and support till information is gathered, then selling can start in earnest	Use the information knowledgeably to make the sale
Foot placed behind calf when standing or seated	It is usually a female's way of expressing negative thoughts	Flatter and encourage this buyer. Patience is a virtue!	Most people like flattery, whether they show it or not. Use it carefully and you will sell

Sender's (buyer's) posture, position or signal (non-verbal communication)	Receiver's (seller's) interpretation of that non-verbal communication & meaning	How seller should respond to that non-verbal communication	The likely reaction/outcome seller could expect from buyer
Seated on chair with chair back facing the buyer's front; also known as the straddle position	Dominating and using the chair back as a shield	You have literally got to pierce this buyer's strong psychological defences with a high-powered presentation. Use 'word bullets' to penetrate the shield	The buyer will be left psychologically demolished
Picking bits of fluff from clothing whilst looking downwards	Disapproval at what is being said	Look sad and dismayed at buyer's reaction	This is a good tactic to play when others have been tried and failed. It can be very effective and make you sales
Nodding head up and down	Agreement. It means YES	Go for it	Sellers who do not ask for the order in this instance are amateurs
Moving head from side to side	It means NO. This is an inborn gesture learned as an infant where it refuses milk from its mother when it does not want to drink	For every two No's imitate the gesture, then stop and move your head up and down and make two YES's till the buyer starts to imitate you	You win over the buyer by conscious manipulation of the buyer's negativism
Head parallel to the floor	Neutral	Play this buyer carefully. What you say and how it is said will swing this buyer	You can win if the strategy is right

Sender's (buyer's) posture, position or signal (non-verbal communication)	Receiver's (seller's) interpretation of that non-verbal communication & meaning	How seller should respond to that non-verbal communication	The likely reaction/outcome seller could expect from buyer
Head tilted to the side	Interested	Close as soon as possible	The buyer is in the act of committing themselves when the head is upright
Head down	Negative or disapproving	Motivate this buyer with bags of enthusiasm coupled with bouts of negativism	This buyer must be coerced into buying
Leaning forward while communicating	Interest	Close once, twice, thrice	When you make the sale, hold onto it tight and run!
Hands behind back of head	Demonstrating superiority	Manipulate the buyer by either copying the posture or looking somewhere else of importance to the buyer while talking	Buyers who purposely use these tactics against sellers are displaying their power status – they are in a sense asking for a 'show down'. Give it and then take the sale
Arms folded and one arm fidgeting fidgeting with cuff, bracelet or wrist watch on the other arm	Nervousness	Offer the buyer something such as a sweet, a complimentary gift such as a pen or key ring. Treat it as if you are giving a nervous child a comforter	Sellers who have the ability to calm nervous people (buyers included) are getting the buyer to give them the sale
Female clutching a bunch of flowers or a handbag	Defensive	It may be due to apprehension, so calm down your sales patter	This should reassure the buyer

Sender's (buyer's) posture, position or signal (non-verbal communication)	Receiver's (seller's) interpretation of that non-verbal communication & meaning	How seller should respond to that non-verbal communication	The likely reaction/outcome seller could expect from buyer
Sticking tongue out	Aversion, disgust	Ignore it and keep on selling	The buyer's tongue will still be sticking out when you take the order!
Standing with hands on hips	Prepared to move into action. It also denotes aggression	Keep adjusting your standing or sitting positions so as to keep the buyer guessing all the time in order to maintain control	If the buyer is allowed to dominate, you might as well send for a hearse!
Seated, leaning forward slightly with middle of right forearm on on right thigh and left-hand open palm pressed against left knee with right leg in front of the left	Ready to go ahead	Ask the buyer whether they want to pay by cheque or cash or to use their pen or yours to sign the order, etc.	You should win by adopting this attitude
Seated, leaning forwards with both hands clutching both knees	Ready to terminate	If you cannot do the 'negative sell' then try your hand at fainting; it is easier to do that before you are thrown out!	The main objective is to hang on by hook or by crook waiting for an opening. Never give up hope, for things can improve suddenly

Sender's (buyer's) posture, position or signal (non-verbal communication)	Receiver's (seller's) interpretation of that non-verbal communication & meaning	How seller should respond to that non-verbal communication	The likely reaction/outcome seller could expect from buyer
Side glance	Could mean interest or hostility	You must think on your feet; every action you take will produce a good or bad reaction; the important thing is knowing how to handle it	If you diagnose the buyer's intention wrongly then the presentation won't be right and the sale will be lost
Nodding off	Either tiredness or lack of interest	Open the door for fresh air or offer the buyer a drink of water to relieve tiredness	It is pointless trying to sell to a very tired buyer. Arrange another meeting if the simple measures recommended fail
Dilated pupils	Positive sign	Go for the close	If you do not close at this obvious signal, then I am afraid selling is not for you
Contracting pupils	Negative sign	Seller must do something to startle buyer. For example, slam portfolio fairly abruptly but not too severely on buyer's desk to highlight a point	Dramatising your point will cause the buyer to pay more attention and also respond positively
Short gaze	Dishonest, nervous or timid	Try to keep this buyer well stroked so that they keep on talking. As long as they are talking, you are winning	Wait for the opportunity to pounce, but lay the ambush first. If you don't, they will run away!
Longer gaze with dilated pupils	Interested	Close early	Ask and you should receive

Sender's (buyer's) posture, position or signal (non-verbal communication)	Receiver's (seller's) interpretation of that non-verbal communication & meaning	How seller should respond to that non-verbal communication	The likely reaction/outcome seller could expect from buyer
Eye to eye contact	Businesslike response	Imitate the buyer and you will indicate that you are on the same plane of thought. Keep the discussion businesslike but occasionally inject a touch of humour	In this way you add flavour to the sales interview, which may otherwise be too strained
Eye-to-eye contact with gaze dropping from upper face to around the mouth area	Friendly response	Act prudently. Do not rush to rash conclusions	Prevention in these matters is better than cure
Eye-to-eye contact with gaze dropping to around the sex areas	Intimate response	There is most likely a sexual encounter to be had as well as the order, if it is so desired. Act with caution	A word of advice: do not mix business with pleasure unless you are a risk taker
Male adjusting tie or stroking hair in the presence of a female, or vice versa Female tossing hair, exposing wrists and palms, rolling her hips, opening her legs, occasionally glancing and having wet lips from saliva or lipstick	Indirectly on intimate signal	These are normal gestures, postures and positions for humans to make when they want to signal their intentions,	If sex is what you are looking for, you have made the sale. But if it is 'the sale' you are after, your chances are slim. My advice is to leave trouble alone because it can lead to guilt, blackmail and emotional involvement,

Sender's (buyer's) posture, position or signal (non-verbal communication)	Receiver's (seller's) interpretation of that non-verbal communication & meaning	How seller should respond to that non-verbal communication	The likely reaction/outcome seller could expect from buyer
Female seated with one leg folded at right angles across seat with other leg folded over shin and pointing downwards exposing thighs in the presence of a male		whether it happens in a business environment or not. This sort of thing has been around since Eve tempted Adam with the apple!	which drain useful energy and make selling an even more difficult task. Such behaviour can also be construed by the buyer subsequently as being unprofessional even though they may have given the lead. I would like to emphasize the point here that 'business is business and pleasure is pleasure and never should you mix one with the other'. Furthermore, sellers, if you are looking for business with the 4 S's (sun, sea, sex and sand) in mind, take a holiday – please do not bring it into selling as you will do yourself more harm than good.
Female seated with one leg crossed over the other exposing thighs and dangling a shoe in the presence of a male	Indirectly an intimate signal	How you should react all depends on the buyer's motives. Does the buyer intend giving the seller the thrill of his or her life or 'the sale'?	
Female with one leg crossed and pressed firmly over the other exposing the thighs in the presence of a male			
Female crossing and uncrossing legs slowly, or crossing thighs and talking in a sexy voice			

Sender's (buyer's) posture, position or signal (non-verbal communication)	Receiver's (seller's) interpretation of that non-verbal communication & meaning	How seller should respond to that non-verbal communication	The likely reaction/outcome seller could expect from buyer
Reaching for cigarette or pipe	Playing for time and indicates the receiver is under stress	Play the waiting game, using questioning techniques with long pauses in between. To hurry this buyer would mean to lose the sale since the usual policy of such buyers is 'when in doubt say NO!'	Patience is a virtue. With time, the most difficult of buyers can be made to mellow and any drawbacks to the sale can be resolved
Blowing smoke upwards	Positive personality	Tickle their ego with compliments	You could expect positive feedback
Blowing smoke downwards	Negative, secretive, suspicious	Provide the buyer with facts and get agreement as you go along	This type of buyer can be nailed down only with hard-hitting facts
Continuous tapping of cigarette on ashtray	Internal conflict	Change the scenario by getting the buyer to join you for lunch, or a brief walk, or watch TV.	When the buyer's mind is relaxed, that is the time to start squeezing the juice out of the fruit!
Sudden extinguishing of cigarette after lighting	Signal to terminate conversation	Quickly wind down the sales talk and get down to asking for the order	Get the sale and get out!
One arm holding the arms of a pair of glasses in the mouth	Stalling and needs reassurance	Use supportive and confidence-building statements	Reassurance works wonders

Sender's (buyer's) posture, position or signal (non-verbal communication)	Receiver's (seller's) interpretation of that non-verbal communication & meaning	How seller should respond to that non-verbal communication	The likely reaction/outcome seller could expect from buyer
Removing glasses	Wants to terminate conversation	Quickly get down to the point that you wish to discuss with the buyer without going off course, or else you could lose the sale	Being alert to such movements and responding with positive alternative reactions is what makes a professional a professional!
Putting glasses on again after removing	Wants to see the details again	Give the details to the buyer in the form of benefits and close	The fact that the buyer wants to see the details again is a good indication that they are interested and want to make a favourable decision
Peering over glasses	Judging	You must be prepared for this buyer to find loopholes and tear the proposition to pieces. Equally, they will withdraw from the transaction only if any serious flaws exist	The outcome will depend on how well you have prepared for the interview
Leaning on your property purposely	Buyer is trying to intimidate or dominate you	Let the buyer lean, but quietly move your property so that the buyer will fall and look foolish	It is only by taking control of such situations that genuine selling can take place

Sender's (buyer's) posture, position or signal (non-verbal communication)	Receiver's (seller's) interpretation of that non-verbal communication & meaning	How seller should respond to that non-verbal communication	The likely reaction/outcome seller could expect from buyer
Touching one's own property	Expressing pride of ownership	Compliment the buyer whenever they show interest by touching their own property. To disregard or ridicule the buyer's personal property means rejecting the buyer and spells danger	When a buyer is complimented honestly it broadens their shoulders. If they deserve it then the compliment should be freely given. You will find that such an act goes down well
One leg over chair arm with one hand over the chair back	Lack of concern	If a buyer shows lack of concern, it obviously stems from their not thinking too highly of you or of the offer. Give the buyer regular doses of praise intermingled with 'I don't care' impressions to distract them from their attitude	This tactic should get the buyer to take the issue more seriously
Both feet on desk	Claiming ownership of property but buyer has hostile intentions	You must play a game like dodgem cars. Whatever the buyer says, you should duck, twist it around and come back like a boomerang	This tactic is the only one I know of that can be deployed in the circumstances. I have tried others without much effect. The main purpose is to bring the buyer down a peg or two

Sender's (buyer's) posture, position or signal (non-verbal communication)	Receiver's (seller's) interpretation of that non-verbal communication & meaning	How seller should respond to that non-verbal communication	The likely reaction/outcome seller could expect from buyer
The buyer copies your gestures, postures or positions	Thinking alike. It is a favourable situation for the seller	Capitalize on the situation and get down to the main points as soon as possible. Extol the benefits of the product, service or idea and close the sale	Failure to capitalize means that you do not know what a favourable situation is or are in the wrong job. Either go back to the classroom or quit selling
Buyer is positioned at a higher level than seller	Commanding authority	By acknowledging and respecting buyers who are big and powerful you can gain strength and knowledge. However, remember always that you are there to make the sale and also grasp the opportunity to gain some knowledge if it is available	You can only learn to become better from those who are better. If in the course of doing business you can also pick the buyer's brains, it is only a fool who wouldn't take advantage of that opportunity
Face pointing towards seller but body pointing in another direction	Indicates that the buyer wishes to go in the direction of the body rather than talk with the seller	Move with the buyer in the direction they wish to go, but return later with the buyer to where you want to be	This like the well-known method of comply and complain. Do it and the buyer will pull along with you
Buyer speaks to you face to face and the body points in the same direction	Communication is taking place properly	This is an optimum position to be in to make sales and make friends. Talk like a maestro and win the buyer like a sportsperson winning a game	If you do a well-structured presentation then you can start singing 'Happy days are here again'!

Sender's (buyer's) posture, position or signal (non-verbal communication)	Receiver's (seller's) interpretation of that non-verbal communication & meaning	How seller should respond to that non-verbal communication	The likely reaction/outcome seller could expect from buyer
Buyer communicating with another person with their bodies pointing towards each other and a third person (you) wishes to enter the discussion, but only the buyer's and other person's faces and not their bodies are turned towards you	It means that you are not accepted accepted into the conversation until the buyer's and the other person's bodies and faces are pointing towards you	Make a critical comment on some general issue so that both the buyer and the other person get 'shell shock' and jointly want to listen to you. When you have taken control try to ease out the other person from the discussion and concentrate on dealing with the buyer unless the other person can influence a decision in your favour	These tactics work when you start using them fearlessly and make them part of your day-to-day selling arsenal
Pointing foot in a particular direction	Subconsciously there is interest in what is being offered	Think of fishing where the fish is being tempted by the bait. Wait till it makes a grab and then start playing it till you land it	The skill in selling is to know when the buyer is hot and then to move into the closing phase. If you cannot determine when the buyer is giving out buying signals I suggest you try another career
Buyer and seller seated close to each other at the corner of a table at right angles to each other	A casual and friendly set-up	If the buyer's disposition is that of a friend, by all means make friends but make money too	There are friends and friends and it is rare to find really good friends in business

Sender's (buyer's) posture, position or signal (non-verbal communication)	Receiver's (seller's) interpretation of that non-verbal communication & meaning	How seller should respond to that non-verbal communication	The likely reaction/outcome seller could expect from buyer
Buyer and seller seated on same side of table and adjacent to each other	Full co-operation and understanding for each other	Same as the preceding example; a nice, comfortable, selling atmosphere that can be very fruitful to both seller and buyer	This buyer is like a special gift. Treat them as extra special
Buyer seated diagonally opposite to seller	Defensive/ competitive	This is my favourite position for most selling situations and the one I feel most comfortable in. Take this position if it is the only one you feel comfortable with	When you understand the psychology of the sales process, nothing in selling will worry you
Buyer seated on corner and seller seated on opposite corner	Buyer does not wish to interact	Give the buyer something to play with like a complimentary key ring or pen, and make it a talking point to lead into a proper selling approach	Treat this buyer as a child and see how that approach works
Buyer seated on a higher chair	Power status	Take control of the situation by standing and delivering your presentation. To sit and sell means an uphill struggle to make the sale	The outcome of the interview will depend on your skill at taking control of the situation and playing the selling game in the presence of pre-existing disadvantages

Sender's (buyer's) posture, position or signal (non-verbal communication)	Receiver's (seller's) interpretation of that non-verbal communication & meaning	How seller should respond to that non-verbal communication	The likely reaction/outcome seller could expect from buyer
Buyer who puts a lock on the telephone or displays testimonials or shows off files marked 'strictly confidential'	Trying to show importance and to subtly intimidate	Show appreciation for the buyer's testimonials and stroke the buyer's ego. You can only win by attaching importance to the buyer's marks of distinction, even though they are basking in their own glory by showing them off as if to say 'Look, I am great', or possibly even 'I am the greatest'	Failure to recognize the buyer's importance or criticising them is a surefire way to lose out on a sale
Head tossed to one side and listening intently	Trying to figure out what is being said	Speak clearly, coherently and get agreement on main selling points from buyer. Build up to the final close with a series of minor closes	A listening buyer is not difficult to close

In all the above examples you may try out what is recommended and can expect either the speculated reaction/outcome or something close to it. The main objective is to resolve the matter at the first meeting or on a subsequent visit.

If you fail it does not mean the end of the world or that the buyer is too good for you or that you are less capable than the buyer. It just happens to be the way things function in life; you have to be philosophical about these matters and try again with a fresh approach.

A buyer's resistance is not 'cast iron' and 'forever'. It changes by the second, minute, hour, day, week, month and over the years. You will be surprised if you analyse two or more meetings you have had with the same buyer – one may have been diabolical whereas the other was very cordial. Never say 'Never' – keep trying, and you should succeed if you know what to do and how to do it – that is the secret of success. Do not lose your cool and insult the buyer. If they are awkward, learn to like them more. I assure you, if you have time, patience and skill on your side and have the fighting spirit, you can, you will and you must win.

CHAPTER 8

The pros and cons of non-verbal communication (body language)

Brilliant communicators talk well, listen better, observe more, close on time and hit their targets near enough every time. If you can read and understand people in the same way you read and understand a book you will be able to sell them even water and fresh air, assuming of course you have the knowledge, skill and experience in what you are selling and they have the Money, Authority and Need.

In the course of my research into body language I had the opportunity to meet Gordon Wainwright, author of *Teach Yourself Body Language* and several business books. Here is the outcome of my conversation with him, in which we discuss the fascinating subject of body language.

PE: I thought it would be a good idea if we could have an exchange of our knowledge on this topic, where you can play the part of a seller, and I could play the part of a buyer, and we could analyse the interaction together. I will give you some non-verbal signals which I would like you not just to interpret, but to translate into selling strategy, so what we will in effect be doing is clinching a hypothetical deal.

Now, I am the decision-maker, seated behind a large desk.

GW: Well that in itself communicates something.

PE: Yes I am aware that it is an extension of my body space and that's what it is intended to do, to intimidate people like yourself, and furthermore it is a very large desk.

GW: That communicates an even stronger message.

PE: Right, now this desk's position is at a higher level than the chair that you are expected to sit on and there am I looking at my watch and saying to you, 'I've got a meeting in five minutes, so tell me what you have to say quickly.' Can you please tell me how would you tackle that one?

GW: I would have to think of something to tell you quickly that would catch your interest and make you delay that meeting. It would have nothing to do with what I have to say but rather the way I say it. I have got to come forward by leaning forward. I would have to establish eye contact with you. I have got to have a nice, positive, friendly facial expression and I would make a statement such as, 'I have a fantastic product for you, Mr Ellis, that is going to be of benefit to you by saving you time, money and effort,' and I would have to look convincing.

PE: That may be so but I am a busy executive – I have to rush off now.

GW: We are all busy executives and I too have to call on my next appointment shortly.

PE: Indeed. Can you get down to the point quickly. I do not intend to be rude but I am in a bit of a hurry. (And then I move my chair backwards and I join my hands behind my neck, you know, into an arrogant position.)

GW: It means rejecting, not wanting to know, which is why when I came in I brought with me some very interesting literature which has got some very fine visual illustrations and details of the kind of tape recorder you will find to be of benefit to you and I lay these in front of you and you cannot resist coming forward because I am coming forward and I am showing interest (enthusiasm) in the literature because I know they are going to meet with your requirements and if you purchase then we both are going to benefit so, how can you not be interested?

PE: Well, Mr Wainwright, seeing that you are so persistent and persuasive, and I am very busy, why don't you see my departmental head?

GW: Yes, but you know the kind of organization that you run, you are the one who makes the decisions and you are the person that I have got to talk to and you are the one that needs to see these illustrations.

Now, Mr Ellis, these illustrations that I brought to show you – and I may even move nearer to you to get you to have a quick look. I wouldn't come too near because you are indicating to me that you do not want me to come too near by not showing a lot of interest at this stage. But the fact that you are still there and haven't kicked me out of your office indicates to me that you are vaguely interested, so I can manoeuvre around for a while until I find an opening. If I can get you into a position where you are in an indirect orientation looking at the product then if I am going to look at it you will also tend to come and look at it.

PE: Now from this position, where I am looking at you and your literature from a distance with my hands behind the back of my neck and my legs in the cocked up position on the desk, I adjust myself on the chair into an upright position and listen to you with my hands covering my mouth. How would you react to this?

GW: Are you saying anything when you are doing that or, are you just listening to me when I am making my sales presentation?

PE: I am listening to you, but my hands are covering my mouth.

GW: That is not necessarily a problem. If you are speaking and your hand is over your mouth then it might be a problem, but as you are not talking and your hand is covering your mouth and you are listening to me you could be thinking about what I am telling you. In fact that is what you are likely to be doing, considering what I am saying, so I have got you hooked.

PE: But could it mean that I may be thinking that you are lying to me, you know, with my hand covering my mouth in this context while I am listening could mean that I do not believe what you are saying or I may be evaluating.

GW: But, I have such an honest face you see, I am looking you straight in the eyes, I could not be possibly lying to you – you might be doing something which might make you think that I am lying to you, but as long as I don't do anything which communicates to you that I am lying to you then we should get on OK. Obviously in a selling situation there is a certain amount of, not lying, but exaggeration that takes place on the seller's part. For example a seller might say, 'Did you know, Mr Ellis, just exactly how good this product I am trying to offer you is? As far as I am concerned it is an absolutely perfect tape recorder, and nothing on the market can compete with it. It can pick up our voices clearly from around six feet, while screening out the background noise from that busy road. Can't you see it is an excellent, high quality product ideal for your requirements?'

Now, if I were to try and exaggerate too much the quality of the tape recorder and say that it would actually talk back and tell you if the message you have recorded is, for example, grammatically wrong, or illogical then the seller would start to exhibit signs of deception.

But I am not doing that and I am deliberately avoiding signs of deception and I am being totally honest with you. I have open hands, I am leaning forward, I am establishing eye contact with a nice friendly facial expression, open posture, open gestures, everything is open and what I am really saying to you non-verbally is that I have nothing to hide, this tape recorder speaks for itself and all you have got to do is order one now.

PE: So what you are saying to me is that if the buyer covers the mouth with the hands in a live selling situation it does not necessarily mean that the buyer does not believe the seller, or in other words thinks that the seller is telling lies?

GW: Oh they may very well do, because all buyers disbelieve sellers anyway and that is axiomatic. If any salesperson is going into a selling situation they have got to assume that whoever is a potential buyer doesn't believe a word the seller is saying because they would have heard it all before. I am not the first person to come with a tape recorder. I may be the second, third or even the tenth but I know that my product is just as good, or even better than, the others.

Let's face it, if you have got any kind of product or service that you are selling, if it is not the best then it is just as good as most of the rest, so you have got at least that amount of confidence in it and you can sell it with a clear conscience. The buyer may not believe you, but as part of the verbal side you draw their particular attention to the USP – the Unique Selling Point – in such a way that there is the openness and the buyer can feel that what the seller is saying is the truth. Now if this is the way the seller is communicating would the buyer then believe the seller?

The chances are if there is eye contact, and if it is maintained and the facial expressions are varied and positive and the gestures and postures are open, the seller leans forward and everything on the non-verbal side is positive then there is a better chance of making the sale than by doing anything else.

Now if I as a seller were to lean back like this with my hands behind my neck and I tell you to buy this tape recorder as it is a very good product, would you believe me when I am sitting there telling you all this with my hands behind my head and my legs crossed away from you?

PE: Well, that would come over to me that you were trying to be too cocky.

GW: Exactly. It would be a totally wrong approach. Similarly if I sat like this with my hands folded across my chest, an all-closed posture, closed gesture and I am saying to you this is an excellent product, a very good tape recorder you wouldn't believe me. Why? Because it doesn't appear to you that I have confidence in it.

PE: When you say closed posture and closed gesture do you mean legs together and hands together?

GW: Yes, legs together, hands together in this kind of artificial steepling effect with elbows resting on a desk top.

Normally, a steeple like that with the thumbs together and finger tips together would be a sign of being authoritative and confident. But in this situation that would be too much for a seller to do in front of a buyer because as a seller you do not want to dominate your buyer, you would want the buyer to dominate you because the buyer is the one who is going to make the decision, so you let non-verbal and the verbal communication be dictated by the buyer. This means you are ready to come back as soon as you can get in with a positive point.

If the buyer moves away, the seller should not do likewise. Again, if the buyer is exhibiting negative language, the seller should not copy that for obvious reasons. But if the buyer is demonstrating positive body language, such as coming forward towards the seller, showing interest, looking at the product, then the seller too must come forward and show interest and look at the product and share the experience together with the buyer. So, *positive non-verbal communication* the *seller shares* the experience with the buyer and *negative non-verbal communication* the *seller does not imitate* because two negatives have a greater tendency to fail. If you, the hypothetical buyer, put your hands behind your head and cross your legs, and I, the hypothetical seller, did the same then it would make a sale much more difficult.

Gerald Nierenberg and Henry Calero in their book *How to read a person like a book* recorded and analyzed 2500 negotiations, and noted the importance of proximity when trying to negotiate a sale. You have got to get close but not too close – as close as the client finds it comfortable and certainly not too positioned far away.

Buyers tend to buy from sellers who are close to them rather than from someone who remains at a distance. Hence many salespeople carry literature and other visual aids with them and sometimes they even take audio aids too, so that they can approach the prospective buyer from close quarters. If the buyer reacts by folding his arms or some other defensive gesture, like you putting your hands behind your head the salesperson must move away until the buyer's behaviour is more relaxed and less defensive and then the seller can move in again. So the seller should be all the time looking towards getting close to the buyer.

PE: It is a game, isn't it?

GW: Well, life is a game and selling certainly is a game, played for real and played for results, and there are winners and losers. The seller makes a sale and wins but the buyer does not lose – the people who lose are the other salespeople who haven't got the business because they just weren't good enough. So, there are winners and losers and it is not a team game, it is an individual game.

PE: It is played on a one-to-one basis.

GW: There is also the game of one against the rest. The seller is not just in competition with the buyer but is in competition with all the other salespeople to make a sale of the product, service or idea and they have to win, so it is a game played to win.

PE: Let's talk about being positive.

GW: The salesperson must always remain positive because salespeople are involved in what broadly speaking you might call public contact work and need to be positive all the time. One of the basic problems with such people is that they are not positive.

You can go into any selling situation and watch people communicating and you can see many of them using negative body language and as a consequence they don't get results.

What the seller has to decide is what the objective is. The objective in a selling context is clearly to get the buyer to make a purchase – that would be what the seller wants and that would be his or her responsibility; in other words the seller would be looking for a positive response and result. How on earth is the seller going to get a positive response from a buyer if he or she is doing things that are setting up negative reactions in the minds of the person the seller is trying to get a positive reaction from? Logically speaking, in my opinion it just isn't possible.

PE: So, with negative feedback coming from a buyer what would you advocate the seller should do to try to get the buyer to switch to a positive and enthusiastic state?

GW: Salespeople need to use plenty of eye contact, head nods and head cocks or head tilts. When you move your head to one side it shows you are interested in what the other person is saying. When a seller is communicating with a buyer and the buyer is revealing his or her needs (after the initial exchange of courtesies of shaking hands have taken place) the sale could be made to the greatest advantage of the seller by the seller displaying a nice friendly disposition to the buyer without awkwardness or uneasiness, by the seller touching for example the buyer's arm or shoulder with the hand.

Some very interesting studies have been done on bodily contact which have nothing to do with selling. In one, the researcher went into a library, took a book and got a ticket and then recorded the same activity as other people did the same thing.

On certain occasions when the librarian handed over the book and ticket to certain people, their fingers would touch for a few seconds (finger to finger contact) while others took hold of the book and ticket without any bodily contact at all. When those people came out of the library and were asked to rate the librarian on a number of different factors, those people with whom there was that brief bodily contact consistently rated the librarian as a much warmer and more pleasant person and easier to get along with.

From this it is obvious that the best way for a seller to approach a buyer would be to start off by shaking the buyer's hand – not a hard handshake nor a limp one, but a reasonably firm handshake, and the same on leaving. That would be one of the most influential things a salesperson could do to establish initial friendly hand-to-hand bodily contact with the person they are going to talk to.

PE: But in my selling life I have come across people who do not like to shake hands.

GW: Sure, I am not saying that all of this is purely mechanical and that it would work every time. All I am saying is where it is possible to do it then it would increase the effectiveness and chances of getting a good result. We are talking in this area of non-verbal communication and whatever you do there is no 'magic' about it. People tend to assume that there is some special power in it because they know so little about it – they know that they are experiencing things intuitively but they have not looked at the underlying reasons and evidence for that non-verbal communication.

Just as with memory training, rapid reading, listening and writing business letters and reports – there is no special secret to them, but they are essential skills every salesperson should acquire.

PE: Getting back to negative gestures and postures, it is known that when somebody is talking with their hand pointing downwards they are giving a negative indication.

GW: Yes, hand down is negative and hand up is positive, but everything is context dependent. There are only one or two gestures that I can think of which are capable of being interpreted as being the same: one is the smile which is almost universally accepted as being a positive response; and the other gesture is the eye brow flash which implies recognition when a person meets another.

You always have to get back to the context and that is why interpretation is so difficult. Hence you can lay down broad guide lines like positive is better than negative, but you cannot lay down iron clad rules. If it is a smile on its own surrounded by negatives then it should be discounted. It is like trying to detect whether somebody is trying to deceive you – you might see them rub their nose and incorrectly think they are deceiving you, but they might just have an itch. So to find the exact meaning of the non-verbal communication one has got to look at the whole rather than the parts of it, for example avoidance of eye contact, turning the head away and similar gestures.

I will tell you an interesting little story someone told me once. A group of people used to meet every lunchtime to play a game of poker. They always knew when one fellow had a bad hand as his face and body wouldn't move, but no sooner did he get a good hand, then his foot would begin to twitch.

PE: That is what is called leakage, isn't it?

GW: Correct, and leakage usually occurs in the lower half of the body and not in the upper half. We are much more able to control what we do with the upper half of the body than with the lower half. We tend to forget about the lower half. Well, who cares about feet – what can feet tell you? Actually, feet can tell you a lot. Watch someone who is nervous and watch the way in which the nervousness comes out through the feet – that person may be perfectly controlled verbally and facially in the upper half of the body but if the feet are moving it is a sign of stress. There is a great advantage in having a knowledge of body language to detect signs of stress. It all helps to keep control of the situation and will indicate to the salesperson whether s/he is coming on too strong. In selling, some sellers do push too hard and if the buyer does indicate signs of stress then that might be a warning to the salesperson to back down a bit, not completely, to a sufficient level and a psychologically advantageous position.

PE: Now I am convinced that the importance of knowing body language is where a buyer may be saying, *'Yes, I want to go ahead,'* verbally, but with the body non-verbally saying, *'No, I do not want to go ahead.'*

For example, if you are a seller, selling to a buyer in a face-to-face selling situation where you have a product, have taken its features and converted them into benefits and shown how those benefits satisfy the needs of the buyer; have competently handled any objections, and in doing so have paved the way to close the sale, then comes the 'crunch point'. You ask the buyer a closing question such as, 'May I have your authority to go ahead on this purchase agreement?' To which the buyer replies in the affirmative with a statement like, 'I think it sounds a good idea,' but with his body saying No non-verbally by having his hands folded and pressed against the chest and his legs pressed together. I would say the seller is in a bit of trouble, don't you agree?

GW: I would say get the signature.

PE: But the next day the buyer may ring up the seller and

say something like, 'You know Mr Seller, regarding that product we were discussing yesterday, I have had a good think about it and I have decided not to go ahead, so I am cancelling the cheque I gave you as a deposit.' The reason for this is that the buyer had a hidden objection to the product which was revealed in the non-verbal communication with a defensive posture. Had the seller been aware of it at the time and attempted to bring out that hidden objection with some open ended questions, followed by some closed ended questions to get agreement, then the hidden objection could have been appropriately answered and this would have relieved the buyer's anxiety which would have resulted in a relaxing of his posture.

GW: Yes, you have to find ways of converting those negative indications into positive ones, and you do that by getting the buyer's decision and signature first and then giving the buyer the option there and then (on the spot) to change his mind. The chances are that it is very unlikely that he would change his mind after having commited themselves.

PE: What I would have done in that situation would have been to go into a full-blooded probing sequence to try and establish precisely what the hidden objection is. It may be that the buyer did not have the finances, or was not completely sold on the offer. Now that non-verbal communication is telling the seller something such as, 'I am a bit apprehensive about this whole thing' or, 'I need a bit more time to consider this proposal' or, 'I have to consult my partner or accountant' or, 'I do not have the necessary deposit at this moment to pay for it' There could be any number of reasons for stalling, so unless the seller knows the reason for the stall exactly at that critical point, it cannot be confronted and handled to pave the way for a water-tight sale to take place.

Moving on to spotting other reactions in buyers. When a seller is giving a presentation, how can they tell the audience is bored?

GW: It could be seen by the person refusing eye contact with you and showing a negative facial expression. They might be doodling, but doodling alone is not a very reliable indication. Some people can be quite interested, alert and attentive but doodle because that is a habit they have. Boredom can also be detected in a hunched posture rather than an upright and forward one or, leaning backwards or to one side, in what is called a asymmetrical posture. You have to add all those things together before you can interpret the way they are feeling.

PE: In a live selling situation at what point, would you say, should a salesperson who is encountering a lot of opposition stop pushing any further and say, 'Right, I have had enough, I had better pack my bags and go.' In other words, at what stage of the interview should the seller take the non-verbal cues from the buyer as being a definite No and what sort of non-verbal signals would the buyer give in that situation?

GW: If the seller has worked consistently through the sales strategy and the buyer is still not giving any kind of positive response, then the thing to do is to look for an accumulation of negative responses because that can give the seller an indication as to how far he or she could go. These might be leaning back and crossing the legs away from you and all the time retreating from the situation. There comes a point, if the seller is unable to convert that negativism into some kind of positive response then you might just have to write that one off. You can only spend a certain amount of time with buyers and you have to discriminate and spend your precious time with those who are most likely to buy and eliminate the time wasters.

PE: When a buyer is getting angry, what other non-verbal signs would they give?

GW: It will show in the face (in the facial expression), in the eyebrows (they may be frowning) and the colour of the face would become either red or white. There would also be various twitches particularly in the feet movements – a restlessness, an itchiness and a desire to move away or aggressive finger-pointing. There would also be a general level of activity that is not necessarily co-ordinated. It would not be very productive to pursue that buyer until he or she has cooled down.

PE: Now I know cases where salespeople (including myself) who on a rare occasion have been thrown out by a buyer in a rude and aggressive manner!

GW: I would say if you push too hard you could expect that sort of reaction. A salesperson must be positive but not aggressive.

PE: You mean the seller is asking to be thrown out by being too persistent or too pushy? I believe persistence to be a very valuable quality in the salesperson, but it must be wrapped up with large doses of empathy for it to be productive.

Now, what signals would you say the buyer would give when showing intense interest in the offer?

GW: The buyer would lean forward, use more eye contact and display positive facial expressions. The pupils will dilate, but I do not know whether you would necessarily spot that, because to notice that they have dilated you would first have to know what their natural position is, and it is very difficult to observe something as detailed as that.

As a general guide, if you want to be a good salesperson and accepted as a good person generally, you should make more eye contact rather than less eye contact. Now you need not stare at people all the time, but the more eye contact there is between people the more likely it is that they will get on with each other, and the less there is then the less they tend to like each other.

PE: If a buyer is critically evaluating a product what sort of signals would he or she give?

GW: Well, chin stroking would be one, having the hands on the side of the face with fingers under the nose, there would possibly be a slight frown; the buyer would be looking tensely upwards rather than not downwards, towards the left or right depending on whether the person is a left looker or right looker.

You do need to be as finely tuned to the various signs and signals as possible – observe yourself and other people in similar situations and practise how to overcome those situations. Knowledge, Observation and Practice (KOP) are the three basic rules.

PE: Now, in the branch of psychology known as Neuro Linguistic Programming (NLP) people are said to process information in three distinct modes: visual, auditory or kinesthetic, and what the salesperson is advised to do to maximize the chances of making the sale is to tailor the sales presentation to suit the mode in which the buyer is processing the information. For example, a visual buyer will move the eyes upwards to the left or right or may look at a point at a short distance ahead with the eyes slightly defocussed and say something like, 'it looks to me' or 'I see what you mean.' The auditory person would move the eyes to the right or left, parallel to the floor, or alternatively move them down to the left and use phrases such as, 'it sounds good' or 'I can hear you.' The kinesthetic person, who reacts through feelings, would move the eyes down to the right and say something such as, 'I like the feeling' or 'it feels just right'.

GW: Yes, that is similar to the seller adjusting his/her body language in positive terms to suit the body language of the buyer.

PE: What if a buyer wants to terminate an interview very quickly? What are the non-verbal signals they would make?

GW: They would have their hands on their knees or chair showing that they are ready to go. They might start folding a document or file.

PE: What if a person is very rude — should you grin and bear insulting behaviour like two-fingered gestures or swearing, give back as hard as you get, or pack your bags and go?

GW: Well, there is a saying, *a soft word turneth away wrath*. Either react in a pleasant manner or deflect it by turning it into a joke. If you say something like, 'Come on, please don't be horrible to me, you are not normally like this, I understand you must be having one of those bad days that we all have from time to time. You know you bought the smaller version of this product last year and upgrading it to this slightly larger version is going to bring you more benefits for only slightly increased payments' – you become persuasive rather than reacting against the person. Sales people in particular have got to be able to take things like that on the chin without reacting negatively or else they will lose more sales than they make.

People will communicate their negative attitudes in other ways without necessarily being openly rude. For example they might do it by making you wait. How many salespeople go into see a buyer with an appointment, and are made to wait and wait with the buyer knowing full well that the seller is sitting there.

PE: Is the buyer trying subtly to dominate or undermine the seller or is the buyer not interested at all?

GW: The buyer is probably testing the seller, or it could be lack of interest – again, you look at the total picture. I do know buyers who habitually deal with salespeople in that manner. They believe that if the seller is any good then it would not upset them and that they should be able to bounce back! The reason they do it is to take control, and by letting them do that you have a better chance of moving in later and taking control of the situation yourself.

PE: Alternatively, you could confront the buyer saying, 'You have kept me waiting for nearly an hour. Are you going to see me now or aren't you, because I have three more people to see this afternoon?' It is a full forward thrust approach I favour.

GW: That's fair enough, as long as you have the nerve to do it. You can take some chances and you may come out the winner in the end, but you are taking chances.

PE: Who Dares Sells!

GW: Big sales come from taking big chances, and maybe on such occasions that is what you have to do.

PE: I am not particularly bothered about what the buyer thinks about me, as long as I know in my heart of hearts that what I am doing for my buyer is legal, decent and honest and I get the sale – that is what matters, everything else is of secondary importance. If I get on well with the buyer that is fine, but if our chemistries do not click so be it, but the show must go on!

It must be clearly understood in selling that the greatest punishment a buyer could give a seller is not to give them the order; and the greatest compliment that the seller could give the buyer is to prevent them from making that negative decision. Having said that, my view is that if the buyer upsets the equilibrium I would make them feel that they have done certain things that are un-businesslike. I believe they will respect you when you show them how you feel.

Another point is that most sellers take a rather submissive type of approach, assuming that the buyer is king in his own domain. In the selling business, the buyer is the king as long as s/he gives an order or makes indications that they are going to give you that order after perusing the benefits. If I, as the seller, am genuine in my proposal I would expect the buyer to respond similarly. When the seller enters the buyer's protected territory, s/he is wandering into a strange kingdom where the buyer would use all manner of animal-like responses to put the seller off-course and take control of the situation. That is standard and you must expect displays of emotional outrage and tantrums at one extreme, to delay tactics or complete indifference at the other. All the games that buyers play are geared towards one thing: to take control of the seller. The true professional salesperson is aware of those tactics and uses counter measures to take control of the situation themselves.

It is the seller who must control the sale, not the buyer. For if the seller lets the buyer control the sale, you run the risk of making unprofitable sales. Play the faithful, lovable dog, but not the underdog.

In your book you refer to the ectomorph, endomorph and mesomorph types of people – would you say that body language signals will vary for these different types of people?

GW: It is bound to. With thin people you get much more activity and movement than you are going to get with fat people, for the simple reason that it requires much more energy for a fat person to be as lively as a thin person.

PE: What about athletic people?

GW: They tend to be much more positive in their body language, and are likely to give a quick decision.

PE: So, to consolidate everything we have been talking about, can you give me some general guidelines that salespeople can bear in mind and observe in all future contact?

GW: Take each situation individually. Eye contact is very important, but obviously there is a line between no eye contact and a total stare. Aim to be somewhere in the middle, with more eye contact rather than less. Facial expressions should be lively, and head movements such as nods, keep an encounter going, signalling that the person can carry on talking. It does not have to be a lot, but a little indication shows that you are listening.

Open palms (indicating honesty), open postures and gestures, a direct orientation rather than an indirect one, closer proximity rather than distance, and smart dress. Follow all this and you will automatically increase your sales and your success.

CHAPTER 9

How to deal with objections

An objection can be looked upon as sales resistance, and without it you cannot expect to make a sale – just as in electricity you cannot expect to have current flowing from one end of a conductor to the other without resistance.

Making a sale is like driving a car from A to B, where you accelerate and decelerate according to the road conditions. If the car were lifted, the wheels would not touch the ground, it would not have resistance, and without friction you won't be able to move forward no matter how fast the wheels are spinning.

Objections can arise from the buyer wanting:

● doubts clarified
● further information
● reassurance on certain points

They may be:

● openly expressed
● implied
● hidden

and if they are hidden it is the salesperson's job to smoke them out, for an objection that is not discovered and dealt with is a lost sale.

Objections can be rational or irrational. In face-to-face selling, most objections come from the buyer – but an inexperienced salesperson could provoke some objections himself if he or she is not vigilant.

Dealing with Objections

Either:

● Pre-empt the objection – kill it off before the buyer thinks of it, or
● Answer it immediately

If you tell the buyer you will deal with the objection later, then forget about it, or – worse – ignore it, you will risk the buyer thinking you are either hedging or ignorant of the answers. In either case the sale could be threatened then or later.

Unprofessional or inexperienced salespeople do not know how to recognize an objection and deal with it, and disregard what the buyer has said. They carry on regardless and hence lose the sale. Salespeople who do a wishy-washy job when selling, by not confronting objections and dealing with them in the right manner will always come out with sob stories to defend their poor selling abilities. Their excuse for losing the sale will be that the buyer gave them a tough time and complained about the product, service or idea. This is not so. What the buyer is telling the seller is that, based on their perceptions of the product, service or idea being offered and what the seller has told them, during the sales presentation is that the buyer could not make a decision.

Objection handling to the seller therefore takes place as a prelude to closing and it is in that context that objections must be viewed rather than suspecting the buyer of throwing in a red herring in order to escape giving the seller a decision, or put him or her off course.

When multiple objections are expressed by the buyer, the seller can treat all of them as one and ask, 'Apart from these objections is there anything else that concerns you?' If not, the seller then says, 'If I could provide you with a solution or a valid explanation to those objections you would be prepared to go ahead, wouldn't you?' The answer to this must naturally be 'Yes' so you deal with them by isolating each objection, writing them down on a piece of paper in the presence of the buyer, answering them to the point, getting agreement with the buyer that each one has been answered to their satisfaction and crossing them out as you proceed, until the sale is made. This technique is called the *final objection closing technique*.

It is very easy for a seller to confuse an **Excuse** with a genuine **Objection**. An excuse is where a buyer is deliberately trying to avoid making a decision. An objection is a concrete opportunity for you to find a way of dealing with whatever is troubling the buyer, and close the sale.

When the buyer starts to make **excuses** you start to **manipulate** them subtly, letting him or her know that you have gauged their game and are aware that they are prevaricating. Be careful, though – you risk making the buyer angry if you use intimidating behaviour and you might reach the stage where you have to withdraw from the meeting. You then allow a cooling-off period, and may then contact the buyer again, apologizing for your supposed 'mistake'. This should pave the way for a fresh selling start.

Objections can be based on the following factors:
- you, your company, product, service or idea
- rumour or hearsay
- cost (the amount of money required to run something) or price (the amount of money you would have to pay to own it)
- quality
- reliability
- durability
- packaging
- competitive advantages or disadvantages
- size
- shape
- colour
- functionability
- weight
- chemical composition
- suitability
- reputation
- past performance
- lack of desire to change
- seasonal demand
- fear, guilt, jealousy, anger
- future growth potential
- product, service or idea does not satisfy need
- unwillingness to take risks
- lack of urgency
- cultural differences

Let us look at some of the sales resistances or objections a seller can expect to encounter in the sales arena, and how to deal with them. The professional salesperson should meet these objections head on, and defuse them just like a bomb disposal officer would neutralize a bomb, rendering it harmless.

EXCUSES

Example 1

Buyer: I don't make decisions to buy on rainy days.

Seller: So, you mean that if it is sunny you will buy? Tell you what, apart from my close involvement with this product, service or idea, one of my hobbies is performing magic tricks. But before I use my skills to make the sun shine – and I promise not to be like the politician who in desperation for farmers' votes promised them rain – will you kindly write me a cheque? I can assure you that I am giving you this first class service or idea at the attractive price of [name it], and you will be the proud owner of it in three weeks' time. Now how does that sound?

Example 2

Buyer: If you had arrived here five minutes earlier, I would have bought from you.

Seller: Let's turn the clock back five minutes and assume you did not have this product, service or idea and it is clearly apparent to both of us that you would be at a great disadvantage without it. Now let us turn the clock ten minutes forward and assume you do own this product, service or idea from which it is plain to see that you will be enjoying some valuable benefits that will strengthen your current position (whatever it is) and give you better advantages than you would have had if you did not take it. So let's assume I came here five minutes ago. May I strongly recommend that you invest in this product, service or idea which I would be pleased to provide to you, with my wholehearted support as I want to see you profit from it. Whose pen do you want to use to sign the cheque, yours or mine?

Example 3

Buyer: You are the best salesperson that I have met offering such a superb product, service or idea. Contact me in another two years' time and I will buy from you then.

Seller: Thank you for the compliment. I appreciate it very much, but the thing that confuses me is that had I been that good you would have purchased from me. Maybe what you really mean is that I am good in my job and you also like my product, service or idea but it is not good enough for you to go ahead at present, and you are prepared to wait for it to improve in a couple of years time. This seems most unlikely as the product, service or idea has been tailor-made to cope with current and future trends. Can you clarify your views to me and kindly be a bit more specific? [The buyer would now be forced to reveal the hidden objection which the seller can isolate, then answer and close.]

Example 4

Buyer: I like your product, service or idea very much, but no thank you. Why don't you try selling it to our competition? Maybe it can help them better!

Seller: So what you are saying to me is that you like to commit business suicide by letting this product, service or idea go to your competitors for them to go up and for you to go down? [If the buyer answers Yes, No, Maybe or remains silent, continue with:] I would hate to be partner to such a crime, but what I can offer you is hope and a successful business life with this product, service or idea. When would you like it – today, tomorrow, this week or next? [Alternatively, you could try discovering what benefits the buyer thinks their competitors will gain from the product.]

Example 5

Buyer: Don't go out of your way to see me, but if you are in the area and doing nothing and I am free, I will have a chat with you.

Seller: With the greatest of respect, I wish to stress that you have got me wrong. I am a professional salesperson and not an amateur entertainer; it is against my rules of conduct to call on you on the off-chance without an appointment, or to waste your valuable time or mine if I did not have something of significant value or benefit to show you. And as I do have something special that will make you money, save you time or effort [tell them which of these it is or whatever else it could be], when can I see you to discuss this matter further – would Wednesday at three or Friday at eleven suit you better?

Example 6
Buyer: Don't contact us, we'll contact you.
Seller: I have always believed that one good turn deserves another, so if you don't contact me I won't contact you and likewise, if you don't contact me I will contact you. Would you prefer me to call on you this week or next?

Example 7
Buyer tells receptionist to tell seller that she is not in.
Seller: [Believing that the buyer is in and is making an excuse should say to the receptionist] 'As I am not a magician I cannot say whether your boss is in or not. I have to take your word for it because you look so honest. Now assuming you were a priest/nun which you resemble so much, and the head priest/nun of your order asked you where your boss was, would you still say the same as you told me, i.e. not in? [The answer to this should be yes, as you wouldn't expect a priest or nun to tell a lie.] The next quick question I would like to ask you is "what is the easiest way that I can make contact with an important person like your boss?" [To this the receptionist should reveal how the boss may be contacted as the seller would have won over the receptionist on to his or her side through subtle manipulation. If the receptionist doesn't want to play the seller's game, it could mean they are shy or have a dislike for religious matters, or that they have been forced to tell a lie to protect their job]. Another strategy is: 'Your boss may have been the winner of my company's special prize or may like to take advantage of a very special offer [something genuine and currently made available to buyers as part of a sales promotion]. Would you therefore please make an appointment for me to discuss this important matter with him or her please?' [Do press forward regardless until the appointment is given – **Who Dares Sells!**]

Irrational Objections

An irrational objection is based on some notion or preconceived idea that is idiosyncratic in nature or personal to the buyer, caused by an unusual prejudiced or abnormal attitude.

Example 1

Buyer: Can you supply this product to me in purple with a sprinkling of gold dust? [The buyer states an unusual colour preference after the seller has informed the buyer that there are only three standard colours available.]

Seller: That is certainly an unusual choice but I guess a nice one [make sure you do not ridicule the buyer's choice]. Now, if I can get you a model custom-made to your specifications, would you have it? [The answer to which will be Yes]. But if I try my best for you and still cannot come up with this special, which of the other three colours would you have, red, blue or white?

Example 2

Buyer: I know more about my business than you do, I don't think you can help me.

Seller: So what you are saying to me is that you are the Einstein of your business, and I am the Newton of mine. I can assure you that I have a lot to offer your business to make it prosper even further. So rather than you minding your own business and me minding mine let us pool our individual resources for mutual benefit – if you are the coffee then I am the cream, together we will make a good cup!

Example 3

Buyer: I am not interested in your offer. (Without even caring to look at the proposal.)

Seller: You come across as a very intelligent person, but I am puzzled as to how you came to this conclusion without even evaluating my offer. If I sent you a gift in an envelope addressed to you stating that it included something special from me to you would you dump it without opening it first? Of course you wouldn't! So how could you come to a conclusion without carefully looking at the pros and cons of my offer which has benefitted numerous other people like yourself. I would appreciate the opportunity to discuss it with you. When would be convenient?

Example 4

Buyer: All you salespeople are the same.

Seller: You may as well say that all cars are the same, which in one sense is right in that all cars transport you from one place to another. But apart from that we know that cars can be as different from each other as a cat is from a tiger. I pride myself on being one of the best in my field, and am a bit upset that you have tarred us all with the same brush. I knew of another buyer who, I must admit, was ten times worse than you because he never listened to any salesperson. Sadly he and his business disappeared into oblivion and today he drives a taxi for a living; but if I were to compare you with him, you come out with flying colours, you are prime minister: when can we have our cabinet meeting, tomorrow or the day after?

Example 5

Buyer: [to a life assurance salesperson] I don't think it is necessary for me to insure myself. I have managed for so long without any problems. Nothing is going to happen to me. I can look after myself if anything goes wrong, and if I die who cares what happens after death? My wife has a good job and she will have my house, and my mother-in-law can continue looking after the children.

Seller: So what you are saying to me is that you have no need for my offer. [The buyer answers Yes to this question.] Now suppose I were to come and offer you a cheque for $60,000, saying you were nominated for it by someone without your knowledge and had won it as a prize, you would be pleased, surprised and possibly suspicious. However, my line of business as a life assurance consultant is not based on a game of luck but is played on the real life table of statistics, which I have here in front of me and it clearly shows that for you as an overweight male of 47 years, smoking 40 cigarettes a day, your chances of living up to the age of seventy are reduced dramatically. But as I am a person that respects human life I can give you my honest, friendly advice which you can either take or leave: give up your smoking, reduce your weight, switch to healthier food and take a little exercise and if you invest with me your money that is going in smoke you would have made the right decision to secure for yourself a nice little nest egg of health, happiness and financial security with a cheque for $60,000 at the age of seventy, if you live that long and when you need it most. And in the event of you not living to see the day, you would have provided financial security for your wife and children. Let us fill in the application for a medical, to check on your suitability at our expense. Your doctor's name is?

[This method can be modified to suit different kinds of buyers and their circumstances, bearing in mind if you cannot sell to the *need* then sell to the *greed*.

Example 6

Buyer: People do not eat ice cream in winter, so it is not the right time for us to make a purchase of your product.

Seller: I do agree that it would be more difficult to sell ice cream in winter, although if you go into most cafés or restaurants in the height of winter you could get yourself an ice cream. But if you take a stock of my product now, I could offer you a very good price on it so that when your peak selling period starts in summer I will be able more or less or maintain the prices even if there is a price increase by then, so you will benefit by making more profit later. Incidentally many people purchase the following year's Christmas cards at around half or quarter the usual price at the end of previous year's Christmas season, thereby saving money and safeguardings against prices increases. That is what you can do for yourself through me by giving me your order at a reduced price. Shall I put you down for 20 units or 10?

Example 7

Buyer: That type of product, service or idea is good for restaurants or estate agents [or whatever it is], but we are builders' merchants [or whatever they are] and it is no good to us.

Seller: How did you come to that conclusion? Are you saying that you are some alien organization working on a different set of business principles from the rest? Come, come, what is sauce for the goose is sauce for the gander. If other businesses are saving money or making it with this product, service or idea, why shouldn't you? You can, if you will start to use it and I am committed to showing you how, and that is my promise when this product, service or idea comes into operation for you in two weeks time. Can you OK this paperwork for me so that I can get everything sorted out for you without any further delay?

Example 8

Buyer: You are wasting your time trying to sell to me; why not try selling to someone else?

Seller: My job is to make contact with people like yourself to offer you the opportunity to improve your circumstances financially or otherwise. To do this I get paid by my company, so you certainly would not be wasting my time. On the other hand if I can offer you my product, service or idea that is going to benefit you not just financially, but in many other ways, then I couldn't be wasting your time. So let's both of us not waste any more time and get down to discussing how I can help you achieve just that!

Example 9

Buyer: You are annoying me.

Seller: I am sorry if you think like that. I never had the slightest intention of upsetting you in any way, so before you throw me out I am going to pack my bags and go, and while I am doing that [physically show the buyer you are doing it], I would like to ask in what way have I annoyed you? [Wait for the buyer to give you the reason, answer it and then get back to selling or make a fresh appointment to go back again when the buyer has cooled down.]

Example 10

Buyer: Goodbye [even before the seller has started].

Seller: Is that the way you deal with all sales people or is it just me that you have singled out to be awkward with? I must say in all my selling encounters this is one of the most outrageous things that anyone has done to me. May I ask you why you have said this to me? [Wait for the reply, answer it, terminate the interview by telling the buyer you are not in the right frame of mind to continue as you are upset at their remarks, pack your bags and then make a new appointment]. Goodbye, I will see you again on *day, date and time.* [You now have control of the situation.]

Example 11
Buyer: No [just after the seller has started].
Seller: No what? No good? No money? No time? I don't understand you, can you please explain what do you really mean and I will see if I can help you out. [Wait for the buyer to explain, and once you have determined the reason for the buyer's hot-headedness then you can smooth it over and continue with the selling.]

Hidden Objections

Hidden objections are objections which are in the buyer's mind but not directly revealed. They come out camouflaged as a different expression.

Example 1
Buyer: I am not sure that your product, service or idea will suit my application.
Seller: That statement of yours has intrigued me and got me trying to figure out whether I am in the right job with all the confidence, extensive training and experience I have at my finger tips on my product, service or idea. Alternatively, perhaps you may have got it wrong because if you are in doubt now I don't think you ever will be sure about it. Let me clear up any doubts or fears you may have. What exactly is bothering you?

Example 2
Buyer: I would like to give your offer some serious consideration.
Seller: From what you have just said it appears that there is something of concern to you. Has it got anything to do with the product, service or idea, or possibly finance, or are you in any way unhappy with my style of selling? Please let me know as I cannot help you resolve these matters if you keep me in the dark; I am not a mushroom!

Example 3
Buyer: You are not the only one selling this product, service or idea, I can get it through a friend who works for one of your competitors.

Seller: Sure, the world is full of people trying to make a living at selling. A small group are good at it. A slightly larger group are fairly good at it, and by far the vast majority are useless at it. On the other extreme, you have a handful of people who are top class and treat their business as a profession. I happen to fall into that last category, as you may have gathered by now. So, having said that and without wasting both of our time, who would you like to deal with? [If the buyer says you, then you are in. If the buyer chooses the friend you can go on to explain that if there were any problems that cropped up after the product, service or idea was purchased and repeatedly had to run after his friend to iron them out, feelings could get strained and h/she could not only lose a friend as a result but could also end up in court to sue the competitor, which could all be avoided by dealing with you.]

Example 4

Buyer: Before I commit myself, let me see how your product, service or idea proves itself; after all it has only recently been introduced.

Seller: I can appreciate your concern but I feel that you may be a little over-anxious. What you have to bear in mind is that this concept has been very carefully researched and meticulously put together and you can be assured that we would not take any chances by releasing it for sale to the public. I can supply you with many names of satisfied customers who are already using and are extremely happy with it. That being the situation, how much longer do you want to wait to enjoy the benefits that others like yourself are already gaining from my product, service or idea?

Example 5

Buyer: I have some good reasons why I do not want to go ahead at present.

Seller: Good, don't go ahead if you have got good reasons for not wanting to, I wouldn't either if there were valid reasons for me not to go ahead. But I must admit I do not know of any major drawbacks, except for a few minor ones I have discovered myself of no real significance, and come to think of it, no product, service or idea is completely faultless. The excellent benefits you will enjoy far outweigh the drawbacks. In order that I may know where our thinking differs and that I may clear up any doubts you have on the so-called disadvantages as opposed to the numerous advantages, what is it that is concerning you?

Example 6
Buyer: I will talk to my bank manager or accountant about it.
Seller: That's fine with me. If they are authorising the finance of course you would need to get their advice, but it does not mean that your bank manager or accountant is a specialist in my product, service or idea. If you want to get your hair done you see your hairdresser, not your bank manager or accountant. So that you may stand the best chance of getting the finance approved, for which your advisers would want a comprehensive cost justification and which I would be only too pleased to provide, why not let me also come with you on this important meeting, after which I will be pleased to treat you and your bank manager to a hearty lunch?

Example 7
Buyer: Either you supply your product, service or idea to us or to our competitors, but you can't do it to both.
Seller: In a democratic country people can choose where and to whom they sell. While I appreciate that there exists some natural, healthy competitive rivalry it is in my interest and yours that I do not divulge any of the secrets of my dealings with you to your competitors, which I solemnly promise to observe as long as you realize and acknowledge that I am in business to offer my products, services or ideas to any company or individual that needs and is willing to pay for them. So, having given you my promise let us ignore the competition and concentrate on how I can help you better your circumstances.

Example 8
Buyer: I would like to think about it.
Seller: I have the greatest of admiration for thinkers. This means that you are genuinely interested in my offer; but there are a few loose ends that need tying up and I would like to assist you to the best of my ability with all the right answers to the questions you have, and have not mentioned, to help you come to the right

decision. To enable me to do this may I ask you what is really of concern to you?

Rational Objections

Rational objections are based on genuine fears, doubts, requests for further information or clarification. They are the easiest of all objections to deal with.

Example 1
Buyer: It costs too much
or: You are too expensive, I can buy it cheaper elsewhere.
Seller: What makes you say that? Can't you see the savings and how the product, service or idea will pay for itself in a few months? Maybe I have not explained it very clearly to you. Let me go through it once again, Rome was not built in a day!

You then go through a step-by-step cost justification sequence with the buyer. Or:

- Promptly pull out from your portfolio (which you must keep ready as part of your contingency measures), at the appropriate time, the writing of John Ruskin (1819-1900) on VALUE, show it to the buyer and keep silent.

Value
'It's unwise to pay too much, but it's unwise to pay too little. When you pay too much you lose a little money, that is all. When you pay too little, you sometimes lose everything, because the thing you bought was incapable of doing the thing you bought it to do.

The common law of business balance prohibits paying a little and getting a lot. It can't be done.

If you deal with the lowest bidder, it's well to add something for the risk you run. And if you do that, you will have enough to pay for something better.

- Or tell the buyer, 'I am aware in practically every area of life you could probably find a cheaper alternative, but don't forget

that the bitterness of poor workmanship remains long after the sweetness of low price is forgotten.'
● Or say, 'A person who buys an expensive product and spends a lot of money cries only once, but a person who buys a cheap product and spends a little money cries often!'

Example 2

Buyer: Can you better your price?
Seller: Why do you want me to put the price down? Are you not satisfied with the value for money you are getting with my asking price? Let me summarize the benefits that you will be getting for that price.

Do it and wait for the reply, as the buyer may concede to paying the asking price. However, if the buyer is not willing to change the demand for a cut in price then start to negotiate:

Suppose I were to cut the price, what sort of figure would you have in mind? [If the figure mentioned by the buyer is agreeable to the seller then the deal may be closed, but if the figure is not acceptable then the seller must negotiate further with the buyer for a mutually acceptable price].

Example 3

Buyer: I am not convinced that the product will last that long.
Seller: You appear to have some clairvoyant qualities about you. Our existing customers are well pleased at the service they have so far had from this product which has gone well past the period we anticipated for it. There are some statements to prove it. Doesn't that track record speak for itself? When do you want to start using it?

Example 4

Buyer: I am too busy.
Seller: That's good, it means you are making money and it tells me you can afford my product, service or idea, but we do need to discuss it in detail. Shall I see you at the end of this week or early next week to discuss the important benefits of my offer, which has received rave reviews and which could be of immense value to your organization?

Example 5

Buyer: It's too big/It's too small.

Seller: What you are saying is that you are concerned about finding a space for it, isn't that so? This question tests whether the buyer is concerned about where the product will best fit into their environment. So what the seller should do is then follow on. Let's see where we can fit it. I reckon that corner is the most convenient location for it. Where would you like to see it positioned, on the table or behind that filing cabinet?

Example 6

Buyer: I do not want to change, I am happy with what I already have.

Seller: That's fine, I do not expect you to change unless you change for the better. As I have clearly shown you that my offer has distinct advantages over your existing system, that in itself is a good reason to change. I understand your apprehension about change. I too would have felt the same if I was in your position and got used to something, but if you do not make the decision to change for the better now, in three, six, nine months time and so on, where would you be?

Example 7

Buyer: I would like to check out a few more facts before I make my decision; you cannot expect me to make up my mind immediately.

Seller: Go right ahead and do just that, I do not expect you to buy gold bars in a bag without looking inside the bag. You are on the right track, and I am right behind you to answer any legitimate and bona fide questions you may have. Let us start the mastermind question and answer session on my product, service or idea right now. You ask the questions and I will answer them. Now what is your first question?

Example 8

Buyer: I have read some bad reports about your product/service in the trade press.

Seller: Well, paper never refuses ink. If some journalists have nothing else to do but spend their time trying to write adverse reports based on hearsay to make news it does not mean that they are right. The press is often full of such stories which are later discredited. The only people who are in a position to criticize are people who are qualified in terms of specialist knowledge and experience, and on that score I can reassure you that you are welcome to bring any known expert whom you wish to nominate to test the product. But they won't have an easy ride when they try to tear down my product or service, which is as good as any in the market place and even better than most. If you have any doubts about it please put forward your fears to me now, or let's change the subject once and for all to when you want to start using it.

Example 9
Buyer: Your delivery schedule (or something else) does not impress me.
Seller: If what we have to offer does not impress you, then what would impress you? [Wait until the buyer answers and reveals what you have to do to get the business, and then say:] If I can do that for you, are we in business?

Example 10
Buyer: We used your product, service or idea before and it gave us a lot of trouble. No amount of reassurance will convince me to change my mind.
Seller: I am troubled to hear you say that and am sorry if you suffered any inconvenience. If you will permit me to look into your predicament in a bit more detail I will endeavour to establish if there was any error on our part. If there were any shortcomings I will seek to remedy them immediately, under no obligation on your part, and give you my renewed pledge to look after your interests from then on to the best of my ability. Now, how does that sound?

Example 11
Buyer: I have decided I am not going ahead.
Seller: You mean that you are not going ahead now but you will take it later. Will that be in a month's time or will it be more like in two months' time? [Wait until the buyer answers. If the

buyer answers Yes, everything is fine. If the buyer answers Maybe, try to uncover the hidden objection, answer it and then get the buyer to commit to an exact date. If the buyer is adamant that he doesn't want the product, service or idea, then revert back to open-ended proving to get feedback to determine why he is reluctant to pursue the offer. Then follow on with specific probes to tie the buyer down to a firm Yes.]

Example 12
Buyer: I am giving you five minutes to tell me all about it.
Seller: It looks as if you are in a terrible hurry to get away and I don't think it is fair on my part to keep you away from whatever you have to attend to. What I will do in four minutes is I will give you the bare bones of my product, service or idea and call later to fill in the finer detail. Now do you want me to do a cat's lick of a job now and call back later when you have more time, or make a fresh appointment for a more meaningful discussion?

In the above examples of objection-handling techniques, and the following closing strategies, I have only given one suggestion for each situation, and obviously you would not have to use these exact words, but about those which come naturally to you. There are literally hundreds of other ways you could overcome objections and then close a sale. I do hope this gives you a starting point for developing your own creative approaches.

WHEN AND HOW TO CLOSE SALES

Immediately after an objection has been handled, the professional salesperson instinctively closes, for otherwise the sale would be lost. So, what is closing?

Closing is getting a commitment from a buyer, or a decision to purchase. Without a commitment from the buyer to see the seller again or to do something specific towards an interim or final decision towards a purchase, no matter how good the seller's demonstration or presentation is, it would be a fruitless exercise for both buyer and seller – neither side would have benefited. The buyer would be without the product, service or idea from which she could gain increased benefit, and the seller would be left with no sale, revenue or profit. To cap it all, both parties would have jointly wasted precious time.

So how could this be avoided, and what needs to be done? The answer is that closing must become a way of life for the salesperson – a second nature. You are paid to close. You keep your employers and yourselves in business by closing. These are the hard facts of the selling business. If you are in the selling profession and think otherwise, do yourself, your employer and your buyer the biggest favour – get out of selling, you are a complete misfit in the profession, you are like a square peg in a round hole!

Closing must be as vital to selling as breathing is to life itself. It must be done as naturally as opening your bowels and without strain, or you could hurt yourself. Those with verbal diarrhoea who close too soon, cannot control themselves and let it go all over the place, causing embarrassment to themselves and revulsion to others.

But the person who knows when to close and how to close is automatically going to be a winner. They will make the sale and help the buyer prosper. It is therefore a very beneficial thing that the seller does to the buyer by closing the sale.

No one can really tell the seller when to close, because no two sales are the same. The professional gets a gut feeling. It is intuitive. At the appropriate time when the buyer gives a buying signal, the professional confidently asks for the order. Depending on how good a selling job they have done, closing will be a logical conclusion to an emotionally made decision. It is as simple as that.

Some schools of thought propound the ABC theory, or Always Be Closing. Research has shown, however, that closing prematurely or too late are both fatal in selling. There is an appropriate time to close and it is at that precise moment, based on the seller's knowledge, skill and experience that closing must be attempted. Let's go back to the fishing analogy. If you tug too hard when the fish makes an initial grab you could break the line, if you give the line too much slack there is a good chance of the fish working itself free and getting away.

All top class sales professionals are the same animal. They are all predators, whichever way they disguise themselves, although they can appear quite harmless. The fact is that they are lean, mean and hungry salespeople. They are closers. Born a leopard, they can never be a cat – leopards never change their spots!

Some sales can be transacted quickly and sharply while others take much longer. Closing may also mean getting a series of minor commitments, over a prolonged period of time leading to the final Yes. The more complex a product, service or idea is the greater the likelihood that it will take longer for the sale to be concluded.

I have witnessed high pressure double glazing and life assurance salespeople spend all night badgering buyers in their own homes with devastating closes, and finally through sheer physical and psychological exhaustion the buyer submits and gives the order just to get rid of the seller only to cancel it later on. This is a grave injustice to the buyer and gives a bad reputation to the profession of selling. It is for that reason that nowadays there are tighter legal controls in some developed countries and a 'cooling off period' to protect the buyer and provide them with an option to cancel. Do not use high pressure tactics – you cannot take a horse to the water and make it drink, but if you can make the horse thirsty and then show it water it will automatically drink!

This means that when selling professionally and ethically, where the seller has whetted the buyer's appetite and the buyer desires the product, service or idea, a good sale must naturally close itself. If the seller is upsetting the buyer by treading on his toes then she must know when to stop pushing or making a nuisance of herself. Once you damage a relationship, salvaging it can be difficult.

Canned closing

Many people used the canned (learnt verbatim) closing techniques without understanding the psychology of the sales process. This leaves the buyer annoyed with the seller for his lack of empathy and understanding. When closing is done in this manner the sales interview often ends in failure. Just think for a moment; how can you close a door properly unless the door hinges are working freely and smoothly and the top and bottom edges of the frame snugly fit against the door and it is

locked into position? That is the way closing should be looked
upon. Do not leave the buyer offended and with a bad taste in
the mouth.

I am going to give you some powerful revolutionary closes which
I recommend that you do not use parrot fashion, but rather grasp
the concepts and adapt them according to the selling situation.

There is a golden rule in selling introduced by the father of
American salesmanship, J. Douglas Edwards, which states:
*Whenever you ask a closing question from a buyer, you must stop
talking – remain dead silent.* Silence is top priority here. The first
person that talks loses! Sellers, take heed of the rule and always
bear it in mind when you are going for the close. Furthermore,
all closing questions must be asked in a manner so as to get a
Yes answer and it can be assumed that the more Yeses a seller
gets from the buyer the closer they are to making the sale. The
average sale is closed on the fifth request for the order. Also
remember that the initiative must be on the seller's side to close
and not the other way around. For those who are expecting
the sale to close itself, they stand a better chance of walking on
water.

The 'let's shake hands' close

This is the most powerful close I have ever used and I have tried
a great number. This close is suitable for any type of product,
service or idea anywhere in the world and it goes like this. When
you sense the buying signal simply put your hand out, reach for
the buyer's hand, smile and say the magic words, 'Can we shake
hands on this deal?' And shut up.

The buyer can only say three things. If the buyer says Yes start
writing out the order, confirmation or contract.

If the buyer says No treat it as an objection, and commute it
to No, because, in which case you handle that objection and
close again. 'Seeing I have provided you with a suitable
explanation, can we now shake hands?'

If the buyer says Maybe with an objection such as 'I want to
think about it' then your line of approach must be to get the
buyer to bring the hidden objection to the surface with an open-
ended probing question from the previous section. Wait for the
buyer to answer and then handle the objection if there is one,

and close again by repeating, 'As I have provided you with a reasonable explanation on the benefits of my product, service or idea, can we now shake hands on it?'

This is strong stuff.

The 'I like the white of your eyes but I prefer the colour of your cheques' close

This close may be used when you want to get a deposit from your buyer who is hesitating about parting with his money. You can try saying, 'It has been very enjoyable talking with you, but like all good things our discussion must now come to an end. And although I like the whites of your eyes I prefer the colour of your cheques! Would you care to give me half or a third of the total cost up front?'

The tossing of a coin close

This close must be used on the price-cutting buyer. You must first establish what the buyer is trying to beat you down to in relation to your asking price (the selling price). What you do is negotiate a price with the buyer, the lowest you are prepared to go down to, but do not give away your product, service or idea until the buyer gambles with you for that lowest price. You tell the buyer that as much as she is looking for a good deal you are also going to be as flexible as you can and like a sportsman play ball with her and try to get her the best deal going.

Tell the buyer that she is the Captain of her business and that you are the Captain of yours and even in sports like cricket and football captains toss a coin, and as part of the game you are going to do the same. If she wins then she can have the offer at the lowest fixed price, but if you win then she must give you your asking (right) price. You can be sure that quite a lot of people will toss for the sake of the challenge.

The 'Don't take the goose, take the golden egg' close

This is a close which is very effective against a buyer who is not just trying to get a good deal but is trying to take all the meat and leave you scraps or just the bare bones. This is the buyer who is trying to grab everything. What you do is say, 'I understand you want a good deal, but please don't take the whole goose, take the golden egg; for if you grab too much and go for the kill you will end up with neither.'

The 'I like to be associated with winners' close

When a buyer says, 'I am doing well and I don't need your product, service or idea', the seller replies, 'I am glad you are doing well, that is what business is all about. I love to be associated with winners but in business one can never foretell the future. You may be aware of the four stages of the trade cycle: Boom, Recession, Depression and Recovery. The time for you to invest in something good like my product, service or idea is when you are doing well. It's like an insurance policy. Even looking at it from the worst angle it is better for you to have insurance and not need it than to need it and not have it, which means that it has immediate benefit of protecting you as soon as you put the policy into operation! Looking at it from another point of view I can also say that the best time for you to stop smoking, take physical exercise and eat wholesome food is when you are fit and well. You don't want to get a heart attack to start a fitness programme, do you?'

The 'asking a question with another question' close

Here you ask a question called a verbal lock. Verbal locks are as follows: aren't you, can't you, don't you, won't you, shouldn't you, mustn't you, isn't it, wouldn't it, wasn't it, couldn't it, shouldn't it, doesn't it? The technique you use goes like this. If you are trying to get the buyer to go ahead on a proposal, you make a statement, then pop the question with a verbal lock like this:

- 'You do want to go ahead on this proposal, don't you?'
- 'Before your competitors get ahead of you with increased production and sales I presume you would want to have the competitive edge by having this equipment installed?'
- 'This motor car's roadholding is superb, isn't it?'
- 'In the event of anything happening to you as the breadwinner in your family, you should have protected all your dependants so that they may have the same standard of living they are accustomed to, shouldn't you?'

Do not forget always to phrase your questions in such a way that it will elicit a Yes reply from the buyer.

The 'Yes, No or Maybe' close

This close is exceptionally good for the buyer who is procrastinating. What you do in this situation is to come out openly and ask the buyer, 'Rather than troubling you or myself any further, I would like you to give me a definite decision on my product, service or idea. I would greatly appreciate if you will tell me it is a Yes, No or Maybe to my offer.' If the buyer says Yes start writing out the order. If it is an outright No treat it as a rational objection and deal with it like this, i.e. instead of an outright No try to change the decision to a No Because. Then you can handle it easily by saying something like this to the buyer: 'So the reason why you are saying No is because of . . .? Wait for the reply, let the buyer state the reasons and then proceed to handle the objection and close the sale. If the buyer says Maybe, probe to find out the hidden objection, answer it and close the sale.

The 'may I ignore that if I can show you or prove to you, that my product, service or idea is of good merit or greater benefit' close

This is a close to be used on the buyer who brings out an objection that leaves the seller stumped for words. Tell her: 'May I ignore that if I can show you or prove to you that my offer is of good merit or greater benefit (compared with something else)?'

The 'Rolls Royces only run on supergrade petrol' close

This is a close you can use when the buyer brings out an objection suggesting what you have to offer is far too expensive. Come straight out and tell the buyer, 'You only get what you pay for – quality at the right price. Rolls Royces only run on four star petrol, so if you are looking for something cheap, I do not know why we are talking!'

The 'without petrol this luxury motor vehicle and chauffeur cannot move' close

This close is for the buyer who has decided to go ahead but is refusing to give you a deposit. Tell the buyer that you are there to provide her with a personalized service by offering her your first class product, service or idea. It is like having a luxury motor vehicle with chauffeur at their beck and call parked in front of the doorway ready to take her wherever she wants to go but, unless they put in the petrol (provide the money) you cannot move.

The 'Please correct me if you think I am wrong' close

This close is a deliberate attempt by the seller to make the buyer (mainly the negative buyer) correct the seller's erroneous statement and in doing so the buyer makes a positive decision in the seller's favour. What the seller does here is to make negative statements, so negative in fact that the negative buyer himself feels that they are so ridiculous that he corrects them by making a positive statement.

For example, in a live presentation or demonstration situation the seller points out several positive characteristics enthusiastically about the product, service or idea which the buyer has been negating right throughout the sales interview. When the seller realizes the buyer's attitude it is time to change tactics. The seller should say something like this, 'Am I right in saying that by your wanting high speed franking impressions from this mailing machine you do not want to save time?' or, 'I presume, as you have been contradicting all my arguments about saving money with this system, on the question of being able to select the exact value of the postage as opposed to putting on too many stamps for the corresponding weight of the item, together with all the other economical features I have advanced to you so far, it is not what you require and I guess the word profit must be a dirty word for you, isn't that so?'

The 'you have squeezed all the juice out of me' close

This is a close you can use when there is no more you can give and you have gone as far as you can on price, delivery, after sales, and so on. Just tell the buyer, 'You have squeezed all the juice out of me, I can't go any further. May I put you down for X amount or Y amount?'

The 'everything I touch turns to gold, but everytime I try to touch you it looks as if it is going to cost me money' close

This is a close you may use if other attempts to get the buyer to make the purchase on your terms are failing and the buyer is really trying to nail you down to the floor boards. Smile and say, 'I must be doing something dreadfully wrong or else we would have concluded this deal a long time ago. You know, everything I touch turns to gold, but everytime I try to touch you it looks as if it is going to cost me money. Please don't be too brutal on me – we both have to eat, you know!'

The 'you have long pockets and short hands' close

This is a close that is used on a buyer that is not just trying to cut the price but is attempting to get a freebie. Laugh and tell the buyer, 'That was a good try. I now realize you have long pockets and a short hand! You are trying to do the salesman on the salesman, aren't you? I like your style but sadly you have picked the wrong person. Do your homework next time. I am not as green as I look! You are playing the business game to win, aren't you? I am here to try and help you win, so please don't do the naughty on me. If I quit it could end up in tragedy for you. So let's be sensible about it and share the loot together. You meet me half way on the price and I will meet you half way too. Now, isn't that fair?'

The mind over matter close

This close, like the Yes, No or Maybe close is good for a buyer who is beating around the bush, but it is a more powerful close.

When the buyer is procrastinating about making a decision after a demonstration or presentation, the seller can say something like this: 'I can see you are having difficulty coming to a decision. Everything in the final analysis boils down to mind over matter. Let me give you a helping hand to make the right decision. Without prolonging this issue any further, it appears to me that you wouldn't mind if I were to get moving on this matter and have this product, service or idea working for you as soon as possible. Let me complete the agreement. Your surname and initials are?'

If the buyer stops you, it means there is a hidden objection in the way preventing you from making the sale. Smoke it out. Handle it and close again.

If she doesn't stop you, get the contract or order details completed and get out as fast as you can.

In this section I have deliberately omitted the more elementary and commonly used types of closes such as the Alternative Choice, Benjamin Franklin, Half Nelson, Order Blank and so on, which are well known among salespeople. Any person who wishes to learn more about these and the more advanced closes not mentioned are welcome to contact me.

So to close this section, may I say to all you sellers out there in the big wide world of selling, *The thing to remember is be once, twice, thrice, four times and five times a closer and you are well on your way to Sales and Financial Success.*

106 Reasons Why Sales Are Lost

This checklist is very important; read it carefully.

1. Lack of punctuality
2. Misrepresentation (deception and blatantly lying)
3. Lack of empathy
4. Monopolizing the conversation
5. Bad planning, pre-call preparation and research
6. Lack of knowledge of own product and competitive products
7. Ridiculing the buyer
8. Talking in terms of features rather than benefits, i.e. concentrating on what your product, service or idea is, rather than what it will do for the buyer
9. Inability to close
10. Lack of enthusiasm and not smiling
11. Inability to handle objections
12. Arguing with the buyer
13. Lack of knowledge of own and competitive company policy, procedures and people
14. Thinking and talking negatively
15. Wrongly channelled aggression: raising voice and talking in a haphazard

fashion rather than in a businesslike manner with a clearcut business objective

16. Inability to keep a promise

17. Lack of self knowledge

18. Not knowing when to stop talking

19. Lack of general business knowledge – financial, legal, marketing

20. Being unprofessional and unethical

21. Using a 'canned' sales presentation

22. Inability to think creatively

23. Inability to control temper and keep cool

24. Denigrating and underestimating the competition

25. Being too friendly, or forgetting to send a greeting card during the festive season or a special occasion, or providing the occasional treat or gift as a token of goodwill or appreciation

26. Part-time effort

27. Inappropriately dressed for the occasion

28. Lack of concentration

29. Inability to persuade, motivate, manipulate and negotiate

30. Using high-pressure tactics

31. Wasting your buyer's time and your own by rambling on after the sale has been made, thereby creating an opportunity to talk your buyer out of the sale

32. Inability to modulate voice

33. Low activity level

34. Guessing

35. Insincerity

36. Fear

37. Poor written communication

38. Poor product image

39. Poor personal hygiene

40. Trying to be too clever

41. Inability to create desire

42. Making wild claims or exaggerations

43. Poor telephone manner and technique

44. Inability to grab the buyer's attention

45. Inability to develop interest

46. Poor personality and personal grooming

47. Not articulate enough

48. Talking in terms of self rather than the buyer, and

not using the YWI formula:

Y = You the buyer (first)
W = We, i.e. You the buyer (first) and Me the seller (second)
I = I the seller (last)

49. Lack of belief in product
50. Boasting, bragging
51. Lack of knowledge of the business
52. Overpriced or underpriced product
53. Lack of patience
54. Carrying on regardless when the best thing to have done would be to reschedule the meeting
55. Behaving immaturely
56. Inability to understand non-verbal communication
57. Lack of confidence in yourself, product, idea, service or company
58. Selling when either your own or your buyer's health is poor
59. Lack of optimism
60. Poor approach, timidity
61. Intimidating the buyer, being too aggressive or violent
62. Poor selling technique
63. Lack of experience
64. Poor self image
65. Inconsistent selling effort
66. Not keeping pace with new developments in your field
67. Inability to probe
68. Worry caused by personal, domestic or business problems
69. Poor listener
70. Bad reputation
71. Lack of publicity
72. Talking too fast or too slowly
73. Inability to maintain eye contact
74. Giving the buyer more information than is required to make a decision
75. Extraneous noises
76. Trying to serve two or more competing clients
77. Showing a political or a religious bias
78. Being too persistent and pushing the buyer too hard
79. Selling equipment and portfolio not in a good and presentable condition
80. Overtiredness
81. Not keeping customer records

82. Poor memory
83. Inability to think logically
84. Inability to handle complaints
85. Being too emotional
86. Not seeing sufficient people
87. Procrastinating
88. Bad territory management
89. Talking to non-decision makers
90. Not knowing why people buy
91. Being inflexible
92. Not knowing how to deal with different types of buyer
93. Lack of persistence
94. Not being courteous or being ill-mannered
95. Not knowing how to identify a need or create a need
96. Inability to read a buying signal
97. Lack of determined effort
98. Not prepared to go out of your way to be of assistance
99. Having prejudices
100. Lack of love
101. Living in a make believe world rather than in reality
102. Jumping to the wrong conclusion
103. Having self pity
104. Lack of discipline
105. Inability to adapt to changing situations
106. Inability to function under stress

Successful Selling by Telephone

The marvellous telephone exists for business and for pleasure. It is a valuable tool you must learn how to use and to treasure! The telephone is one of the most fantastic money-making business tools ever to be invented, but in order to make it profitable for you it must be handled with care.

Ever since its invention in 1876 by Alexander Graham Bell, the telephone has remained an indispensible and time saving device to business people all over the world, providing them with an open ticket to create success for themselves, their companies and their countries by trading locally, nationally and internationally.

Though the telephone gives business people limitless opportunities to create wealth, unless that little electro-mechanical device is kept under strict control it can either make or break you in the business scenario.

Today you can have the whole world in the palm of your hand with your telephone. The telephone has contributed immensely towards civilization and progress in the twentieth century. You can brighten up your life or sort out a worrying problem by calling your family or friends or an expert on the telephone. A life could be saved or lost as much as business could be saved or lost depending whether there is access to a telephone and our ability to communicate through it to the right people, at the right place, at the right time, in the right manner!

Modern civilization, progress and business would come to a grinding halt without the telephone. Let us now focus on some of the important functions your telephone can perform in the buying and selling arena.

The main uses of the telephone for business and pleasure

- To make appointments (prospecting).
- To confirm appointments.
- Pre-call research.
- To take an order (incoming).
- To place an order (outgoing).
- To communicate internally or externally for business, pleasure and in an emergency.
- To receive messages through a telephone receptionist, answering machine, telephone bureau.
- To send a telex through a computer or a facsimile through a fax machine linked to a telephone system.
- To operate a local, regional, national or international telephone sales campaign.
- To gain access to information.
- To operate a debt collection service.
- To train other telesales people.
- To assess changes in attitude.
- To gain rapid feedback.
- To save time, money and effort travelling several miles to be

present at a meeting when it could be discussed on the telephone.

- To advertise through a pre-recorded message played on a telephone answering machine.
- To sell products (e.g. consumer repeatables), services (e.g. advertising) or ideas (e.g. educational material) by tele-salespeople.
- To buy products, services or ideas such as:
  - Dial-your-pizza
  - Dial-your-minicab
  - Dial-your-plumber
  - Dial-your-electrician
  - Dial-your-emergency services
  - Dial-your-medical knowledge
- To avoid face-to-face contact.
- To handle complaints.

Unless you have a system of measuring the duration and cost, and a method of recording the message, it is difficult to monitor your performance and improve on it. There is no fully comprehensive system that I know that does all of these things together, but there are one or two effective products available with limitations for this purpose.

Over-indulgence on the telephone can erode a business's profits severely and could even threaten its survival if there are not sufficient sales. Furthermore, if you do not make your calls *short and sweet* you cannot call as many people as it would be necessary to arrange the required number of appointments to make demonstrations or presentations to close sales. Make no mistake, achieving good selling results for most types of products, services or ideas is often a numbers game, unless you are highly trained and an experienced individual who through sheer exposure to different types of selling situations knows what to do and how to do it as quickly as possible!

The more people the seller is seeing and selling to, the more results statistically will be made.

Because of the basic in born dislike many salespeople have of telephone selling, to help you motivate yourself to use your

phone more enthusiastically here is a bit of business thinking
well known in selling circles.

In one hour (60 mins) you make 25 calls
Out of 25 calls you establish 20 contacts (prospective buyers)
Out of 20 contacts you make 5 appointments
Out of 5 appointments you make 1 sale (by closing the sale
you have converted a prospective buyer into a buyer)
Let us say that the sales value of this sale you made was £100
i.e. 20 contacts produced £100
Each contact is worth $\frac{£100}{20} = £5$

Also, it took 25 calls to produce £100
Each call is worth $\frac{£100}{25} = £4$

What this analysis means is that you can look at the telephone
selling process in a positive light no matter how many people
you call and who refuse your offer. Someone will buy, so you
must carry on dialling regardless. Even an unemployed person
looking for a job can use this analogy to find themselves one.
However to continue dialling and have people slam the
telephone down on you because of bad telephone selling manner
indicates that there is something disastrously wrong with your
technique.

Before we have a look at some of the causes of your failure,
just suppose someone has slammed the phone down on you,
catching you unawares and leaving you shattered. How do you
deal with it? You should call back immediately and say sorry
you got cut off and apologize for having left the prospective buyer
angry about your call, which you are now going to put right. Then
shoot straight into your sales talk by saying, 'Tell me, how did
you come to that conclusion about my product, service or idea?'
Then wait for the reply and go on from there.

Reasons for telesales failures

● Not using the Attention, Interest, Desire and Action formula
(AIDA).
● Lack of clear-cut objectives and pre-call preparation.

- Sticking to a 'canned' sales presentation and not being creative.
- Not persuading, motivating, manipulating and negotiating when it is required.
- Not listening.
- Trying to sell on the phone. This must be positively avoided on a first-time call. Sell the appointment only.
- Lack of product, service, idea, self, competitive and customer knowledge.
- Spending too much time on the telephone, particularly on a cold call. The amount of time a person should spend on such a call should not exceed six minutes, but on average up to three minutes should be more than adequate to make the appointment.
- Not smiling while talking (Dial-a-smile).
- Distractions at the buyer's or seller's end.
- Negative approach.
- Trying to do too many things at the same time while on the phone.
- Not modulating the voice.
- Not taking control of the conversation.
- Not being polite and courteous.
- Not speaking to the decision maker.
- Not probing properly.

I have covered some of the important closing techniques under the section on Closing previously and what I am going to give you here are three different techniques to gain an appointment on a cold call to pave the way for the seller to sell a product, service or idea.

Example 1
You are trying to make an appointment to sell a product, a motor car make X, to a prospective buyer, who is currently using a competitive make Y.
'Good morning, my name is Ellis, Patrick Ellis from the Reliability Motor Company, and may I ask to whom I am talking?' or you could say, 'Your name is?'
  The prospect replies, 'Mr Jones.'

You reply, 'Thank you Mr Jones. Now before I proceed any further is it convenient for me to talk to you now?'

The prospect replies: 'Go ahead.'

You reply, 'Thank you Mr Jones. I understand you are using a motor car make Y, is that right?'

Your prospect replies, 'Yes, that is correct.'

You reply, 'For how long, may I ask?'

Your prospect replies, 'For two and a half years.'

You reply, 'I understand that you change your motor vehicle every three years, isn't that so?'

Your prospect replies, 'That is correct.'

You reply, 'The make of car you currently own is a fine one [always remember not to denigrate the competition], and the chances are that you may want to re-order the same make and model with some additional extras, that's natural – I would be inclined to do the same if I was in your position.

'As you are considering changing your vehicle, Mr Jones, what I would like to do is to give you an opportunity to view, under no obligation, a competitive make and model on the market which is my company's newest car X, which compares exceptionally well with your make and model car Y on both price and quality.

'It also has many luxury extras fitted at no extra charge. But, above all my company is offering a superb trade-in discount which I am sure you will find hard to resist. Would you like to view it at your home at 5.30pm today or would you prefer to see it at our showroom at 6.30pm tomorrow?'

Example 2
You are trying to make an appointment with a middle aged single woman to try and sell her a savings plan including life assurance cover.

'Hello Miss Smith, this is Patrick Ellis calling from the XYZ life assurance company. Thank you for giving me the opportunity to explain how I may be of use to you. To see if I could be of help to you, save you precious time and give you the chance to plan your financial security for the future, I would like to ask you a couple of quick questions if I may.'

Your prospect replies, 'Yes, alright.'

You reply, 'Thank you for your cooperation. Do you currently have a savings plan with another company?' If Miss Smith replies 'Yes', you then say, 'Fine, which company are you with and what type of plan, may I ask?' Once you find out the name of the company and the type of plan that she has got, you then go on to say, 'That is a great company you are with and a fairly good policy too, however I must be honest and say that my plan has more advantages which I would like to show you, and there would be no pressure for you to change unless it would be for your betterment, is that fair?'

You then suggest an appointment to discuss face-to-face with her what you have to offer. If she agrees you close by making a firm time and date.

If Miss Smith had said she did not have a savings plan and did not want one, you can point out that her lack of interest is tantamount to turning down a gift of a thousand pounds. Mention you are going to be in her area the following week and you would welcome the opportunity of introducing her to a plan that has been specially designed for working people like herself. If you are tactful and friendly, persistent without being pushy, you should be able to secure an appointment in this way.

Example 3
You are trying to get an appointment with a company managing director to sell him a consultancy service.
To be successful by telephone and get the appointment, your plan of attack should be as follows:

1. Undertake pre-call research. Let us say that you discover that the decision-maker you are going to call is an awkward person to deal with.
2. Pluck up courage and dial the company. Use the AIDA formula already discussed.
3. A receptionist will probably try to deflect you by asking what you are calling in connection with. Give him or her your name, your company, and explain that you have something of importance to discuss with the decision-maker.
4. When you have been put through to the decision-maker again give your name and your company. Explain the purpose of

your call, which is to show him or her how you can increase their sales, profits, efficiency, or whatever it is.

5. Make sure that the person you are talking to is listening to your sales talk with interest. Give him or her information on your offer. Concentrate throughout on the benefits the buyer will enjoy.

6. After whetting their appetite, close by asking for an appointment to discuss the matter further. Remember, the purpose of your call is to secure an appointment, where you can then start selling face to face. If the response is No, handle the objection in the usual way, and close again and again until the appointment is made.

Do you have what it takes to be a busy bee?

A worker honey bee has to travel around 46,500 miles to make one pound in weight of honey.

MORAL

Work like a bee
Bee very busy
Bee your best
Sell Honey
Make Money!

CHAPTER 10

Neuro–Linguistic Programming: the fine art of communication excellence

Neuro-Linguistic Programming, or NLP, is one of the fastest growing and most exciting developments in the communications business. Getting acquainted with NLP can help to put you several strides ahead of the competition in the selling game.

What is NLP? It has been defined in several different ways, for example:

- a study of subjective experience
- a model of behaviour
- a thought and communication process
- a set of techniques to facilitate personal change and change in others
- a set of modelling skills

It originated in the early 1970's, when John Grinder, a linguist, and Richard Bandler, a mathematician, set out to model the common factors found in excellent communicators. The three people they studied were Fritz Perls, a gestalt therapist, Milton Erikson, a hypnotherapist, and Virginia Satir, a family therapist. They discovered that although these people were working in different fields, they were using a similar pattern of behaviour and language. What this meant that any form of human excellence could be modelled by emulating observable behaviour patterns.

On top of their respective knowledge of Linguistics and Mathematics, Grinder and Bandler delved into the disciplines of Neurology, Psychology and Computing.

NEURO = Our perceptions of the outside world are derived through our senses and nervous system.

LINGUISTIC = Our perceptions that are stored in the mind (memory) are coded, organized, recalled, transformed and transmitted primarily through the voice (language).

PROGRAMMING = Our knowledge and experience is made up of a series of programmes – programming the subconscious mind, or the human bio-computer.

Grinder and Bandler did their research looking for linguistic structure patterns, thinking the way people put words together in sentences would be the clue. There clearly was something there, a link to be found in the *syntax* of communication which has an impact on the way a communication is received and the way the communicator is thinking. For example, in English, 'The cat chased the rat' infers the same meaning as 'The rat was chased by the cat', produced by only a subtle shift in perceptual position of the speaker in the two statements. Of course, a simple repositioning of the words (syntax) without changing the words 'the cat chased the rat' or the 'rat chased the cat' profoundly alters the meaning. What we are talking about here is sequence of behaviour expressed in terms of pattern.

From their original work with language structures they concentrated on paying attention to non-verbal behaviour in terms of posture, gesture, breathing patterns, facial expressions, colour changes and then on to a model of what occurs when people think, because the behaviourists always said 'you can't look inside the black box (the mind), you can only measure observable behaviour', or external behaviour. The latest research seems to suggest that brain activity is analogous to a hologram in nature and has at least 12 dimensions. The hologram can recall thousands of different images on the same plate and any of the images can be reconstructed from any part of the plate. The human brain, being holographic in nature, is the most sophisticated information storing system on the planet.

This is probably a bit beyond what most of us can think about, so what Grinder and Bandler concluded was 'OK, we do not know what is going on inside the brain, but as modellers, we can construct a model that is useful, based on the way people think and speak. We can establish certain patterns of communication.'

How can NLP help in day to day communication? Some people tend to use expressions like 'I see what you mean', 'It looks to me', 'Can we focus in on' or 'The perspective is brightening up' – they use words that make reference to some kind of imagery or visual activity.

Others use words like 'I feel I am coming to grips with the situation', 'I am getting a handle on this', 'things are pretty rough', 'it's smoothing out', 'the pressure's on', 'it's coming through' and so on, suggesting some kind of feeling, or kinesthetic, ways of thinking and relating to the world, if you like by sorting their thinking according to the sense of feeling.

Yet others use words like 'tune into', 'listen', 'I hear you', suggesting auditory activity or thinking based on the sense of sound. Grinder and Bandler proposes that the language which people use indicates which senses are being processed internally. We have five senses: sight, sound, touch, taste and smell, but predominantly three seem to be involved in the thinking process: seeing, hearing and feeling. One can hear in people's language which sensory system they are using for thinking in any given moment in time.

This information, of course, can be of tremendous value to the salesperson when trying to establish the buyer's needs and wants. For example, in a car showroom the buyer says, 'I want a good, solid, comfortable car', (suggesting kinesthetic feeling).

In this selling situation, if the salesperson responds by saying, 'Well, let me show you this one', 'look at these features', 'see this', 'let's focus on that then', the seller is not responding to the way the buyer is thinking about the car. On the other hand, if the seller talks in the same way the buyer is processing internally (kinesthetically) by saying something like, 'I think you would feel comfortable with this model' or 'Let me go through the quality features of this car so you can weigh them up yourself', it would be more advantageous.

Grinder and Bandler formulated Neuro-Linguistic Programming which was a model of thinking according to the senses associated with things that had been discovered about eye and muscular movements and other non-verbal signals. The model they came up with was this:

● When people are making images in their mind (thinking visually), they look upwards.
● When they are experiencing feelings, thinking factually (kinesthically) in a particular fashion or direction, they tend to look downwards to the dominant hand.
● When they are thinking auditorily (with sound), or talking to themselves (internal dialogue), they look downwards to the non-dominant hand, probably tilt the head to the side and very often put a hand on the chin or near the mouth; sometimes you will even see tiny lip movements.

What are the processes involved in NLP?

Some people have adopted the idea that people behave like computers and have applied that willy nilly to psychology and communication. It is from that kind of reasoning that the 'resistant buyer' arises.

Communication is evidently a two-way continuous loop. If the listener is present then it is possible for the speaker to see the response from moment to moment and ascertain whether the listener is agreeing or disagreeing, understanding or misunderstanding.

Body Language only takes into account half the loop. This leads us into the whole question of *rapport*, which is the relationship between the verbal (voice, words, tone, tempo, volume and pitch) and non-verbal behaviour (posture, gesture, facial expressions and so on).

Words provide the content of communication and are usually extremely ambiguous. Almost every word in the dictionary has several possible meanings. The non-verbal behaviour sets the context through which to make sense of these words. Think how many ways you have of saying Yes and No: it's not what you say but the way you say it! This has a tremendous impact on the information the buyer receives from the salesperson. The non-verbal communication from the buyer is what the seller intuitively responds to, which tells the seller what is important and unimportant, the main considerations which will provide a lead into what to do or say next.

How would you use NLP to deal with different types of buyers?

NLP can show which words you should use to get optimum responses by tuning in to the customer's responses. In order to become more sensitive to these factors the seller must pay careful attention to the sales interview by noticing all the minute changes in the prospect as regards breathing, voice quality, posture and so on. The reason one trains in this way is because when the seller is in front of the prospect he needs full focus on the task at hand. It is very much like training pilots in simulators to deal with all kinds of emergencies so that in the aeroplane they don't need to think about it, they just do it.

There is another area of NLP that is worth talking about in sales and that is the idea of language as a map. Korzibsksi said, 'The map is not the territory,' referring to the internal maps that provide a coherence for us, that enable us to go through the world picking up required information we need to operate from and disregarding the rest. One of the most common maps that we use to make sense of the world around us is the map of language.

Language is a rather curious map. Say you are navigating from Marble Arch in London to John O'Groats in Scotland, you would require two maps, one large scale for London and another for motorway driving. It is still the same real world that is made of the same sort of things but one chooses the scale of map to correspond to the type of journey one is making.

Language maps do not indicate any information about scale, nor does language have borders defined that tell you the limits of possibility on the map.

Take as an example the word 'aeroplane'. You know what is meant by that word, but it is probably quite clear that 'aeroplane' not only describes a product but also describes a class of products. Every aeroplane could be described by the word 'aeroplane' which means that if you heard the word you would not know what the speaker has in mind. We naturally gather information by asking a question. We listen to what the other person says and make some sort of internal map of what is meant; but there could be holes, gaps in the map, so we ask another question to fill in the gap. The problem with this technique is we presuppose we understood what was meant by the first set of words and that could be an error.

A lot of salespeople get confused and collect misleading information on which they act, with erroneous results. NLP can provide the seller with a way to ask questions that doesn't depend on the meaning of the words in general but what the words mean to the buyer. What is being referred to here is not just how people process their internal maps of seeing, hearing or feeling but the limitations. So when people say, 'I can't do this or that', or 'that's not done' or 'it's impossible' they are not necessarily describing a true thing in the world or a real-life situation, but you hear about, you get to know, the other person's internal maps. By training in NLP skills the salesperson can build in appropriate questions to ask in such situations and thereby bury negative issues with a tremendous degree of flexibility. By moving around the other person's maps they can pinpoint exactly what's on them and bring out what is positive and useful to achieve satisfactory results.

They may even be able to acquire the ability to extend and develop these maps so that they can broaden and develop the buyer's thinking: this is 'consultancy selling' – a secure and valuable selling position to be held in high esteem in the prospect's eyes.

It is only by establishing a context of rapport, by communicating outwards, by becoming sensitive to verbal and non-verbal behaviour and exploring with the prospect their maps and your own map of the situation, products, needs, benefits and so on, that a true win – win relationship can be built.

You cannot 'code' buyers in NLP but you can think of it as a set of tools that can be applied to each unique set of individuals. Though it appears that some people tend to be more visual or auditory or kinesthetic, it is not appropriate always to label people in those ways. Each individual will have their own unique style at any time. The whole point is to develop awareness, sensibility and sensitivity, to pay attention to what the buyer is saying and doing at a given moment in the sales interview, and adjust the way you put across the sales message accordingly.

How can NLP be used in conflict resolution and dealing with aggression?

Basically there are two points to it:

1. By developing awareness of the other person's state of mind it is possible to avoid conflict even before it arises by being sensitive at the earlier stages of such a conflict and by exploring the differences between the other person's map of the world and your own, because that is where the conflict typically arises. Then you must discover what are the elements that are not understood, known or detected, or distorted or generalized, that produce the conflict.

2. Given that inevitably in any human relationship, no matter how good the intention of the salesperson and his company or that of the buyer and his company conflict will arise, people will get aggressive, irritable or angry. There are two ways of helping them. The first would be the simple development of the rapport skill of matching, pacing and leading: the salesperson becomes agitated as well, and to some extent shares in the prospect's map of the world. By staying in that loop of behaviour the salesperson can pace and lead the client back to a calmer approach. This is the exact opposite to when somebody is getting very agitated while the other person is becoming very calm and saying 'take it easy and calm down'

which as we all know seldom works. Here, the technique of self-anchoring, which provides a trigger to the salesperson's resources, could be used to help the salesperson maintain or regain their composure and abilities. One of the curious things is that so many of us are highly capable, resourceful and competent in some situations and in others it is almost as if those resources just vanish into thin air. The skills of NLP provide people with the possibility of getting access to their resources in tough situations.

What benefits are there from using NLP to achieve sales excellence?

The responsibility of the salesperson is not just to make the one-off sale but to make long-term profitable sales. Technical and market knowledge are the bottom line in selling, but what distinguishes the top performers from the mediocre is their remarkable ability to manage a continuing relationship with the buyer. It follows therefore that the more efficiently a win – win relationship can be built with the buyer, the easier will be the task of selling.

Every experienced top flight salesperson has had moments of great satisfaction with their performance but they are usually unaware how these moments of high performance occur. The outstanding salespeople are not the ones who unleash the killer closes that may achieve transitory success; it is not this success that builds business. The outstanding salespeople are those whose approach is that of the professional ambassador, standing between supplier and buyer, and by serving the client they serve their employer, building win – win relationships that make business sense.

There are four characteristics of outstanding salespeople:

1. They have the ability to manage their personal performance, to cope with set-backs and problems and focus on the task at hand, to utilize their powerful resources to move forward with competence even in the face of adversity.

2. They have the ability to establish rapport with a wide range of people quickly, to tune into the prospect and make 'real' contact to build a lasting relationship rapidly.
3. They have the ability to think in terms of practical outcomes and track progress towards them, to think and move forwards rather than backwards, re-sorting problems into alternative outcomes or likely solutions in precise language terms.
4. They have the flexibility to respond appropriately to different buyers and changing circumstances and to be able to notice the prospect's responses and adjust words and behaviour from one moment to the next in pursuit of appropriate outcomes.

Perhaps their greatest art lies in their endless creativity – that ability to respond appropriately, no matter what happens. In cybernetics (the study of systems, such as two people communicating), it may be worth noting that the component with the greatest flexibility will end up controlling the system. It is called the *law of requisite variety* which enables the professional salesperson better to serve the buyer and their own company.

Who are the types of people that can benefit from NLP?

NLP techniques can be profitably used by salespeople, managing directors, airline pilots, scuba divers, doctors, scientists, programmers, and so on – in fact in any area where human performance is vital and communication between people is critical it has a valid application and great benefit.

CHAPTER 11

On your journey to success your memory is like a compass–without it you are lost!

In the jungle, the mighty jungle, the lion, the king of beasts reigns supreme.

In your powerful, computer-like brain lies your wonderful memory that reigns supreme. It has unlimited potential for storage of data and recall, but your ability to use it depends on how well you have trained and looked after it.

The good and bad events that take place today will become the good and bad memories of tomorrow, because everything which takes place in our lives is recorded in the brain. It may be stored for a short time, a long time or a very long time, but I can assure you that it is recorded and may be recalled under hypnosis.

Before I delve into the scientific aspects of memory I would like you to focus on good and bad memories that we all have to contend with in this complex world and how we can understand and learn to live with them.

If you have experienced more bad memories in your lifetime than good then they are going to have adverse effects on the way you think and act. This will affect your mental stability and outlook and how you will influence other human beings. An horrific event, particularly a childhood experience, may cause a deep psychological wound that may heal with time, but nevertheless it will leave a bad scar. Pleasant experiences however, can only lead to good memories, add to an enhancement of one's thinking capabilities and therefore produce clear, positive actions and outcomes. This does not mean that you will have a happy life without any problems or drawbacks. It also does not automatically follow that you will always be a psychologically well balanced person. Life does not come with that sort of guarantee.

So memories are made of good input and bad output. How we use those experiences could mean success or failure, and it is not how intrinsically bad or good the experience was that matters. The point that I am trying to illustrate is that every individual is entitled to a more meaningful and enjoyable existence which I believe can be achieved by getting our thinking apparatus straightened out. But many of us, due to clouded thinking, recalling bad memories, focussing on the wrong

objective and setting the wrong priorities are not getting what we want and consequently end up at the incorrect destination.

By training the memory we can shut out bad experiences and call on the good to help us. A better method is to live without harming others through evil thoughts, words and actions, and you will automatically become a better person. So I say to you seek the good soon and dwell on it and those good memories will help you succeed.

You cannot practise memory but you can train it. In order to train your memory you have to know how it works. There are three kinds of memory store which receive information via the senses. These three kinds of memory store are called:

1. The SENSORY INFORMATION MEMORY, in which we store a precise picture of the outside world based on the way we view it in a fraction of a second.
2. The SHORT-TERM MEMORY, in which small amounts of information can be stored for a short period of time.

The Memory Pyramid

A	line 1, 1 letter
O R	line 2, 2 letters
A P E	line 3, 3 letters
A P E S	line 4, 4 letters
G A P E S	line 5, 5 letters
G R O A N S	line 6, 6 letters
M A S S I V E	line 7, 7 letters
G R A P P L E S	line 8, 8 letters
A A P E G A P E S	line 9, 9 letters
A A P E G R O A N S	line 10, 10 letters
A M A S S I V E A P E	line 11, 11 letters
A A P E G R A P P L E S	line 12, 12 letters
M A S S I V E G R O A N S	line 13, 13 letters
A P E G A P E S G R O A N S	line 14, 14 letters
M A S S I V E G R A P P L E S	line 15, 15 letters
M A S S I V E A P E O R A P E S	line 16, 16 letters

If you look at line 1 which has only 1 letter you would not have difficulty in remembering just one letter on its own. But by the time you get to line 16 with 16 letters you would have difficulty in remembering. Line 7 with 7 letters is about the ideal number of letters or numbers which the average person can remember, which is why telephone numbers and car numbers are usually kept at seven digits.

When you look up a telephone directory to get a number which you locate and enter into your short-term memory, and you then open your purse to get your phone card or coins out to make the call, you will probably keep repeating the number over and over again. This process is called REHEARSAL.

Now let's assume that there is a sudden interruption by an accident occurring in front of you such as a child falling or hurting itself. This involves information that is entered into the short term memory for a short time, which results in the loss of the number, which has to be reviewed again or recalled from the long term memory.

3. The LONG TERM MEMORY is where all our day-to-day experiences and all the knowledge we have gained is stored for years and years, perhaps throughout our entire life. This is demonstrated by our being able to find our way to work and back. Our long-term memory rarely fails in its obligation to help us remember the everyday tasks which we have taken for granted. We also remember many past events and childhood experiences that are stored in our long-term memory.

The long-term memory is a highly complex system and its capacity for storing information is unlimited.

You will see how the sensory information memory, the short-term memory and the long-term memory all work together when trying to do a simple task such as locating a company offering a product you saw advertised in a newspaper a few weeks previously.

a. You use your long-term memory to find the newspaper.
b. You use your sensory information memory to transfer the details of the advert and telephone number to your short-term memory.
c. You go over the advert and telephone number in your short

term memory (REHEARSING) to check and consolidate the information before you make contact with the business that is advertising its products.

Techniques for remembering better

There are several techniques for improving recall:

- Using a MNEMONIC
  For remembering the seven colours of the spectrum in the rainbow, you can use the mnemonic Richard Of York Goes Battling In Vain – the first letters of each word representing Red, Orange, Yellow, Green, Blue, Indigo, Violet.
- A mnemonic originates from the Greek word 'mneme', meaning 'to remember'.
- USING PICTURES
  A picture paints a thousand words! Furthermore, we think first in pictures then in words. For example, if I say House or Car to you, then you would first picture a house or a car and then allocate the corresponding word to it.
- GROUPING INDIVIDUAL LETTERS TOGETHER TO GET A PICTURE
  If we go back to line 16 which has 16 letters in the short term memory diagram (The Memory Pyramid) and group them together, you will find that it gives you MASSIVE APE OR APES which is easier to remember in pictures than REHEARSING: 16 letters with no meaning.
- ASSOCIATION
  This is the most commonly used system for remembering. Let us assume you want to remember the following shopping list of ten items:

1. book	6. shirt
2. apple	7. cup
3. pencil	8. onion
4. envelopes	9. milk
5. stamps	10. bread

The best way to remember these items is to associate the number against each item on the shopping list with a rhyming word system of the numbers one to ten such as:

1. Bun	3. Tree	5. Hive	7. Heaven	9. Vine
2. Shoe	4. Door	6. Sticks	8. Gate	10. Hen

You can formulate your own rhyming word and link it to the shopping list.

To associate the shopping list with the rhyming word system you have to imagine an out-of-proportion link between the two which then will be absorbed strongly into the memory and can be easily recalled. You can make this possible in the following ways:

EXAGGERATE: the image must be exceptionally or grotesquely large or loud.

ABSURD: wherever possible the linked image must form a new image which is both humorous and ridiculous

SEXUAL: sexual connotations can aid recall, so the advice is use it.

VULGAR: obscene things are recalled more easily. You will do no harm to your power of recall by being obscene when you want to improve your memory.

SENSUAL: use the six bodily senses of sight, sound, smell, taste, touch and intuition when trying to put your image into a language that will be easily understood by the memory.

MOVING: a moving image is better than a static one.

COLOURED: a coloured object gaudily presented with a bright appearance is better for the memory than one which is not coloured or bright.

IMAGINATIVE: let your imagination run riot.

PURE AND NOT MIXED UP: two linked items must be matched only to each other as opposed to being linked to other items in the shopping list. A link which is not humorous, or is abstract or confused will not be of help to the memory.

Now the association we have to form between our shopping list and the rhyming word system using the nine keys above is as follows:

1. Bun and book	6. Stick and shirt
2. Shoe and apple	7. Heaven and cup
3. Tree and pencil	8. Gate and onion
4. Door and envelopes	9. Vine and milk
5. Hive and stamps	10. Hen and bread

1. Imagine a bright red *book* sitting on a giant *bun*.
2. Imagine you are wearing your favourite *shoe* on one foot and hopping towards a juicy *apple* you want to get at.
3. Imagine you are trying to climb a banana *tree* where there is a big *pencil* hanging down.
4. Imagine you are walking through a department store *door* and you can see a sales assistant clutching a big box of *envelopes*.
5. Imagine you have entered a *hive* where there is a colony of bees depositing honey like gum on the back of *stamps*.
6. Imagine you have a walking *stick* in your hand and you are trying to chase off a man wearing a *shirt* with a vulgar sign and words written across it.

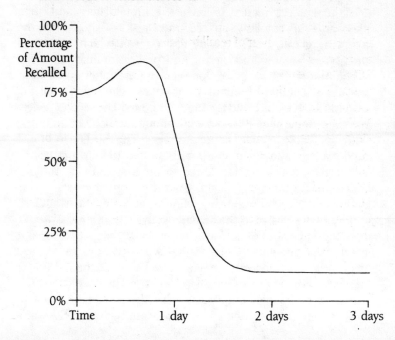

7. Imagine that you are flying with your hands wide open to *heaven* and you can see a pure white angel holding a blue *cup* calling you.

8. Imagine that you have come to the front *gate* of a friend's house and you can see a massive *onion* cut into two and the juice is causing your eyes to water like mad.

9. Imagine you are carrying a *vine* wrapped around a huge bottle of *milk* on the road and people are all turning around towards you and laughing.

10. Imagine you are feeding a big fat *hen* with a freshly *baked* loaf of bread.

● REVIEWING

At regular intervals increases your powers of recall and retention.

The graph on page 305 shows how human recall rises for a short while after learning and then falls steeply. It is disturbing to note that 80% of detail is lost within 24 hours.

If the subject matter is reviewed immediately and then afterwards at regularly spaced intervals, as shown in the following graph, it will greatly assist recall which is vital to professional selling and buying and processing information.

The first review must be done ten minutes after a one hour learning encounter for about ten minutes, which will keep the material fresh in the mind for about 24 hours. The second review must be done after 24 hours for about two to four minutes, which will hold good for about one week. The third review must be done after about a month for about two to four minutes by which time it will be transferred to the long term memory.

One of the most significant aspects of regular review is the overall effect it has on learning, thinking and remembering. This is why I have designed the activity analysis form in Chapter 11 in a particular way to help you review what happened in your previous selling encounters, so that when you talk to or meet the buyer on a subsequent meeting you can use the full power of your memory to produce good sales results.

It must be strongly emphasized that the person who fails to review after any learning encounter is putting themselves at a

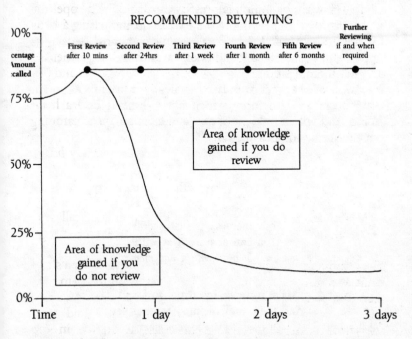

RECOMMENDED REVIEWING

| | First Review after 10 mins | Second Review after 24hrs | Third Review after 1 week | Fourth Review after 1 month | Fifth Review after 6 months | Further Reviewing if and when required |

Area of knowledge gained if you do review

Area of knowledge gained if you do not review

serious disadvantage: they would not have a base to build on and their understanding of any new material will be very weak. I am not just referring to learning from a book but also to any information-exchanging conversation.

By not reviewing, even the general memory suffers because the material entered into the mind is not present at a conscious level. This means that when you are exposed to any new material unexpectedly you won't be able to make the connections, because memory works by a linking and association process.

Conversely speaking, the advantage to the person who does review is enormous. It is like a snowball effect. Each time the snowball starts rolling it gets bigger and bigger as it gathers more snow under its own momentum.

A commonly asked question I would like to answer is whether memory declines with age. It is true that the growth of mental aptitude starts from 0 and reaches its peak between the ages of 18 and 25, after which time it gradually declines by about 5% to 10% over a whole lifetime, which is insignificant when compared with the brain's enormous capacity. The truth of the matter is that if the mind were continually used and its capabilities expanded then recall would be almost perfect, as opposed to being stagnant and poor, for the mind that is unused and left in cold storage.

In the space between your two ears lies your magnificent brain that houses your memory which has unlimited potential for storage and with a little bit of care and attention, you can bring out the magic in your memory.

RULES FOR A BETTER MEMORY

Your memory is just a skill
You can acquire it at will
(you are not born with a bad memory)

Make up your mind not to forget
And then your memory trace is set
(it is up to you to remember)

First treat your brain with constant care
Correct nutrition and fresh air
(give your brain the attention it needs)

Forgetting takes place very fast
Revise at once to make it last
(if you want to remember exercise your brain constantly)

An organized and well trained mind
Makes mental treasures easy to find
(whatever you do, do it well, think about what you do and your memory will assist you)

Link memory into a chain
And you will rarely search in vain
(memory works by association)

Use your senses – sight, sound, touch and smell
One of them will ring a bell
(using your senses will help to form a picture. Use movement too)

Relax and to yourself be kind
With love and patience train your mind
(praise yourself when you do right before
you reprimand yourself for doing wrong. Also,
relax, breathe out, don't hold your breath if
you want to recall something!)

Your memory needs peace and rest
To understand, reflect and digest
(to make your memory function better, study, rest, exercise and a
good diet are essential)

Learning and recall

- We can learn by observation, by being instructed through the written and spoken word and from experience. We then take the material we have learnt (knowledge) and store it in our memory which is our understanding of the planet and its processes. The understanding we have acquired influences our thoughts and actions and in fact we very often will do things just in order to test our understanding of the knowledge we have gained. This process is ever changing as you learn new things and add to or subtract from your existing bank of knowledge.
- Learning may involve getting acquainted with new skills, such as where our senses and muscles interact to produce the skill.
- We learn by experience, storing information in our memories about real objects (tangibles) gained through our senses which we distinguish from one another by likeness (similarity) or unlikeness (difference).
- We learn to distinguish faces, numbers, letters, forms, shapes and sizes, and their individual characteristics and, by giving these a label such as aggressive, jealous, kind, jovial, big, small, first, last, round, square, it is possible for us to learn more

about the world we live in. The sorting out, classifying and storing of information we are experiencing in itself is a learning situation whether we realise it or not.

- To remember something is to recall it from our memory. Some answers to questions come easily from the memory while others take longer because we have to search the memory for them.

Some points to consider to help you get the best from your memory and help you think clearly

- The conscious mind works in the present. The unconscious mind works from the past. The subconscious mind works for the future. These three minds overlap into each other to help you and constitute your thought processes. Subconscious thoughts can *help* or *hinder* your present thoughts.
- Do not try to do too much at one time. Do one thing at a time and do it well. Be specific – it begins with your brain and not with your mouth.
- Correct breathing is very important for a better memory and clear thinking. When a baby enters the world it does so in a state of shock and breathing therefore becomes a very traumatic experience. Memory problems can be due to incorrect breathing. When you get tense oxygen to the brain gets cut off. Don't hold your breath and say you have forgotten. Breathe out, relax and you will automatically breathe in. Breathing can be looked upon as the bridge between the conscious and the subconscious.
- If you do not think clearly the memory gets affected. Clear thinking gives you confidence and helps a great deal in problem solving.

INPUT	STORAGE	OUTPUT
	(Retain what is necessary and throw out what is not)	(what we have been thinking clearly must be communicated)

- Get an overview first and then go for detail.
- To get the best from your memory use all your senses. Link and associate.
- Mental and physical exercise is important. Mental keep fit is done by effective reading.
- Memory is like a path we go many times over. Seven times is the magic number that stays in the memory.
- Yawning is due to the brain asking for more oxygen. Sometimes you yawn until your eyes water which is caused by tiredness. Expose yourself to fresh air and practise some deep breathing to overcome it.
- Thinking without fear means a better memory.
- The memory can get overloaded sometimes, which leads to forgetting. The best way to deal with it is always to find a reason not to forget and then to make a plan on how not to forget.

Breathing for Relaxation

1. Find a quiet room where you will be undisturbed for about ten to fifteen minutes. Lie down on the bed or floor. Undo tight clothing and remove your shoes. Spend a few moments settling yourself down.
2. Close your eyes, spread your feet 12-18 inches (30cm) apart, and check that your head, neck and spine are in a straight line. Focus your attention on your breathing. Do not try to change your breathing for the moment. Become aware of how fast or slow you are breathing, whether you are breathing with your chest or diaphragm. Notice whether there are any gaps or pauses between your inhalation or exhalation.
3. Now, put one hand on your upper chest and one hand on your abdomen just below your rib cage. Relax the shoulders and hands. As you exhale gently, press the lower hand to flatten your abdomen. As you inhale, allow the abdomen to expand. There should be little or no movement in the chest.
4. Allow yourself a little time to get into a regular rhythm. It may help to imagine that as you are breathing in, you draw half a circle with your breath around your body, and as you

breathe out, you complete the other half of the circle. Allow your breath to become smooth, easy and regular.

5. Now, slow down your exhalation, and allow your inhalation to follow smoothly and easily. Smooth out any gaps or pauses in your breathing. If any distractions, thoughts or worries come into your mind, allow them to come, then allow them to go, and bring your attention back to your breathing.

6. When you are ready to end this exercise, take a few deeper breaths in. Bring some feeling back into your fingers and toes. Open your eyes slowly, and turn over onto one side before gently sitting up.

CHAPTER 12

Activity analysis

Activity analysis is the method by which you can determine your performance and results mathematically against a standard set either by yourself or by your company. All businesses are profit-orientated unless they are in the charity business, in which case they obtain their revenue from donations, trusts and special fund-raising activities.

In the direct selling business, profit comes from salespeople making appointments and doing demonstrations or presentations in order to sell products, services or ideas backed by management who will be there to motivate and manage the sales force to produce profitable results according to their company policy and trading procedures.

What must be well and truly grasped about the profession of selling is that a seller may be the most knowledgeable and highly skilled salesperson in an organization but if he or she does not talk to prospective buyers no sales will be made. No one will give you money unless you work for it.

Unless you are in great demand through widespread media exposure, publicity or personal recommendations, or unless you are a super-star your chance of making it big in selling are very, very remote except through hard work, perseverance and building up a reputation as an acknowledged expert in your field. Once you build a good reputation for yourself, then the task of making big ticket sales becomes easier, but you still have to struggle. There is no escape from that.

Start on the right foot, keep on the right track, work hard and have a clean conscience, but have an open mind and learn the secrets from the cowboys, crooks and con men, and the true success you are entitled to must come your way if you are doing what you have to do the right way. It is just like making a cake. If you put in all the right ingredients and prepare it in the right way then you have a perfect cake. If you cut corners on that which is important, then you have a recipe for disaster!

Success in selling means having a suitable product, service or idea and showing it to as many people as is necessary to generate the sales you want to make and learning the right selling methods and duplicating that behaviour throughout your selling life. Those who sell their professional expertise, such as doctors, lawyers, accountants, consulting engineers and dentists do build up a clientele, but they cannot depend solely on their know-how to maintain customer loyalty. The old saying, 'business is only as secure as a buyer's emotions', is very true. One has only got to make a mistake once and you will build up a bad reputation that will spread like wildfire which in turn can affect your business. These people should make an effort to learn and practice some of the 'people business' skills offered in WHO DARES SELLS and other books, videos and audio tapes on improving personal effectiveness.

Some of these people may already be doing their job in the right way without any formal professional selling skills training, having learnt by making mistakes coupled with years of practical experience.

Even with all the selling points of a product, service or idea being in the seller's favour and a salesperson having all the personal qualities, they can still lose the sale if they are not aware of the psychology of the sales process. For similar reasons other skilled people in non-selling occupations sometimes fail either because they did not know how to overcome problems when they cropped up, or disregarded the rules of their trade.

Furthermore, business could be lost in several other ways.

People do go off one another from time to time for various reasons. There could be a price increase, or a delay in delivery, or bad service. A rude word which was said innocently may have been misconstrued and upset someone. The competition might have gained access. Any small or unimportant little thing as much as something more serious can cause a change in either the seller's or buyer's attitude and can produce a 'ping-pong' effect leading to strained feelings on both sides, which in turn can lead to a lost sale that can affect both parties.

A seller has no divine mandate over the way a buyer thinks or acts and that is what you have to be prepared to put up with – the favourable and the unfavourable. You must be prepared to accept it unconditionally and be fully prepared to handle it or leave the business of selling. The cream of the profession of selling screams for drivers, not passengers, and leaders, not followers! When a company or any individual seller loses or gains buyers it needs to know How, When, Where, Why, Who and What caused the situation in order to forecast future business potential and have contingency measures for difficult times. This information is required on a daily, weekly, monthly, quarterly and annual basis.

Activity analysis can provide this information so that both the salesperson and the management can detect any shortcomings in performance and put it right early before any serious outcome follows. So, activity analysis is a method by which you lay down your objectives and record your performance against those objectives and in doing so you can predict how you will perform in the future (forecasting). If your activity/performance is sliding down against a set standard it may pinpoint areas of weakness that could be put right by consultation with other experts and experienced people from within the organization or with outside help.

I am now going to give a very simple but comprehensive activity planner for you to operate, no matter what personal or company system you are operating at present. This system, if followed without fail, will only help you win the war in selling. I recommend you put it into operation immediately and you are bound to score big hits provided you have all the other attributes of a good salesperson.

Remember, this book has been written for you, whoever you may be, to help you become a winner personally and financially. You should be thinking big and believe that you are the best, which is a pat on the back you owe to yourself if you want to influence others' thinking. However that thinking must be based on the real world and not on the make-believe world. You are doing no one harm by thinking you are the cream of the cream even though there are some people who would try to label you a clot. Never let that worry you as long as you know what your strengths are. That supreme confidence can only come when you have analysed your weaknesses and conquered them. Until then you may fall prey to the critics.

Daily Activity Objectives

Daily sales target to achieve = £...
Daily telephone calls to make (cold) = ...
Daily telephone calls to make (call-backs) = ...
Daily canvass calls to make (cold) = ...
Daily canvass calls to make (call-backs) = ...
Daily demonstrations or presentations to make = ...
Daily product mix to sell to users (U) = ...
Daily product mix to sell to competitive users (CU) = ...
Daily product mix to sell to non users (NU) = ...
Daily written quotations to send = ...

Daily Pre-Call Research/Data and Checklist

(To be reviewed daily before each call till it becomes part of you)

1. What is the objective of my first call?.....................................
2. Did I speak to the right person?..
3. What is the additional action required on my subsequent call?..
   Have I done it prior to the follow-up?.....................................

4. Do I have sufficient personal details about the main contact such as Name?...
Age? ....
Country of Origin?..
Family details?...
Religion?..
Business and leisure interests? ....
Academic achievements?..
Mental and physical health?...
Any other information?...
....
....

5. What is the contact's position within the organization and the part they would play in influencing the final decision?
....
Do I need to find out more about him or her? (remember, the more you know about the person you are dealing with the easier it is going to be)...

6. Do I have sufficient personal details about the decision maker as in 4 above and what his/her buying style is like (e.g. aggressive, talkative, silent etc)?...
Name? ....
Age? ....
Country of Origin?..
Family details?...
Business and leisure interests? ....
Religion?..
Academic achievements?..
Mental and physical health?...
Any other information?...
....
....

Has this person the Money, Authority and Need or is there a joint decision maker (such as wife/husband, accountant, bank manager, partner, director, technical expert etc) and do I know enough about them too?..

7. Is my competition making a bid for the business?..................
If so what are their strengths and weaknesses and how would I sell against them?..

Do I know my product, service or idea (the features/benefits, and the advantages/disadvantages of those features and benefits) inside out, and also those of my competitors? ....

8. What knowledge do I have about this company: its size, turnover, the products, services or ideas it buys and sells, its competitors and the people who work in it. Have I upgraded my records on any changes?...............................

9. Do I know the legal and financial implications of the transaction?..

10. What sort of sales approach should I take and what sort of sales resistance can I expect? ....

11. What contingency measures do I have? ....

12. Are my selling skills in tip-top condition (polished until they glisten) or do I need to brush up on areas such as probing, listening, objection handling, closing, body language and sales talk?..

13. Is my sales talk constructed with logical and emotional appeal and is it aimed at the six senses: sight, sound, smell, taste, touch and intuition (as many as you can aim at)?...

14. Have I got all the necessary paraphernalia ready (e.g. equipment, paperwork, plan, proposal, estimate, contract, pen, ruler, briefcase, portfolio, audio visual aids) and are they in good condition, or do they need to be replaced?
....

15. Is my personal hygiene, grooming and clothing suitable for the occasion?...

16. How long will it take to travel to my appointment, park my car and get to the buyer's establishment? ....

17. How long do I intend to spend with the buyer and have I left sufficient time to overlap if necessary before I have to leave for my next appointment, and how much time should I give to relaxing after each presentation/demonstration?...
....

18. If I overshoot my time limit with this client have I jotted it down in my mind that I should ring my next client to inform him or her about my delay and reschedule

accordingly? ....

19. Am I under far too much stress due to domestic or business reasons, and if so, in the interest of giving the best professional service to the buyer, would it not be better for me to reschedule my meeting till my problem is sorted out? ....

20. Have I made it a habit to ask for referrals after each encounter I have had with a buyer, whether a sale was made or not? ....

21. Am I going to persuade, motivate, manipulate or negotiate with this buyer? ....

22. Do I think positively or negatively (I have only one choice: Positive Thinking or getting out of selling)? ....

23. Am I courteous and polite to buyers, and do I empathize with them? ....

24. Am I persistent enough, but not too much? ....

25. Do I know the 106 reasons why sales are lost, 31 reasons why people buy products, services or ideas, 63 different types of buyers and how to deal with them, and do I know them all backwards and forwards? ....

26. Do I know the definition of salespersonality by heart?
   ....

I give you my cast iron guarantee, if you can honestly say that you have a profound understanding of all the 26 activities listed above and religiously practice these recommendations, and yet in spite of it you still say you cannot make sales, you must be some sort of freak from outer space, and that is where you belong – not in the business of selling.

How to Forecast and Plan Your Activity

Let's assume your company sells three products: A, B and C.

Product A
Cost price   = £200
Add profit   = £150
∴ Selling price = £350

Product B

Cost price   = £400
Add profit   = £250
∴ Selling price = £650

Product C

Cost price   = £600
Add profit   = £400
∴ Selling price= £1000

You budget to make a gross profit (Selling price minus Cost price) of £800 per week in order to cover the running cost of your business (your overhead expenses) and to make a reasonable profit. This you forecast to achieve by selling the following product mix in the next four weeks bearing in mind that both the product mix and the price could change week by week.

Dangers on the Road

One of the biggest bug-bears of modern business is the matter of car parking. Traffic wardens and wheel clamps are a perpetual threat. Unless you can avoid these two menaces sales can become very costly trips. I have been unfortunate enough to have collected parking tickets for stopping for only a few minutes to unload equipment in a restricted area through absolute necessity. Unless you are watchful of things such as traffic patrols, parking garages and meters, wheel clamps, motoring law enforcement personnel, the car can become a very costly and hassle-producing tool of your trade that eats into profits and leaves you in bad spirits. This drawback in the selling business often demotivates even the best of us in the profession who need to think positively to do the job properly.

I know of salespeople who systematically collect around ten parking tickets a week which is what someone else may earn as a weekly income to support themselves and a family. The answer is to be careful with the car and its parking. Don't just accept parking fines as one of the perils of the job, when they could be avoided and a suitable alternative found, such as a taxi or public transport. You could also consider giving a brochure

Day:

Date:

DAILY ACTIVITY RECORDER

(must be filled in after each call)

Tick the last column to indicate whether NU, CU or U

Week No:

Week Ending:

Time	Call Number	Call type Tel or Direct	Purpose of call Tel (Cold) Tel (Call-back) Direct (Cold) Direct (Call-back)	Company Address Tel No.	Business Type Contact & Decision Maker	Result	Classification Non-User (NU) Competitive User (CU) or User (U)
	1						NU
							CU
							U
	2						NU
							CU
							U

Time	Call Number	Call type Tel or Direct	Purpose of call Tel (Cold) Tel (Call-back) Direct (Cold) Direct (Call-back)	Company Address Tel No.	Business Type Contact & Decision Maker	Result	Classification Non-User (NU) Competitive User (CU) or User (U)	
	3						NU	
							CU	
							U	
	4						NU	
							CU	
							U	
	5						NU	
							CU	
							U	
	6						NU	
							CU	
							U	

Time	Call Number	Call type Tel or Direct	Purpose of call Tel (Cold) Tel (Call-back) Direct (Cold) Direct (Call-back)	Company Address Tel No.	Business Type Contact & Decision Maker	Result	Classification Non-User (NU) Competitive User (CU) or User (U)
	7						NU
							CU
							U
	8						NU
							CU
							U
	9						NU
							CU
							U
	10						NU
							CU
							U

MUST BE FILLED IN EVERY DAY WITHOUT FAIL

DAILY ACTIVITY ANALYSIS

WEEK NO: WEEK ENDING

Weekly S/V Target £		MON	TUE	WED	THUR	FRI	SAT	SUN	Total Wkly Calls	Daily Target to Achieve
TELEPHONE CALLS (COLD)	NU								NU	Required
	U								U	£............
	CU								CU	Actual £............
TELEPHONE CALLS (CALL-BACKS)	NU								NU	Required
	U								U	£............
	CU								CU	Actual £............
CANVASS CALLS (COLD)	NU								NU	Required
	U								U	£............
	CU								CU	Actual £............
CANVASS CALLS (CALL-BACKS)	NU								NU	Required
	U								U	£............
	CU								CU	Actual £............
APPOINTMENTS (FROM TELEPHONE CALLS)	NU								NU	Required
	U								U	£............
	CU								CU	Actual £............
APPOINTMENTS (FROM CANVASS CALLS)	NU								NU	Required
	U								U	£............
	CU								CU	Actual £............

Weekly S/V Target £	MON	TUE	WED	THUR	FRI	SAT	SUN	Total Wkly Calls	Daily Target to Achieve
PRES OR DEMS (FROM APPOINTMENTS MADE BY TELEPHONE CALLS)	NU	NU	NU	NU	NU	NU	NU	NU	Required
	U	U	U	U	U	U	U	U	£........
	CU	CU	CU	CU	CU	CU	CU	CU	Actual £........
PRES OR DEMS (FROM APPOINTMENTS FROM CANVASS CALLS)	NU	NU	NU	NU	NU	NU	NU	NU	Required
	U	U	U	U	U	U	U	U	£........
	CU	CU	CU	CU	CU	CU	CU	CU	Actual £........
LEADS OBTAINED (FROM TELEPHONE CALLS)	NU	NU	NU	NU	NU	NU	NU	NU	Required
	U	U	U	U	U	U	U	U	£........
	CU	CU	CU	CU	CU	CU	CU	CU	Actual £........
LEADS OBTAINED (FROM CANVASS CALLS)	NU	NU	NU	NU	NU	NU	NU	NU	Required
	U	U	U	U	U	U	U	U	£........
	CU	CU	CU	CU	CU	CU	CU	CU	Actual £........
REPEAT ORDERS OBTAINED (FROM FIRST CALLS)	NU	NU	NU	NU	NU	NU	NU	NU	Required
	U	U	U	U	U	U	U	U	£........
	CU	CU	CU	CU	CU	CU	CU	CU	Actual £........
REPEAT ORDERS OBTAINED (FROM CANVASS CALLS)	NU	NU	NU	NU	NU	NU	NU	NU	Required
	U	U	U	U	U	U	U	U	£........
	CU	CU	CU	CU	CU	CU	CU	CU	Actual £........
TELEPHONE CALLS (DAILY)	NU	NU	NU	NU	NU	NU	NU	NU	Required
	U	U	U	U	U	U	U	U	£........
	CU	CU	CU	CU	CU	CU	CU	CU	Actual £........
CANVASS CALLS (DAILY)	NU	NU	NU	NU	NU	NU	NU	NU	Required
	U	U	U	U	U	U	U	U	£........
	CU	CU	CU	CU	CU	CU	CU	CU	Actual £........

Weekly S/V Target £	MON	TUE	WED	THUR	FRI	SAT	SUN	Total Wkly Calls	Daily Target to Achieve
APPOINTMENTS (DAILY)	NU	NU	NU	NU	NU	NU	NU	NU	Required
	U	U	U	U	U	U	U	U	£........................
	CU	CU	CU	CU	CU	CU	CU	CU	Actual £..................
DEMONSTRATIONS OR PRESENTATIONS (DAILY)	NU	NU	NU	NU	NU	NU	NU	NU	Required
	U	U	U	U	U	U	U	U	£........................
	CU	CU	CU	CU	CU	CU	CU	CU	Actual £..................
SALES MADE (DAILY)	NU	NU	NU	NU	NU	NU	NU	NU	Required
	U	U	U	U	U	U	U	U	£........................
	CU	CU	CU	CU	CU	CU	CU	CU	Actual £..................
PACKAGES SOLD DAILY (MADE FROM PRODUCTS MIX)	NU	NU	NU	NU	NU	NU	NU	NU	Required
	U	U	U	U	U	U	U	U	£........................
	CU	CU	CU	CU	CU	CU	CU	CU	Actual £..................
LEADS OBTAINED (DAILY)	NU	NU	NU	NU	NU	NU	NU	NU	Required
	U	U	U	U	U	U	U	U	£........................
	CU	CU	CU	CU	CU	CU	CU	CU	Actual £..................
REPEAT ORDERS OBTAINED (DAILY)	NU	NU	NU	NU	NU	NU	NU	NU	Required
	U	U	U	U	U	U	U	U	£........................
	CU	CU	CU	CU	CU	CU	CU	CU	Actual £..................
SALES VALUE (S/V DAILY)	NU	NU	NU	NU	NU	NU	NU	NU	Required
	U	U	U	U	U	U	U	U	£........................
	CU	CU	CU	CU	CU	CU	CU	CU	Actual £..................
NETT PROFIT (DAILY)	NU	NU	NU	NU	NU	NU	NU	NU	Required
	U	U	U	U	U	U	U	U	£........................
	CU	CU	CU	CU	CU	CU	CU	CU	Actual £..................

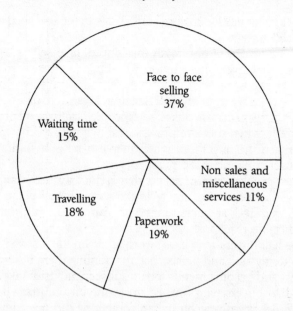

The Pie chart of a salesperson's working day

demonstration or asking the buyer to visit your establishment or that of a nearby user for a viewing. Always be on your guard for ways to save time and money and provide peace of mind.

Think about this chart. Notice how little time the average salesperson has for actual face-to-face selling. In fact, in a nine-and-a-half hour day, one hour forty minutes is spent travelling, one hour twenty minutes goes in waiting time, paperwork takes up one hour fifty minutes, and only three and a half hours will be spent selling. If you can increase the time spent in face-to-face selling your sales can only go up and up!

Your territory will function without you even if you are not there. You need your territory more than your territory needs you. If you want to make sales you must get out there as soon as you can, call into every nook and cranny: small, medium and large companies alike, and you will be surprised at what business you can generate. I have done business, and good business too, in the spookiest, tiniest hell-holes in town with relative ease and yet had to fight hard to make a similar sale in the so-called best-bet establishments.

Don't be misled by the myth that buyers hate sellers calling on them. A relatively small minority do, but even those hard nuts can be cracked.

On the contrary from my experience and research, prospective buyers in general do like salespeople calling on them, particularly when they are professional, when they know how to approach the buyer and when they can be of assistance to their success or increased prosperity.

It is the 'mickey mouse' sellers that are not wanted. Catching the buyer at the wrong time or in the wrong mood is the only real danger, and at such times you can expect all sorts of unpredictable reactions.

I have had buyers who have sworn at me on the first visit, but thanks to my skill and persistence in handling them have done business and become friends too on subsequent visits. Likewise, I have had buyers who opened up to me on the first visit all sweet and lovey-dovey, but when something did not come up to their expectations, like a delivery, or when an unexpected fault cropped up, they turned nasty and even threatened legal action if I did not put the matter right straight away!

Then there are other instances where I have met buyers who not only gave me business but also made me tea, took me out to lunch or dinner and also gave me free samples of what they were selling, with big discounts on all future purchases I made through them. In fact I have often got massive discounts on many things, such as restaurant bills, videos, TVs, hi-fis, motor spares, clothing, tailoring repairs, shoes, wines and spirits . . . you name it, I have negotiated good prices for myself even in the biggest stores all over the world because I learned how and when to do it, and because I *dared* to do it. You can also do the same, when you learn to master the techniques and use them regularly. If you don't have the total ability to sell, sail and make a sale through troubled waters, please don't try to play around with the business of selling; you could end up with a badly bruised ego and your knee-caps blown off (your morale battered and your thinking bewildered). If you have not undergone the survival training for hitting your target in selling you could end up having a very tough time battling for business. In other words, without professional training, a seller can easily fall victim to a buyer's dirty-tricks department and not only lose the sale but also lose face!

Cold-calling

I am a professional salesman. This is the proud title I have earned, starting from the bottom rung of the ladder and climbing to the top. I do not know and I now don't want to know anything else that does not have its links with selling, because I believe selling ability is the greatest asset any human being can possess, no matter what occupation they are in, because selling is a vital part of life itself and involves getting the best out of it. I sell every day, to anybody and everybody, anything that comes up. It is my life, my love, and I have a feeling it will be the death of me! I call on prospective buyers cold, by telephone and canvassing them, as second nature. I very rarely depend on referrals, but not because I do not believe in it or do not use them. Referrals to me are the easy way to sell. The lead generated through a referral is lukewarm. I am a glutton for punishment: I go in the hard way. I go in cold, day in and day out if I have the time, sometimes seven days a week. If you work by referrals and make sales, good luck to you – if that is your personal choice. My belief is that going in cold into the unknown demands a very high degree of professionalism to be able to make sales and survive in business. It is the truest test of selling ability. The other reason is that people who can be coaxed into giving a referral will usually do so if they like, trust and are satisfied with the seller and his or her offer, but there can be drawbacks.

Now just for a moment imagine something goes wrong on an after-sales matter between the buyer who gave the referral and the seller, leading to strained relations. This could have an adverse effect for the seller. Good news travels fast, bad news travels ten times faster, which means the seller could end up making a rod for her own back if she falls short on something or upsets the buyer. I know of a case where something went wrong after a sale was made between a seller and the first buyer in a referral chain. It led to bad relations which were communicated to other buyers in the chain, unleashing a lack of confidence, loss of business and bad reputation for the salesperson who depended mainly on referrals.

I must admit I have a very high regard for the cold-calling salesperson who braves all sorts of sales resistance. In my view he or she is a much better salesperson than the one who takes a casual approach to selling and expects everything handed to them on a plate through referrals. Cold-calling salespeople are the types who will borrow a buyer's watch to tell the buyer the time. Cold calling also keeps your selling skills well greased and oiled, because you have to be constantly prepared to use them in awkward situations. So my opinion on cold calling, which you can either take or leave as you see fit for your situation is that the meat and potatoes part of your business must come from good, solid cold calls and the cake and ice-cream should come from referrals.

In my early cold-calling days I conducted business with all kinds of buyer/s. There was one buyer who had a textile shop and was closing down. I persuaded him to allow me to promote his closing down sale, which left the guy slightly embarrassed, because the reason he was closing down was that he was going bust. I told him that by promoting his closing down sale I would help him close down quicker and in so doing I would relieve him of his anxiety. He thought this was funny so he let me do just that.

The only business that I have not promoted is that of an undertaker! So watch out, undertakers, you could be approached by Ellis the overtaker for some advertising which could put some life back into your dying business!

As I am a professional salesman, it is my job to sell. I rely heavily on my training, my experience, my will to win, not confined to any one single place, but wherever I go, anywhere, anytime I will attempt to sell to anyone. It is as much a part of me as breathing in and out. This does not mean that I do not have fear meeting the unknown. Of course I do, but my fear has been put under control by investing in knowledge, removing the blinkers and conditioning myself to do my job.

You may already be aware how people condition themselves by setting their own limits. The following example I learnt in my discussions with another salesman, a long time ago. How far it is scientifically true I do not know, because I have not verified it myself nor do I know of anybody who has, but it nevertheless serves as a good example to illustrate the point on how we set our own limitations.

If you take a jar, put some fleas into it and cover the top with a lid, you will find that the fleas have a tendency to jump up and down and in doing so they hit themselves against the lid. If the lid is kept in the same position for some time, the fleas condition themselves to that set limit and do not jump any higher even if the lid is removed.

Looking at that analogy from a human standpoint, it is a crying shame when people set their own self-imposed limits without realizing that a journey of a thousand miles starts with one single step. Why should one human being fear another when they are both born the same way and leave the planet in the same way through death? When you can remove this psychological barrier of inbuilt fear through ignorance, hate and negative thinking and put on a positive thinking cap and say to yourself, 'I love this person because he or she is different' then you can sell to them, whoever they are. I know it, because I have done it – WHO DARES SELLS!

No one can be truly happy when they engage in clandestine operations where everything they do is purely for their own personal gain without benefit to others, unless their thinking is warped. No one wins the battle of life in that way. Those who do such things are born to lose the battle of life and the ongoing sales battles too. You are not going to take your loot with you, there are no pockets in shrouds!

Now, all my sales experiences I see as the fun part. For without them selling would be lack-lustre and boring. You certainly would not have had this book, as I wouldn't have been around to write about it without the excitement in the game of selling. And in spite of all the drawbacks, I have gone back and sold to the very buyers who resort to 'dirty business games' by meeting them head on with smart business tactics. I do not hold anything personal against these people. I have no time to do so and it is totally unproductive to have and hold bad feelings against another human being when we are all fallible.

Back to territory management.

Territory management starts with a journey. The journey plan, to be effective, must be designed in such a way that it becomes the shortest travelling distance between your workplace and your territory. By doing this you will not only save time and save fuel, which is another important way of making profit but you will also avoid unnecessary frustration.

Here is something for you to bear in mind and follow, whether you work for yourself or for a company. You must always consider and have respect for the company that employs and feeds you. Just because they provide you with a car and petrol expenses to enable you to perform your job, it is an unwritten obligation on your part to save your company unnecessary expense on fuel bills caused by bad journey planning. The reason why salespeople abuse this privilege and cost their companies more money than is necessary is because management often does not know how to sell the idea of saving money, sometimes even abusing the privilege themselves. They then use fear tactics on salespeople by saying, 'you are expected to do up to so many miles per day and if you exceed that privilege you will have to pay the price.' They use the stick rather than the carrot (in other words instead of motivating they intimidate), which often results in the salesperson falsifying the mileage sheet.

I believe that to use fear tactics and to put additional pressure on salespeople who bring home the bacon and who already have to put up with a lot of hassle from buyers is wrong. In certain cases, when management have to start getting tough with some salespeople who take undue advantage, it has got to be done but only as a last resort and then very diplomatically and only when it is apparent that the seller is taking the boss as an idiot for being kind.

Doing it this way does not mean that the sales force hasn't got to be controlled. Of course it should, but rather than using the autocratic term 'control' I would prefer to replace it with the word 'directed' for that way results are achieved. Start kicking a few asses around only when it is necessary, rather than making it normal practice. Sell them, don't tell them. Joe Louis, the great boxer, had a saying 'one in the eye is better than two on the ears'.

If salespeople like their bosses they will do things to please them. For that to happen the boss must sell him- or herself to the subordinate – that is the Japanese way of management. You can derive some sort of appreciation of this in the expression, *If you love something, let it be free and don't try to fence it in. If it loves you it will remain with you. If it does not it will leave you. And if it leaves you, then there was nothing between the two of you in the first place.* Adopt the live-and-let-live policy in life even when things are not going in your favour, and you can sleep well at night.

Similarly management can control the sales force far more productively through persuasion, motivation, manipulation and negotiation rather than using bully boy tactics: have a soft smile but iron teeth. When the boss is nice to subordinates they respond affectionately. When they are given small kisses they respond with mighty hugs. Furthermore, when the boss is normally nice and turns angry the subordinates will sense the change in climate and be surprised and cooperative which will make it easier for the boss to control the mob.

Cold-Call Countdown

1. Before you 'work the territory', do a quick drive past in order to get an overview of the area. Some unexpected changes may have occurred since your last visit.
2. Review your 'tools of the trade':
   - pen
   - business card
   - activity planner
   - brochures/information leaflets
   - demonstration equipment
   - contracts/order forms
   - calculator
3. Park your car in a safe area.
4. Work in a tight pattern, combing the area street by street. Start on one side of the road and visit all businesses in ascending order, including all side streets.
5. Cross to the opposite side of the road and do the same in a numerically descending order.

This is one of the best systems of cold-calling I know, and like a hungry dog searching for food I have done it many times,

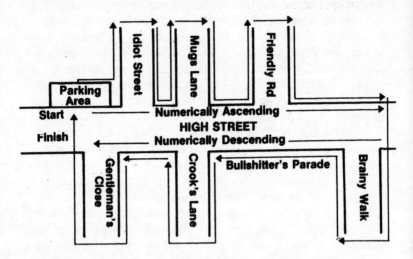

calling on every living human being in business until my objective is met – whether it is to make an appointment or to sell a product, service or idea, it is doing what comes naturally to me.

COLOUR AND ITS EFFECT ON US

You will be familiar with the following expressions, used to describe characteristics, behaviour, or mood states:

- Red with anger
- Tickled pink
- Black look
- The blues
- White with fear
- Browned off
- Green-eyed
- Yellow
- Grey

In the same way that emotions can be expressed in terms of colour, so colour can affect the emotions. Colours contribute to practically everything in life, and an understanding of the way colour works – scientifically, in its impact on buyers, and how we can use it to enhance and interpret our daily lives – is crucial for successful selling.

Colour Consciousness

Colour consciousness covers a wide variety of fields:

- Colour tests in psychology give us a quick guide to our mental health, stress levels and emotional conflicts
- Chromotherapy uses colours to heal the sick
- Colourgenics is the technical term for colour in dress
- Colour plays an important part in the decor of our homes and offices
- Colour in illumination
- Colour in beauty
- Colour in music

Where does Colour come from?

Colour comes from the sun in the form of sunlight (or white light) which is made up of heat and electromagnetic radiation. The sun is responsible directly or indirectly for innumerable energy-requiring processes, such as the growth of every plant and animal. Colour is caused by the inter-reaction between light and darkness.

What is Colour?

The spectrum is the result of the refraction of light against darkness. The spectrum, which can be described as a wide band of seven different colours – violet, indigo, blue, green, yellow, orange and red – enters the eye at different wavelengths to produce a sensation. A colour will have qualities such as hue, saturation, lightness or brightness.

The *hue* which describes the colour as being red or green is called *chromatic*.

A colour without *hue*, such as black, white, grey and silver is called *achromatic*.

Saturation of the colour is dependent on the amount of *achromatic* colour mixed in it.

Achromatic colours have zero saturation.

The *lightness* of an object depends on its ability to reflect or transmit more or less light.

The *brightness* depends on the quality of the light emitted varying from invisible to dim to highly visible.

A *shade* is a colour containing some black, and a tint is a colour containing some white.

As far as light is concerned, red, blue and green are called *primary colours*. Yellow, cyan (blue) and magenta are called *secondary colours* and are made by mixing the primary colours. (Don't confuse this with *pigment* and *paint* where the primary colours are red, blue and yellow.)

The name 'spectrum' was given to the dispersion of white light into the seven different colours above by the British scientist, Sir Isaac Newton, in the 17th Century, when he performed an experiment where he made a small hole in his window shutter to allow sunlight to pass through to make a white circle on the opposite side wall. He then placed a triangular prism in the path of the sunlight which broke the white light into an elongated bank of seven different colours. This was changed to eight by Theo Gimbel, because between blue and green the colour turquoise can be seen, and just before it disappears into ultra-violet light the colour magenta can be seen. The colours of the spectrum, herewith, are: Magenta, Violet, Blue, Turquoise, Green, Yellow, Orange, Red (MVBTGYOR).

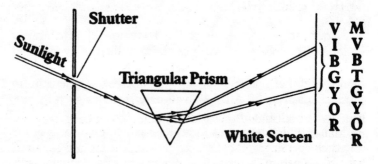

Sir Isaac Newton's spectrum experiment

At either end of this band which is called the visible spectrum is invisible energy called ultra violet to the left and infra red to the right, as shown in the following diagram.

The Visible spectrum and its borders

	VIBGYOR **MVBTGYOR**	

| Ultra-violet | Visible spectrum | Infra-red |

The bank of seven different colours has been presumably seen by everyone at some time in their life in one of nature's spectacular displays of colour, the rainbow, that has long been a symbol of hope, good fortune and happiness. The rainbow, which is a circle, is usually seen as an arc of concentric bands in the sky in the colours of the spectrum, caused by the reflection and refraction of sunlight in rain drops.

When you mix coloured light you get the following result:

Red + Green	=	Yellow
Red + Blue	=	Magenta
Blue + Green	=	Cyan (Blue)
Primary Colours		Secondary Colours

The following combinations of coloured lights when mixed together produce white light and are called complementary colours.

Red + Cyan (Blue)	=	White
Green + Magenta	=	White
Blue + Yellow	=	White

It must be understood that there is a clear distinction between *pigment* and *illumination*.

Pigment is a fusing of colour energy with matter, and coloured light (illumination) is the fusing of pure darkness and light with atmospheric conditions. Surprisingly, in paint mixing which is pigment, to get a green paint for example, the process would be far more complicated than mixing coloured lights to get a green. The reason is that the yellow and blue pigments in paints are impure colours. Blue and yellow, because of their purity in light, will create white. Yellow pigment, on the other hand, in yellow paint is *compound yellow*, which is an impure yellow, and when illuminated by white light it reflects the red and yellow and green light and absorbs blue light. Likewise, the blue pigment in blue paint, which is an impure blue, reflects the blue and green light and absorbs the red and yellow. Now, when the yellow and blue are mixed together between each other they absorb the red, yellow and blue light and reflect green light. The process of mixing coloured pigments of paints to get another colour is called colour mixing by subtraction. However, the mixing of coloured lights by reflection from a white source is called colour mixing by addition.

Eureka, you've got it by now, I guess!

How others (buyers) choose and use these colours together with the seller's preference will give sellers some valuable clues about the psychology of others and themselves, enabling the seller to speculate on the best way to act and react in any situation involving two or more people, in order to achieve a predetermined objective.

In selling, what you are trying to do is to get a total (real) or close enough picture of the buyer's personality so that you can use appropriate strategies to persuade, motivate, manipulate or negotiate.

Colours are closely linked to the emotions. When someone uses a particular colour or a preference of colours in the home or the office, or in clothing, jewellery, personal effects or footwear, they are letting you know something non-verbally. In fact, the deliberate choice of colours reveals how the person views themselves: if you interpret these messages you can always be one step ahead when selling. Consider for a moment when you go to your wardrobe first thing in the morning and you are drawn to a particular piece of clothing – the colour you choose says something!

Dr R. J. Wurtman of the Massachusetts Institute of Technology in Boston considers that after food, light is the next most important influence on our bodily functions, because colour affects us at a deep psychological level and the electro-magnetic energy of colour has far-reaching effects on the endocrine system.

Dr Malcolm Carruthers, a Stress Researcher in the UK, believes that light affects our stress levels. Now let's look at some of the colours themselves and what they indicate.

Colours in Psychology

Violet   =   Creates inner balance, feelings of reverence and peace. It promotes balance of mind and can raise sensuality and be a stimulant.

Indigo   =   Frees fears and inhibitions, broadens the mind, purifies and stabilizes.

Blue   =   Is relaxing and gives a feeling of space and calm, diminishing excitability and urgency.

Turquoise =   Is for coolness and spaciousness, freshness and renewal. It is calming and soothing.

Green   =   Is balancing, but it can lead to indecision because it holds static and arrests movement.

Yellow   =   Can encourage self-control over despondency. It is the colour of intellect and reason.

White   =   Is the colour of purity, completeness, openness, cleanliness, closeness – white bodies reflect heat.

Black   =   Is the colour of concealment, mystery, unknown. Black bodies absorb heat energy.

Orange   =   Creates a feeling of lightness, cheerfulness, and gives a carefree attitude.

Red   =   Is for energy and vitality. It is stimulating, exciting and uplifting.

Pink   =   Is a mixture of red and white and is a toned-down version between these two colours that expresses love, warmth, kindness and compassion. The male and female genital organs are dark pink in colour and if men, rather than using other macho methods to prove their masculinity, used more pink, particularly the lighter shades, it might contribute to better male/female relationships.

Magenta = Is a colour that raises the energy level.

Brown = A mixture between yellow and red. This colour indicates a link with the earth and nature. It is a colour that nourishes the green leaves of trees through the roots and trunk.

Colour in Dress and Decoration

Violet = In dress it promotes peace and love, the sense of involvement but not anxiety, concern without worry, authority without demands. In dress it is conducive to meditation, balance and concentration. In decoration it is good for anywhere dignified, for religious devotion, in festive areas and grand interiors. It is not good for hospitals or treatment rooms.

Indigo = In dress it gives the idea of security. In decoration it makes a room look larger.

Blue = In dress it makes the wearer quiet, settled and in control and allows others to come nearer. It denotes a lively person who receives calm and offers peace. In decoration blue brings harmony, calmness and a spacious environment. It is good for hospitals and consulting rooms where it can minimize anxiety. It is not so good for dining and entertainment areas.

Green = Is the colour of balance. In dress it is good for those who are hyperactive or need to be very active, but not emotionally involved. In decoration it places a person in a static environment and depletes energy. The occupant of a room has to be active or has to relax with this colour being present. Green can have a cleansing effect. It tends to negate in decoration by giving the room a flat and empty effect as opposed to its balancing effect in nature. It is good for external walls in towns, operating theatres and for parts of conference rooms. A total green environment is not recommended for living and activity areas.

Yellow = In dress it is good for those who wish to be alone, detached and non-involved. Creates slight instability and insecurity. In decoration it makes the room look smaller. It is good in areas where the intellect has to be stimulated and in conversation areas, but it is not good as a computer decoration scheme. Don't use it too extensively. Too much of it can remove anchors to stable behaviour. It is not recommended for offices, bedrooms or work areas.

Turquoise = In dress it is a good support for people who are easily involved. It calms nervous tension and does not dominate. In decoration it makes an area look larger, but still static. It is calming to people of a nervous disposition and is suitable for hospitals or for the office of someone who is stressed and over-taxed. Often, it is a very successful colour to use in interior decoration.

Orange = In dress it is good for inducing feelings of joy. It is an antidepressant. Wear when in light, slightly detached mood, not if you need to be in authority. In decoration it makes the room look smaller. It is suitable for entertainment rooms, dining areas, kitchens, passages, playrooms and rooms for young people wanting or needing to be seen. It is not recommended for bedrooms, studies or stressful areas.

Red = In dress it is good for a lethargic person who lacks vitality but is in good health and for people wanting or needing to be seen. It is a colour that commands attention and it is bad for people who tire easily. In decoration it makes rooms appear smaller. Red ceilings create feelings of oppression and weight. Red rooms can cause claustrophobia. It stimulates activity so it is good for rooms where you need to be alert, and for entertaining and dancing places. Over-exposure to a red environment can create anxiety and pressure.

White = All the colours of the spectrum combine to give you white. In dress it is the colour of purity, innocence, chastity – consider the bride in a white gown making her way to the altar and the hospital doctor in white overalls showing the clean, clinical appearance. In decoration it gives an open look and white blends beautifully with all colours. White reflects heat energy.

Black = Attracts other energies. Often used when people are lonely and depressed. Black is a beautiful colour and, like white, it can be used freely to match with most colours and show contrast.

Brown = Indicates commitment and sacrifice. It uses the energy to be in touch with physical experience.

Magenta = Is the colour of letting go and dissolving – giving freely of oneself. It is a colour of independence – a colour which is used when you do not want anyone else to be in touch with you.

I have listed above the various colours and their meaning in dress and decoration. Our human perceptions are based on input from the six senses – sight, sound, smell, taste, touch and intuition. Shape, form, colour and sound act as primary intake doors complemented by the other senses. The human eye is the organ of perception and the stimulants of shape, form, colour, lightness or brightness, and shade all contribute to how something is viewed, accepted or rejected.

It is generally accepted that audio and visual communication in colour together have a far greater impact (attention-getting and attention-holding) than audio or visual alone. But, from an advertising standpoint, it is known that although TV gets the advertising message across very quickly and effectively, the housewife while ironing clothes and listening to the radio, or the busy executive after a hard day's work who browses through the newspaper, has a better recall of the same advert, in the long run. It is a well-known fact that if one of the senses is restricted or impaired, the other senses will work harder to compensate for the inadequacy, and therefore when something is committed to memory as a consequence of having to work harder to assimilate the message, it will leave a greater impression on the memory and will therefore be easier to recall.

While we are on this topic of colour, I would like to put forward a challenging question: why is it we have to hate and discriminate against one another based on the colour of their skins? We all, in principle, eat, drink, sleep, procreate, laugh, cry etc. Why should we attack the difference? We must instead admire and appreciate the difference. As children we were not born to dislike and discriminate against one another. This has been learnt. We all are on this planet for only a short period of time. Man can communicate with one another from thousands of miles across space and the oceans, yet cannot communicate with their next-door neighbour.

Browsing through the English Dictionary, I stumbled across the following words under Black and White used to describe both the good meaning and bad meaning of both colours:

Good Value	**Good Value**
Black Monk	White Friar
Black Board	White Smith
Black Currant	White Flag
Black Forest	White Ensign
Black Bird	White Cap
Black Sea	White Paper

Bad Value	**Bad Value**
Black Eye	White Cash
Black Magic	White Slave
Black Mail	White Elephant
Black Guard	White Lie
Black Listed	White Damp
Black Sheep	White Feather

BLACK & WHITE

So why should we seek to differ rather than be like brothers and sisters in the struggle of life? As Francis Bacon said, 'All colours agree in the dark!'

Before I wind up this section, I am going to relate a true story that happened to me a few years ago. I was out shopping with my wife, my son aged six and my daughter aged four. I, being of Asiatic origin and brown-skinned, and my wife, being European and white, have one child after each of our skin colours.

I was standing with my fair-skinned daughter at one end of a grocery store while my son was with my wife some distance away making some purchases when my daughter decided to join them, but having run a little distance could not find them and started crying and calling for her mum. I walked up to her and there was I, a 180 lb mass of salesman, having my most awkward customer of all. I tried to pacify her through motivation by saying what a sweet little darling she was and that she was my girl and therefore she should not cry, but she wouldn't stop. I then tried to persuade her by carrying and rocking her. It was a no-go. This was followed quickly by manipulation and a threat to leave if she did not stop screaming and finally by negotiating: *if* she stopped making a noise *then* I would buy her sweeties – all to no avail. I must admit I was embarrassed when she did not calm down.

A (white) old lady saw me with the yelling kid and presumably could not figure out what a brown man was doing with a white kid. I say, didn't she confront me! She marched up to me and asked in a stern voice, 'Are you the chauffeur? Why is this child crying? Where is her mother?'

I replied, 'That's right, I am the chauffeur!'

'Are you telling me the truth?' she asked.

'Of course,' I replied. 'I understand your concern; they say paternity is a matter of doubt, but maternity is a matter of fact, but I am her dad, and I can assure you it was not the milkman. Her mother is over there with her brother, shopping. After all this time it took to produce the two of them I should know. By the way, it took me ten years to produce him and twelve years to produce her after firing blanks for so long, and it all took place during trips to California when I visited friends. It all happened during an earthquake, you know! I got that extra push I needed: now does that answer your question? I hope I have shed some light on your darkness as much as you have made it a colourful day for me. Thank you for showing your concern.'

She smiled, said nothing and walked away.

I told you events can happen out of the blue, and when they do you do not look awestruck and flabbergasted, but deal with them on the spur of the moment in the most effective way, without losing your cool.

The reason I have approached this section in a rather unusual way is to make a valid point: *How can you expect to become an expert seller to anybody, anywhere, if you harbour prejudice, hatred and preconceived ideas about your fellow humans?* You may be a master of your products and those of the competition, but as soon as you open your mouth you will give out bad vibrations, and that coupled with the way you look, will give your buyer the creeps, like opening a can of worms, destined to kill the sale as your dislike is conveyed to the buyer. Buyers can be very difficult no doubt, but you can always get by if you love them. However, if you intensely dislike the buyer for what he or she is and for the way he or she behaves, you will have a more profitable time communicating with the silent population in graveyards than trying to get those buyers to buy from you.

The Subtle Difference between Black and White

When I am born, I am **black**
When I am a baby, I am **black**
When I fall down and hurt myself, I am **black**
When I am a young man, I am **black**
When I stay in the sun, I am **black**
When I fall sick, I am **black**
When I am angry, I am **black**
When I am terrified, I am **black**
When I make love, I am **black**
When I grow old, I am **black**
When I die, I am **black**

When you are born, you are **pink**
When you are a baby, you are **pink**
When you fall down and bruise yourself, you turn **blue**
When you are a young man, you are **white**
When you fall sick, you turn pale **white**
When you lay in the sun, you turn **brown**
When you are angry, you turn **red**
When you are terrified, you turn whiter than **white**
When you make love, you turn reddish **pink**
When you become old, you become extra **white**
When you die, you turn bluish **grey**

CHAPTER 13

An introduction to human psychology

Psychology is a scientific study of human or animal behaviour and also the mental and behavioural characteristics of a person or group. Psychology can also be described as the mental characteristics associated with a particular kind of behaviour. A psychologist is a specialist in psychology. Some of the most favoured and often quoted people as far as sales psychology and graphology, the topics covered in this book, are concerned are Jung, Le Senne, Pophal, Hippocrates, St Morand and Kretschmer. Valuable contributions from Freud, Maslow, Eysenck, Fromm and others are also included.

Psychology is not only about finding out the wrong (abnormal). It is also about seeing the right and establishing the facts as they are in a given person. It is the equivalent of describing a man as being, for example, 5'10" tall, with black hair, brown eyes, aquiline nose, and so on. Psychology describes the non-physical as clearly as the visible parts of a person. Psychology is not concerned with the pathology of a person, nor does it make moral judgments. It is about establishing the facts about a person's behaviour.

Psychology is a field of study which has its limits. If we go beyond the limits we find ourselves in the neighbouring areas of philosophy, medicine, religion, physics, and so on.

There is nothing wrong with visiting neighbouring fields, of course, but what is of interest to us here is the specific subject of psychology. We do not know enough about it as yet and never will get the complete picture of something unique as a person's mind. It appears, however, that we have discovered its limits.

First, Sigmund Freud, the Austrian psychiatrist (1856-1939) and founder of psycho-analysis, started by observing the field. His work consisted of describing the two dominant features of the mind: the pleasure-pain and repression-compulsion complexes, and the natural tendency (instinctive drive) of an organism to go back to its previous state. In his last work on the Ego and Id in 1923, he put forward a theory suggesting that the ego and superego were constantly in tension with each other, resulting in morbid mental attitudes such as guilt feelings, inferiority complexes and so on. His earlier work consisted of the treatment of hysteria by hypnosis and dream analysis. He placed great emphasis on the part played by the unconscious mind in the development of a person's personality, the importance of sexuality in very young children and the Oedipus complex.

The Swiss psychologist Carl Gustav Jung (11875–1961) went further until he found the boundaries with other fields. His work was similar to Freud's in many ways but he did not consider the sexual side to be as important as Freud saw it which he replaced with the hero and mother goddess archetype and all the unconscious and racial associations that stem from it. Jung was an illuminated man and had the 'sacred flame' in him. Although he has been criticized as a metaphysical mystic, he simply discovered connections that, unless we follow through with the same process of thinking, we cannot understand. It is very worthwhile to read Jung without prejudice and with an open mind. He was a gnostic who managed to go very deep into the human soul, well beyond the conscious, and reach the concept of Christ.

Having discovered the boundaries does not mean that we know everything in that field. Far from it, we are still discovering.

Consider intelligence: what exactly is it? How does it affect the psychological structure of the individual? How many kinds of intelligence are there? Are there many? And is talent a form of intelligence? The same applies to habits, behaviour, emotivity and activity. We are only at the beginning.

There are many ideas and systems, which have been developed over the last seventy years, on how to assess people from their personality and handwriting. Most of these have been tried and tested for decades and the ones that have been proved correct and scientific have been adopted as common practice.

Some Common Terms in Psychology

Ego is the term coined by the German philosopher Fichte to express the 'I', the subject, which is conscious of itself, and has experience of, and determines, the outside world (the object or non-ego). It is also the personal identity looked on as an organized being distinct from others. It is commonly known as one's image of oneself, and in psychoanalysis it means the conscious personality as opposed to the unconscious.

Id as defined by Freud is the reservoir of man's instinctive drive.

Superego is the idealized image a person builds up of himself in response to authority and social pressure. It is basically unconscious but rises to consciousness on critical occasions and serves as a sort of 'guard' of the personality.

Altruism is consideration for others without any thought of self. It is commonly known as unselfishness.

Egotism is an independent frame of mind which causes a person to pay too much attention to himself, to be conceited and selfish, or refer to himself often whilst speaking or writing.

Egoism is used in the context where a person's concern about his or her own good is the basis for morality.

Egocentric is looking at everything only to see how it affects oneself, or from one's own selfish point of view.

Psyche is life itself. It is the non-physical aspect of life, the abstract side. Wisdom, heroism, will, wish, genius and spirit are part of psyche. It is not, as it is sometimes thought to be, 'spirit', 'soul' or God. Psyche does not involve faith nor does it need saving. Good and evil do not apply and death does not affect it. When a person dies, he surrenders his psyche with his last breath. The ancient Egyptians were the first to say that after a person dies, his psyche flies about and rests before it enters another person. As a pure definition the *Psyche* is the soul and the mind, both conscious and unconscious.

Self-awareness – as previously mentioned, the average human being is thought to use probably 1% of their brain capacity, although it is more likely to be 0.1% or less. Jung said our conscious is like a nutshell floating on the ocean of the unconscious. So **self-awareness** is a colossal task unlikely ever to be fully achieved, but if we start the right way, we stand a better chance of living in harmony with ourselves and others.

Psychiatry is the branch of medicine concerned with the treatment and study of mental and emotional disorders.

Psychotherapy is the treatment of mental illness through psychological methods.

Psychoanalysis is a technique of psychotherapy which renders conscious the contents of the unconscious mind through a dialogue between an analyst and the person being analysed.

A **Psychoanalyst** is a person who practises psychoanalysis.

A **Psychiatrist** is a doctor who specialises in psychiatry.

Psychopathology is the scientific study of the psychological causes of mental illness.

Psychoneurosis is a nervous disorder of mainly psychic origin.

Psychosis is a serious mental derangement (madness).

A **Psychotic** is a person suffering from psychosis.

Psychic concerns the mind or spirit.

A **Psychic** is someone who apparently is able to respond to non-physical forces or influences.

Psychometric relates to the measurement of mental data.

A **Delusion** is a false opinion or idea or an unshakeable belief indicating a severe mental disorder.

Neurosis is a nervous disorder which is not accompanied by an organic change in the nervous system and can be diagnosed by symptoms of hysteria, anxiety, obsessions and compulsions.

A **Neurotic** is a person who is affected by neurosis.

Anxiety is an intense dread or apprehension, or a nagging worry.

Depression is a state of low mental vitality or dejection. It could also be a condition of being less active than usual.

Hysteria is a condition due to a psychic or nervous disturbance characterized by excessive excitability and anxiety.

A **Hysterical** person is someone with a fit of uncontrolled laughing or crying.

Hypnosis is an artificially induced state resembling sleep but characterized by exaggerated suggestibility and continued responsiveness to the voice of the hypnotist. It is used in the medical treatment of a variety of nervous and bodily disorders. In non-medical treatment it is used effectively for a whole range of behavioural and attitude problems.

Hypnotherapy is the treatment of disease by hypnotism.

Hypnotism is the practice of inducing hypnosis.

A **Hypnotic** is a hypnotized person or someone susceptible to hypnotism.

Mesmerism is a state of being hypnotized and a means of exercising an influence over the will and actions of another.

Dementia is insanity.

Paranoia is a mental disorder in which the suffer believes that other people suspect, despise or persecute him or, less commonly, in which the sufferer has delusions of grandeur.

Megalomania is excessive self-esteem as a form of insanity.

Mania is a form of mental disorder marked by great elation and violent action. A maniac is a person affected by mania.

A **Psychopath** is a person who suffers from a character disorder.

Schizophrenia is a common mental disease whose characteristics may include separation of the intellect from the emotions, as well as in appropriate emotional reactions. Symptoms also include distortions in normal logical thought processes, withdrawal from social relationships, delusions and hallucinations.

Oedipus complex comes from Freudian psychology and relates especially to a male child. It is the psychological, and particularly sexual, drives developing usually from the ages of three to six, associated with the child's attachment to the parent of the opposite sex, and resentment of the parent of the same sex, whom the child considers his rival.

There are two types of personalities described by Jung. They are the **extrovert**, whose general attitude and energy are mainly directed outwards, and the **introvert** whose general attitude and energy are directed inwards. These two personality types have existed from time immemorial, from primitive man to the most learned of the present age, and are also found in animals like dogs, cats, horses and dolphins.

The descriptions given by Jung dovetail neatly with the psychomorphological description of the human being (psycho meaning mind, and morphological meaning shape and form of the body) given by Colman, Sheldon and Kreschner which they cited as the following three types:

Ectomorph, being thin and bony.
Endomorph, being fat.
Mesomorph, being muscular.

It is said that the **ectomorph** is perceived by others as being quiet and tense; the **endomorph** as warm hearted, agreeable and dependant, and the **mesomorph** as adventurous and self-reliant.

The American psychologist Dr William James reported that the 'tender' spirit comes from the extrovert whilst the 'resistant' spirit comes from the introvert. The following table gives the main distinguishing features between the extrovert and the introvert:

EXTROVERT	INTROVERT
● The libido (the psychic energy is directed outwards.	● Libido (psychic energy) is directed inwards.
● Reactions to events are spontaneous and immediate.	● Feels threatened in the presence of the extrovert and is usually embarrassed in the presence of one.
● Has much interest in people and things (objects).	● Is considered egoistic or egocentric.
● Is sociable, and sees, thinks and acts in the way the world is perceived by him or her, and is objective.	● Sees the world the way he or she wishes to, i.e. subjective.
● Is a charmer, likes people	● Often is clumsy, timid, closed and nervous.

and dislikes solitude.

- Is outgoing and gives freely of him- or herself. Loves enjoying life.
- Tries to achieve a lot rather than aim for perfection.
- Adapts quickly and easily to changing circumstances.
- Solves problems through people. When problems crop up the extrovert likes to give the impression, 'I will lick it,' and through over-confidence, possibly do the opposite.
- Too much extroversion can lead to hysteria.

- Is reserved.
- Lacks adaptability and suppleness.
- Fears conflict.
- Tries to solve problems by him- or herself and is slow and thorough.
- Too much introversion leads to neurosis and, in psychiatric cases, to schizophrenia.

Libido is the combination of all the functions (psychic energy) which enable us to survive and adapt to the environment. Libido is the intensity of the psychic activity. Throughout life the quantity of the libido remains the same though the quality changes due to the energetic process. If we do not have an objective in life to expend the psychic energy, then subconsciously the libido will find a substitute in the form of a new activity or a new outlet to spend the inherent energy, or it could lead to neurosis or even physical illness. For example, if a man has been working all his life and is then suddenly made redundant, this would produce an altered state of living to which he is unaccustomed, but since his quantity of libido is the same, unless he finds a replacement activity, it can use him to get depressed or aggressive to release his psyhic energy. The psychic energy can be either progressive or regressive.

Progressive libido is when the psyhic energy is used to adapt to new circumstances.

Regressive libido is when the psychic energy is used to go back (retreat) to take the pressure off so that we can recharge the batteries to come back and attack with renewed vim and vigour.

It must be noted that if we do not regress and always stay in a state of high tension it can lead to a breakdown. Progressive libido gives a feeling of power, hope and optimism towards the future and accomplishment. It represents a dynamic and positive attitude which gives confidence and attracts success, good health and harmony.

Regressive libido produces depression, tiredness, discouragement and finds the going tough. Consequently people give up the fight and go back to their childhood where they did not have any cares or worries. This is not good because such an attitude leads to disappointment, a breakdown in confidence and to eventual failure. People who have been forced to direct their libido inwards because of prison or physical disability have produced spectacular works such as the Birdman of Alcatraz.

The libido can get blocked in extreme cases of regression. It happens when a person has had such overwhelming problems that he or she cannot see the light at the end of the tunnel and becomes severely depressed, with underlying anxiety that may even lead to suicidal tendencies.

The condition is called neurosis because most regressive states are a form of neurosis. A sudden unfavourable event can cause shock which affects the libido by impeding the natural flow of the psychic energy.

Dreams express the libido and handwriting expresses fluctuations in it, but it is difficult to comprehend the libido accurately from the handwriting because a mixture of conscious and unconscious actions comes out when writing takes place. There are four psychic functions that help an individual adapt to the environment. These are **Thinking**, **Feeling**, **Sensation** and **Intuition**.

These four functions act independently of each other but any one of them can be dominant, which will indicate, and show a bias towards the way a person perceives the world. It does not follow that the dominant function indicates the intensity with which a person perceives the environment.

The four functions are mainly unconscious and partly conscious, and the more conscious they become the more productive the person becomes.

1. **Thinking** – gives the significance of the things we perceive, what they are and what they mean.

2. **Feeling** – gives value to the things we perceive. It establishes our connection with things (objects) and produces a climate for acceptance or rejection.
3. **Sensation** – perceives and gives a meaning to everything that surrounds us.
4. **Intuition** – gives the likely outcome from things we perceive and is directed from the subconscious mind.

The four functions are present in everybody in different degrees, the dominant function being called the principal or main function. The second most important function is called the auxiliary, with the third and fourth being less prominent and literally being pushed into the unconscious mind. Sometimes, one function is very well developed while the other three are very weak. However it is also possible that all four functions are very weak or well developed.

A person with a dominant function of thinking is logical and objective and disregards feeling and its subjective influence. A person with a dominant function of feeling quickly decides whether 'I like it' or 'I do not'.

A person with a dominant function of sensation feels vividly about all that touches the senses. This person may not be intuitive.

A person with a dominant function of intuition has a profound understanding of things immediately but may be useless when it comes down to practicalities.

Thinking being a logical process can be *passive* or *active*. *Passive thinking* is not under control of the *will* whereas *active thinking* is. Jung called the *active thinking intellect*, and *passive thinking intellectual intuition*.

Feelings (sentiments) coome from the heart. They are subjective and revolve around the person. When feelings become intense they turn into affection (love) or dislike (hatred). Feelings, like thinking, are an evaluating process and can be either active or passive. They are passive when someone is at the receiving end causing a decision to be made in favour or not in favour of the stimulus. In other words yes – no – or maybe. They are active when someone is displaying his or her feelings. Both thinking and feeling are rational functions.

Intuition is guided from, and is an aspect of, the subconscious mind, and is known to be the basis for certainty and infallibility. Sensations are caused by internal and external factors and come into the mind in five ways – sight, sound, smell, taste and touch. Externally, any stimulus that affects the senses can trigger the appropriate reaction. Internally, in mental or physical situations, the stimulus affects the senses which work regardless of

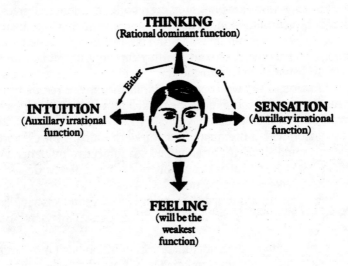

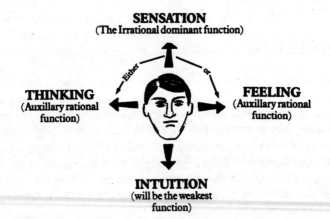

judgment or reason. Intuition and sensation are irrational functions.

The rational dominant functions of either thinking or feeling can have only one auxiliary irrational function. For thinking it can be either intuition or sensation, and feeling will be the weakest. Likewise, an irrational dominant function can have only one rational function as an auxiliary.

The following diagram shows the position of dominant, auxiliary and weakest functions in relation to one another. There are eight possible combinations.

Animus/Anima

Animus is the male element found in a female and **anima** is the female element found in a male. The two dynamic forces co-exist in both sexes to a greater or lesser extent. To Jung, anima represented all the female tendencies of the male such as sentimentality, prophetic intuitions, vague moods, feelings towards nature, artistic inclinations, the capacity to love and contact with the unconscious. A male possessing anima will become sentimental, emotional, artistic, intuitive, subjective, moody and introspective. Animus is all the masculine tendencies found in the female such as objectivity, practical reasoning, morality and intellectuality which make a woman's personality aggressive, authoritarian, intellectual, creative and shows strength of character.

Persona

Persona is a mask we wear when we communicate with others. It is not our true selves and is complex because it is used as an adaptation to the environment and for our convenience and survival, and is a 'false self'.

Every human has a persona which they use on others when they communicate, because every person, whatever their role in life, is consciously or unconsciously craving for attention and will use their persona in different ways in different situations to get that attention. Some use it more and some use it less, for whatever reason they see fit. There is no such thing as human behaviour without a reason behind it.

Some people blend the persona with their role in life, but because this persona is not as they truly are it stops them from growing – these people have a low opinion of their true self which they do not wish to reveal. They hide behind their mask throughout life and their secret fear is of being unmasked. For example, if someone comes from humble beginnings and achieves a high position, their intention may be to hide their past and pretend they were privileged and gifted all along, to give others what they think is a good impression. If it is true, say so and be proud of it. If it is not, don't try to paint the wrong picture and make a fool of somebody else.

A point I would like to make here is, why try to hide your past? Be open, come out of your shell and don't suffer unnecessarily trying to hide behind your past sins. People can smell a dead rat if there is one, so it is no point trying to cover it up pretending everything is rosy. It is your life, and what matters is the truth and your love for others. Be true to yourself first and then you will be true to others. If you have any weakness, seek to conquer it and you will not let the cat out of the bag unconsciously, which is the thing you are trying to hide behind and is blatantly obvious to the sharp eye.

Characterology

Characterology is the science of the study of character. Numerous scientists have been involved in this work from which two schools of thought have emerged: the narrow approach which suggests that character is congenital and is a permanent feature of the mental structure; and the wide approach (mainly the German view) of what the mental structure has upon the person.

Alfred Adler (1870–1937) of Vienna, who analysed the nature of character, also tried to discover what a person does with it, but like all the others he got lost trying to understand destiny. Earlier this century Rene Le Senne, who studied the differences of character in people for many years, defined character as having three distinctive elements:

1. Character is not the whole being. It is only what we possess as a result of our heredity, a fundamental structure formed by our genes, passed on to us by our distant and recent ancestors. There is nothing in a character that is not congenital.
2. The character is solid and permanent. It is the structural identity of the individual.
3. The structural identity is mental but is only the skeleton of psychological life.

Le Senne further postulated that character is an integral part of the body and conditions the mind, and that the body develops in conjunction with the character. Character must not be confused with personality which is defined as follows:

Personality

Personality includes both character and all the elements that are acquired in the course of life. It is the total self of which character is the fundamental and unchangeable part among others. To sum up, each individual has his/her own character from birth which is unchangeable.

The Factors that Constitute Character

There are three factors that make up a character. These are **Emotivity, Activity** and **Responsiveness**. It must be clearly understood that people are only recognized and classified according to, and depending on, the degree of intensity of these three factors, not by whether they were present or absent.

Emotivity (E)

This means there is an inherent tendency in the person to be moved by events. Everyone, of course, has this tendency, but some of us have it more than others. The more emotive a person is the greater will be the reaction from the person they are communicating with. When any event occurs it provides a stimulus to the mind which acts as a trigger or motivating agent which produces input energy that is released as output energy, or action. The intensity of emotion is seen not only in action but can also be found in knowledge. In actions, as long as there is no change in the direction of the action, it can result in it being more or less aggressive. For example, we can make a statement angrily in a raised voice and with a red face or we can say it cooly in a calm voice and with a poised attitude. In knowledge, emotivity is seen in how a person pursues knowledge – with great interest or little interest.

The intensity of feeling (sentiment) has a profound effect on the whole being, in that it motivates the total being whether the individual is an active or non-active person. He or she will react in a way that he perceives the stimulus. Because emotivity is a force, an energy which has to be directed, the outward manifestation of this energy will be in the direction it takes and will be dependent on whether the person is active or inactive. For example, an emotive and active person will express his or her feelings (output energy) in thought, word and action which ends up in some form of action, whereas the emotive and non-active person will direct the outward energy inwards so that the force remains within, and the body could then be said to be in a state of stress.

When studying emotivity there are two important considerations you must remember:

Firstly, the basis of emotivity lies in the fact that emotivity rests on the predisposition of the human animal to be moved by events of minimal importance, something which varies from person to person depending on tendencies and interest. For example, an emotive and ambitious man might be moved by success, fame, fortune and position, whereas an emotive and ambitious mother might be concerned on how well her child is performing in school so that it will be successful and her interest and objectives will probably be different from those of the emotive and ambitious man. Hence, her reaction would be different and possibly even cold when compared to that of the man, which would be understandable.

To be able to judge the level of emotivity in a person you need a fair amount of knowledge of the person and their interests. Even on issues like fear of death or disease, which cause us all to be concerned to varying degrees, there should be no doubt that the emotive person will react with greater intensity than the non-emotive person because of how it affects him or her personally.

Secondly, some individuals hide their emotivity, for example in the face of terror. They show fear which escapes observation, but with greater insight and 'fine tuning' one can detect that the person is under tension from a slight change in tone of voice, from statements made, judgment errors and memory lapses. If the individual concerned is an introverted type, he or she will show **Responsiveness** (the third factor that constitutes character) as a secondary factor, and for the extroverted type it will be the primary one.

The main characteristics of an emotive person

- How the person reacts to an event: the level of intensity of feelings expressed from a cool, calm attitude, to rage, aggression and violence.
- Concern, which shows elements of anxiety, restlessness and uneasiness.
- Mental flexibility.
- Change of mood which is both visible and invisible.
- Alteration of mood from ecstasy to depression and from enthusiasm to hate.
- Impulsiveness is also a characteristic of emotivity. It is closely related to responsiveness. To some people who live in the present, impulsiveness is immediate and reactive; and to others who suppress their feelings, the end result could be explosive. This is caused by harbouring past gathered experiences which have to find a way of expression.
- Excitability, because it takes only a little to excite an emotive person.
- Intolerance. Due to the intensity of the feelings the emotive person is usually not tolerant.
- The amount of reaction an emotive person displays is based on the intensity of the emotivity. The increase or decrease of

the reaction will be based on the increase or decrease in the intensity of emotivity and correspondingly with it there will be an increase or decrease in anxiety, activity and expressiveness, with a tendency towards an increase in sympathy and a decrease in indifference.

To conclude the topic of emotivity, it can be said that although there is a difference between emotive and non-emotive people as regards the intensity of feeling, it often follows that even though emotive people interpret non-emotive people as being 'hard' or 'unintelligent', they resent them subconsciously, and likewise the non-emotive person finds the emotive person difficult to understand.

Activity (A)

Activity can be two-fold: activity because of emotivity; and activity which is self-generated (characterological).

The non-active individual acts against his or her liking and will do so because he or she does not find satisfaction. He or she acts only when forced to, whereas the active individual acts because he must and because of a congenital impulse that drives him to do so. To put it another way, the active person acts to live and lives to act. When the active person is confronted with an obstacle it is looked upon as a challenge for action. Some active individuals will select a task to engage in purely because of the obstacle it poses. These are the daredevils, the front-line people, whereas the inactive armchair critics choose to write about it instead.

The emotive and active individual is an 'action man' who is eager and ambitious to produce results. An emotive and non-active individual is a private person whose feelings control him or her, while the emotive and active person controls his or her own feelings. Active people live life to the fullest every second, every minute and every hour even during leisure. They could be workaholics and rarely postpone a job. Do it now, is the rule they live by. They will demonstrate qualities of perseverance, independence, liveliness, agility, punctuality, objectivity, practicality and truthfulness.

Responsiveness (P+S)

Otto Gross, in 1902 in Leipzig, discovered there was a slow and rapid reaction of the nervous tissue of the brain which was later used by the Dutch (Heymans and Wiersman) School to describe the primary and secondary ways of response. Primary Response (P) individuals live in the present, and their joys and sorrow are short lived. They react to situations fast and explosively, but it quickly dies out. On the other hand, individuals of the Secondary Response (S) are influenced for prolonged periods by their feelings. These individuals live in the future and assume their present as a basis for the future, which in turn depends on the past.

A stimulus triggers a reaction, and no one is immune to the effects of a stimulus in the present or its effects on the past, but when the effects of a primary stimulus recall the past, then the person is of a primary character. If past events, on the other hand, persist and remain in the present, then the individual is of secondary character. Therefore, to conclude, it can be said that in primary character people you will find maximum effects for short periods of time, where the word experience means the live presence of a fact or situation; and for secondary character people experience is a gradual build-up of maximum effects which is longer lasting.

Rene Le Senne said, 'You can write easily on sand, but it can be wiped off without difficulty; but you carve on marble with difficulty and it lasts indefinitely.'

The Eight Characters

The combination of the three fundamental factors – Emotivity, Activity, Responsiveness – gives eight characters:

The Emotive, Active, Secondary (EAS)	Passionate
The Emotive, Active, Primary (EAP)	Choleric
The Emotive, non-Active, Secondary (EnAS)	Sentimental
The Emotive, non-Active, Primary (EnAP)	Nervous
The non-Emotive, Active, Secondary (nEAS)	Phlegmatic

The non-Emotive, Active, Primary (nEAP)   Sanguine
The non-Emotive, non-Active, Secondary (nEnAS)   Apathetic
The non-Emotive, non-Active, Primary (nEnAP)   Amorphous

These are the basic, pure characters, but because of the variability in the degree of the components (E, A, S or P), each of the eight characters may have one or two of the others as auxiliary, for example the Passionate can also be paraCholeric, paraSentimental or paraPhlegmatic. No character, however, may have, as an auxiliary, its opposite – the Passionate cannot be paraAmorphous, the Choleric paraApathetic and so on, at least not without producing a highly explosive mix which can be called genius or madness.

The pure EAS (Passionate) is aggressive, decisive, practical, efficient, active, persevering, observant, objective, precise, devoted, patriotic, ascetic, honourable, natural, indifferent towards food and sex, kind towards people inferior to him, prudent, loyal, serious, attached to tradition, a collector. He has a good memory, is compassionate, has no vanity, a vigorous reaction to obstacles, great working ability, a taste for grandeur, sense of social values, and a rapid conception of situations. He likes order and cleanliness, and there is harmony between words and actions. Because of his strong attachment to tradition, his political ideas are not always progressive.

Among the great Passionates are Napoleon, Nietzsche, Carlyle, Michelangelo, Pasteur, Dante, Gladstone, Newton, Tolstoy, Beethoven, Louix XIV, Goethe and Plato.

The Pure EAP (Choleric) is impulsive, authoritative, excitable, optimistic, versatile, inventive, combative, violent, subjective, touchy (but will not sulk), mobile, busy, decisive, extroverted, demonstrative, natural, talkative, materialistic, sociable, cordial, obliging, popular, dynamic, quick witted, keen on politics, good humoured, confident with people, easily adaptable, a motivator of people, a keen and uninhibited public speaker with lively sentiments, practical.

He has a taste for change, a fast emotional response to the environment, has desires for honour, taste for action, a tendency to exaggerate, vitality, appetite, strong sexuality, taste for new things and no fear of obstacles. He lacks discipline in action, patience when waiting for results. He also likes to satisfy his physical needs.

Among the great Cholerics are Dickens, Danton, Scott, Fielding, Cellini, George Sand, Casanova, Victor Hugo, Diderot, Leon Gambetta and François I.

The pure EnAS (Sentimental) is unobservant, subjective, retrospective, scrupulous, melancholic, obsessive, sulky, spiteful, grudging, timid, stubborn, prudent, attached to habits, very sensitive to changes and new things, displeased with himself, inclined to boredom, nagging, easily discouraged, honourable, an idealist, romantic, vulnerable, mistrustful, introspective, interested in meditation.

He has variable sensitivity, long-lasting emotional hurt, lasting impressionability, taste for solitude, variable moods, slow reactions, taste for collecting, poor adaptability, moral feelings, dignity, tendency towards half measures, a rapport with nature. He likes old memories (mental rumination). He avoids tragedies. His words and actions are in accord (agreement).

He lacks élan (vitality), confidence in himself and the future, aptitude for practical solutions, interest in machines. He feels the need for protection, seeks security, and can be violent. He reacts against social conformities. He is dogmatic, dislikes commands or being commanded.

He loves animals and transfers his affections to them, avoids closeness with people since he is easily hurt. He may, therefore, be mistaken for a hard person.

Some famous Sentimentals are Thackeray, Rousseau, Robespierre, Calvin, Kierkegaard, Amiel, Louis XIII and Alfred de Vigny.

The Pure EnAP (Nervous) is impulsive, mobile, busy, negligent, unstable, artistic, prevaricating, playful, susceptible, excitable, frivolous, artificial, seductive, indecisive, not persevering, easily discouraged, self-contented, affected, vain, mistrustful, unreliable, unpunctual, sarcastic and capricious or sad and sorrowful, rapidly consoled. He is a vagrant in friendship, love and profession.

He has rapid and superficial judgments, big projects which never take off, taste for fashion, taste for entertainment, variability of moods, mobile sympathies, reactive impulsiveness, emotional violence, vivacity of sentiments, poetic feelings, desires for honour, liking for change. He talks much – mainly about himself. He embellishes his talk. He laughs and talks loudly. Laughs at his own jokes. He needs new impressions. Expects immediate results. There is contradiction betweeen his thoughts and his life.

His feelings are exceptionally mobile, moving him promptly from tears to laughter, from depression to enthusiasm, and vice versa. His emotional energy is wasted on impulsive decisions. There is debility of moral sentiment and disorderly sexuality. He is a big spender. He has a taste for the macabre, absurd and horrible.

Some famous Nervous characters are Baudelaire, Alfred de Musset, Edgar Allan Poe, Oscar Wilde, Byron, Heine, Chopin, Mozart, Dostoyevsky, Jean Cocteau, Chateaubriand, Alphonse Daudet, Lamartine and d'Annunzio.

The Pure nEAS (Phlegmatic) is calm, even-tempered, well controlled, silent, contained, wary, reflective, circumspect, tolerant, intelligent, constantly occupied, patient, persevering, tenacious, methodical, concise, punctual, patriotic, virtuous, sober, impassive, honourable, a person of habits and principles, interested more in things than people, ceremonious. He has cold kindness, sexual continence, apparent indifference, dignity, a wide mind, independence of opinions, long-lasting sympathies, objectivity, objective observation, sense of humour, slow decisions. He worries about the future. He has little sympathy but great understanding for his fellow human beings. There is accordance between words and actions.

He may lack imagination but he has a very open mind and great intellectual abilities. He is kind and attached to principles. He is courageous and stoic and if it were not for his tremendous sense of humour he could be considered the greatest bore of all.

Some great Phlegmatics are Hume, Darwin, Bergson,

Cavendish, Addison, Gibbon, Montaigne, Owen, Washington, Turgot, and Kant (a truly rare pure Phlegmatic).

The Pure nEAP (Sanguine) is calm, polite, witty, constantly working, a lover of wealth, practical, courageous, egoistic, observant, objective, positive, tolerant, indifferent, benevolent, sceptical, cynical, adaptable.

He has rapid understanding, a talent for improvised public speaking, independent judgment, easy rapport with people, easy adaptation, a taste for the abstract, a taste for science, rough sexuality, negative and critical attitude to religion. He lacks depth, sense of continuity, and solves problems fast. He prefers useful things. His words and actions accord.

He likes wealth (and knows how to make it) and all the pleasures that go with it. He is a great diplomat, somewhat ironical but with a quick mind. He is a realist and likes sport.

Among the great Sanguines are Machiavelli, Mazarin, Bacon, Voltaire, Shaftesbury, Talleyrand, Metternich, Haekel, Montesquieu, Colette and Henri IV.

The Pure nEnAS (Apathetic) is sombre, placid, closed, stubborn, unconsolable, introspective, unsociable, secretive, a person of principle, even tempered, honourable, sexually indifferent, not particularly religious.

He has a tendency to melancholia and economical living. He dislikes changes and novelties. He has no strong predisposition towards mental disturbance.

He bears grudges, though not spiteful, and also likes solitude. He sticks to his principles, is conservative and, when he is not thrifty, is avaricious. He dislikes children and as a teacher may prove cruel. He endures danger and hardship without emotion (since he has little). He thrives under discipline and is a happy soldier. Lacking in imagination, initiative and curiosity of the mind, he floats over life, frustrating people and boring himself. He usually ends his existence drinking heavily as if to fill up the void within.

No Apathetic has left his name in history except Louis XVI, and only through heredity of power.

The Pure nEnAP (Amorphous) is inactive, placid, impulsive, laconic, lazy, insensitive, courageous, selfish, indecisive, tolerant through indifference, difficult to convince, sexually undisciplined, non-demonstrative. He has no religious fervour. He is the servant of his physical and egoistic interests.

He lacks practical sense and his predominant interests are selfish and materialistic. He is brave but not especially patriotic. Although lacking many qualities of character, he is usually gifted with various talents, more than any of the other seven characters: he can 'act' any of them.

He likes being with people, spending money and entertaining. This makes him a charmer which, together with his lack of personality, often misleads people into saying about him, 'He is a mystery to me; I can't quite grasp him.' Of course there is little to grasp. He is the mirror of any one he chooses – when he can be bothered. Many entertainers, actors, comedians belong to this character.

As far as can be ascertained, no Amorphous has reached immortality, except for Louix XV, but he, too, was born to it.

The similarities between the eight characters are due to the similarities of the components (E,A, S or P). For instance, the Passionate and the Choleric share the same two factors (E and A) and are bound to have similar character traits.

No one of the eight characters is better or worse than the others. Each can be good or evil, kind or selfish, depending on education, upbringing and circumstances of life. Prisons are full of all eight characters. It is behaviour that counts, and behaviour can be learned at any age in life.

Le Senne added three supplementary factors to the three fundamental factors of character already described. These are:

1. Broadness of the field of consciousness.
2. Analytical intelligence.
3. Egocentricity/allocentricity.
4. Will.

Broadness of the Field of Consciousness

During our lifetime the field of consciousness may vary from large to narrow, and vice versa, depending on the influencing factors. If the mind is focused on a specific object without any distraction and in isolation from other perceptions, then the field of consciousness is said to be narrow; and if the ideas and sensations from the mind are continuously flowing, then the field of consciousness is large. In any emergency, the field of consciousness is narrowed to deal with the threat, and the degree to which the desired effect is produced depends on the character of the person, some minds being larger than others. Prof. G. Heymans suggests that on average the intensity of consciousness is narrower in women than in men. The impressions received by the mind of a person with a narrow consciousness are more intense because they shut off other extraneous impressions. The person with a large field of consciousness tends to perceive things in a different light, with less intensity and focus than the narrow-charactered individual.

Analytical Intelligence

Prof. Heymans also defines an intelligent person as 'the one that arrives quicker and more competently than others to the right conclusion'. Le Senne defines intelligence as being (1) pure appreciation of value and (2) the ability to reflect abstractly and consequently analyse the meaning. It can therefore be interpreted that intelligence is the ability to understand quickly and accurately and to make quick deductions from the logical combination of accumulated information and experience using imagination and memory. There are two types of intelligence: generalized and particularized, and both stem from the same source of intelligence.

Egocentricity/Allocentrism

There are two primordial tendencies of the human conscious mind: 'I' and the 'Other'. When the 'I' is the focus of attention, the tendency is egocentric and when the 'Other' becomes an object and the conscious is put on the side of the 'Other' and can see the 'I', from the other's point of view, then the tendency becomes allocentric.

Will

The word 'will' is not specifically a term used in psychology. What it means is that it is the inclination of an individual to make one's interests become reality, where every voluntary action directed by an idea requires intelligence and responsibility. Actions that do not conform to this rule are not dependent on the will.

The modus operandi of the will is made up of four stages:

1. The concept of the project.
2. The deliberation (to weigh up the pros and cons of alternative actions).
3. The decision (to select the best possible action).
4. The execution (to actualize the concept).

The main problem areas of the will happen at the deliberation stage where the individual weighs up the pros and cons and stops there, being unable to make the decision. Some will go around subconsciously asking others to make the decision for them, because they find it painful to do so and find it the easiest way to avoid the responsibility of making the decision. It must be noted here that the impulsive and erratic individual is doomed to fail through lack of consistency. The will is exercised intentionally and is done so because of the individual's needs, and is the expression of the total personality, unconscious motivations and sociability of the individual.

We will now look at some other psychological traits.

Temperament

Dr Paul Carton, in his book on temperament says, 'The study of temperaments is one of the most important means to the overall understanding of the human being' and supports the idea that the inherent structures and patterns of a person's temperament must be known if we want to direct, orient or treat them. Temperament is a mental tendency in the person – it can be congenital or acquired, 'a dynamic state represented by the totality of physical, psychological and biological possibilities of the individual,' says Dr Vannier. It dominates one or more of the four fundamental instincts of life: the **motor** instinct (also called 'unifying') which co-ordinates decisions taken according to aptitudes, tastes and the physiological and intellectual possibilities of the individual; the **cerebral** (also called 'psychic') which directs thinking, reasoning, searching and understanding the **vital** (or thoracic) which incites respiration and development; and the **nutritive** (or abdominal or 'material') instinct which sees to the nutritive and reproductive needs.

There are four anatomical systems that serve these dominant and fundamental instincts: the **osteomuscular** system which holds the whole body together and is therefore called the 'unifying' system; the **nervous** system which, incorporating the brain, the cerebellum, the medulla and plexus of nerves, co-ordinates, regulates, conserves, warns, protects, and so on; the **respiratory** system, which incorporates the heart, veins, arteries and lungs which feed the whole body with oxygen and keep us alive; and the **digestive** and **reproductive** systems, incorporating the digestive organs (stomach, intestines), the transforming organs (kidneys, bladder) and the reproductive organs (genitals, external and internal) which constitute the abdominal factory that sees to our material needs of growth and reproduction.

The ancient Greeks, from Hippocrates, the 5th century BC physician who made a connection between the body fluids and temperament, the Egyptians, the Jews and the Indians all believed that there are four body fluids (also called 'humours') and that each temperament is caused by the predominance of one over the others.

These four body fluids are:

- bile or green bile – corresponding to the Choleric temperament
- atrabile or black bile – corresponding to the Melancholic temperament

- blood – corresponding to the Sanguine temperament
- phlegm or mucus – corresponding to the Phlegmatic temperament.

They went on to say that the fluids correspond with the four primordial elements of fire, earth, air and water, and with the four fundamental qualities of matter: dry, cold, hot and humid, which, in turn, correspond with the four states of matter: ether, solid, gas and liquid.

Dr Carton gives an interesting table of correspondence of the four temperaments:

Temperament	Phlegmatic (lymphatic)	Sanguine (sanguine)	Choleric (bilious)	Melancholic (nervous)
Elements	Water	Air	Fire	Earth
States of matter	Liquid	Gas	Ether	Solid
Organic chemistry	Hydrogen	Oxygen	Nitrogen	Carbon
Vital qualities	Humid	Hot	Dry	Cold
Force	Physical	Vital	Unifying	Spiritual
Sphere	Instinctive	Animistic	Volitive	Intellectual
Parts of the body	Abdomen	Thorax	Limbs	Head
Systems	Digestive	Cardio-pulmonary	Osteo-muscular	Nervous
Humour	Phlegm	Blood	Bile	Atrabile
Functions	Digestion	Respiration	Execution	Reflection
Manifestations	Instinct	Sentiment	Will	Intelligence
Expressions	Material	Life	Synthesis	Thinking
Ages	Childhood	Adolescence	Old	Adult
Seasons	Winter	Spring	Autumn	Summer
Vices	Sensuality	Hatred	Indiscipline	Foolishness
Qualities	Asceticism	Love	Saintliness	Genius
Nation	Agriculture	Communications	Government	Finance
Industry	Manufacture	Commerce	Direction	Research
Arithmetic	Division	Multiplication	Addition	Subtraction
Colours	Blue	Red	White	Yellow

It is a fact that, among company directors, the vast majority are of a Choleric temperament; the Melancholic temperament is better in research than any other; and people who suffer from, say cardiovascular discomfort tend to belong to the Sanguine temperament.

Everybody has at least three (if not all four temperaments) in their biological make-up, but in differing proportions. A temperament in equilibrium has the four elements – water, air, fire and earth – in balance.

A person of **Phlegmatic** temperament is calm and stable, passive and slow, relatively unconscious. She needs time to absorb situations and impressions. Few things ever trouble her. She likes routine in her life and in her business. She is consistent and wise, loyal in her feelings and traditional in her habits. She avoids exalted and agitated people; they trouble her. She has no enthusiasm in her activities and is slow in the execution of her job. She is precise and punctual, capable and competent, despite her apparent carelessness. She doesn't misuse her energy. Her movements are sober, precise and slow. She is very observant and has a good memory, particularly for concrete and physical things. But her imagination is weak. She prefers to use instruments of precision. Her instinct of preservation is very developed. She is prudent and fears the unknown, danger, fights and violence and avoids them without shame. But if she finds herself involved in such a situation, she defends herself with ferocious and astonishing tenacity.

She can be an engineer, mechanic, scientist, employee; because of her ability for repetition, execution, comparison and measure, she could do any job requiring these qualities.

A person of **Sanguine** temperament is sociable, passionate, impulsive and jovial. She is full of joie de vivre, likes nature and adapts easily to every environment. Dazzling and overflowing, she is destined to exteriorization. She likes movement, physical activities, contact, adventures and amorous conquests. She has a practical mind and a great heart. She likes travelling and she is usually optimistic, sensual, greedy and full of vitality. She switches readily from cordial behaviour to combative, aggressive reactions.

She may be a commercial traveller, industrialist, financier, good in public relations, marketing, executive positions, advertising, artistic work.

A person of **Choleric** temperament is disciplined and organized, energetic, firm, serious, sober, reflective, decisive. Her intelligence is profound, prompt and brilliant but her memory often fails her. She is dignified, laconic, ethical and just, objective and positive. She respects others and expects them to keep to their word, as she does. She has great ability to concentrate, think and reason. She is the intellectual *par excellence*. She prefers the concrete to the abstract and, as her feelings are not very well developed, she sees, or prefers to see, only the evident. Emotionally she is vulnerable.

She is particularly suited to academic work. She is also a director in business. Her creative and executive talents, together with her tenacity, will-power and energy, could make her an apostle, a leader or a fanatic.

A person of **Melancholic** temperament is perpetually dissatisfied, pessimistic, introverted, reflective, orderly, anxious, meticulous, serious and reserved. She worries, she feels badly placed, unadapted, uprooted in the real world. She rebels against her surroundings, feels hostile in society, she is distrustful. Extremely sensitive and emotive, she can be vindictive, susceptible and grudging, irritable, versatile and egocentric. She has an inquisitive mind and needs to know everything that goes on around her. She has a very creative imagination and speculates on abstract thought. She is the great intuitive thinker. Her intelligence is profound and prompt, her mind is complicated. She is usually unstable in her profession until she comes to terms with her instability. She could be a researcher, philosopher, psychologist, teacher, lawyer, poet or painter.

These are the four temperaments. But almost no one has only one, pure temperament. We all have one dominant, a second auxiliary, a third and a fourth, which may vary or alter, sometimes after a traumatic experience or dramatic change in life. Therefore, the written signs in the handwriting (which you will learn more about in the next section) are always modified by the second and third temperament's influence.

MASLOW'S THEORY OF MOTIVATION

Abraham Maslow, the American humanistic psychologist, devised a theory of motivation based on a hierarchy of needs (see below). The inner nature of individuals, says Maslow, is either neutral or positively 'good'. What we call evil behaviour appears to be a secondary reaction to frustration of this intrinsic nature.

Human beings can be loving, noble and creative, and are capable of pursuing the highest values and aspirations. The

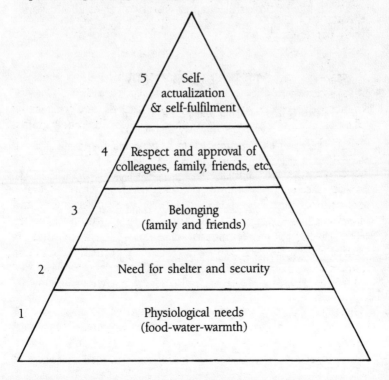

5 — Self-actualization & self-fulfilment

4 — Respect and approval of colleagues, family, friends, etc.

3 — Belonging (family and friends)

2 — Need for shelter and security

1 — Physiological needs (food-water-warmth)

constitutional differences in an individual generate personal values, i.e. he must satisfy his needs, for example, for salt or love. If deprived of satisfaction, the individual 'sickens and withers' and his growth is stunted.

All these basic needs, says Maslow, may be considered to be simply steps along the 'time path' to general self-actualization, under which all other needs can be subsumed. If the inner nature is permitted to guide our life, we grow healthy, fruitful and happy. For Maslow, self-actualization is a goal towards which all human beings move, and is experienced as unity of personality, spontaneous expressiveness and full individual identity.

Psychology is a fascinating and highly complex subject. In this chapter I hope I have given you an insight into some of the basics. Remember that the more you know about the way someone's mind works, the easier it will be to persuade, motivate, manipulate and negotiate with them.

I would like to close this chapter with two verses about work, and the way people approach it and relate to each other.

IT'S NOT MY JOB

This is a story about four people, named Everybody,
Somebody, Anybody and Nobody.
There was an important job to be done and Everybody
was sure that Somebody would do it.
Anybody could have done it, but Nobody did it.
Somebody got angry about that, because it was Everybody's job.
Everybody thought Anybody could do it.
but Nobody realized that Everybody wouldn't do it.
It ended up that Everybody blamed Somebody,
when Nobody did what Anybody could have.

(Author unknown)

MY BOSS & I

When I take a long time,
I am slow.
When my boss takes a long time,
He is thorough.
When I don't do it,
I am lazy.
When my boss doesn't do it,
He is too busy.
When I do something without being told,
I am trying to be smart.
When my boss does the same,
that is initiative.
When I please my boss,
I'm apple–polishing.
When my boss pleases his boss,
He's co-operating.
When I do good, my boss never remembers.
When I do wrong, he never forgets.

(Author unknown)

CHAPTER 14

Graphology, the science and art of handwriting analysis

HOW IT CAN MAKE YOU A BETTER MANAGER OF PEOPLE

Graphology can be used as an additional tool to all the others given in this book to help you pinpoint your buyer and discover the right time to persuade, motivate, manipulate or negotiate when selling a product, service or idea. It is also of great value to the buyer in understanding the seller. To do this would necessitate one of two approaches.

- A quick glance at some handwriting of the buyer or seller while you are face-to-face, your observations and conclusions.
- An in-depth analysis of a few pages of handwritten material for a detail picture of the buyer or seller.

My interests in graphology lie in the broader context of its uses, not just in buying and selling alone.

So what is graphology, and how can it help you communicate better? These and other questions on graphology will be answered in the next few pages in a factual way, but if you wish to develop your knowledge further, I can recommend *Graphology* by Reena Nezos.

Graphology is the study of the psychological make-up of a human being through the handwriting. It is derived from the Greek language – **Graphe** meaning writing and **logos** meaning definition. It is a social science which is based on research and experimentation, not on magic or mystery.

The sixth sense, intuition, plays an important part in the analysis and diagnosis of handwriting, as it does in the other professions such as medicine, psychology, law, physics, chemistry and philosophy. Science calls for the systematic and organized search for knowledge with a precise objective to discover the truth. Science being non-fictional is dependent on logic and is based on reality.

Graphology has a long and well-authenticated history. Here are some historical facts. The following people have been involved in graphology since ancient times. The Greek philosopher Aristotle (322–384 BC) and the Greek orator and writer Demetrios Falirefs (309 BC) made reference to it, as did the Greek poet Menandros Athenaios and the Greek writer Dionysos Alikarnasefs. The Italian physician, writer and professor of philosophy Camillo Baldo (in 1622) produced the first book on how to know the nature of a person from the handwriting. The German Grohman (in 1792) published a book where he said it was possible even to assess the physique, voice, hair and eye colour from the handwriting. Goethe found a connection between speech, walk and writing in the majority of people. Lavater found a pattern of consistency where you will never find an active man dragging his legs while walking or speaking or writing in a slow, bored manner, just as much as a non-active person will never be found having swift, perky writing.

The French writer Eduard Hocquart (in 1814) wrote about the art of judging the mind and character of men and women from their handwriting. Abbé Flandarin, a French graphology researcher, opened the first school for the interpretation of writing in 1830. Jean Crépieux-Jamin (1858–1940), a pupil of Michon, revised his teacher's work after his death by reclassifying and regrouping the sign system and establishing new laws on sign classification which are observed to date. The author of ten books, in his last one titled *L'ABC de la Graphologie*, a masterpiece, he gives his conclusions on fifty years of research and gives graphology a firm scientific basis.

Towards the end of the nineteenth century, the Germans took the lead in graphological research. Professor of Physiology William Thierry Preyer at Jena showed that handwriting is in fact brain writing. People who have lost their writing arm and have had to adjust to the use of the other one will find difficulty initially, but in time, the writing will become identical to that of the lost limb.

Dr Ludwig Klages (1872–1956), a German physicist, chemist, philosopher, psychologist, characterologist and graphologist added his own ideas to Crépieux-Jamin's suggesting that the movement in handwriting had soul and spirit and was either positive (+) or negative (−). He also introduced the concept of rhythm which is described further on. He explains that in a regular piece of handwriting, the form level (FL) which is the spontaneity and identity which symbolizes the happy meeting between uneven and monotonous writing, and the succession of movements in the writing if it is not even repeated in the same form, will show an unconscious order and natural balance.

Klages suggested that in a regular piece of writing if the form level is high (+) it is the power of the will, and if it is low (−) it means there is a lack of depth of feeling. In an irregular writing, if the FL is high (+) it means there is a power of depth of feeling and if the FL is low (−) there is the lack of will power.

Klages developed the Form Level which consists of six basic elements:

1. The degree of **organization** of the writing.
2. The **spontaneity** of the handwriting.
3. The **originality** of the style.
4. The **dynamism** of the stroke.
5. The **harmony**.
6. The **rhythm**.

1. The **organization** of the writing has four degrees: **unorganized**, **organized**, **combined** and **disorganized**.
- **unorganized** writing is the crude early childhood form.

– **organized** writing is the spontaneous real writing which is acquired around teenage years or later.

– **combined** writing is the highest form of organized writing achieved by writing masters through thought and action. This degree is not common.

– **disorganized** writing is usually caused by disease, intoxication or old age, and is characterized by shakiness, unevenness, fading pressure, thinning of tail and lack of precision. Disorganized writing can happen at any time of life and is not confined to old age. It is important to let the graphologist know the age of the writer to prevent any error of interpretation.

2. The **spontaneity** of the handwriting can be seen when the writer's movement is fluent and free from any signs of effort or constraint. Spontaneity is a sign of honesty and self-confidence.

3. The **originality** of the style has a personal, original and spontaneous presentation rather than a calligraphic style. If the original form is crude, unpleasant and illegible, so will be the writing.

4. The **dynamism** of writing reflects vigour, good pressure, flowing movement, decisiveness and spontaneity.

5. The **harmony** of writing consists of six elements: **proportion**, **order**, **clarity**, **simplicity**, **sobriety** and **freedom of movement**, and indicates a well-balanced and mature personality.

– **Proportion**: when all the proportions of the writing are in harmony and there are no exaggerations.

– **Order**: the writing is well-placed on the page, the layout, date, paragraphs and signature are presented in an orderly fashion.

– **Clarity**: where there are no erasings, scratchings or crossings out.

– **Simplicity**: without too much verbosity.

– **Sobriety**: presented within moderate dimensions.

– **Freedom of movement**: in an easy, flowing style.

6. The **rhythm**, according to Klages, is the manifestation of life itself and embraces the living world. It can be seen in the beat of the wings of migrating birds, the trot of a horse, the swimming

activities of fish, the inhaling and exhaling of air in human breathing. Likewise, the handwriting of each person will have a certain rhythm. The rhythm in writing can be affected by anger, hesitation, hastiness, depression, cold, and so on.

Rhythm can mean the occasional reproduction of similar phenomena in the writing. Small inequalities constantly reproduced and non-identical still give it a rhythm. Good rhythm indicates a well-balanced character and a brilliant personality, with optimism, inspiration, confidence, sensibility, feeling, sensation and intuition. Rhythm is one of the few signs that has no negative interpretation. A short rhythm applies to words alone. A long rhythm applies to writing that moves symmetrically along a line or passage.

A graphologist starts by examining the form level in a sample of handwriting before anything else. This is very important because each sign has more than one significance, depending on the standard of the form level and the rest of the signs. This is the reason why on their own the signs mean nothing else. Education and culture play a very important role in the form level by making the writing more expressive.

Conventional, calligraphic, commercial and indeed all stylized writing is defined as persona. The personal writing is seen when a personal mask is adapted to cover the true self of the writer, and when the buyer's behaviour is seen in the writing, it contributes to a select or non-expressive style. It is caused when the individuality of the person is hidden, suppressed or so weak that it is virtually non-existent.

Another element that affects the form level is integrity, which encompasses such things as deceit, discipline and justice. Integrity is one of the most difficult signs to assess in writing. Conscious honesty is reflected in every man, woman and child to a greater or lesser extent, and when we refer to integrity what we are talking about is its manifestation in one's actions. We can all think and act honestly or dishonestly for conscious or unconscious reasons. A person can be honest in his dealings with money but dishonest when dealing with people. What really matters in life is how our behaviour affects our feelings as well as what it does to other people. Both modesty and pomposity have either a positive or negative influence on the person's honesty. Niceness coupled with positive thinking and kindness also affects the form level greatly, even in the absence of good education, and meanness diminishes it, even in spite of the best of education.

From the above, it can be seen that the elements that effect the form level are education, culture, personal development, integrity, kindness, intelligence and dynamism. The question we must ask is: how do all these factors appear in the handwriting? This is a difficult question to answer as there is no one sign that indicates a specific thing. The conclusion we can draw is that writing which is spontaneous, simplified, original, harmonious, with rhythm and well-combined letters with no exaggerations tends towards a high form level, and writing with exaggerations and disproportions has a negative interpretation.

So, to summarize the signs in the form level:

A high form level is indicated in the handwriting by rhythm, i.e. a succession of similar but never strictly identical movements, good distribution of black and white aesthetically appealing letters with proportion, consistency and regularity, and not too rigid in appearance.

A low form level is indicated by a mechanical movement of hand showing emptiness, monotony, exaggeration, of messiness and lacking lustre.

Now let us see the 'aura', or the 'uniqueness' of each individual's handwriting which is visible to the graphologist as well as to the non-graphologist.

A cardinal rule in graphology is that you should never try to allocate a meaning to a sign on its own, that this means egoism or that means pessimism – this would be very incorrect. What you must do is look for consistency and repetitiveness – it is only then that they will mean something.

When we receive a letter from a friend we can instinctively say who it is because we have identified the signs.

Handwriting is the smallest movement of the human hand and also the most revealing. It consists of minute movements flying in all directions – vertical, horizontal, diagonally upwards or downwards, right and left, curved, straight, heavy or light pressure, rapid or slow. Writing is most often done with the right or left hand, and on rare occasion with some other part of the body which is governed by the central nervous system and is therefore unconscious and very revealing.

This diagram shows the main writing movements, directions and meaning.

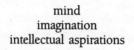

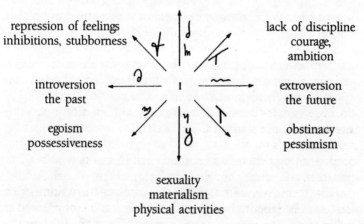

mind
imagination
intellectual aspirations

repression of feelings
inhibitions, stubbornness

lack of discipline
courage,
ambition

introversion ←——————→ extroversion
the past   the future

egoism
possessiveness

obstinacy
pessimism

sexuality
materialism
physical activities

The Laws of Writing

There are five basic and universal laws upon which graphology depends. These laws are essentially independent of the alphabet used. The types of letters are irrelevant. Alphabets are human inventions based on local needs. The laws of writing, on the other hand, are natural phenomena.

However, there are two remarks to be made:

- Each one of these laws is manifested more frequently or in a more tangible way in a particular alphabet rather than another.
- To understand them, it helps if we take examples of phenomena appearing in a specific alphabet.

Equally, we must not lose sight of a principle, the ignorance of which has caused much misunderstanding. This principle is: even though the laws of writing are exact, the same cause has the same effect. Similar written phenomena may derive from different sources. In this respect, graphology does not differ from other natural sciences.

Let us specify these laws of writing:

The **first law** is an acknowledgement of source and is of primary importance:

The written movement is under the direct influence of the central nervous system, which comprises the brain, the cerebellum and the spinal liquid. The form of the written movement is not modified by the writing organ (hand, foot, mouth, etc.), if this functions normally and is sufficiently adapted to its function.

Fifty years ago there was a difference of opinion about this principle and some thought it to be mistaken. The misunderstanding came from the fact that the action of the writing organ is seen to be laboured and unnatural when it is not adapted to its function. The writing organ, however – right or left hand or foot, mouth, arm, neck and shoulder – will only act as an imperfect transmitter if it is defective or if it has not yet acquired the necessary training.

The cerebral influence on writing is also supported by the fact that physiologists have never been able to discover a criterion which will permit them to tell, with certainty, the differences between the brains of the two sexes; neither have graphologists ever discovered any certain differences between the writing of the two sexes. So the conclusion is evident that in all human beings, tendencies of the opposite sex exist, more or less unconscious and more or less able to manifest themselves. Handwriting, having its origins in the whole personality, shows these tendencies, even the most unconscious ones. But although we can see a feminine or masculine tendency in writing, the physical organs that constitute the differences between the sexes do not make their owner behave in a certain fashion. They only construct a part of the personality which may be the most visible, but the underlying tendencies are much more complex and definitely more important.

We all have met men who behave like women and women who behave like men. If sexual differences were as all-important as some psychologists, such as Freud, made them out to be, then all sexually normal men (or all sexually normal women) would have a better psychological structure and behaviour, which they do not.

Now we come to the **second law**:

When we write, the 'ego' is active but is not always active to the same degree. Its activity comes and goes, waxes and wanes, being at its highest level when the motion of the writing organ has gained momentum and is driven by it (e.g. at the end of words).

This is a phenomenon that exists in a more or less continuous way in normal people who are aware that they write, when they write. This ability may disappear in alienated people. If they write at that time, their writing will be a series of words put on paper as if by an automaton.

This law justifies what graphologists have always stated about capital letters which are the start of the writing effort: that under the influence of pride, vanity or arrogance, these initial letters take ample dimensions.

The **third law** says that:

We cannot voluntarily modify our natural writing at any given time without putting in it the marks of the effort required to obtain the change.

The marks of the effort required to change our writing are many, such as brusque stops, hooks, breakings, deviations, unnatural thinning or thickening of the strokes. They can be confused with signs of distraction or uncertainty, the difference being that an effort to change the writing is voluntary and conscious, whereas distraction and uncertainty are not voluntary or conscious. Long practice may make fluent an artificial or disguised writing by more or less eliminating the marks of effort; the disguise, however, will always be limited because, if we chase away nature, she will return galloping! Graphologists will be helped by the study of the 'will' in writing, since it is natural, as we know, for initial attention and effort stimulated by the will to diminish in accordance with the degree of intensity of the will.

To detect this attention and effort, there is no better way than to study the written signs of speed and form, especially in the independent elements of the handwriting. These are layout, dimension, pressure, form, speed, continuity, direction and particular signs (e.g. the signature, punctuation marks, diacritics and figures). These are described in greater detail further on.

The **fourth law** concerns the circumstances under which we write:

The writer who writes under circumstances where the action of writing is particularly difficult will instinctively use either the forms of letters which are more familiar to him, or forms of letters which are simple and easy to write.

This law is, of course, based on the principle of the 'easiest way out'.

The law covers all manner of situations, such as:

- People who wish to try to write with their other hand
- People who need to add a word or a group of words between the lines of a manuscript
- People who write in moving vehicles
- Ill, weakened people who have to write a testament by hand but who are in an uncomfortable position, probably in bed

The third and fourth laws are particularly important for the expert in graphological crime (anonymous, letters, verification of the identity of the writer or suspected fraud, particularly in wills).

The **fifth law** states:

The physiological mechanisms which produce the written movement are in correlation with the state of the central nervous system and vary in accordance with it. The written strokes, therefore, are in correspondence with the constitutional varieties of the nervous system and with the momentary modifications of each nervous system.

Briefly, writing varies in accordance with the mental particularities and the temporary dispositions of each one of us.

It has been argued, in connection with this law, that people can imitate its effects. The possibility necessitates education, great care and, particularly, great suppleness of the writing organ, the combination of which, in reality, is the privilege of a very small number of people. Here it must be pointed out once more that if we try voluntarily to modify our writing, nature's revenge is instantaneous.

The interpretation of the sign forms the basis from which the analysis of handwriting is done, but the accuracy of the reading will be dependent on how knowledgeable the graphologist is and the following considerations will have to be borne in mind to facilitate a proper interpretation:

- The correct assessment of the form level.
- To discover harmony.
- To observe rhythm.
- The right classification.
- The right definition.
- The right interpretation.

As mentioned earlier, the cardinal rule in graphology is that the value of a sign on its own means nothing, but the value of the sign is dependent on the following four factors:

1. The number of times the sign is repeated on the same page.
2. The written zone in which it appears (Max Pulver's symbolism of space – see below).
3. The rest of the signs that can be seen.

4. The form level of the handwriting (as defined by Dr Ludwig Klages, already explained).

Symbolism of Space

Discovered by Max Pulver (1890–1953), Swiss writer, poet, philosopher and lecturer in Graphology

Pulver said ambivalence, which is a state of internal conflict covering the sexual, emotional or spiritual in human nature, can occur unless there are compensating opposing forces, and when it occurs it can be seen in the handwriting, showing irregularities in all categories (i.e. the main movements shown above) and in all three zones (i.e. the upper, middle and lower zone in the diagram below).

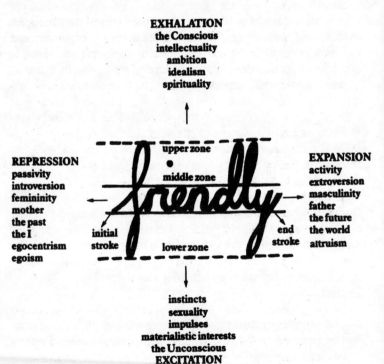

EXHALATION
the Conscious
intellectuality
ambition
idealism
spirituality

REPRESSION
passivity
introversion
femininity
mother
the past
the I
egocentrism
egoism

upper zone
middle zone

EXPANSION
activity
extroversion
masculinity
father
the future
the world
altruism

initial stroke
lower zone
end stroke

instincts
sexuality
impulses
materialistic interests
the Unconscious
EXCITATION

Pulver studied insincerity and dishonesty in depth. He believed that lying is a symptom with a psychological basis, and pointed out that fast writing shows greater sincerity than slow writing, which in itself did not indicate insincerity, and he developed an elaborate list of signs indicative of dishonesty under certain conditions.

After the Second World War, Rudolf Pophal, a German neurologist at the University of Hamburg, taught graphology and its connection with the motor-physiological and then his student Heinrich Pfnanne followed by developing a connection between the brain centres and handwriting.

During the last fifty years or so, significant advances have been made by numerous scientific people into various fields, e.g. graphometry, graphotherapy and criminological graphology. One of the pioneers in this field was the German graphologist, Walter Hegar, a strong critic of Klages who dismissed the form level as fiction and who developed his own system on the stroke alone, based on the principle that the stroke is measurable and is the only thing that makes contact with the paper. There is much truth in this, but it has its limitations.

Another great researcher was Dr Paul Carton, who discovered that the graphological signs could be classified into four temperaments: choleric, melancholic, sanguine and phlegmatic. This has already been covered earlier in chapter 13.

There are three other laws concerning the science of graphology that Crépieux-Jamin himself established.

First law:
One must examine the significance of a handwriting trait by considering it as a physiological movement and by comparing the quality, overall size, regularity and consistency of energy with the corresponding psychological movement.

Second law:
There are no independent signs; there are only general indications which may have different forms. The significance of these general indications can be assessed accurately by tracing them back to their origins and adapting the meaning of the latter to the conditions of the milieu in which the form appears.

Third law:

One graphological sign does not necessarily represent a single character trait. For example, rising handwriting may indicate ardour, activity, ambition, momentary joy or folly. The value of the sign depends on its cause, its context and its intensity. Handwriting which slopes downwards, for instance, may reveal a passing anxiety, habitual depression or simply bad positioning of the paper.

These, Crépieux-Jamin's own laws, are evidently the golden rules of graphology today. Every serious scientific graphologist abides by them. If not, he or she is an artist in fortune-telling rather than a graphologist.

The Signs

Eye training means learning to look at a handwriting, exercising the brain to observe the slightest movements of pen on paper and noticing all the different ways the letters are formed.

In graphology no sign is insignificant. Every little thing counts. The smallest hook or irregularity can be significant and indicative of a mood or trait of character, a good quality or a fault. Some signs may look similar to the untrained eye. Experience and devoted study clarify the confusion.

As we saw in the Introduction and in the laws of writing, no one sign indicates one trait of the writer's personality. The same trait of character in different people may appear under a different combination of signs. That is why we can never take a sign out of context and also why we can never have a complete list of signs as such.

In the pages that follow you will find the interpretation of each sign. Combinations of signs are infinite, like people.

The order of the categories is unimportant, although it is advisable to start with layout and to finish with the particular signs. This makes sense since the first thing we notice in a writing is usually the layout, and the last, more often than not, the 'i' dots, the punctuation, and so on.

After we have learned how to look at each writing and to see the various signs and write them down in their order of dominance (and before we start with their interpretation), we must remember that:

1. No sign should be interpreted alone. All signs are invalid when taken out of context
2. All signs can be contradictory, complementary, predominant, confirmatory or compensatory
3. All signs have value only when they are constant and repetitive
4. The FL must always be considered in order to interpret a sign correctly.

THE ANATOMY OF WRITING

Letters are written symbols and consist of nine elements:

1. Traits – any strokes made by the pen in one move
2. Down strokes – any vertical strokes drawn downwards
3. Up strokes – any vertical strokes drawn upwards
4. Ovals – the 'eyes' of the letters in the middle zones, e.g. a, o, g, d, etc.
5. Upper extensions – all the down strokes of the letters l, k, t, b, h, d and f to the baseline, also of the capital letters
6. Lower extensions – all down strokes of the letters g, j, y, p, q and f from the baseline down
7. Loops – all upward strokes of the upper and lower extensions which curve and cross the upper or lower extension, forming loops
8. The essential parts – the skeleton of the letter which is indispensable to its structure
9. The secondary parts (or accessories) – ornamentations or parts which are not essential to the structure of the letter.

The letters have five different zones:

1. Initial zone – the point where the letter starts
2. Final zone – the point where the letter ends

3. Upper zone – all upper extensions, i dots, t bars, accents and a part of the capital letters
4. Middle zone – all letters or parts of letters which occupy the space between the baseline and the top of the letters a, o, etc.
5. Lower zone – the lower extensions of the letters g, y, f, etc. the lower extensions of capital letters and all that extends below the baseline.

Writing has three dimensions:

1. Vertical
2. Horizontal
3. Depth.

THE CATEGORIES AND THEIR SIGNS

The following list of signs are amplified under their respective categories and will be found in *Graphology* by Renna Nezos, published by Random Century.

Layout

Layout covers the distribution and organization of the text on the page. It indicates the adaptability of the writer to the environment, the method and sense of organization, time, space, and so on.

The sheet of paper represents the world, the space within which we evolve. The 'guiding images' (ideas which dissect thought) are also represented by layout.

Layout contains eighteen signs. These are: aerated, chimneys, clear, compact, confused, disorderly, envelopes, invasive, irregular, margins, messy, neat, orderly, spaced out, spacing, tangled lines, underlined, unnecessary dots.

Dimension

Dimension deals with the size of the letters. It indicates the writer's opinion of himself and, consequently, the way he affirms his personality. It also shows the adaptability of the writer. Dimension covers variability in height, amplitude or spread (width or breadth).

The symbolism of space (discussed earlier) is also applicable to the evaluation of dimension: upwards symbolizes mind, imagination, intellectual aspirations; downwards symbolizes sexuality, materialism or physical activities.

Dimension contains twenty-four signs: compensatory, diminishing, disproportionate, enlarged, enlarging, exaggerated, expanded, extensive movements, full, irregular, large, low, prolonged downwards and upwards, prolonged downwards, prolonged upwards, proportionate, reduced, small, sober, squeezed, superelevated, tall, very large, wide.

Pressure

Pressure includes the study of the pressure of the writing instrument on the paper and the quality of the stroke. It indicates the intensity and originality of the personality, the vitality, the importance of instinct and material values, the state of health, and gives an indication of the influence of psychic health upon physical health.

The choice and handling of the writing instrument are determined by the totality of the personality, with very few exceptions.

Pressure contains thirty signs altogether, eighteen of which refer to the weight of the stroke, as follows: clubbed, deviated, flat, heavy, irregular, light, medium, notched, pale, in relief, robust, sharp-pointed, spasmodic, spindle-shaped, superficial, trenchant, weak, well-nourished.

Twelve signs refer to the quality of the stroke: blurred, congested, dry, fine, firm, medium, tension, pasty, precise, runny, smeary, thick, thin.

In order to assess pressure correctly we need the original document rather than a photocopy.

The signs which are not apparent in a photocopied document are as follows: flat, heavy, light, medium tension, pale, robust, superficial, trenchant, weak, well nourished, congested (sometimes photocopying fills in the little ovals), and thick.

It is also advisable to use a magnifying glass; the naked eye is not always adequate.

Form

Form is one of the most important categories. It has two parts. It deals with the way letters are formed and with the way letters are connected. It indicates the character, personality, memory (to some degree), attention, tastes, ideals, virtues, attitudes, aptitudes and originality of the writer.

The formation of the letters tells us whether the writer is rich or poor in imagination, whether he is close to, or far from, his unconscious with its eternal images or archetypes. It also tells us whether a person is endowed as an artist, has latent artistic possibilities, an imposing personality or otherwise, and is dependent or independent.

It is important, when considering form, to know the style of writing which is taught in each particular country as this will affect an individual's form.

Form contains sixty-three signs: ample, angular, animated, arabesques, arcades, artificial, bizarre, bow-ties or loops, closed, complicated, confused, conventional, copy-book, covering strokes, cramped, disguised, distinguished, double curves, double joins, elegant, filiform (thready-horizontal, elongated, wavy stroke), formless, garlands, graceful, gross (see following Particular signs), harmonious, illegible, impersonal, inharmonious, irregular, lassos, limpid, looped garlands, lower extensions, mannered, mirror writing, mixed (semi-angular, semi-garlanded), narrow letters, natural, negligent, open, original, ornate, proteiform (many styles of forming one letter), regular, round, rounded, shark's tooth, simple, simplified, soaring, spelling, spirals, square, stylized, supported, swords (see Particular signs), triangles (see Particular signs), typographic, upper extensions, vulgar, whips.

There are eight forms of connection of the stroke.

Angles – 𝑀𝑀 𝑀𝑀𝑀

Garlands – 𝑢𝑙 𝑢𝑙𝑙

Arcades – 𝑚 𝑚𝑚

Loops – 𝑙 𝑙𝑙 𝑙𝑙

Filiform – ⁓ = 𝑚

Double curves – 𝑣𝑣𝑣

See also Continuity when considering connections.

Supported – 𝑀𝑀𝑀

Square – ⊔⊔⊔ ⊓⊓⊓

Speed

Speed indicates the ways of reacting, manifested or not, the speed of thought and response of the writer, the degree of intelligence (see Form and Continuity), natural vivacity, creativity and nervous tension.

In a general way, fast writing is more favourably considered than slow. Two kinds of speed can be differentiated: absolute speed which indicates a writer's intelligence and culture, and relative speed, or that at a given time in one specimen of writing. Slowing down of speed reveals hesitation, sometimes inhibition, complexes and the tendency to conceal something.

Speed contains eighteen signs: abbreviated, accelerated, carried away, constrained, controlled, dynamic, effervescent, flying strokes, illegible (see Form), irregular (see Continuity), poised, precipitated, rapid, resolute, slack, slowed down, spontaneous.

Continuity

Continuity indicates the continuity of reasoning and action of the writer, logic, perseverance and capacity to achieve or otherwise. It indicates independence or lack of it and spontaneity of feeling.

The activity of the unconscious, which is often opposed to the writer's conscious ideals and ideas, may momentarily influence the writing trail. Retouches and corrections of all kinds interrupt the spontaneous flow of the writing by an intervention of the unconscious.

Continuity contains forty-two signs: agitated, amended, automatic, broken, calm, combined, comfortable, connected, constant, disconnected, discordant, disorganized, false connections, faltering, fragmented, free, grouped, hesitant, homogeneous, hopping, inhibited, irregular, jerky, lapses of continuity, mingling letters, monotonous, nuances (slight irregularities which do not affect the harmony of the writing), organized, overconnected, resting dots, rhythmic, shaky, stable, sticks, structured, sublimated, suspended, unfinished, unnecessary lines, unorganized, unvarying, variable.

There are ten forms of continuity. These are: angular, arcades, combined, connected, double curves, filiform, garlands, grouped, looped, supported.

Direction

Direction, like Form and Pressure, has two parts: the direction of the lines, which indicates the stability of behaviour, orientation, fluctuation of the mood and state of mind (moral and intellectual) of the writer; and the slant of the stroke, which shows the degree of impetuosity and ardour in action, the impulsiveness or restraint of the emotions and the moods.

The symbolism of space contributes towards an evaluation of direction: rightwards is the 'You', the outside world, the future, masculinity, action, goals; leftwards symbolizes the 'I', introspection and the past.

Direction contains twenty-five signs altogether. Thirteen refer to the direction of the lines: concave, convex, descending, diving, galloping downwards, galloping upwards, horizontal, irregular (see Continuity), rigid, rising, stable baseline, undulating words, wavy lines.

Twelve refer to the direction of the stroke and the slant: centrifugal, centripetal, irregular (see Continuity), leftward, progressive, regressive, reverse, rightward, rigid, twisted, vertical, very slanted to the right.

Particular Signs

These include all the small particularities which do not fit into any of the above categories, such as figures, punctuation marks, diacritics and the signature. Each sign is studied individually. If a sign is not constant and repetitive it must be considered a particular sign and not as belonging to any of the other categories. For example, if, in writing, the majority of the lower extensions (or the t bars) are in the shape of triangles, then this sign belongs to form; if, however, there is only one or two (for instance in the signature) then it is a particular sign.

Some of the most common particular signs are: accents, capital letters in the middle of words, final strokes, hooks, lassos, lyrical, shark's tooth (see Form), signature, spirals (see Form), starting strokes, strong regressive strokes, swords, triangles, wavy strokes.

The first two categories, Layout and Dimension, show adaptability of the writer and his respect for others.

The third and fourth, Pressure and Form, reveal character, temperament, personality, will and vitality.

The fifth and sixth, Speed and Continuity, indicate the rhythm activity and intellectual abilities.

The seventh, Direction, expresses stability, sensibility, health and the ability to express feelings.

SIGNATURE

Category: particular sign.
The signature can never be interpreted as an isolated sign, it can only be studied in connection with the text to help complete and confirm an interpretation of the writing as a whole. Whatever the qualities of the writing, we cannot be certain of these without the signature. In truth, we know little about the writer without his or her signature.

In order to analyse someone's writing, therefore, the signature is needed. Its role is decisive – whatever we have deciphered from the handwriting may be confirmed or rejected by the signature. In cases of disparity the signature is pre-eminent; it is the key to the writer's real personality and inner life.

The first thing a signature reveals is the writer's vitality: his or her ability to realize his potential; the direction he gives to his life; how he puts his abilities to use.

In the writing we see the writer's potential; in the signature, whether and how he uses this potential. The choice depends more on history and psychic strength than on personality and temperament.

The second element revealed in the signature is the writer's own evaluation of himself: his personality and how he rates himself among his fellow beings.

The third element expressed is the degree of reliability and morality, sinceritty and honesty, or otherwise.

The fourth element deals with the writer's family history: the whole of his childhood, personal history, situation in the family home and the way he felt about it; the attachment, or not, to a memory of past happiness or misery – all reflected in his future, directing it this way or that.

In analysing a signature we should first have a proper signature, not just initials. Also, it helps if we know the exact name – and its spelling – of the writer.

The symbolism of space is very useful in an interpretation of signatures, in the same way as a compass helps a navigator map out a journey. If the extensions tend to the north, the writer's tendencies reflect the activities of the brain, through intellectuality, spirituality, to psychic utopianism. If the extensions point due south, the writer is more oriented towards practical activities, instincts and materialistic interests. If there is a tendency towards the east, the writer looks towards the future with open arms. If the strokes turn west, it indicates a denial of the present, fear for the future, withdrawal and dissimulation; the writer's activity in life.

Often his profession is pictured quite clearly in its design. In this case, it helps if we know more about the writer than sex and age. For example, the following signature   could be interpreted as that of an intellectual – however, this does not apply here. He is, in fact, a man who has made his fortune in shipping and his signature is clearly the outline of a three-masted ship.

The text will tell us about the writer's attitudes towards his environment, towards the world, and his social behaviour. The signature will express the writer's attitude towards himself; his inner feelings about his own value.

Hundreds or even thousands of pages have been written about the study of signatures. There is hardly room here to elaborate in detail on this subject, important and even imperative as it may be for the building-up of a portrait. We shall concentrate, therefore, on the basic, general rules of interpreting the signature in connection with the text.

1(a) If the *forms*, e.g. angular writing in a filiform sign, are *different* from those of the rest of the text (discordance between signature and text), there is disassociation between social and intimate behaviour. Duality of personality. Lack of harmony between the writer's social attitudes and private reality. At the extreme, it indicates dishonesty, amorality, hypocrisy, etc.

 (b) If all categories are similar (continuity, speed, pressure, etc.), but as a whole, *inharmonious*, it is a sign of deeply rooted neurosis. The writer is unaware of his own situation, whatever this may be. He identifies completely with the social role he has adopted, thus blocking any chance of allowing himself room to evolve and progress.

   If the whole is *harmonious* the writer is in harmony with himself. His behaviour is always in accord with the circumstances of his life, in private or in public. He is loyal, natural and honest (with supporting signs).

2(a) If the signature is the same in form and style but is *larger* than the text, there is a discrepancy between what the writer is and how he likes to appear. This may (with supporting signs) indicate an inferiority complex compensated by arrogance or pride. If there are no supporting signs for this, however, then it shows only that the writer values himself higher than, at the least, the person he is writing to.

Also (with supporting signs) self-admiration, narcissism, vanity, neurosis, paranoia (with disproportionate upper extensions).

(b) If the signature is *smaller* than the text, then it shows an inferiority complex (always with supporting signs), or humbleness, timidity, inhibition, or unsatisfactory attitudes at home, e.g. meanness.

3(a) If the signature shows signs of *greater* speed than the rest of the text, the writer is really more confident in himself, than he shows. He has good potential for improvement in many fields of his activity.

(b) If it is *slower* than the text, the writer is trying to master his impulses. He is reserved. His attitude may be defensive (with supporting signs). He is careful, he slows down to give himself time to control his impulses.

4(a) If the *pressure* of the signature is *heavier*, the writer is avoiding compromises and has fear of confrontation. He feels stronger alone; his self-confidence is greater.

(b) If it is *lighter*, the writer needs to retreat into the comfort of his privacy. Social contacts threaten his self-confidence. He dislikes expressions of feeling. He has to force himself to communicate with others.

5(a) If the letters of the signature are *more connected* than those in the text, it shows fluency of thought (in a high form level with medium-to-small letters). The writer can 'think' better when he is alone. He tends to get distracted by the presence of others. In a low form level it indicates anxiety and social inhibitions.

(b) If the letters are *less connected* in the signature, the writer may be tired, he needs to 'go home', or rest alone, to recover strength and recharge his batteries.

6(a) If the signature *slants* more to the *right* than the text, the writer is more at ease in intimate circles. He can communicate more easily and express his feelings better.

(b) If the signature is *vertical*, but the text slanted, the writer is reserved by nature; he dislikes intimacy and feels more comfortable in the presence of others. He may be displeased with his present private situation.

7(a) If the signature is *placed* to the *right* of the page, it is where it should be, as taught in European schools.

It shows extroversion (always in accordance with the text and the rest of the signs), easy communication with others, activity, initiative, optimism.

In the United States, the fashion is to sign to the left of the page. The electric typewriter prefers it! The organization of the page is such as to force the person to sign on the left.

(b) If the signature is placed in the *middle* of the text, it shows inhibition. The writer is hesitant, possibly shy and withdrawn (with supporting signs).

(c) The more the signature moves to the *left*, unless it is part of the American 'block style' (see above) which will be evident from the rest of the text, the more the writer is withdrawn, discouraged and depressed. His self-confidence is punctured, he tends towards melancholia, isolation, possibly suicidal tendencies (Pulver).

8. When the signature is *rising*, it shows optimism, ambition, activity, *élan*, possibly an *arriviste.*

9. If it is *descending,* it indicates pessimism, discouragement, stubbornness, obsession or tiredness.

10. A signature followed by a *full stop* shows prudence, inhibition, mistrustful attitude towards the world.

11. A signature *underlined* with a firm horizontal stroke indicates confidence, will-power, tenacity. If the line is undulating it shows coquetry.

12. A *centrifugal* (upwards) end stroke shows élan and physical courage.

13. A *large paraph encircling* the name indicates that the writer feels a need to protect himself from danger. Feebleness, general inhibition, anxiety. Often, agoraphobic people encircle their signatures. It is also a form of dissimulation or dishonesty.

14. The *paraph* in lasso is usually a sign of suppleness. The writer has mental agility, diplomacy, cleverness.

15. When the final stroke of a signature extends firmly downwards (*centripetal*) and stops abruptly, nervousness and irritability are indicated. Also, firmness and will-power of the writer. He is the achiever in concrete, material things. If this lower extension is barred by another stroke, forming

a cross, it shows combativity.

16. If a final paraph *returns towards the left* in the shape of lightning, *underlining* the name, it shows hardness, ruthlessness, vindictive instincts. If it returns over the top of the signature it shows egoism and apprehension of society.

17. If the final stroke *returns to the left over* the signature, crossing it out, it is a sign of self-destruction. In this case the signature will rarely be on the right – it will be either in the middle or on the left under the text.

18. If the signature is *illegible*, the writer is distrustful, mean and petty.

19. If the signature is *simple, clear* and *without any paraph*, it indicates an honest, open character, confident of his value, who has nothing to hide. Also (depending on the form level and the rest of the signs), simplicity of mind or naivity.

20. If the signature *runs between two parallel lines*, it shows that the writer likes to follow a set path of action. He feels more comfortable 'on rails'.

All the above interpretations are basic and general. Everything depends on the form level and the signs in the rest of the text.

Signs of Insincerity

We all lie at some time in our life and we hide something from someone if need be. There is no one sign which indicates insincerity, hypocrisy or criminality, as such. There is, however, a combination of signs which, when present, should be examined with particular attention and care.

The following signs (listed in alphabetical order) may be completely innocent and normal, but could become indicative of insincerity, hypocrisy or even criminality if present in specific combinations and under certain conditions.

These are: ambiguous forms, amended, arcades, artificial, bizarre, clubbed, covering strokes, diminishing (excessive), double curves, enlarging, fragmented, irregularity of forms, lapses of continuity, left slant, mingling letters in middle zone, negligent, one letter replaces another, ovals open on the left or underneath, in reverse, shark's tooth, slow, spirals, supported, trenchant, unnecessary dots, wavy lines.

Take note also: if there are marked differences between text and signature, excessive irregularity of pressure, exaggerated width or height of letters, exaggerated ornamentations. It is not advisable for students or inexperienced graphologists to interpret any of the above signs as insincerity, hypocrisy or criminality, as these can only be assessed when present in certain combinations and in a specific context.

Graphology is a constructive science. It does not judge or put a value on people. Positive thinking, objectivity and understanding are fundamental qualities for all serious graphologists.

Pathological Signs
Some graphological signs may indicate a malfunction in certain areas of the body or mind.

These are: amended, automatic, broken, congested, constrained, cramped, descending, discordant, disorganized, diving, faltering, fragmented, jerky, pale, shaky, spasmodic, twisted, unnecessary, dots, weak.

Although these signs, when present, indicate a certain malfunction, it is not wise to try to make a full medical diagnosis from them alone.

Whereas it has been proven that early medical detection of a malfunction (say, in the respiratory system) is possible from the written signs, it is impossible to tell what causes it (pneumonia, tuberculosis, cancer or simply smoking too much). It is therefore wiser to advise a general medical check-up rather than presume on a risky diagnosis. It is not improbable that one day graphology will be able to help medical doctors more accurately, and perhaps this day is not far off. It is only a matter of research and organized documentation.

Interpretation of Signs

The purpose of graphology is to understand the human mentality, character and general psychological make-up through handwriting. In this process we trace the cause from the effect, through logical connections only.

Before starting work on a person's writing, establish the age and sex of the writer and whether he is left- or right-handed. It is also important to discover whether the writer is fluent in the language in which he is writing. Other useful information concerns nationality, level of education, profession, and so on.

The document must be adequate, i.e. one full page of prose (not poetry or copy from another text) on unlined paper, handwritten with a fountain pen or ball point (not felt-tip pen or pencil), fully signed and dated. Ideally, we should have more than one document, preferably with an interval of about six months between each.

After setting the document in front of you, first open your mind to it and all its favourable and unfavourable aspects. Chase away any personal preoccupations or feelings in order to stay receptive to the writing.

Look at the totality of the writing to get a first general impression, e.g. its intensity of energy or lack of it.

Establish a few basic factors: whether it is harmonious or otherwise, organized or disorganized, spontaneous or artificial, natural or copy-book, typographic or any other style, and the form level.

It helps to retrace the movement of the stroke with a pointed instrument or pencil without lead.

Now start the definition. Observe all the particularities of the writing and write them down. Pick out the dominants; these are the most striking signs, the ones which give the writing its special character. They can be almost any of the signs. Each writing has six to twelve dominants and from twenty-five to fifty or sixty signs.

Write down all signs, even the smallest and most insignificant. A magnifying glass is helpful at this stage. It is surprising how many details the naked eye can miss. Read carefully the description of each sign before you decide to attribute it or reject it.

To make sure nothing has been overlooked, use the list of signs for each category and check each one against the sample of writing. Mark down the ones that apply.

At this stage, a determining frame emerges and we proceed with the synthesis of signs. This is the stage at which one group of signs gives an indication of the writer's intellectual potential, a second group shows emotional state and depth and a third highlights the writer's activity, energy, motivation, etc.

The next stage is the psychological typology.

From the work already done, it becomes clear which is the dominant psychological function, temperament and character of the writer. At this stage, choose the psychological typology you wish to use; the more information the better.

Now we can build up the writer's psychological portrait from the synthesis of signs and psychological classification. This portrait is the only part of graphology that relies on subjective elements.

Personality can be viewed from many angles. Which angle the graphologist chooses should depend solely on the use to which the portrait is to be put. Portraits of the same writing done by different graphologists will differ, however, because each graphologist will tend to emphasize one or other trait of the writer's personality, depending on his or her own concept of life, particular tastes, or character and temperament.

Questions & Answers on Graphology

What are the uses of graphology in business?
Graphology is used in interviewing and recruiting staff where you do not need to have the candidate present and all the graphologist requires is the handwriting to work with, from which a very accurate and in depth analysis can be made. It avoids the difficulty of people who go for interviews and often become nervous, or who are on their best behaviour and therefore put forward qualities they either do not possess, or wish they had and are not able to put forward the good qualities they have, because of the nervousness created by an artificial situation.

If you have a totally spontaneous piece of writing which the writer was not aware was going to be analysed, then you get the true, natural person coming out. From this you can get a picture of what the person really is and not what he or she is trying to project in the interview. Furthermore, in an interview there is a certain rapport or lack of it between the interviewer and the interviewee and a great deal depends on whether they like each other or not, which very often has nothing to do with the job or the person's suitability for the job. Graphology totally circumnavigates that disadvantage.

Is graphology an art or science?

Graphology is a combination of both art and science. The art is in interpreting what you can find scientifically – there is a well tested scientific basis to graphology where many, many years of scientific testing has been done to establish its validity.

The essence of graphology is the message sent by the nerves in the brain directly down the arm to the fingers through the pen and then onto the paper, and the picture that emerges on the paper through the handwriting is the inner workings of that person – the very soul of that person – and it cannot be changed. People who say they can change their handwriting to give a different impression may be able to fool the layman. Some people may indeed have two or three different kinds of handwriting which to the layman may look completely different, but the graphologist cannot be fooled.

Is handwriting controlled by the subconscious mind?

Absolutely. The handwriting is directed by the subconscious mind but the conscious mind is also involved in the production of the writing. The subconscious mind always expresses the truth and the conscious mind may sometimes try to block the truth from emerging, and this conflict of intentions will be revealed in the handwriting.

In handwriting, how are a person's strengths and weaknesses determined?

There are various handwriting movements such as pressure, speed, the way the letters are connected or not connected, the different lengths, the form of the upper and lower loops, the bits that are on the baseline, whether the small letters are small and narrow, how broad or narrow the writing is, the margins and the space between the words and lines. All these are like the parts of a jigsaw puzzle and when you put all these bits together you get the real person.

Does stress reveal itself in the handwriting?

Very much so. If you were to see the handwriting of a very stressed person and that of a very calm person, you should be able to tell the difference even without any training whatsoever.

If a person is, for instance, straight, devious, homely, God-fearing, loving, aggressive, etc, can it be detected in the writing?

All these qualities can be accurately pinpointed but it takes many hours to sit down and go through the handwriting very carefully because so many signs in graphology can contradict, complement, or confirm other signs and it requires skill to know what is what. The same shades of grey you would find in a simple black and white painting will appear very different in a beautiful full-colour oil painting which the trained eye can spot.

Can a quick glance at a piece of handwriting reveal any clues to a graphologist?

If you are an expert graphologist, yes, it could. One thing you can tell very quickly is whether the person wants an analytical, bare-bones approach, i.e. getting to the essentials, or whether a more colourful or flamboyant approach is necessary. This could be done very easily.

Does the handwriting change periodically?

Yes, you can see moods of depression, optimism and buoyancy which show themselves in the writing from day to day. If there has been a great crisis in the life of the writer then this will, as it does in the body, take a little bit longer to manifest itself in the writing, but if somebody is in a dreadful accident they show signs of shock in their writing immediately. The kind of injury that was made to the inner self would take longer to manifest itself in the writing as it would do in the body.

Why is the handwriting of certain professional people like doctors illegible?

A lot of it is due to tiredness or speed, and sometimes in the case of doctors it is an affectation which the layman should not know about. Illegibility can be caused by various things. It can be haste, carelessness or dishonesty, depending on the other signs present in the writing, but what it very often means if it really is illegible is inconsideration; because the purpose of writing is to communicate and if the writer's efforts at communication are illegible it implies he doesn't want to be understood or he doesn't want to be bothered to make an effort to make it easy for the reader to understand him.

Why do some companies ask candidates to apply for a job in their own writing?

It may be because they intend to have it graphologically analysed and also because some employers instinctively get a feel about the person by looking at the writing. Even a layman will get a feeling through the handwriting. Every time a letter drops through your letter box you know instinctively, if this is from a friend or relative. It is like a photograph, which is individual, because no two sets of handwriting are identical.

Can the personality and mental stability of a growing child be read through the handwriting?

Yes. The handwriting develops with the child from cradle to grave. The manifestation of the person comes out in the handwriting with personal development. There have been studies done with children learning to write and copying sentences off the board in a classroom and in all of these samples of handwriting from a class of twenty children, no two samples were the same, even though to the layperson they all look like a school child's handwriting, but they are all very, very different according to the rules of graphology.

How long does it take to become a competent graphologist?

It depends entirely on how much dedication you put into it, how much reading you do and what degree of competence you wish to achieve.

Can you learn graphology from a book or have you got to undergo formalized training?

It is very hard to learn graphology from a book. It requires one-to-one teaching because your questions could be very difficult and individual, requiring evaluating and correct answers. It is possible to learn a certain amount from books but this can be dangerous without proper guidance. Most of the really good books are hard to obtain and in any event you will still need some explanation from an expert.

Is graphology more widely practised in America than in the United Kingdom?

Yes it is. In the United Kingdom it is still in its infancy. It is still not fully accepted as an important branch of psychology and psychiatry, but is now gaining widespread acceptance.

In banks, to determine whether cheques are genuine or bogus, is it done by a graphologist or a bank clerk?

Examining documents is a speciality in its own right and this job is performed by an examiner of question documents, which is a complete science in itself.

If a signature is forged, can it be recognized by someone without training?

It requires more training to be able to detect a forgery and all banks have someone with the extra training for this purpose.

What does the left slant and the right slant of the handwriting mean?

The left orientation can mean sensitive, bloody-minded or anti-social. A slant to the right indicates extroversion. A lot of the books published show only the nice things about people. They do not go into great depth to show anything of real value. You can never take one character on its own, such as a slant, and try to analyse it. You have to take it in combination with other characteristics and the slant is the easiest thing to change and it can vary very much according to your mood and to whom you are writing. There are a lot of people who will slope quite markedly to the right on personal correspondence, but in business they are upright.

How can graphology make a manager's job more productive?
It will cut through a lot of the first and second interviews in recruiting, by shortlisting candidates through the graphological process. The manager can send a graphologist a complete list of applications together with the job specification with a list of requirements he would want the applicant to perform in a specific environment, and on evaluation of the handwriting and job requirements, the graphologist can put comments in the form of answers to questions posed on the subject, in the form of yes, yes, no, no, most likely, least likely, and an opinion expressed as to the most suitable candidate for the job.

After this the manager will have to have a face-to-face interview and choose the most likely one. The graphologist is not in the business of recruiting. He is in the business of giving employers valuable information so they can make intelligent choices and save time and money taking on undesirable candidates who appear ideal when taken on but who fail to deliver and never carry out their duties properly, and leave the employer in dire straits when he is most dependent on the employee. In this way the graphologist can help a great deal.

One of the most useful pointers which can be revealed accurately is whether a person is good at working alone or in the company of others. Many employers fail in this area when selecting staff. They take on someone and put him or her in an office to work alone when the person is best suited to, and is stimulated by, working with others.

It must be emphasized from a graphological point of view, that irrespective of whatever a person says, if it is not in the handwriting, it is not in the person.

What are the other uses of graphology?
Graphology can be used effectively to improve business and personal life. In a business situation where someone is thinking of going into partnership with another, compatibility can be shown from the handwriting by comparison. The individuals concerned can write down their plans, and their suitability can

be matched from the writing. Likewise, in private life it has its uses between husband and wife, parents and children, boyfriend and girlfriend. Graphology also has its advantages in identifying and treating problems in mentally disturbed children and monitoring the progress of normal children. Graphotherapy is a science that enables the therapist to diagnose and treat mental problems by reversing the process, i.e. looking at the writing on paper and then trying to search for the cause from the source (brain and mind).

In conclusion, then, graphology is a highly complex discipline that requires training and practice. Despite this, it is possible for the layperson to gain a good deal of insight into a person's character from their handwriting. As a salesperson, being able to decipher some general facts about a person from their writing will help you establish what kind of a person you are dealing with. And when you know this you will have the key to formulating your sales strategy.

CHAPTER 15

How to win the battle of life

You will realize by now that this book is based on the techniques of acquiring personal power and selling power through human psychology and extra-sharp communication skills. We will now leave the science and art of professional selling and move onto the purpose of acquiring power, how we should use it, and what the ultimate goal of everyone's life should be.

Anyone who views their own success and that of others in terms of fame, money and status, which they believe are going to make them the 'king pins' in this world are only kidding themselves unless that power and wealth are acquired by fair means (ethically and with love for their fellow man) and not by foul methods (unethically and with hate for their fellow man).

To some misguided people who have acquired power, their fellow men only become a 'number' and in the same way that some people ruthlessly exploit the God-given natural resources, they apply that philosophy of exploitation, superimpose deprivation onto it, orchestrate their activities and then dish it out regardless to their fellow men.

It is never too late to stop, and I mean stop and help or let nature start the restorative process on the harmful practices that man himself has inflicted through his so-called progressive thinking but which in fact has produced a detrimental outcome. To fail to do so would leave the planet in jeopardy.

We have seen that all differences of opinion and conflict start with words and are resolved with words, and that armaments are used only in between. If we cut the armaments out the end result will still be the same: demands, threats, irrational sentiments, blackmail and so on and, if they are faced up to with the full force of persuasion, motivation, manipulation and negotiation (think sharp and talk smart, not tough!), I am confident that they can be dealt with effectively.

All religions teach respect of life. Let us not be hypocritical about this, all human life is precious irrespective of colour, shape, size, financial status, culture, race, and religion. The cardinal code that I have developed for myself which I hope others can take the lead from is that all people in power must learn (bear in mind I used the word learn) to appreciate and accommodate the difference of others, and resolve their differences verbally, as opposed to physically annihilating (killing) another by any means they would see fit and for whatever reason, and if we all can do that the magic of love will permeate to produce wonderful results throughout the world.

If we spend the time and know what to do and how to do it, with love in our hearts, there are many ways to solve most human problems. Persuasion, Motivation, Manipulation and Negotiation is the key!

If the belief system or set of ideals of another individual or group is different from yours, learn to tolerate another's way of life and, if there are shortcomings, help others conquer their deficiencies, help them succeed and then reap the rewards of their efforts without killing them off. If the difference is great, why cannot that difference be resolved effectively as it is done everyday in the business of professional selling with the use of some of the selling skills mentioned. I would say that if a genuine salesperson who loved God and humanity ruled a nation as opposed to a bunch of hotheads and extremists that country would be the one to raise our hats to!

To kill does not require intelligence and nerve, but to save man requires both intelligence, nerve and goodwill to fellow man. What defence has human flesh and blood got against metal or chemical armaments? None! It is therefore morally and ethically wrong to even consider making them, let alone using them. It would be a different story if someone was personally attacked and, in self-defence, as a last resort, had to resort to some drastic violent measures with whatever he or she had at their disposal to protect their own skin, family and home from invasion. I believe misery and suffering can be avoided if we can get our thinking changed the world over.

We are not born with hate, we learn it or are taught it. If it is learnt then it can also be unlearnt.

The famous English mathematician, physicist, astronomer and philosopher Sir Isaac Newton's third law of motion in physics states, 'To every action there is an equal and opposite reaction.' The Bible says, 'Those who live by the sword will die by the sword' and 'as you sow so shall you reap'.

What we have to get into our minds is that we were all conceived in the same way by a distinct act of creation, are born uniquely different as persons but are uniquely the same, which some people seem to forget. We were given a free will with a choice to live a good life or a bad one. By the same token we also have our exits.

While you are reading this book somebody, somewhere in the world is leaving the planet by the most violent means imaginable. I cannot change the whole world's thinking, that would be an impossible task. Only the world can change itself. All I am trying to do is to give my fellow brothers and sisters an insight from what I have gathered from the real world, which is now firmly implanted in my thinking apparatus and memory as food for thought for others. I want to give to others as much as others have given to me the facility of knowledge for which I am deeply indebted and grateful, from whichever source it came, as it is those people who have made me stable today when I started off from very shaky beginnings. I now try to make all my activities God-guided (sometimes I fail like we all do) instead of being man-directed.

If we want to live in harmony with our fellow brothers and sisters then we should teach a balanced view of life by creating in our education system a method of helping everyone, everywhere, to learn scientific facts and artistic ways of living together happily and peacefully. We should solve mental and physical deprivations of unfortunate people as they are part of the extended brotherhood of man. It would mean providing everybody, everywhere, with a means of earning a living with at least the bare essentials of life. This would not necessarily have to mean that we would not have trouble and strife and our differences. Of course we would, just as the best of engineered products break down from time to time. Life would be meaningless without problems. Just imagine a problem-free world – it is hard even to conceive.

Solving problems does not mean creating problems in order to solve them. People spend time and money on material things in life to adorn their external self which they can see and use, but if only we could realize that what lies underneath our skins which is a living miracle, we would marvel at it. It is the most intricate, delicate and important mechanism of all, that functions regardless. By giving it a little attention, it can pay big dividends to enrich our lives. The happiness of each and every individual is what we all humans must strive to achieve.

What we need is not more bombs and bullets, but more love, understanding and a bigger wallet and a more compassionate hand to win hearts over. Think of the millions of people who have died in vain, or in treacherous wars, or are the victims of brutality under the most horrific circumstances caused by man's hatred and ignorance of his fellow man, or who have been the victims of natural disasters. We must rally round to support all victims of such heinous crimes and tragedies in their hour of need, but above all we must seek to remedy the cause of the matter by education and preventative methods.

Learning from nature

To discover more about how animals behave, and how to relate this to human behaviour I had the privilege of interviewing a very enlightened and experienced veterinary surgeon, Gavin Deans BVSc, MRCVS, in his surgery. He provided me with a most fascinating insight into real-life animal behaviour, which when accepted and understood can only assist in the better understanding of our fellow human beings and facilitate communication, producing effective results for the benefit of both seller and buyer. My interview was conducted informally and the answers provided to my questions by Gavin only showed without a shadow of a doubt what an important area this is for anyone wanting to achieve excellence. What follows is a summary of our discussion.

PE: The first thing I would like to raise with you is that I see a very close parallel between the animal world and the human set-up. Let us start by looking at aggression. For example, as a professional salesperson, I may walk in to see a prospective buyer, happy with myself, and beaming with smiles. I am visiting this person to be of service, to do everything within my capabilities to help him benefit from my offer. I am nice to this person and approach him in the most civilized and respectable way and then all of a sudden the man who started off by shaking my hand and who was nice and friendly has, within a few minutes, become a very aggressive, irrational being and this I find extremely strange. It is very much like petting a dog which then quite unexpectedly starts growling and tries to bite you. In order that I may try to understand humans better why would you say that a dog that is friendly should suddenly swing to a very aggressive mood and try to attack you?

GD: Well, the main reason for this is *territory*, which always seems to be involved with animals. Territory with dogs is a big thing. For example a dog meets another dog on the street (neutral territory), one dog goes to the other dog, sniffs it, probably wags its tail, and one of them will usually give up and walk away.

But in a different situation, such as where a dog is chained to its own kennel in a garden, the dog that strayed into the property will walk over to the dog that is chained up, and the dog that is chained up becomes aggressive because the other dog is going towards it and it cannot get to it, nor can it stop the other dog advancing on it. Eventually you will find that the dog that is coming onto the territory gets to a certain position, close enough to the dog that is chained up, and is eventually frightened off by the dog barking at close range rather than fighting. That is called 'Property Protection' and is quite a well known territorial thing between dogs.

PE: It is also known that we as humans have an invisible bubble that surrounds us, which is sometimes called the aura, or body space in body language terms. If for example you are talking with me from a safe distance, then you would feel comfortable talking to me from that distance, but the closer I approach your body space, you would start to respond either favourably or unfavourably. I would guess the same thing takes place with animals due to electro-magnetic activity which is controlled by the mind.

GD: That would be right, they would react aggressively

(unfavourably) when protecting their own property, but the same animal can be approached in a different area and there may not be any sign of aggression and the two dogs will not bite each other. Usually one dog becomes submissive and moves away. As you say that may involve an aura – one dog may perceive the other's aura as less dominant.

PE: When animals fight, do they fight to destruction or do they do so only if trained? And is it a natural tendency to fight to death or to fight to appease?

GD: It depends on species, but with intraspecies fighting, in dog fighting dog, it happens in two ways: (i) where they fight to death or (ii) where they fight to appease, and it can be either natural aggression or learnt aggression. I know of an experiment carried out with mice. Mice can run around together with very little squabbling at all. You can have one hundred mice in a box, for instance in a pet shop, with no fighting taking place. However, you can actually train an individual mouse to become aggressive. This is the way it was done by some researchers – you have an individual mouse in a cage and everyday you intimidate it by dangling another live mouse by its tail in front of it. Each day you do this you provoke aggression and the time taken for the mouse to become aggressive becomes shorter and shorter day by day. That was one part of the experiment. The researchers then conditioned a whole group of mice in the same way and then introduced them to a non-conditioned control group. They then found that if they mixed the two groups, the aggressors and the non-aggressors, the aggressive mice would attack the non-aggressive mice straight away and the non-aggressive did not fight back. They were submissive. This experiment could be repeated with the same mice that were kept together for, say, several months, then split the group up and condition the aggression and submission into the same group of mice, showing that submission as well as dominance was conditioned in this case.

PE: When an attacking mouse approaches another mouse has the size of either mouse got anything to do with it at all?

GD: The size has no bearing at all and the age too has no bearing.

PE: Would you say the anatomy of a mouse or dog is very much like that of a human being?

GD: The anatomy is basically the same, but more developed in humans. A mouse has a heart, lungs, nervous system (the same similar type of nerves), a brain (a smaller brain obviously), intestines, muscles, so basically all mammals (excluding whales) have a very similar type of anatomy.

PE: Do animals suffer pain and do they have emotions?

GD: Certainly they do feel pain – a dog that has been run over will definitely have pain and a mouse that has a pin pricked into it will certainly feel pain. Emotions are a little bit different and that is a question that vets are always asked.

PE: I have seen dogs actually crying – tears streaming out of their eyes when upset. How can you account for this?

GD: Dogs will howl, dogs will whimper and you could call that emotion, but certainly not to the same degree as humans, because their nervous system is not as advanced as ours. For example, two family dogs are kept together. They get on well with each other. One of them dies, and the other one may start pining. The same thing may well happen if the owner dies. We see this where a dog comes in, hasn't eaten for a week, and lost weight.

PE: Is it expressing its grief?

GD: Certainly, they do know something has gone wrong and they do start to pine physically because of it.

PE: We've got our six senses of sight, sound, smell, touch, taste and intuition – do the other animals function on a similar basis?

GD: Yes, they do, but the degree to which their senses are developed varies with species. For example, a dog pining over its missing owner shows intuition – it would not know whether the owner had died naturally, had been killed by someone or had left the country. But certainly it does perceive that things don't appear to be the way they should and its reactions must be due to intuition.

PE: Let us now assume that a person has characteristics that describe him as being timid, sly and mean. If I were to communicate with this type of person in a selling context by manoeuvring according to his psychological make-up, if I were to start by being pushy and overpowering, then this person because he is timid, may withdraw into a shell and I would have to go in very, very gently to establish rapport and build up confidence with the objective of trying to achieve a sale or a specific end result. Likewise, if I were trying to approach the bold, courageous lion type of person with a timid sales presentation I could lose.

As a veterinary surgeon, if you were dealing with an aggressive animal and a timid animal what would your techniques be for handling these two types?

GD: Well, that's an easy one! This afternoon we had a German Shepherd which is a dog that many people are frightened of. As soon as the German Shepherd saw me it cowered away, turning its back, which to me in that situation meant that if it's an aggressive animal or a timid animal I was likely to get bitten. The aggressive animal attacks you because of its inbuilt aggression and the timid animal attacks you in fright. Hence, in that situation both animals have to be handled differently to prevent being bitten. For example the timid German Shepherd that came in today may have been beaten by its owner, may not like men because the last person who beat it was a man, or it doesn't like a veterinary surgery because the last veterinary surgery it went into it was hurt. Whatever reason the dog may have, its reaction would be the same.

PE: Do animals have a memory where they can recall past events and experiences?

GD: Most certainly they do. Some dogs will run into my veterinary surgery and in other instances the owners sometimes have physically to drag their dogs through my front gates. The approach I make is gradual. What I normally do is talk to the owner. I do not stand above the animal towering over it. I do not rapidly approach the animal. What I do is I get down to its level. It can be dangerous. It can actually lunge at you at that level, but usually I find that it works very well to crouch down to the dog's level, talk quietly, not overpowering it, talk to the owner, ask the owner just to pat the dog, then get as close as I can to it so that I can get down to its own level without actually doing anything to it, without shouting at it, and genuinely wanting to make physical contact with the dog. There is usually an instance where the dog will retreat but as I make physical contact by touching, it reassures the dog and the animal calms down quite quickly. As long as you do not raise your voice, lose your temper, lean over it or approach the dog too rapidly you are usually OK.

Some vets mistake a timid dog for an aggressive dog and start shouting at it to sit down and keep still, which in the case of a timid dog only makes it more and more timid and frightened and therefore this approach perpetuates itself, probably into a difficult situation. It is always worthwhile spending more time the first time with a nervous dog, and when it meets you again it will be less frightened.

PE: Are there times when you have to shout at a dog to do something specific?

GD: Well, with the aggressive dog it is slightly different. With the aggressive dog it really does not matter how much you try to reassure it. It wouldn't make any difference. For example another German Shepherd that was used as a threat was tied to a garage as a guard dog, used to bark at anyone and everyone it saw or heard, and would try to bite someone if they came in. Your approach to such a dog is (1) approach it quickly (2) approach it gently or (3) get down to its level. Trying to make physical contact with such an animal would get you nowhere and you would probably end up getting bitten, so my approach to such an animal is to be strict and actually try to dominate the dog by shouting.

PE: So what you are saying is if you have an aggressive dog you have to use different tactics.

GD: Definitely, in my own interest.

PE: So, being nice to an aggressive dog wouldn't work, would it?

GD: Nine times out of ten it is a waste of time trying to calm the dog down because it is trained to be aggressive. An aggressive dog quite often has its emotions far more charged up, and trying to defuse that situation in a fifteen minute consultation is just about impossible. If at all possible, that would take many, many months for the owner to defuse in his own time. It is far easier to train a timid dog to calm down than a fully grown aggressive dog.

PE: Now what about the type of dog that is downright stubborn – it is not timid, nor aggressive but is really stubborn, it just won't budge! How would you deal with that type of animal?

GD: In my situation I would use force. When stubbornness is part of the animal's behaviour I would use force as long as aggression is not associated with it. If the animal, for example, is refusing to swallow a tablet I would then physically force the animal to swallow the tablet by putting it into its mouth and holding the upper and lower jaw together until the animal swallowed it.

PE: In other words you would either use the carrot or the stick?

GD: Yes, that's right, one of those two. Usually it has to be the stick (shouting at it) with stubbornness, but the carrot – patting it, speaking to it in a friendly fashion and offering it a reward such as a biscuit or toffee can often work as well. I will give you an example of an unusual case which I had to deal with a few weeks ago with one of my clients. A dog came in with bad ears. I had to look down its ears with an instrument that is called an oroscope. This I was unable to do at first and because it was painful, the dog would not let me put medicine down its ears. Eventually, I managed to look down and gave the owner some ear drops to use and asked her to come back with the dog in a week. In a week's time she came back and said there was no problem whatsoever getting ear drops down the dog's ears. Believe it or not, she did it by getting a dog biscuit and balancing it on the dog's nose. She then held the biscuit on the dog's nose for a while and then with the dog sitting there with the biscuit on its nose she put the ear drops down. I just looked on in amazement. As soon as she had finished the owner took the biscuit off the dog's nose, put it on the table and the dog ate it. That is more the 'carrot' method where there was a reward at the end of it.

PE: Let's assume you have two dogs and you want to share a can of dog food with both. Let's say I take the can and divide it into two and I put half on one plate and half on the other plate. Let's take it that one dog has gobbled its share and is now eating the other one's food. How would you stop this?

GD: To stop that is not very easy. One dog is probably a fast eater and the other dog is probably a slow eater. In a household of two dogs, one may be dominant, eating more quickly than the other. A dog will have a social grading in the same family. If you find that the dominant (not aggressive) dog is going to the submissive dog while eating it is a problem to correct if you want to continue feeding both dogs at the same time in the same room.

PE: Can you give it a little treat to stop it eating the other dog's food?

GD: That may work, but the question is what is it that is driving it there? Its hunger may not be hunger but a greed to satisfy a very, very basic natural urge. So what will make it contented, and also discourage it from eating the other dog's food is to provide it with an equally satisfying experience, which may mean food. It may prefer to eat a small prawn or toffee rather than have a whole bowl of filling dog food, so if you use an alternative stimulus that is rewarding to the dog and it gets satisfaction from it then it would respond to that approach.

PE: To put this into its proper perspective, may I ask what method you would actually use to prevent the fast eating dog from snatching the slow-eating dog's food?

GD: It is possible to discourage the dominant dog's feeding behaviour by the use of a desirable stimulus such as a sweet. When the dominant dog has finished its own food and attempts to devour the other dog's food, it is first discouraged with a firm NO and then offered the sweet instead as a reward.

PE: Now I do not know whether you have realized it, but with your answers to my questions you have just confirmed how you use some techniques of Persuasion, Motivation, Manipulation and Negotiation when dealing with animals.

GD: Have I?

PE: The first example was the timid dog, where you persuaded it by going down to its own level. The second example was the aggressive dog where you had to manipulate it by shouting at it and controlling it. The third example was the case of motivation by offering the animal either the carrot or the stick. The last example was that of negotiation, 'If you do not go and eat the other dog's food then I will give you a treat.' It is very similar to what goes on in human communication as far as selling and buying goes, but obviously it can sometimes be more complex.

Let us now move on to another very interesting aspect of animal behaviour: animal magnetism or mesmerism. We know in the wild about the predator/prey relationship; wherever you find wildebeest, gazelles or sambar you will also find big wild cats like lions, tigers and cheetahs hovering around. I believe before these cats kill their prey for food they stalk it and only one in so many hunts are successful, is that right?

GD: Yes, that's right. The way lions eat is they gorge-feed themselves. They are very practical when they have got food, they make the most of it – they bloat themselves full. In fact many dogs to the same: they eat only once every couple of days rather than eat three small meals a day. That's a natural thing they have adapted to with their limited supply of food they often gorge-feed at the time.

PE: I understand the predator actually watches its prey with intense concentration and an eye fix. Is this called animal magnetism or mesmerism?

GD: Yes, you could call it that.

PE: Let me rephrase that. When the predator's eyes appear to be glued onto its prey during the hunt is that really the case? In other words has the prey been hypnotized (mesmerized) by the predator, has it fallen under the spell of the predator and submits, before it is devoured?

GD: That's a very difficult question to answer because in that situation it is hard to tell whether the predator is keeping its eye on the prey waiting for some movement. For example, a tiger stalks its prey. It does not come running with its eyes fixed, it actually crawls. It is the same way a cat goes for a mouse, it crawls and stalks it. It is difficult to say whether the animal is staring intently at the prey, waiting for the slightest sudden move, as in the case of, say, a gazelle beginning to run or a bird just starting to fly off, before making the sudden rush and pounce. For example, you watch a cat in the back garden, it crawls on the floor very, very slowly just staring at an individual bird and it can be within five feet of the bird and then suddenly the bird flies off.

Likewise, with a very quick reflex action the cat will sprint straight away towards the bird and quite often pull the bird out of the air because it has been so quick off the mark with its reflexes. It would appear that as soon as the bird has made a movement, the cat gets as close as it can towards it, but no sooner has the distance become so short that the bird realizes there is a threat to its survival that the whole-hearted attack begins. I would imagine that is probably why the intense eye contact is there, to give the predator a very quick reflex action to attack its prey.

PE: Then in your opinion what exactly is animal magnetism or mesmerism?

GD: It is difficult to say precisely what animal magnetism is. It is probably used to explain eye-to-eye contact as already discussed. For example, say two male cats are about to fight, this is the standard and natural way they would do it. They would stalk each other, staring at each other. They would both be treading very cautiously and concentrating on each other. Now, if you watch these animals, you will find that if one cat is staring at its opponent, nine times out of ten you will discover the cats just sitting there and staring at each other.

The two cats can get to within a couple of inches of each other but as long as they are staring at each other then more often than not a fight will not ensue. As soon as one of the cats loses concentration then the other cat will immediately take advantage of that and attack.

PE: What I am really trying to get out of this discussion on mesmerism is this, Gavin. If a professional salesperson wishes to go out into the market-place and get an order then he or she has got to keep their eyes firmly fixed on that target. Now the target is to make a sale, but salespeople make the sale through another human being, and if they use their eyes in conjunction with their selling skills in the same way the predator uses its eyes and hunting skills when approaching the prey, I am of the opinion that it would produce a satisfactory result when it is done correctly. This means making the sale just like the cat catches a mouse and the lioness brings down the wildebeest.

GD: People, as you say, can portray things such as aggression, fear and love but with animals it is not as complex as that. The eyes would probably convey a greeting or aggression between two animals to an extent, but that is about as far as it goes.

  The difference between humans and animals is this: two people could be standing and communicating by talking and visual means. With animals there are a lot of other factors. For example, in mating between animals certainly the eyes come into it, but it is also the way the animal actually moves itself, the noises it makes and the mating behaviour pattern itself.

PE: If we did not have language to communicate with, how would we put our message across? Right now I am talking to you with a language that has been learned by both of us, but if we go back to prehistoric times I wonder what it would have sounded like and what meaning was conveyed. I presume it must have been all gestures, postures and positions, with sounds (grunts and groans) that may have been some primitive form of language which had meaning. Now we humans are similar to animals in terms of our anatomy and physiology. How would you say we would have communicated in those early days? Wouldn't we have communicated then like the animals do today without a sophisticated language?

GD: We don't really know what really happened in primaeval times, but going back over the evolutionary scale, animals all basically came from the same origin and they gradually diverged out, and as they did so each animal, or each part of life – mammals, fish and insects – all separated and went further and further apart. The animals diverged from so-called strata sources and the more and more advanced they became, the further apart the neighbouring lines went. If we go down the evolutionary scale our behaviour is closer, of course, to chimps and other primates. Now, the main way they communicate involves noises and movements. Lower down the evolutionary scale animals use behavioural patterns to communicate, with a group of behavioural patterns involving body language, emotions, noises, barks, growls and whimpers.

PE: This is what we call in human body language the various gestures, postures and movements that constitute non-verbal communication and supplement the verbal expressions. Each one of the non-verbal cues is like a word and a group of individual cues is like a series of words that constitute a sentence. If you want to find the true meaning of what is being conveyed you do not look at an individual word in isolation, but you look at the sentence and even the paragraph. Isn't that similar in the animal world?

GD: That's right. For example, if you are out in the park you will often find other people's dogs running around. If one dog comes up to another and wants to play it will quite often stand up on its hind legs and get down in front of the other dog, conveying a message which says, 'come and play'. The other dog may walk off or may join in play.

PE: But back home in their own little environment they could be aggressive animals, even attacking the postman. When a fight does start do animals go for the kill or do they stop at a danger point when one could be seriously harmed, or do they fight to appease one another?

GD: They rarely kill each other when it is a fight between individuals of the same species of animal, but they can kill each other in, for example, dog fights between Staffordshire bull terriers, but they usually have to be trained.

PE: But it is known, if there is a pride of lions, for example, where there is a male that is servicing some of his females and another male tries to intrude, then the male will resist the intrusion by fiercely attacking the intruder to safeguard his position, isn't that the case?

GD: Yes, that certainly does happen, especially where a male has a group of females and forms a herd or a social group. If another male tries to creep into that social group then the fighting can be quite aggressive.

PE: Is there a peer group amongst animals?

GD: Oh yes, most definitely. In fact, the same male that is being fought off by the male of a group may go and challenge another group. If it comes across a weaker male in another group it can actually displace that male and direct the group. It is especially so if the male is gradually getting older and natural selection means a younger male will emerge and displace that older male. This of course is nature's way of perpetuating itself.

PE: Going back to this question of appeasement, what I am trying to figure out is this: you said dogs can be trained to fight to death. Let's suppose they are not trained and one dog displays an inherent dominance factor over a submissive dog by attacking the weaker one; will the dominant dog pounce on the weaker one without any reason or will it have to be provoked or challenged before it attacks the weaker animal?

GD: There are dogs that are very, very dominant and if another dog passes it on the street that shows no sign of aggression towards it, it may bite and possibly do the same with people passing by. Without any challenge at all that type of dog may turn and bite.

PE: What causes this? As a puppy was it a learnt thing or is it stress or conditioning?

GD: It is probably conditioning. You will quite often find if you go right back to the start with dogs that they go through two different periods of socialization; when they are a few weeks old they learn whether they like or dislike other animals, and a few weeks later comes the human socialization period in which dogs are very strongly influenced with regard to people. So it depends on what's happening during those few weeks that could possibly influence it for the rest of its life. If during the human socialization period it is treated badly or hit repeatedly then in that short period it will learn that aggression is the norm.

PE: Now, let's say this dominant dog meets a meek and submissive dog that doesn't want to fight at all and totally submits to the aggressive one. Will the submission be accepted by the dominant dog where it would growl, do a U-turn and walk away or will it still attack the weaker one? And how will the submissive animal show that it does not want to fight? What would a dominant/aggressive dog do if it met an equally vicious dog?

GD: It all depends on how dominant and aggressive it is. There is a very small dividing line between dominance and aggression. In a park you may find a dominant dog repeatedly challenging a submissive dog just to reinforce its dominance over it, rather than challenging an equally dominant dog. The submissive dog will indicate its submission either by sitting or lying down or retreating.

PE: When I refer to aggression from a human point of view I do not necessarily mean violence. You can have aggressive behaviour, where you talk loudly and act boisterously, without violence. When I refer to violence I mean physical violence. There is a saying that barking dogs do not bite. I am inclined to believe that barking dogs seldom bite.

GD: I agree with you, but there are many variations.

PE: If a human being is attacked by an aggressive dog, what is the best way of dealing with that situation and why would you recommend that action?

GD: My advice to anyone being attacked by a dog is to freeze and stand still. By doing this you will leave the animal puzzled. If you fight back, the dog may interpret it as a challenge, or if you run away it will perceive it as fear and then also attack you.

PE: To go into this a little further, can we humans learn from the behaviour of other species? I am sure that if a human being is cornered and it cannot flee or doesn't want to submit it will be a natural instinct to fight back in response to the threat. Now for example, in the way a bee behaves I see its behaviour telling me something that we can learn from. The bee leaves the hive in search of nectar and pollen which it brings back and deposits in the cells of the honeycomb, after which it does a special dance as if to celebrate its efforts.

I see this activity as analogous to a salesperson leaving the office, going out into their territory, doing demonstrations or presentations and bringing back the orders and celebrating the occasion. Can you please tell me in a little more detail how the honey-bee works?

GD: Yes, certainly I will give you a concise version of it. In the case of the bee there is the forager bee that goes out into the field and finds the pollen from somewhere, brings it back and then deposits it on the honeycomb in the hive. What it then does is it performs one of two dances called a 'waggle dance' or a 'round dance'. The hive is dark, and the bee performs the round dance inside with various movements in circles; the other bees tagging on behind by using touch and smell. This enables them to get to the source of the honey by mimicking the circles. Now what that circle does to the other bees is tell them that the honey is close to the hive but outside. The other dance, the 'waggle dance', that the forager bee does involves a lot of body movements where it keeps waggling around on its return until it is inside the hive to give precise information to the other bees about the distance, direction and where the honey is so that the other bees can locate it up to around half a mile away. So the round dance is a simple version of communication amongst bees where it tells the other bees that the honey is located close outside the hive. It doesn't tell the direction or anything else, but with the waggle dance, specific information is given through nature's intricate system of communication when the forager bee brings back a sample of honey, so that the other bees can be guided precisely to the honey and large amounts of it can be collected and brought back to the hive.

PE: So the forager bees are like the front line salespeople are to their managing director as workers are to the queen bee who never leaves the hive.

GD: Yes, they are the ones that are scouting around for the

honey and the queen only leaves the hive during swarming.

PE: What happens during swarming?

GD: Towards the end of the year the bees will swarm. Basically it is a rooting-out process. It means that they are going well. So what the main aim of a beekeeper would be is to maintain the queen which stays in the hive over the winter months until the next spring. If you lose the queen you have lost the hive irrespective of whether it is full or partly filled with bees. If the hive is wiped out during the winter you will have to find another queen and put her in to start off a new colony. So, the queen is certainly like the managing director, and the rest of the hive is centred around her.

PE: Without the managing director or the captain of a ship in command, directing and taking responsibility for the running of the organization it is difficult to see how progress can be made.

Bees are a very peaceful community. When I see soldiers in action it reminds me of the predator/prey relationship in the wild and the predator hunts a prey from another species and not its own.

GD: Unless mankind realizes that there is more to life than killing and doing harm to one another and that mutual respect and understanding amongst people irrespective of colour, creed and age is the criteria for a stable world, then I am afraid that we will have to live with some of the horrors we all witness during our lifetime. Animals only kill for a need, for food; they usually do not kill their own species.

PE: Amongst animal groups is there always a leader?

GD: Not always, and it is debatable. Between one herd of cows and another herd of cows there aren't leaders, but quite often you will find social groups, in a herd you will find three or four social groups. So not all species have a leader and follower, by any means. Most animals live together in harmony, whether they survive individually or in a large group.

PE: If animals live in harmony, that means we can learn

something from them, even though we are superior to them in intelligence. We can learn how they cohabit, how they face danger, how they seek a companion, how they procreate and look after their young, how they grow up and fight for their survival and how they prepare for death.

PE: Apart from what we have discussed so far is there any other example in the animal world that you know of that we can relate to business?

GD: I will give you some interesting facts you can consider using aggression as an example. Some species of fish will show increased aggression between each other if they are separated for a long time. The yellow-tailed Damsell fish, on the contrary, shows decreased aggression to each other. So you could say that the motivation is either increased or diminished after separation. Damsell fish very quickly learn to swim through a maze into a glass bottle to display superiority to a rival competitor. It supports the theory that an aggressive display in which the fish doesn't get hurt is a challenge that is welcomed and is a rewarding experience.

A mother hen, seeing a fox come towards her to attack her and her chicks will show aggression by fluttering her wings and flying towards the fox's face; in other words throwing herself at the fox to protect herself and the chicks. So she is actually showing aggression to the fox, a much more dangerous animal. If she did not have any chicks and a fox approached her she would run off in fright.

PE: In selling there is a technique called the funnel technique. The task of the salesperson is to bring back the orders, or get the buyer to jump into the funnel through persuasion, motivation, manipulation and negotiation, slide down the funnel into the bucket, and as the funnel narrows the options to escape from making the commitment get fewer and fewer and finally the sale is made.

Now, the buyer may have a hundred reasons for not wanting to go ahead, but the salesperson needs to find only one good reason which appeals to the buyer and which the buyer agrees is of benefit and then homes in on it.

Going back to the animal situation, the funnel technique is very much like trying to get a hen to lay an egg: you catch it, put it into a basket and cover it and by creating the right climate it will lay the egg, whereas if you let it roam free it wouldn't lay the egg where you want it to and when you want it to, so the funnel technique is useful. What I have been doing in this discussion with you is to heighten the seller's and buyer's awareness of each other by showing with your assistance the various behaviours, their reasons and their interpretations as seen in the animal world. What about sounds that animals give out when they are angry – do they become boisterous or belligerent in the real sense of the word? If they do so, why would you say it happens?

GD: Well, when they are angry animals become more excited and they are inclined to change their voices slightly or heighten it. For example with cats there are two different voices; they meow or they hiss. They meow when they are looking for attention or food or showing signs of friendliness. They don't hiss unless they are provoked by another cat or person, and that means extreme warning.

PE: There are also some animals that show their contempt or ridicule by urinating. Is that correct?

GD: Yes, it happens with dogs. If two dogs meet on the street they lick each other's noses not in greeting, but as an identification. What they do quite often is they both urinate in the same place which people in general interpret as being, 'I am open to further offer.' I do not think that is what it actually means. Cats quite often do it as well usually at a fight or just after the fall. It is more a marking of the territory to show, 'I am bigger, smarter and tougher than you think I am, now scram.' It is like writing graffiti on the wall rather than offering direct offence.

PE: Other than using those sort of ridiculing gestures are there any other gestures that they use?

GD: As to whether animals ridicule each other, it is difficult to say. For example with Siamese Fighting Fish, which quite a lot of people keep as pets, when two males are challenging each other they push out their gills when they are angry, and their fins will also become heightened and elevated just to enlarge themselves so that they look more fearsome to the attacking fish. That sort of 'put-on appearance' is quite common throughout the animal world. You may have even witnessed the changing of shape yourself amongst dogs and cats when they are angry; dogs will quite often lift up the hackles (the hair) on their back.

PE: Why do dogs urinate on trees?

GD: It is mainly scent marking. You will find if there is a tree in a street corner where a dog has urinated, if you walk past it with your own dog it will go and sniff all around it and smell the scent left by the other dog, and it too will treat it as a marking post and leave its scent there by urinating on it.

PE: Referring to the stress factor in mammals, I would like you to explain the displacement theory. Say we put a wild tiger or fox in a cage and keep it confined to a specific area, by virtue of the stress imposed upon the caged animal it would be forced to move within a confined area. If, about six months or a year later you were to put it into a larger cage the animal would still tend to move within the smaller boundaries. What is the reason for this?

GD: When the animal is caged it can be interpreted as being subjected to unnatural stress which leads to adjacent behaviour, reflected in them pacing the floor from one side of the cage to the other. They pace to and fro all day long. This is called 'displacement behaviour'. When put into a different environment they behave in a different manner, but when put into a different cage, their previous behaviour will tag along. However, after a short period of time I would imagine that they would adjust to the larger width of the cage and use the whole width of it.

PE: Are there any behaviour characteristics of psychological origin that affect the physiology of animals that can be referred to as mind over matter, which is commonly known as psychosomatic in human terms?

GD: Oh yes. There is a nice experiment that was performed in Gothenburg, Sweden in 1958. Experimenters introduced an antigen to some guinea pigs in a room, which produced an asthmatic attack to whatever they were allergic to in the antigen. They conditioned them by putting them into a specific room over and over again and introducing the antigen to produce the asthmatic attack. There came a point when they put them into the same room without the antigen and they still developed the asthmatic attack. These were very primitive animals with simple brains.

PE: Birds such as parrots, minahs and budgerigars have been taught and conditioned to talk. What is the process behind this?

GD: They don't talk in the real sense. All they do is mimic the sound. If you keep hammering away at a word or short sentence, some of these birds will pick it up whereas others won't. I would say that the minah bird is the most prolific of talkers – some are known to mimic wolf-whistles, car engines and other birds like starlings.

PE: How do they train circus animals to perform obediently?

GD: There are two methods commonly used, fear and reward. Putting this into human terms, if a salesperson performs badly and has pay deducted, it will cause dissatisfaction for being reprimanded and his or her quality of work may deteriorate even further. A better method would be to give a firm pep talk but not to dock his or her pay, and reward handsomely for good results.

★　　★　　★

To conclude this section I should like to reiterate the reason why I wrote on this subject in the first instance. It was done to make selling, buying and life in general understood better, to make life more fun and happier to live and above all to appreciate and respect the beauty of the world. From now on, when the seller is in front of the buyer and vice versa, if you look through the clothing you will no longer see just a unique human being, but also an animal with some of the best and the worst qualities.

An old friend of mine told me this poem many years ago. He is now ninety four years old, and said he learnt it in school when he was a young lad.

> *Dogs they like to bark and bite,*
> *For God has made them so,*
> *Let bears and lions growl and fight,*
> *It is their nature so.*
> *So children you should never let,*
> *Your angry passions rise,*
> *Your little hands were never meant,*
> *To tear each other's eyes.*

Earl De Zylva (born 1 March 1896)

CHAPTER 17

The voice of reason, freedom, caring, compassion and understanding

If you are concerned about the world you live in, you may be interested to find out more about the work of organizations such as the following:

Some information on World Society for the Protection of Animals

- WSPA is the widest-ranging animal protection society, having over 300 member humane organizations in 60 countries around the world, as well as thousands of individual members.
- WSPA works to protect all animal life, whether domestic pets, farm livestock, wild animals, experimental animals and others – world-wide.
- WSPA has consultative status with the United Nations and works through its member societies and at governmental level to operate effectively on an international scale.
- WSPA has been actively involved in animal protection since 1959 and some major areas of work include: sealing, whaling, the fur trade, illegal trafficking of wild life, livestock

transportation, humane slaughter, stray animal control, bullfighting, experimentation and disaster relief.

The Friends Of The Earth Trust

Friends of the Earth's one concern is protecting the environment to make our planet habitable for our children and their children. Ensuring that we use the Earth's resources sustainably, reduce pollution and stop exploitation and unnecessary waste are their priorities.

Recycle paper, protect wildlife, reuse bottles, stop waste, reduce pollution, save energy are what FoE campaigns for as a charity to further its beliefs through non-political, research and educational work. Their message is a simple one: it is only by protecting the earth that we can protect ourselves – against pollution, the destruction of our urban and rural environment, mass unemployment and the horrors of global famine and war.

The National Anti-Vivisection Society

says, 'Animals Cannot Protest – Please Help Us To Help Them!'

National Anti-Vivisection Society Policy

- To advocate total prohibition of the performance on living animals of all experiments and, pending the achievement of this fundamental aim, to support, sponsor, and promote partial measures of reform as steps towards the total abolition of vivisection.
- To encourage the development and adoption of research techniques not involving experiments on animals.

Save The Children Fund

Save The Children Fund is the leading international children's charity.

Their work is connected with:

- Day care centres for under fives
- Support for families
- Equal opportunities for disabled children
- A fresh start for young offenders
- Help for refugee children

Save The Children Fund's overseas work is connected with:

- Improving health care
- Training local health and welfare workers
- Day care centres for under fives
- Support for street children and orphans
- Income generating schemes for families
- Opportunities for education

The Anti-Slavery Society

The Anti-Slavery Society was founded in 1839, but there are more slaves now than when the Society was founded.
  Their work involves:

- Investigating and exposing abuse of basic human rights.
- Lobbying national governments to introduce, reform or enforce protective laws.
- Reporting violations of international standards to the United Nations for actions.

Survival International

Survival International is a leading international organization working for the rights of threatened tribal peoples. It does not seek to preserve them as though in a zoo or museum, but to ensure that they have a future in which they can adapt to outside society in their own way and at their own pace.
  Survival International promotes awareness of the value of tribal societies as well as publicising their current plight.

Amnesty International

Amnesty International is an independent worldwide movement working impartially for the release of all prisoners of conscience, fair and prompt trials for political prisoners, and an end to torture and executions.

Amnesty International urges:

- An immediate and permanent halt to executions and the commutation of all death sentences.
- The abolition of the death penalty for all offences by all state governments which retain it.
- That, pending the abolition of the death penalty in law, state laws should preclude the imposition of the death penalty on juvenile offenders or mentally ill and broaden the criteria for the granting of clemency in capital cases.
- The setting up, as a matter of urgency, of a thorough and impartial inquiry into evidence of racial discrimination in the application of the death penalty.

Greenpeace

Greenpeace stands for a safe and nuclear-free world, fresh air, clean water, the protection of wildlife and their habitats. Against all odds Greenpeace campaigns:

- to save the whales
- to stop nuclear weapons tests
- to protect seals, dolphins, porpoises and sea turtles
- to stop the disposal of radioactive waste and dangerous chemicals at sea
- to close down nuclear power stations and nuclear reprocessing plants
- to stop acid rain and protect the atmosphere
- to reduce the trade in endangered species products.

If you are keen to get more involved in the activities of these organisations or any others, you should find their addresses in your local telephone directory.

CHAPTER 18

Religion, your purpose for living and business ethics

Good and evil are two sides of the same coin – one side represents winning and the other defeat. All along this book has been emphasizing winning, and winning the ultimate victory – the trophy of trophies in life must be for all humans to aim to win a place with their Creator where they can attain eternal peace and happiness, a taste of which can be found for a temporary period in this world.

Good represents everything flowing from righteousness and love; and evil represents everything flowing from wrong doings and hate. As humans we all have a choice to follow good or evil.

Whatever religious belief you hold, and whatever label you give it, it does not really matter; the principle does not change.

There is only one, God our Creator, for us all even though we may have different interpretations of him. He is the source of light, hope, future, happiness, love, mercy, power – all that is good and righteous, and nourishes all living things. Whether you are a Christian, Jew, Muslim, Buddhist, Hindu or Sikh, He is the source of light to us all.

Now, there may be different interpretations of his Word, and I am not here to do an in depth analysis of the various religions and their comparisons. But I would like to give you a general survey of the main religions of the world and what they teach. To be able to understand and respect other religions is an absolute necessity for us all to live happily on the planet – everyone is our brother and sister, even though their thinking, words and actions may be different – this is also a civilized view. And in order to be able to make selling to anyone in the world easier, you need to understand their religion.

All religions tell us to do good and avoid evil. In selling, we will come across people from all denominations so I am including information on many people's religions and customs so that you can appreciate the message given by their religions which you will come across in the English-speaking world. I have researched relevant material from the teachings of Christianity, Buddhism, Islam, Hinduism and Judaism. Even though there are so many different religions and variations in worshipping a supernatural being, they are all talking about the same origin – God the Creator of the World and Everything in it. Here is what I mean.

The following illustration shows a light source representing God, around which there is a hexagonal lamp shade.

Each side of the lamp shade has got a panel representing a religion. When the light is switched on the person facing the

Christian panel would say, 'I see nothing but Christianity' – which is right. The man facing the Islam panel says, 'I see Islam and nothing else' – he is right. The man on the Jewish side says, 'I see Judaism and nothing else' – he is right. In order for the Jew to respect the Muslim's view, he must move to the other person's way of thinking, without necessarily agreeing, in order to live in tolerance and peace.

For those disbelievers in any religion, who say there is no God, I'd like to ask a few simple questions to get you thinking about your very own being:

1. Who keeps your heart beating when you are asleep and awake?
2. Who keeps your breathing system functioning, your thoughts and blood circulation flowing regardless?
3. Who controls night and day, darkness and light, life and death?
4. Who controls your process of ingestion, digestion and excretion?
5. Who controls the tide, rain, sunshine, insects, wildlife, plants and trees?

Since I was a youngster, I have always remembered a poem called 'Trees' written by Alfred Joyce Kilmer in 1914 which was later sung by the American singer, Paul Robeson.

TREES

I think that I shall never see
A poem lovely as a tree
A tree whose hungry mouth is pressed
Against the earth's sweet flowing breast
A tree that looks at God all day
And lifts her leafy arms to pray
A tree that may in Summer wear
A nest of robins in her hair
Upon whose bosom snow has lain
Who intimately lives with rain
Poems are made by fools like me
But only God can make a tree

To me, Roman Catholicism is my cherished faith because I was born to Catholic parents, and due to my upbringing in the Catholic faith, just as much as to someone else another religion will be their dominant faith for similar reasons. However, I deeply respect, appreciate, admire and value the richness and diversity of all other religions equally, as much as I would like any car of any make and any size as long as it will take me to my destination in reasonable comfort. I have no bone to pick on colour, interior design, shape, and the only area of disapproval I would have is with a person who has no belief in any religion at all, when all the facts are available.

It is just like the buyer in Selling who needs the product, has the ability to purchase and has been given all the benefits to purchase, but who doesn't say yes, no or maybe and just remains silent, and does not air his or her views – may God give me patience to suffer this type of individual, who in my opinion is the clown of clowns who requires a special hymn to be sung for his or her salvation – and I would be the first one to sing

it! It is as if you offered someone a free golden nugget that most people would grab if given the opportunity, but some people show total indifference or lack of comprehension.

Some people spend their whole lives making and accumulating millions! That's great, if they can help others too. For what can millions do when you are pulling your last breath? There are no pockets in shrouds. But if you know in your mind you have done good in this world to alleviate pain and suffering, you can fearlessly meet your Maker.

Let's now look at some of the most widely worshipped religions on the planet, their origins and their message from a non-business angle, and then in the context of business ethics.

Islam

Islam is the second largest religion in the world next to Christianity. With around 600 million followers, the countries with the highest concentration (over 90%) of Muslims are Algeria, Afghanistan, Egypt, Iraq, Iran, Indonesia, Morocco, Pakistan, Saudi Arabia and Turkey. Indonesia alone has 100 million followers, Pakistan 80 million, followed by India and Bangladesh.

The prophet Mohammed, the founder of Islam, was born in Mecca in AD 570. Islam began in 622 with the flight of Mohammed from Mecca to Medina. His followers ruled virtually the whole of Arabia till he died in AD 632. Around AD 750 Muslim Armies had conquered North Africa, Spain, Persia (Iran), Palestine and parts of India. Muslim civilization from then onwards contributed greatly to the fields of science and medicine from which Europe benefited so much. Muslim beliefs are similar to those of Jews and Christians, i.e. in heaven or hell after death. The term *Allah*, used by the Muslims, means *God* in Arabic, and the term *Islam* means *submission to God*. A Muslim is one who gives himself to the service of God. Muslims acknowledge Moses and Abraham of the Old Testament, and Jesus Christ as great prophets, and Mohammed as the last and the greatest prophet.

If you are a true Muslim you are forbidden to eat pork and

must eat only halal meat, which is meat of animals slaughtered and prayed over while it is bleeding to death; you must not fight except for the cause of Islam; you must be kind to strangers and not gamble.

Islam permits a man to have up to four wives if he can afford to maintain them, but the general rule in most countries now is one wife.

A mosque is where a Muslim worships, and it is built so that the worshippers face Mecca. It has a dome and a tower called a minaret. The largest mosque, with the largest gatherings can be found in Damascus, Syria, and is called the Umayyad Mosque; the tallest minaret (86 metres high) can be found in the Sultan Hussan Mosque in Cairo, Egypt. The worshippers are first required to remove their shoes and enter the mosque barefoot as a sign of respect to God. They then perform a purifying ceremony known as Al-Wudhu, which starts by reading the name of God, which is then followed by washing the hands, mouth, nostrils, face and arms (from wrist to elbow). This is followed by the right arm, then the head, ears and finally both feet up to the ankles.

The *Quran* is the Holy Book and Muslims believe it contains God's actual words spoken to the prophet Mohammed through the angel Gabriel. Muslim law, which is to be found in the Quran, has five distinct duties the Muslim has to perform.

Duty 1: **Shahada (Affirmation)**, which declares there is no other God but one God, and that Mohammed is his messenger.

Duty 2: **Salat (Prayer)**, which means you have to pray at least five times per day.

Duty 3: **Zakat (Almsgiving)**, which means you have to donate money to worthwhile causes.

Duty 4: **Siyam (Fast)**, which means that in the month of Ramadan (the ninth month of the Muslim year), healthy Muslims must fast (not eat or drink) from dawn to dusk.

Duty 5: **Hajj (make a pilgrimage)** to the holy city of Mecca.

The prayers in a mosque last for around ten minutes and are led by a prayer leader called an Imam, and on Fridays there is a sermon. Women are not allowed to pray with the men – they pray in a different part of the mosque.

Here are some teachings of Islam direct from the Holy Quran (translated from Arabic to English) which states how a person should live his life, which all of us can learn something from, whichever walk of life we belong to. The divine revelation was given from God to the prophet Mohammed in the 6th century AD.

1. The initiate shall solemnly promise that he shall abstain from Shirk (association of any partner with God) right up to the day of his death.

2. That he shall keep away from falsehood, fornication, adultery, trespasses of the eye, debauchery, dissipation, cruelty, dishonesty, mischief and rebellion; and will not permit himself to be carried away by passions, however strong they may be.

3. That he shall regularly offer the five daily prayers in accordance with the commandments of God and the Holy Prophet; and shall try his best to be regular in offering the Tahajjud (pre-dawn supererogatory prayers) and invoking Darood (blessings) on the Holy Prophet; that he shall make it his daily routine to ask forgiveness for his sins, to remember the bounties of God and to praise and glorify Him.

4. That under the impulse of any passions, he shall cause no harm whatsoever to the creatures of Allah in general, and to Muslims in particular, neither by his tongue nor by his hands nor by any other means.

5. That he shall remain faithful to God in all circumstances of life, in sorrow and happiness, adversity and prosperity, in felicity and trials; and shall in all conditions remain resigned to the decree of Allah and keep himself ready to face all kinds of indignities and sufferings in His way and shall never turn away from it at the onslaught of any misfortune; on the contrary, he shall march forward.

6. That he shall refrain from following un-Islamic customs and lustful inclinations, and shall completely submit himself to the authority of the Holy Quran and shall make the word of God and the sayings of the Holy Prophet the guiding principles in every walk of his life.

7. That he shall entirely give up pride and vanity and shall pass all his life in lowliness, humbleness, cheerfulness, forbearance and meekness.

8. That he shall hold faith, the honour of faith, and the cause of Islam dearer to him than his life, wealth, honour, children and all other dear ones.

9. That he shall keep himself occupied in the service of God's creatures, for His sake only; and shall endeavour to benefit mankind to the best of his God-given abilities and powers.

Judaism

Jewish people rarely intermarry, which means it is a custom that Jewish children are born from Jewish parents and therefore many ancient traditions and customs, particularly with regard to religion, are handed down from generation to generation.

This means that the Jewish way of life is preserved and revolves around the family, home and the community centre – the synagogue – the place where religious services are held and religious education is taught to children. It is also the place where Jewish events are celebrated.

A Jewish custom is to give presents to one another as a token of caring for others. The preparation and eating of food is done in a special way to give reverence to God. Jewish men wear a skull cap called a kipa when saying prayers as a mark of respect to God.

Every week Shabbat, which is the Jewish day of rest and celebration, is considered a special day. It starts on Friday at sunset and ends on the following Saturday evening. The Christian holy day Sunday, is named after Shabbat. To demonstrate that Shabbat is a bright and festive day, candles are lit, eyes are shut and prayers are said by Jewish mothers, followed by a blessing by Jewish fathers to their children to commemorate the very same blessing given well over two thousand years ago, to be found in the Jewish Bible (known as the Old Testament by Christians) in the temple at Jerusalem. The blessing asks God to bless everyone and shower peace on them.

The temple built by King Solomon in Jerusalem around 3000 years ago was destroyed by the Romans. Although most of it was demolished, a part of the western wall, also known as the wailing wall of tears, remains and is the main place of worship for Jews from all over the world.

The best cutlery and crockery are used for the three Shabbat meals. Celebrations start with a cup of wine for supper and between courses Shabbat songs are sung. Drinking of wine, and a special blessing with Shabbat songs at the table, and prayers are ways of thanking God for providing food. On Saturday evening Shabbat ends with Havdalla, a ceremony which marks the end of Shabbat, in which a cup is filled till it overflows to demonstrate how the joy of Shabbat should flow to the new week. The scent given off from spices are inhaled in order to continue with the joy of Shabbat.

Jewish people mainly eat kosher food. It is food that is prepared and eaten according to biblical and talmudic rules. On Shabbat Jews make their own plaited bread at home or get it from a kosher bakery.

One rule is that meat must be kept separate from milk or foods made from dairy products. Because Jewish rules are very strict about the slaughter of animals in a religious ritual, Jews buy meat produce from a kosher butcher. Even foods that are made from animal fat or meat must be kosher.

It is customary for Jews to go to the synagogue on Saturday for a service in which the Torah (scrolls) is taken out from the ark and read.

The Torah comprises the first five books of the Bible which contain the law given by God to Moses on Mount Sinai about 3,500 years ago. It is written in Hebrew and the word Torah means 'Law' or 'Teachings'. Men and women sit separately in the synagogue. Parts of the Torah are read every week in the synagogue and during a whole year the entire Torah is finished. At the final stage of the reading, a ritual called 'Simhat Torah' is performed where worshippers perform a dance around the synagogue. The Torah, being sacred, is not touched by hand but is pointed to with a silver pen-like instrument called a *Yad* when read.

The scrolls are very carefully made by hand, and this is done by taking the dried skin of an animal which is stretched and hung by means of strings attached to the skin and then onto pegs secured to a wall and inscribed by hand with a quill pen. It usually takes about a year to make. The ends of the skins are then fastened onto two wooden rollers to form a scroll.

The Torah scrolls are read from right to left and the five books that make up the Torah (Bible) are: Genesis, Exodus, Leviticus, Numbers and Deuteronomy. The Hebrew Bible contains history, laws, poems, prophecy and ethics. Judaism is an ancient religion, for Abraham lived 1800 years before Christianity and 2400 years before Islam. The Christian and Islam beliefs in one God originate from the revelations to Abraham.

Less than 400 years after Abraham, the Israelites became slaves of Egypt. Moses was chosen by God to lead them out of Egypt across the Red Sea to freedom. They then entered the Sinai Desert where God appeared to Moses and told him how Jews should live and gave him the Ten Commandments.

The Ten Commandments

"I am the Lord your God:

1. You shall not have strange gods before me.
2. You shall not take the name of the Lord your God in vain.
3. Remember to keep holy the Lord's day.
4. Honour your father and your mother.
5. You shall not kill.
6. You shall not commit adultery.
7. You shall not steal.
8. You shall not bear false witness against your neighbour.
9. You shall not covet your neighbour's wife.
10. You shall not covet your neighbour's goods."

(Exodus 20:1-17)

These are the words found in the Torah, called *Mitzvot* which means Commandments of God, and is the fundamental basis for the Jewish religion.

Jews believe that God will send his Messiah, as foretold in the

Torah, to bring peace and justice to the world and they do not, like Christians, believe Jesus is the awaited Messiah.

The Jews finally settled in Canaan (God's promised land), now called Israel, and they built the Holy Temple in Jerusalem and placed the ark in it to house the tablets of stone. This is why synagogues today are built to face Jerusalem.

Around 900 years after Moses, in the year 586 BC, the temple in Jerusalem was destroyed and the Jews were expelled to Babylon and other far-off destinations around the world. It was rebuilt and opened. It was a further 500 years later that the Jews came under Roman rule and during that time Jesus of Nazareth lived.

In the year AD 70, the Romans destroyed the temple again and it has remained thus ever since. For about 1,900 years, the Jews were scattered all over the world, but in 1948, in the land that was once called Canaan, the state of Israel was set up and since then the Jews have been migrating back to their historical homeland. Today there are still around five million Jews in the USA, three and a half million in Israel, one third of a million in Britain. The Jews have excelled in all spheres of the professions, including politics, law, music, business, medicine, science and journalism. But they have been subjected to some of the most horrific suffering known to man throughout their existence as a race.

Jews today are of many nationalities, and they form different denominations: Orthodox, Hasidic and Progressive Jews. There are also sects called Reform, Liberal and Conservative Jews, who are similar to Progressive Jews.

A rabbi is a Jewish teacher. They have to study for many years and can come from any employment background, not necessarily that of a tutor or community leader. Orthodox Jews are ones who practice Judaism very strictly as laid down in the Torah. You would call them Jewish fundamentalists. Hasidic Jews have been East European town dwellers who were forced to live in ghettos. Though they suffered much poverty and hardship, because they were led by wise and holy men, they flourished – they even had their own hospitals, schools, shops and religious law courts. Hasidic Jews can be found in most parts of the world today but they mainly mix with their own kind and they speak their own dialect, called Yiddish. They are very conservative in their religious beliefs and they cannot be influenced to change their religious customs. They can be recognized by their dress because the men wear a long black coat, large fur hat and a beard, whilst the boys have short hair with long side locks.

Progressive Jews are those who from about the year 1800 onwards started to mix freely with the citizens of their countries of domicile by going to University, engaging in business and politics and so on. Some of these Jews wanted to modernize their religion, and they did so by reading the Torah in the synagogue in modern languages and the men were allowed to sit with women during services. Women were allowed to become rabbis and not all the strict kosher laws were observed. These actions have caused friction between the Progressive and the Orthodox Jews.

There are more than a dozen Jewish festivals.

Before a boy reaches the age of thirteen, he takes lessons to sing from the Torah to celebrate his coming of age. It is called 'Barmitzvah' and a similar ceremony is performed for girls at the age of twelve which is called 'Batmitzvah'. After these events, Jewish boys and girls are expected to take responsibility for their actions and follow the Jewish customs and way of life in a mature fashion.

Passover is the festival of freedom which reminds Jews of their escape from Egyptian slavery 3,500 years ago. During the festival, all members of the family get together during springtime for the Seder meal, which consists of bitter herbs, which remind Jews of the misery they had to undergo under the Egyptians, and a flat bread called matza which reminds them of the time when during their hurry to escape to freedom, they did not even have time to let the bread rise. There are also a variety of questions, stories, games and songs which the family participates in, and one such game is that children have to find the piece of matza bread hidden on a special plate positioned in the middle of the table.

Sukkot is the harvest festival. The sukka, a temporary shed made with a roof of leaves, is decorated with fruits and pictures. The sukka is made in Autumn and it is where the festival is held. Meals are consumed in the sukka. Sukkot reminds Jews of their past when their ancestors lived in tents while wandering through the desert to escape from Egypt to Israel.

Hannuka is the victory festival for when Jews won back the temple at Jerusalem around 2,150 years ago. The festival lasts for eight days during winter. Children play a game called dredle (spinning top) and give presents to their family and friends. Legend tells that the oil used to light the temple light was almost depleted, but lasted for eight days giving the Jews time to make more oil and the dredle has inscribed on it in Hebrew 'A great miracle happened here'.

Purim is carnival time and during this festival, the story of Esther is read from the Bible. It takes place at the end of winter and it tells how Queen Esther saved the Jews in Persia from being killed by Haman, and when the name of Haman is said rattles are shaken violently to demonstrate the happiness of Jews at what Queen Esther did for them. It is a time of great happiness and celebration for Jews.

From birth to death, these are some of the special customs practised by Jews:

A Jewish baby has a Hebrew name and a non-Hebrew name. The Hebrew name is used in the synagogue and on religious documents (a Ketubah). Jewish baby boys are circumcised eight days after birth and the ceremony is performed by a Mohel (a Jew specially trained in the skill of cutting off the skin of the baby's penis) according to God's law. Baby girls are given a blessing on the Shabbat day after birth and are also given their names.

At Jewish weddings, the bride and groom stand under a canopy called a huppah, which represents the home they will share together. The bridegroom gives the bride a plain golden ring and the marriage agreement, called the Ketubah, is read out which holds the promise that the groom makes to the bride. A blessing is said over two glasses of wine which the couple take, and then the groom crushes the glass under his foot to show life is not easy and they must stay together in good times as in bad and always remember those who are suffering. As the couple descend from the Huppah, all the guests say 'Mazel Tov' which means 'good luck'. In death, the last words a Jew will say, if he can are, 'Hear, O Israel, the Lord our God is one.'

Jewish Ethics

1. Loyalty to the Community.
2. Loyalty to the State.
3. Brotherly Love.
4. The Sanctity of Human Life.
5. The Sanctity of Property.

Chapter 19 of Leviticus contains many guiding principles for regulating everyday conduct. Jews are commanded to respect their parents, be kind to the poor, pay wages promptly to employees, deal honourably in business, not be a tale-bearer, love their neighbour, show friendship to the alien, and be just to both rich and poor. In many ways they correspond to the Ten Commandments. Significantly, we read at the very beginning of the chapter, **You shall be holy for I the Lord your God am holy**. The duty of carrying out these and all other righteous principles is an integral part of the Torah.

Buddhism

In the world today there are about 1,000 million Buddhists, of which 700 million can be found in Communist countries such as China, North Korea and Vietnam. There are about 60,000 Buddhists in Great Britain, mainly of Sri Lankan, Indian, Chinese, Burmese and Tibetan origin, whereas in the USA there are over 200,000 mainly of Chinese and Japanese background.

There are two main sects, even though there are many offshoots from the mainstream Buddhists. One sect, the '**Mahayana Buddhists**' spread northwards from India (the birthplace of Buddhism) to China, Mongolia, Korea, Japan, Tibet and Vietnam. **Zen Buddhists** of Japan are also included here.

The other sect, called '**Theravada Buddhists**' spread southwards to Sri Lanka, Burma, Thailand, Laos and Kampuchea. Prince Siddhartha Gautama, who became the spiritual leader of the Buddhists, called the 'Buddha,' was born in India in 560 BC. Up until the age of 29 he lived a life of luxury. His own enlightenment led him to conclude that most people's lives were made up of suffering and hardship. He then decided to go in search of the true meaning and understanding of life which he eventually found.

The word '**Buddha**' means '**Enlightened One**'. The Buddha and his followers set out to preach the **Four Noble Truths** and the **Eight-fold Path**, travelling to different places during the Indian dry season and remaining in one place during the rainy season preaching to local villages. It is from here that the Buddhists Monks we see to-day evolved.

The **Four Noble Truths** are:

1. All life is suffering.
2. Suffering is caused by our selfish attachment.
3. We can escape from suffering by eradicating selfish attachment.
4. This can be achieved by being moderate in life.

By following the **Eight-fold Path** below, we can avoid extremes:

1. Right understanding.
2. Right intention.
3. Right speech.
4. Right conduct.
5. Right occupation.
6. Right endeavour.
7. Right contemplation.
8. Right concentration.

Buddhists also make five voluntarily accepted daily vows in front of the Buddha's statue. These are called the **Five Precepts**, which are:

1. I take the Precept to abstain from killing (i.e. killing any living being).
2. I take the Precept to abstain from taking that which is not given (i.e. any form of stealing, such as unfair advantage of labour, forgery, theft).
3. I take the Precept to abstain from sexual misconduct (i.e. unlawful sex and adultery).

4. I take the Precept to abstain from false speech (i.e. lying, gossip, backbiting, slander and rude and improper words in speech).

5. I take the Precept to abstain from intoxication (i.e. intoxicating drink and drugs).

The Buddha taught that beings go through many stages of life on this earth until they reach the last stage, which is a stage of peace called **Nirvana**, through merit. The Buddha eventually attained this state in the final years of his lifetime.

Buddhists, unlike in some other religions, are not required to visit the temple at any specific time or day. They usually congregate at the Buddhist temple, which is called a **vihara**.

The vihara has a shrine room in which there is a large image of the Buddha, statues of his disciples, relics and manuscripts of his teachings, a religious library, and a lecture and meditation room. When entering the shrine room Buddhists remove their shoes as a mark of respect to the Buddha. They then light candles and incense sticks and recite special verses. Buddhists do not look at the Buddha as God but as a great teacher.

Buddhists make special offerings to the Buddha with flowers or food, and whilst they are making their offerings, they recite the special verses called **gathas**. They remind themselves of the fact that, just like flowers perish, so will they. Devotees also offer gifts of food to the monks called a **dana** (almsgiving to the monks, poor or needy) as they do not have a means of obtaining such necessities because they are involved in religious duties. By giving alms to the monks, the Buddhists view it as an action on their part that will help them attain **nirvana**. Monks usually have shaven heads and carry a bowl for food, clothing and other requirements and wear a saffron coloured robe as the Buddha's first followers used to do.

The dana ceremony takes place almost everyday at the temple where food is offered to the monks before midday, as the monks do not eat after that time. On special occasions the dana is given at the devotees' homes where the monks are invited, fed, given gifts of robes and other necessities are provided, and the monks in return give their blessings to their host.

Monks chant sacred verses from the Holy Books which are

called **pirith** – a custom that has been in existence since Buddhism itself. Pirith chanting is often made at the end of a ceremony, or, as some families do, before going to bed each night. Sometimes on special occasions the chanting can go on without interruption for several days.

Sermons, called **sutras** made by the Buddha are felt by Buddhists to have a special importance or power.

The monks help the devotees understand the message of the Buddha by participating in **vandana** which is paying homage to the Buddha, which is then followed by deep meditation on a special theme, for example on loving kindness which is a very important part of the Buddhist way of life. A holy thread is then tied onto the wrists of the devotees by the monk at the end of some ceremonies, which signifies protection from evil.

The Buddha featured in different positions is said to signify something to Buddhist followers. For example, the Buddha with his right hand pointing downwards is said to represent his triumphs over earthly temptations. Another position which shows the Buddha with his fingers near his heart and palms touching it represents the Buddha making his first sermon.

The main teachings of the Buddha can be found iin the **Tripitaka** or **Three baskets**, which comprises 31 books divided into three sections. One of the books is Jataka which relates 500 stories of the life of the Buddha. Each book has a moral theme which the monks use in sermons. The holy books are written in the **Pali** language which originated in India and is very ancient (over 2500 years old), and many Buddhist temples have been used as a place for education. Hence, there are religious books written in Pali and in the native languages of the country, to be found in temples.

Children attend religious classes on Sundays at the Vihara. The Buddha's teachings were written down many years after his death and they were written on **ola** (palm) leaves.

Many deeply religious Buddhists are vegetarian, eating only a strict diet that contains no meat, fish or eggs, but the non-vegetarian Buddhists usually, on full-moon days, become vegetarian.

On full-moon days, when visiting the temple, devotees wear white clothes and observe **Attha Sila** or the eight vows, which encompass the five precepts above and three others:

1. Not to eat after midday and not to dance or sing.
2. Not to adorn or beautify oneself and use perfumes.
3. Not to use luxury beds or chairs.

Buddhist weddings are usually arranged by the parents of the bride and groom and the wedding ceremony is performed on a **poruwa** (a platform) and is called the poruwa ceremony. The platform is beautifully decorated with white flowers. Rings are exchanged between the bride and groom and the bride's and groom's thumbs are joined together with a piece of string by the bride's uncle. The wedding celebrations and feastings go on for many days afterwards.

Buddhists in many countries have colourful festivals and processions on full-moon day. In Sri Lanka there is a world-renowned festival of the August mooon called the Kandy Perahera where hundreds of magnificently dressed elephants, drummers and dancers take the relic of the tooth of the Buddha in procession around the gaily decorated and well-lit city of Kandy.

The following is the extract of a sermon given by the Buddha in the 6th century BC on loving kindness and can be used as an excellent foundation for business ethics as much as it is the guiding principles for the life of a Buddhist, or even a non-Buddhist.

The Discourse on Loving Kindness
(*Translated from Pali*)

1. One who is skilled in his good and who wishes to attain that state of calm, Nibbana, should act thus: he should be able, upright and conscientious, of soft speech, gentle and not proud.
2. Contented, living simply, at leisure and unburdened, with senses calmed, prudent, modest, and without showing anxiety for support.
3. He should not commit any slight wrong on account of which wise men might censure him.

4-5. May all beings be happy and secure, may their hearts be wholesome! Whatever living beings there be – feeble or strong, long, stout or medium, short, small or large, seen or unseen, those dwelling far or near, those who are born and those who are to be born – may they be happy-minded!

6. Let none deceive another nor despise any person whosoever in any place, neither in anger nor in ill-will, let one not wish any harm to another.

7. Just as a mother would protect her only child at the risk of her own life, even so, let one cultivate a boundless heart towards all beings.

8. Let thoughts of boundless love pervade the whole world – above, below and across without any obstruction, without any hatred, without any enmity.

9. Whether standing, walking, sitting or lying down, as long as one is awake, this mindfulness should be developed. This, they say, is the Highest Conduct here.

10. Not embracing false views, virtuous and endowed with insight, giving up attachment to sense-desires; of a truth, such a person does not come again for repeated becoming (for rebirth).

Hinduism

Hinduism is thought to be one of the oldest religions of the world and is the third-largest religion, with around 700 million followers. Its origins can be traced to 2500 years BC in ancient India. The word 'Hindu' was first used to describe people who dwelt near the river Indus and their beliefs and way of life eventually became a religion that spread all over India.

Hindus believe there is only one supreme god called '**Brahma**', even though some Hindus believe there are manifestations of this god in other gods that look like humans or animals. Some of these gods are named as follows:

Brahma   Is the god that creates life.
Vishnu   A kind and gentle god who assists mankind to escape from evil.

Shiva   The god who rules life and death and is the god that destroys everything found in the universe. Shiva has many forms – some are goddesses such as Kali and Durga.

Ganesha   The elephant-headed god (is worshipped usually at the start of events and religious ceremonies).

Krishna   Is the god who appeared on the earth for the salvation of mankind. This god is also known as the god of love.

The largest number of Hindus in the world can be found in India where over 80% are followers of the Hindu faith. Pakistan has only 11% and East Africa has the most outside India and Pakistan. Hindu communities are also to be found in Sri Lanka, Nepal, Bali (Indonesia), Europe, Canada and the USA. Britain has around 300,000 who mostly came from East Africa, and the rest from India and Pakistan.

The Hindu Holy Book, called the **Rig-Veda**, was written in Sanskrit around 1000 BC and includes four **Vedas** (the oldest written statements on the Hindu belief).

The first is called *Rig, Sama, Yajur and Atharvan*. The second, the *Upanishads*, contains the most important statements in Hinduism, written around 500 BC. The Upanishads tell of man's place in the Universe and about rebirth and how our actions and behaviour will determine what form, human or animal, one will take after death. After several rebirths, depending on merit, one will be united in perfect harmony with God with no more life or death. Third is *Ramayana*. Fourth is *Mahabharata* which contains the famous verses from **Bhagavad Gita**. The **Bhagavad Gita** tells about the various duties which man has to perform in life. The Vedas are a collection of hymns that describe nature and how to worship God. For hundreds of years they were not written, but committed to memory by Brahmin children.

The essential Hindu belief is that everything in the world is united through the spirit of God. Brahma is said to be found in every living thing – humans, animals and plants. It also includes the following beliefs:

Ahimsa   that it is wrong to hurt any living thing.

Samara   the cycle of life and death in which the person is reborn into another form after death until the highest state called **moksha** is achieved. Moksha means freedom from the cycle of life and death where one ends up in unity with God.

Karma   how one's actions and behaviour in their present life will affect the next.

Dharma   a person's obligations to God, family and clan.

The Hindu religion divides people into castes (social group) and people are born into their own caste. The highest caste is the **Brahmins** (priests) followed by **Kshatriyas** (warriors and rulers) followed by **Vaishyas** (merchants and farmers) followed by **Shudras** (peasants and labourers). There is a further caste called the **Untouchables** (coolies) who do all the menial jobs. Nowadays, most Hindus tend to ignore the strict caste system. Many Hindus keep statues or pictures of their gods in their homes. It is a custom that the day is started by waking the gods and washing the statues. They are put onto a platform by day and onto a special bed at night. During the day special prayers are recited and ceremonies performed to the gods. The red powder dot worn on the head by Hindus signifies their belief in the religion. Food is offered to the gods with prayers and hymns which then becomes holy and when this consecrated food is eaten by the worshippers, it is called **prasad**, which means food shared with the gods. This ceremony is performed throughout the day before the Gods are put to bed at night.

Many Hindus go to the river Ganges in India to bathe as it is considered holy and the river washes away their sins. Asian Hindu women usually wear sarees, but can adapt like the men to wearing the dress of the country of residence (which usually is western clothes). Because of their religious beliefs that it is wrong to kill, most Hindus are vegetarian. For the Hindus who do eat meat, beef is not taken as the cow is considered a holy animal.

Arranged marriages by parents are a Hindu custom to find a compatible partner for their sons and daughters. A Hindu Priest then checks the couple's horoscopes to fix the best time and date for the wedding. The father of the bride is required to give a dowry (money) to the bridegroom. There are numerous wedding ceremonies and feasting can go on for three days.

There are many Hindu celebrations and festivals. One such event is the name giving ceremony for a child which is done before the child's first birthday – the child is fed its first spoon of rice.

Diwali is a big festival for Hindus every year in honour of Lexhmi, the goddess of wealth and to celebrate this event homes are decorated and lit with lamps, candles, sparklers and firework displays are held. **Holi** is another festival where coloured powder and water are thrown at each other. It signifies the start of spring and remembers the gods **Radha** and **Krishna**.

The following are the ten principles of Hinduism made by the first great teacher of Hindu philosophy, translated from Sanskrit and Hindi. They form an ethical approach to life and business.

Ten Principles of Hinduism
(Translated from Sanskrit & Hindi)

1. **DHARITH (Firmness)**: Patience or Self-Command both in days of rise and days of fall. Never be overjoyed or depressed. Have full faith in the Lord.
2. **KSAMA (Forbearance or Forgiveness)**: If one does some harm to another person and the other person does not try to take revenge, such an act is called forbearance or forgiveness. It is the quality of mighty people and must be applied to both friends and foes.
3. **DAMO (Control over mind)**: This is an important means of salvation because without it one cannot meditate, and without meditation one cannot acquire self-realization, without which there is no salvation.
4. **ASTEYAM (Not to steal)**: It is a pious human quality very useful for social welfare. The Scriptures command that one should earn his living by lawful means. To take anything without the knowledge or permission of his master is an act of stealing. Lord Krishna commands man to worship God through Vedic sacrifices. God bestows on him all that he requires for a happy life. The person who enjoys the gifts bestowed by God without offering a part of it to God or in charity is a thief.

5. **SAUCAM (Purity or cleanliness)**: It is of two kinds, internal and external. External purity is acquired through truthfulness. God is perfectly pure. One who wishes to come near him must purify himself in both respects. The great Saints have said, 'The more one is purified, the nearer he is to God'. Saucam, or purity, can be called the backbone of righteousness.

6. **INDRIYANI GRAHAN (Control over senses or restraint)**: The senses are attracted by objects of the outer world. The senses also possess some extraordinary natural power when attracted by the objects – they forcibly drag the mind towards it and, within a moment, the mind is immersed in thinking of that object; it never gives any chance to the intellect to think of the result. The soul is neutral, like steam of an engine, but never interferes in its direction, so the mind runs to the direction where senses are already attracted. So the senses must be trained to follow the mind and the mind must be trained to follow the intellect.

7. **DHIR (Right Knowledge of Scripture)**: Right knowledge of the Sastras is absolutely necessary to take a firm decision about one's own duty. Bhagwan Manu has said in his Smriti that those virtuous people who are anxious to know what merit and demerit are must remember that the Vedas are the supreme authority to decide what is righteousness and what is not. Lord Krishna also commands that the persons who cast aside the teachings of the Scriptures and act accordingly to their own sweet will shall attain neither perfection nor happiness nor salvation. Therefore, one should accept the authority of Scriptures in what ought to be done and what ought not.

8. **VIDYA (Brahm-Vidya or Knowledge of the Spiritual Science)**: Man must learn Brahm-Vidya since god-realization or the realization of the identity between the Self and Absolute is the highest aim of human life. The study of spiritual science has more importance than the study of material science. Disregarding the study of Brahm Science does far more damage to man than the study of material science. Neglecting the study of Brahm Science means misery in human life. Deep study of Vedant is an essential requisite to man.

9. **SATYAM (Truth)**: The Scriptures, commonly known as the truth, mean we must endeavour to attain the Truth. The Vedanta says that truth is known by truthfulness. One who knows the reality by the constant practice of truthfulness shall undoubtedly attain immortality.

   Everyone must speak the truth because truthfulness of the people can make a better society – a society of divine nature. Thus truth is nectar for social welfare which a man must possess.

10. **AKRODHO (Absence of Anger)**: For spiritual uplift it is absolutely necessary to control anger. The Scriptures say that one who has conquered anger completely has won the whole universe. Anger gives rise to destructive sentiments. The mind of an angry man is so confused that he loses the right thinking or discriminating power. Anger burns the energy in the body and is one reason that an angry man is always found weak and thin. Absence of anger shall bring health to the individual and a peace-loving society to mankind. Control of anger is indeed a good quality of human conduct.

Sikhism

A Sikh temple or shrine is called a **Gurdwara**, which originates from linking the two words Guru and Dwara together to mean 'The teacher's place'; **Guru** meaning teacher and **Dwara** meaning place.

Outside the Gurdwara a yellow triangular flag called a **Nishan Sahib** flies, identifying it as a holy place for Sikhs. Removing the shoes is customary for Sikhs before entering the Gurdwara as a token of respect to the **Guru Granth Sahib**, which is the holy book containing the sacred writings of early Sikh religious leaders. Inside the hall both men and women keep their heads covered, again as a mark of respect to the holy book which is mounted on a platform for all to see. Sikhs visit the Gurdwara for **sangat** (prayer) and worship before the holy book. This is done by bowing and touching the floor with the forehead after the person sits down on the floor.

The Guru Granth Sahib is wrapped in a fine, bright-coloured

cloth and it is positioned beneath a canopy in the centre of the worship area. Sikhs make offerings of money to the book. In the Gurdwara, the religious service begins with **Kirtan** (singing hymns from the holy book) with musical accompaniment on the **tabla** (a small pair of drums) and the **harmonium**. The holy priest, called a **Granthi**, then reads from the Guru Granth Sahib and explains its meaning. At the end of the service, the congregation fold their hands while the sacrament **prasad** (made of flour, butter and sugar) is handed out to the followers.

Sikhs hold the belief that there is only one true God and the gurus were the teachers who strengthened the faith of the followers through their writings by stressing the importance of good conduct and a peaceful and happy society. Even practices like smoking and drinking are forbidden.

The Guru Granth Sahib tells about God, creation, man and his place in God's kingdom and how man can obtain enlightenment and salvation. The ten Great Gurus in chronological order are:

Guru Nanak (1469–1539), who was originally a Hindu, started the Sikh religion in the Punjab, North West India. From him, nine other gurus followed on. They were:

Guru Angad (1504–1552), who used the Punjabi language in religious ceremonies as opposed to the Sanskrit language of the Hindus.

Guru Amar Das (1479–1552). He taught the importance of living a clean life and of being good to others.

Guru Ram Das (1534–1581). He founded Amritsar, where the Sikhs' holy temple is built.

Guru Arjan (1563–1606) was responsible for compiling the Sikhs' Holy Book.

Guru Har Gobind (1595–1644) was a great religious teacher and military leader.

Guru Har Rai (1630–1661). He taught the importance of doing good and not causing pain or suffering to others.

Guru Har Krishan (1656–1664) aged eight, and the youngest guru.

Guru Tegh Bahadur (1621–1675). He preferred death to being converted to Islam.

Guru Gobind Singh (1666–1708). He formed the brotherhood of Sikhs called the **Khalsa** and named the holy book Guru Granth Sahib and declared himself as the last Guru (teacher) to Sikhs. The Ten Gurus have written rules by which Sikhs should live:

- That there is only one God who created the universe.
- To earn an honest living and to share it with others.
- Not to take alcohol, tobacco or drugs.
- Not to follow the Hindu system of upper and lower caste.

There are five Sikh symbols starting with the letter 'K' which must be worn all the time by Sikhs. These are **Kara, Kangha, Kacchera, Kirpan** and **Kesh**. It was introduced by the tenth and last Guru, Gobind Singh, to signify that the Sikhs were 'Khalsa' meaning 'Pure' or 'God's Own', but these days not all Sikhs wear the five symbols, whilst some even cut their hair.

The five symbols are:

1. **Kara**: A bangle or steel bracelet. It is the sign of eternity.
2. **Kangha**: A comb. It is a sign of cleanliness and tidiness which keeps the hair knot in place.
3. **Kacchera**: A pair of shorts. It is a sign of action and goodness.
4. **Kirpan**: A sword (dagger) worn by Sikhs. It is a sign of strength.
5. **Kesha** (Hair): It is the sign of wisdom.

The emblem of Sikhs is the **Khanda** – a double-edged sword, circle and two scimitars.

Sikhs number around 11 million in India, about 2% of the population. They have emigrated to Europe, East Africa, USA, Canada and Malaysia, and excelled in all spheres in those countries, since the Indian Independence in 1947. Britain has the largest number of Sikhs (over ¼ million) outside India.

Sikh men grow their beards and do not cut their hair. A turban is worn over the long hair which is combed into a bun and is held in place with a cloth called a **patka**. A band of cloth called a **fifti** is used to hold the knot of hair in place and the turban is wrapped round the head. Sikh women usually wear Punjabi dress called a *salwar kameez* which are trousers gathered in at the ankle and worn with a tunic.

Most Sikh men wear European clothes in daily life, but when attending religious ceremonies, some change into Punjabi clothes, i.e. a white turban, white shirt and trousers.

Sikhs are usually vegetarian, as the generally held view is that it is an injustice to kill animals for food, though some Sikhs are meat eaters.

Christianity

Roman Catholics, Baptists, Church of England, Church of Scotland, Orthodox Christian, Pentecostal, Methodists, United Reformed Church and Quakers are all denominations of Christians who have one common belief that Jesus Christ was God on Earth. But they have disagreed with how His teachings should be followed, resulting in the different denominations of Christianity and methods of worship.

The name Jesus Christ is described as **Jesus**, meaning '**God Saves**' and **Christ** meaning '**Anointed One**'. The word **Messiah** also has the same meaning.

The origins of Christianity can be traced to Jerusalem where Christian groups first met and spread the faith to many other countries such as Italy, Egypt, Turkey and Greece, which resulted in different Christian customs developing.

From time to time, Christian leaders called bishops would meet to discuss matters of mutual interest and faith, and during these discussions there ensued a power struggle between the Roman bishop and the Constantinople bishop which resulted in a split in the Christian Church in the year 1054.

The Eastern Orthodox Christians (Orthodox meaning 'right belief') made Constantinople their main centre of affairs and the Roman Catholic bishops made Rome their headquarters and their head was later to become known as the **Pope** (which means father) with the main centre of worship being St Peter's Basilica in the Vatican. Half the Christians in the world belong to the Roman Catholic Church (Catholic meaning worldwide). Today the largest number of Orthodox Christians can be found in

Greece, Russia, Cyprus, Yugoslavia and the USA, with a relatively small number to be found in the United Kingdom. The head of the Orthodox Church is called the **Patriarch**.

Martin Luther, a German priest, protested to the Pope that the Church, with all its power, riches, rules and priests, interfered with the way in which ordinary people came close to God, which angered the Pope and caused his expulsion. He and his followers gained acceptance from many people and, as a consequence, many Protestant Churches were established in many countries – the Church of England, also known as the Anglican Church, is one of them and Anglicans can be found all over the world today. The head of the Anglican Church is the Queen, and the chief primate is the **Archbishop of Canterbury**.

Christians believe that Jesus Christ is the Messiah and that there are three sides to God – the eternal triangle like the three sides of an equilateral triangle: God the Father who created the world, God the Son who was Jesus Christ who was sent to save the world from sin and God the Holy Spirit which is the supernatural phenomenon of God to be experienced on the Earth.

Though Jesus was a Jew, Jewish people do not believe he was the Messiah – they have been waiting patiently for hundreds of years and are still waiting for the Messiah to come. Christians, however, believe that Jesus was the Messiah and He, being God, did not sin.

It is written in the Bible that a young virgin woman named Mary was told by one of God's Angels that she was to carry the infant Jesus.

Jesus was born very poor. He had no money and no possessions of his own. When He reached the age of 30, he travelled on foot everywhere with His disciples telling people about God. The Jews did not believe that this poor and holy man could be God, and the Messiah they were expecting because they thought the Messiah would be a powerful king.

However, there were many people who were astonished and were drawn to Jesus' miraculous powers and way of life. He healed the sick, walked on water, cared for the poor, which can be read about in the Gospels (part of the Bible about the life and work of Jesus – the word Gospel means good news). Whilst

Jesus was preaching God's holy Word and performing miracles, the converted people followed Him for three years, but there were others who feared Him and were jealous of His supreme power and consequently plotted and were responsible for His death by crucifixion, the prevalent system of capital punishment at that time. He died aged thirty-three. However, the Bible tells how Jesus, being God, was resurrected from death and now there are around 1,000 million Christians in the world, making Christianity the largest religion in the world.

The Bible, which is the Christians' holy book describes God, His creation and how people should worship God. The Bible contains documents of the history and lives of holy men, stories, poems and songs of praise. Christians believe the Bible tells the truth of how people should live and give reverence and praise to God, as it was written through divine inspiration.

There are two parts to the Bible, The Old Testament and the New Testament. The Old Testament tells about the beliefs and way of life of the Jewish people before Jesus Christ was born and about the coming of the Messiah who would bring peace and joy to the world. The New Testament reveals the life and work of Jesus who came to teach people about God and how to avoid sin and gain salvation.

Four of Jesus's disciples, Matthew, Mark, Luke and John, wrote about Jesus and their belief in Him and what transpired up to 70 years after his death. These accounts can be read in the 27 books of the New Testament, which cover the life of Christ and how a true Christian life should be lived.

Jesus taught love and peace. He said, 'love God and love your neighbour as yourself', which is the essence of Jewish Law. And he told how God the Father had sent Him to remind the Jews about their laws – the Ten Commandments which God gave to their leader, Moses, a long time ago, which they were not observing, and he spoke of what would happen to them as a consequence.

The Ten Commandments are all the same for Christians as for Jews. One can examine one's conscience from a business and a non-business angle in relation to the Ten Commandments, as they are a marvellous set of rules for anyone (Christian or non-Christian) to live by.

Jesus communicated through parables, which are short stories, that were said in such a way as to make understanding God better.

One such parable was how a man owed a king a large sum of money. The worried man begged the king time to pay it back; the merciful king let him go. It then happened that another man had borrowed a small amount of money from this man but the man who was pardoned by the king ruthlessly demanded the sum back from his debtor. When the king got to know about this he summoned his debtor and angrily told him, 'You worthless slave, I forgave you your debt and you should have shown mercy to your fellow servant. Now go to prison.' Jesus said that this is how God will treat each person if they did not forgive their brother from the heart. In *selling*, the parable style is a very effective way to get the message across and achieve results. There are 39 parables told in the Bible about farmers, fishermen and family life and there is always a hidden message in them about, for example, pride, greed or forgiveness.

CHAPTER 19

A
final word

This book has been laboriously researched and written at great personal cost to me with the assistance of many experts and my primary intention all along has been to provide it as an inspirational and sharp-edged cutting tool to help my fellow brothers and sisters whoever you are and wherever you may be on this planet, to journey through the labyrinth of life's drawbacks, pitfalls and hurdles, caused by humanity itself less painfully and to help you achieve success by adopting a dynamic, rational, reasonable and fair live-and-let-live philosophy.

It consolidates the best from the best of us and the best from the worst of us. When you fuse the two you get a cocktail mix of 'how to' that cannot be rivalled. I would like to mention in passing a little verse I know of:

> *There is so much evil in the best of us*
> *And so much good in the worst of us*
> *That it wouldn't be fair for any of us*
> *To talk about the rest of us.*

For those in power, the lawmakers, the do-gooders, the rich and famous – it offers an enlightened view and sensible outlook of the other side, and for those who are powerless, weak and deprived – it offers hope and consolation to become stronger and provides the all-important guidance and know-how to help develop into a better person and contribute towards a more prosperous company, community and country. As humans, we are all mortals and vulnerable mentally and physically. The circumstances may be different, but the end result is nearly always the same. We cannot fail to ignore this. All we can do in life as living beings is to learn to survive and take out an insurance policy by strengthening ourselves for any eventuality.

WHEN TIMES ARE HARD

When times are hard and you are feeling blue
Think about others who have worries too.
Because you feel your problems are many
It doesn't mean that others haven't any.

Life is a mixture of smiles and tears,
Joy and sorrow and many a fear.
To some of us, though, it appears one-sided,
You can bet trouble is pretty well divided.

If you can peer into everyone's heart
You will discover each one has their fair share
And those who travel the fortunes road
Sometimes have to carry the biggest load

From the cradle, life was meant for living, loving, laughing, evolving, exploring and achieving until death, just like a small plant grows – taking nourishment from the earth, energy from the sun, water from the rain to grow into a tree and bear flowers and fruit. But, invariably, and sadly, what happens in life is people put the mental brakes on with self-inflicted negativism and complacency, and rather than blaming themselves for their current situation, they start blaming others for the hell-hole they are in that they themselves have created. They moan and groan and try to bring down others who are making it or have made it and try to grab the other's trophy by fair or foul means. What they must do is fight the disease within and look towards bettering themselves from now and forever on and believe in the power of their subconscious mind to solve life's dilemmas by feeding it with success ingredients and positive thoughts, rather than the mental junk food of negative thinking. God helps those who help themselves and the late John F. Kennedy told the American people, 'Ask not what your country can do for you, but what you can do for your country.' The only way a person can contribute to his home, his workplace, his community and his country is by being strong and powerful himself. It is only the good use of power that benefits one and all of us that matters. Power is a wonderful thing. It means the person who's got it has energy. What is in question here is the direction of the energy for constructive and not for destructive purposes. Unquestionably, it is the good use of power that benefits one and all, not the misuse of it which counts. The ultimate objective of acquiring power, therefore, must be to benefit other human beings.

One of the best ways of preventing, avoiding or dealing with man made conflict and misery is knowing when and how to start, when and how to change tactics, when and how to review and take a fresh approach, when and how to heal and, if the matter has gone too far and is out of control, to know when and how to stop one's actions dead in their track.

All life's problems resulting from mental anguish can be managed and made more palatable if we can accept and accommodate change, think positively and fight our problems on a day-to-day basis.

For the misguided and those who have a grudge against life, please think before you let the animal out of you. What these people have to realize is that there is much good flowing out of human nature, and if they accept that their vision may be clouded, they could genuinely benefit from it themselves rather than abusing that goodness – they should look for it, reach for it, and when they find it make use of it by grasping the opportunity when it arises and take full advantage of it in order to make it useful to themselves and then in turn give it to others. There is nothing more soul-destroying than to see an inactive human that was built for action.

'I am going to do something positive and good in life for the love of myself and of others and I am going to do it now,' must be the motto of all well-balanced human beings. Aspire to be among the 5% of achievers in the universe or reconcile yourself without remorse to the pile of non-achievers. This book, I hope, will encourage you to say to yourself these magic words 'I can, I will and I have changed my situation for the better and I totally reject all negative, unproductive and evil influences from now on,' simply start acting that wish out, and just watch your powerful subconscious mind move to make your dreams come true.

I am thankful to my Creator for having given me a mere *speck of intelligence* and a *pinhead of knowledge, skill and experience* to know the difference between what is right and what is wrong and the *wisdom* to steer myself through the jungle of the good, the bad and ugly and still maintain my sanity. I love them one and all just the same. I hope you can love them in the same way too. **That's the real secret of success and successful living!**

Professional Salespeople play their cards right

Ace
Declare yourself an ACE in selling.

1. Do one thing at a time and do it well.
2. There are two words you must always use in selling: PLEASE and THANK YOU.
3. Don't forget the THREE SIDES PRINCIPLE (No – Maybe – Yes) and how to deal with it.
4. Know the four techniques of PERSUASION, MOTIVATION, MANIPULATION and NEGOTIATION – how to and when to. Also adopt the four attributes **WISDOM**, **JUSTICE**, **POWER** and **LOVE** when you have any business or private dealings with others.
5. Learn the message of the FIVE PRECEPTS OF BUDDHISM, the FIVE DISTINCT DUTIES OF ISLAM and adapt it to your personal life for its goodness and purity, whatever other

religion or your belief structure, and also realize that the average sale is closed at the FIFTH attempt.

6. Use your own SIX SENSES of SIGHT, SOUND, TASTE, TOUCH, SMELL and INTUITION with greater awareness and effectiveness. Interpret and adapt to the feedback given through the senses of others and respond to it accordingly.

7. If somebody has done you wrong in life, try to forgive not just seven times but SEVENTY TIMES SEVEN – to err is human, but to be able to forgive is a divine quality. Remember that up to seven digits is the optimum number to memorize.

8. Always consider the EIGHT COLOURS of the SPECTRUM – Magenta, Violet, Blue, Turquoise, Green, Yellow, Orange, Red – your preference for a particular colour, what that tells you and what it means when someone else expresses a choice of colour.

9. Don't forget the NINE P's of the Professional Salesperson: **Positive · Persuasive · Patient · Precise · Polite · Plans · Prepared · Punctual · Professional**.

10. Obey the TEN COMMANDMENTS, and learn the message of the TEN PRINCIPLES OF HINDUISM and adapt it to your personal life whatever your faith is or isn't.

Jack

Be a **Jack** of all trades but a master of one – if it is not selling then whatever it is.

Queen

For every king of selling there is a queen. Female intuition can help you become a Queen quicker than it would take to make a King.

King
From a jack to a king of selling is easy when you have knowledge, skill and experience behind you to back you.

Joker
Laugh and joke about life, and it will help you through the good times and bad times. Only a Joker looks for respect without earning it. Think and work like a professional in life, then respect and success will automatically follow.

Spade	**Heart**	**Diamond**	**Club**
Dig for gold: work for rewards.	Have a good heart and be a kind and understanding person.	Be precious and hard. Be a person who has value attached because of your knowledge, skill and experience. Be mentally tough and you will cut through the most difficult of resistances.	Be a fighter, like a primeval man with a club in his hand hunting for food. In other words, cultivate the fighting spirit.

Our Alternative Approach

- Fight poverty with work.
- The salesperson who ends up in bed exhausted with the most number of deals is the winner.
- Love your job but please don't hate the work.
- Always go for a definite maybe when you are selling, and use flattery because it will get you everywhere.
- Don't be led into temptation, just go out and find it for yourself.
- Never let old age and treachery deter your youth and skill.
- Don't get mad with people, just get even.
- Word bullets will help you win when selling, but verbal volleyball won't!

Critics can make you, but never let them break you

In life you will experience critics of all shades. Critics are like Crickets – they make a lot of irritating noise in their darkness, which can be a nuisance, but they are really harmless when you know how to deal with them.

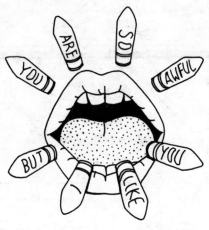

Word bullets

When you know who you are, your strengths, your weaknesses and the hidden power of knowledge that lies within you in reserve and which you can draw upon when required, never let the annoying nuisance called a critic ever worry you. Let them say whatever they like for you can't stop people talking – you can tie a fence around a person's house but you can't tie a fence around a person's thoughts and verbal expressions.

To those superior minded and knowledgeable critics who think they know a better system than what has been taught in this book, I say, please let it be known to me. If you can prove to me that you are right and I am wrong then claim your prize. I look forward to hearing from you soon, the quicker the

YOUR HOTLINE TO SUCCESS

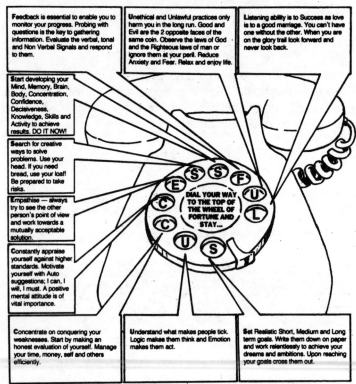

Feedback is essential to enable you to monitor your progress. Probing with questions is the key to gathering information. Evaluate the verbal, tonal and Non Verbal Signals and respond to them.

Unethical and Unlawful practices only harm you in the long run. Good and Evil are the 2 opposite faces of the same coin. Observe the laws of God and the Righteous laws of man or ignore them at your peril. Reduce Anxiety and Fear. Relax and enjoy life.

Listening ability is to Success as love is to a good marriage. You can't have one without the other. When you are on the glory trail look forward and never look back.

Start developing your Mind, Memory, Brain, Body, Concentration, Confidence, Decisiveness, Knowledge, Skills and Activity to achieve results. DO IT NOW!

Search for creative ways to solve problems. Use your head. If you need bread, use your loaf! Be prepared to take risks.

Empathise — always try to see the other person's point of view and work towards a mutually acceptable solution.

Constantly appraise yourself against higher standards. Motivate yourself with Auto suggestions; I can, I will, I must. A positive mental attitude is of vital importance.

DIAL YOUR WAY TO THE TOP OF THE WHEEL OF FORTUNE AND STAY...

Concentrate on conquering your weaknesses. Start by making an honest evaluation of yourself. Manage your time, money, self and others efficiently.

Understand what makes people tick. Logic makes them think and Emotion makes them act.

Set Realistic Short, Medium and Long term goals. Write them down on paper and work relentlessly to achieve your dreams and ambitions. Upon reaching your goals cross them out.

better. So until I hear from you, may I sign off and as you will have all the skills of success by now may I wish you Good fortune, God Bless, and **WHO DARES SELLS**.

May the road rise to meet you
May the wind be always at your back
May the sun shine warm upon your face
The rain fall soft upon your fields
And, until we meet again
May God hold you in the palm of His hand.

THIS IS LIFE

Life is a gift....................Accept it
Life is a beauty....................Admire it
Life is a sorrow....................Face it
Life is a struggle....................Fight it
Life is a joy....................Sing it
Life is a promise....................Fulfil it
Life is a tragedy....................Overcome it
Life is a misery....................Bear it
Life is an adventure....................Explore it
Life is a pleasure....................Enjoy it
Life is a hope....................Dream it
Life is a journey....................Complete it
Life is a problem....................Solve it
Life is a goal....................Achieve it
Life is a game....................Play it
Life is a challenge....................Dare it

WHO DARES SELLS!

THE POWER TO SUCCEED

Who Dares Sells

Keeps You Winning!
For further information on Creative Dynamic Selling Seminars, Courses and other products please contact: Patrick Ellis

c/o HarperCollins*Publishers*
77–85 Fulham Palace Road
Hammersmith
London W6 8JB

Free Membership – Who Dares Sells Winner's Club
As the owner of the most powerful self-improvement book ever written, you automatically qualify for FREE membership of the above club.

As a member of this elite club you will have access to a wide range of training, support services and events at reduced rates. This will ensure that your progress towards cherished goals gathers momentum as your personal power grows, just like a snowball gets bigger and bigger as it rolls along. You can positively look forward to glittering success as you start to apply the most powerful secrets from WHO DARES SELLS. Recommend a business colleague or friend to WHO DARES SELLS and you will qualify for a 25% commission on any product or service they have from us.

LET US KEEP IN TOUCH with you as a valued member by sending us your full name and address, telephone, telex and fax numbers.

CONGRATULATIONS on making WHO DARES SELLS your guiding light and welcome to the club.

Index

Also available . . .

TALK AND GROW RICH

How to create wealth without capital

RON HOLLAND

How often have you tried and tried to remember some elusive fact that hovers just out of reach, only to find that when you've given up and stopped trying, the information simply pops into your head? How often have you found that when you stop worrying about a problem, the solution suddenly becomes obvious? This is the secret behind Ron Holland's amazing formula: SSS – silence, stillness and solitude at work.

In this remarkable book, Ron Holland explains how anyone can tap the unlimited and infallible power of their unconscious mind any time they want to. He shows us how we can, at will, use SSS to solve quickly and easily problems that we have been thinking about unsuccessfully. He describes how SSS can be used to discover ways and means to acquire anything we desire simply by talking to people. He demonstrates:

- How to persuade people to do what you want, but have them think that it was all their idea.
- How to sell anything to anybody, including the most hardened and demanding buyer.
- How to generate so many fool proof ideas that you will need to carry a pen and paper around with you to write them all down.

This book truly is the handbook for all Apprentice Millionaires!

ONE MAN BAND

How to set up your own service business

JOHN VINEY & STEPHANIE JONES

One Man Band is *the* book for you if you are thinking about (or have already started) setting up your own business in the service sector.

More and more companies are using outside consultants for specialist work, and at the same time consumers buying services are increasingly looking for value and personal attention. These are opportunities for *One Man Bands*.

One Man Band will take you through stage by stage to ensure your chance of success, with wide-ranging, detailed and useful case studies of 'one man bands' – including both those selling services to other businesses, and those selling directly to the public.

One Man Band addresses the following issues:

- do you have the right motivation and personality to 'go it alone'?
- how can you capitalize on your skills and experience?
- how can you differentiate yourself from your competitors?
- what do you need to know about law, tax and accountancy?
- how do you pitch for business for yourself?
- what are the problems and pitfalls?
- why small is beautiful – and highly profitable

One Man Band answers these questions and many more, and includes inspiring ideas on choosing a one man band, and how to get started!

DO IT!

A guide to living your dreams

JOHN-ROGER & PETER McWILLIAMS

We all cherish at least one dream – a heart's desire. Moreover, it is a fact that most of us do have the time and the ability to fulfil our dreams – if we put our mind to it. Unfortunately, we spend all our precious time and energy on other things, often completely unrelated to what we really want to do. What is it that makes us procrastinate?

The answer is the comfort zone – the old, safe, practised thoughts, responses and actions we feel comfortable with. Pursuing a dream involves ways of thinking and acting that are outside the boundaries of this comfort zone. But how can we overcome such a problem when we probably aren't even aware that it exists?

This book provides the answer.

- recognize your comfort zone and learn to go beyond it
- discover, or rediscover, your dreams
- choose which dreams to pursue
- work out practical solutions for achieving them

As the authors say, 'LET'S GET OFF OUR "BUTS".' So stop making excuses, and start living your dreams!

INTRODUCING NEURO-LINGUISTIC PROGRAMMING

The new psychology of personal excellence

JOSEPH O'CONNOR & JOHN SEYMOUR

Neuro-Linguistic Programming is one of the fastest growing developments in applied psychology. This book will show you why. Some people appear more gifted than others. NLP describes in simple terms what they do differently, and enables you to learn these patterns of excellence. This approach gives the practical skills used by outstanding communicators. Excellent communication is the basis of creating excellent results.

The purpose of NLP is to increase personal choice; it provides powerful and elegant tools for change in a changing world. NLP skills are proving invaluable for personal development and professional excellence in counselling, education and business.

Introducing Neuro-Linguistic Programming includes:

- How to create rapport with others
- Influencing skills
- Understanding and using body language
- How to think about and achieve the results you want
- The art of asking key questions
- Effective meetings, negotiations and selling
- Accelerated learning strategies
- How to run your nervous system

As well as covering the classic NLP therapy techniques in depth, Joseph O'Connor and John Seymour list the books currently available on NLP and give advice on further reading and choosing an appropriate training course. Here in one book are the ideas that are enabling more people to achieve outstanding results in important areas of their lives.

TNT

The power within you

CLAUDE M. BRISTOL & HAROLD SHERMAN

Open the door to the unlimited resources within you!

This amazing bestseller shows you how you can achieve whatever you want to tapping the hidden power of your own mind. We all have this inner power – but it will only work for us if we believe in it and know how to use it. Find out how *you* can use this ability to:

- turn 'pipe dreams' into realities
- achieve health, wealth, success and happiness
- share your good fortune with others.

Claude M. Bristol and Harold Sherman demonstrate, through practical examples as well as fascinating theory, how to decide what you want out of life and then achieve it. This compelling and inspirational book will convince you of the tremendous power of belief.

THE SHORTER MBA

A practical approach to business skills

Edited by BARRIE PEARSON & NEIL THOMAS

The Shorter MBA is a unique distillation of the skills that you need to acquire in order to be considered successful in business. Not everyone is able to devote a year or two of their time to study for a Masters in Business Administration, but in today's highly competitive environment it is crucial to have a thorough understanding of the issues involved in the smooth and successful running of a business.

This book concentrates on practical tips and techniques in the key areas of Personal Development, Management Skills and Business Development. Each chapter has been written by an acknowledged expert, and will give you the essential tools syosu need to become a high flier in your own field.

The Shorter MBA is a complete course in:

- Finance and Accounting
- Project Management
- Human Resource Management
- Competitive Marketing Strategy
- Business Development Strategy
- Turnaround of a Loss-Making Business
- Business Plans
- Acquisitions and Divestments
- Selling & Negotiating Skills
- Time Management
- Decision Making
- Problem Solving
- Communication Skills

TALK AND GROW RICH	0 7225 1955 9	£5.99	☐
ONE MAN BAND	0 7225 2646 6	£7.99	☐
DO IT!	0 7225 2695 4	£7.99	☐
INTRODUCING NLP	1 85274 073 6	£7.99	☐
TNT: THE POWER WITHIN YOU	0 7225 2493 5	£4.99	☐
THE SHORTER MBA h/b	0 7225 2507 9	£25.00	☐

All these books are available from your local bookseller or can be ordered direct from the publishers.

To order direct just tick the titles you want and fill in the form below:

Name:_____

Address: _____

_____

_____ Postcode: _____

Send to: Thorsons Mail Order, Dept 31U, HarperCollins*Publishers*, Westerhill Road, Bishopbriggs, Glasgow G64 2QT.

Please enclose a cheque or postal order or your authority to debit your Visa/Access account —

Credit card no: _____

Expiry date: _____

Signature:_____

— to the value of the cover price plus:

UK & BFPO: Add £1.00 for the first book and 25p for each additional book ordered.

Overseas orders including Eire: Please add £2.95 service charge. Books will be sent by surface mail but quotes for airmail despatches will be given on request.

24 HOUR TELEPHONE ORDERING SERVICE FOR ACCESS/VISA CARDHOLDERS — TEL: **041 772 2281**.